CW00802111

Cambridge

International AS and A Level Mathematics

Pure Mathematics 1

Sophie Goldie

Series Editor: Roger Porkess

HODDER
EDUCATION
AN HACHETTE UK COMPANY

Questions from the Cambridge International AS & A Level Mathematics papers
are reproduced by permission of Cambridge International Examinations.

Questions from the MEI AS & A Level Mathematics papers are reproduced by permission of OCR.

We are grateful to the following companies, institutions and individuals who have given permission
to reproduce photographs in this book.
page 106, © Jack Sullivan / Alamy; page 167, © RTimages / Fotolia; page 254, © Hunta / Fotolia;
page 258, © Olga Iermolaieva / Fotolia

Every effort has been made to trace and acknowledge ownership of copyright. The publishers will be
glad to make suitable arrangements with any copyright holders whom it has not been possible to contact.

®IGCSE is the registered trademark of Cambridge International Examinations.

Hachette UK's policy is to use papers that are natural, renewable and recyclable products and
made from wood grown in sustainable forests. The logging and manufacturing processes are
expected to conform to the environmental regulations of the country of origin.

Orders: please contact Bookpoint Ltd, 130 Milton Park, Abingdon, Oxon OX14 4SB.
Telephone: (44) 01235 827720. Fax: (44) 01235 400454. Lines are open 9.00–5.00, Monday
to Saturday, with a 24-hour message answering service. Visit our website at www.hoddereducation.com

Much of the material in this book was published originally as part of the MEI Structured
Mathematics series. It has been carefully adapted for the Cambridge International AS & A level
Mathematics syllabus.

The original MEI author team for Pure Mathematics comprised Catherine Berry, Bob Francis,
Val Hanrahan, Terry Heard, David Martin, Jean Matthews, Bernard Murphy, Roger Porkess and Peter Secker.

© in this format Roger Porkess and Sophie Goldie 2012

First published in 2012 by
Hodder Education, an Hachette UK company,
Carmelite House, 50 Victoria Embankment,
London EC4Y 0DZ

Impression number   5 4
Year   2016 2015

All rights reserved. Apart from any use permitted under UK copyright law, no part of this
publication may be reproduced or transmitted in any form or by any means, electronic or
mechanical, including photocopying and recording, or held within any information storage
and retrieval system, without permission in writing from the publisher or under licence from
the Copyright Licensing Agency Limited. Further details of such licences (for reprographic
reproduction) may be obtained from the Copyright Licensing Agency Limited, Saffron
House, 6–10 Kirby Street, London EC1N 8TS.

Cover photo by © Joy Fera / Fotolia
Illustrations by Pantek Media, Maidstone, Kent
Typeset in 10.5pt Minion by Pantek Media, Maidstone, Kent
Printed in Dubai

A catalogue record for this title is available from the British Library

ISBN 978 1444 14644 8

Contents

Key to symbols in this book

? This symbol means that you want to discuss a point with your teacher. If you are working on your own there are answers in the back of the book. It is important, however, that you have a go at answering the questions before looking up the answers if you are to understand the mathematics fully.

p This symbol invites you to join in a discussion about proof. The answers to these questions are given in the back of the book.

⚠ This is a warning sign. It is used where a common mistake, misunderstanding or tricky point is being described.

▫ This is the ICT icon. It indicates where you could use a graphic calculator or a computer. Graphical calculators and computers are not permitted in any of the examinations for the Cambridge International AS & A Level Mathematics 9709 syllabus, however, so these activities are optional.

b This symbol and a dotted line down the right-hand side of the page indicates material that you are likely to have met before. You need to be familiar with the material before you move on to develop it further.

e This symbol and a dotted line down the right-hand side of the page indicates material which is beyond the syllabus for the unit but which is included for completeness.

Introduction

This is the first of a series of books for the Cambridge International Examinations syllabus for Cambridge International AS & A Level Mathematics 9709. The eight chapters of this book cover the pure mathematics in AS level. The series also contains a more advanced book for pure mathematics and one each for mechanics and statistics.

These books are based on the highly successful series for the Mathematics in Education and Industry (MEI) syllabus in the UK but they have been redesigned for Cambridge users; where appropriate new material has been written and the exercises contain many past Cambridge examination questions. An overview of the units making up the Cambridge International AS & A Level Mathematics 9709 syllabus is given in the diagram on the next page.

Throughout the series the emphasis is on understanding the mathematics as well as routine calculations. The various exercises provide plenty of scope for practising basic techniques; they also contain many typical examination questions.

An important feature of this series is the electronic support. There is an accompanying disc containing two types of Personal Tutor presentation: examination-style questions, in which the solutions are written out, step by step, with an accompanying verbal explanation, and test yourself questions; these are multiple-choice with explanations of the mistakes that lead to the wrong answers as well as full solutions for the correct ones. In addition, extensive online support is available via the MEI website, www.mei.org.uk.

The books are written on the assumption that students have covered and understood the work in the Cambridge IGCSE® syllabus. However, some of the early material is designed to provide an overlap and this is designated 'Background'. There are also places where the books show how the ideas can be taken further or where fundamental underpinning work is explored and such work is marked as 'Extension'.

The original MEI author team would like to thank Sophie Goldie who has carried out the extensive task of presenting their work in a suitable form for Cambridge International students and for her many original contributions. They would also like to thank Cambridge International Examinations for their detailed advice in preparing the books and for permission to use many past examination questions.

Roger Porkess
Series Editor

The Cambridge International AS & A Level Mathematics 9709 syllabus

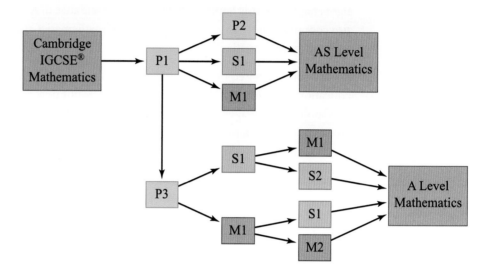

1 Algebra

Sherlock Holmes: 'Now the skillful workman is very careful indeed ... He will have nothing but the tools which may help him in doing his work, but of these he has a large assortment, and all in the most perfect order.'

A. Conan Doyle

ⓑ Background algebra

Manipulating algebraic expressions

You will often wish to tidy up an expression, or to rearrange it so that it is easier to read its meaning. The following examples show you how to do this. You should practise the techniques for yourself on the questions in Exercise 1A.

Collecting terms

Very often you just need to collect like terms together, in this example those in x, those in y and those in z.

❓ What are 'like' and 'unlike' terms?

EXAMPLE 1.1

Simplify the expression $2x + 4y - 5z - 5x - 9y + 2z + 4x - 7y + 8z$.

SOLUTION

Expression $= 2x + 4x - 5x + 4y - 9y - 7y + 2z + 8z - 5z$ ← Collect like terms

$= 6x - 5x + 4y - 16y + 10z - 5z$ ← Tidy up

$= x - 12y + 5z$ ← This cannot be simplified further and so it is the answer.

Removing brackets

Sometimes you need to remove brackets before collecting like terms together.

EXAMPLE 1.2   Simplify the expression $3(2x - 4y) - 4(x - 5y)$.

SOLUTION

Open the brackets

Expression $= 6x - 12y - 4x + 20y$

Notice $(-4) \times (-5y) = +20y$

$= 6x - 4x + 20y - 12y$ ← Collect like terms

$= 2x + 8y$ ← Answer

EXAMPLE 1.3   Simplify $x(x + 2) - (x - 4)$.

SOLUTION

Expression $= x^2 + 2x - x + 4$ ← Open the brackets

$= x^2 + x + 4$ ← Answer

EXAMPLE 1.4   Simplify $a(b + c) - ac$.

SOLUTION

Expression $= ab + ac - ac$ ← Open the brackets

$= ab$ ← Answer

Factorisation

It is often possible to rewrite an expression as the product of two or more numbers or expressions, its *factors*. This usually involves using brackets and is called *factorisation*. Factorisation may make an expression easier to use and neater to write, or it may help you to interpret its meaning.

EXAMPLE 1.5   Factorise $12x - 18y$.

SOLUTION

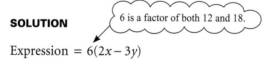

6 is a factor of both 12 and 18.

Expression $= 6(2x - 3y)$

EXAMPLE 1.6   Factorise $x^2 - 2xy + 3xz$.

SOLUTION

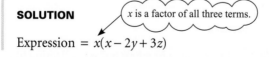

x is a factor of all three terms.

Expression $= x(x - 2y + 3z)$

Multiplication

Several of the previous examples have involved multiplication of variables: cases like

$$a \times b = ab \quad \text{and} \quad x \times x = x^2.$$

In the next example the principles are the same but the expressions are not quite so simple.

EXAMPLE 1.7

Multiply $3p^2qr \times 4pq^3 \times 5qr^2$.

You might well do this line in your head.

SOLUTION

$$\begin{aligned}
\text{Expression} &= 3 \times 4 \times 5 \times p^2 \times p \times q \times q^3 \times q \times r \times r^2 \\
&= 60 \times p^3 \times q^5 \times r^3 \\
&= 60p^3q^5r^3
\end{aligned}$$

Fractions

The rules for working with fractions in algebra are exactly the same as those used in arithmetic.

EXAMPLE 1.8

Simplify $\dfrac{x}{2} - \dfrac{2y}{10} + \dfrac{z}{4}$.

SOLUTION

As in arithmetic you start by finding the common denominator. For 2, 10 and 4 this is 20.

Then you write each part as the equivalent fraction with 20 as its denominator, as follows.

$$\begin{aligned}
\text{Expression} &= \frac{10x}{20} - \frac{4y}{20} + \frac{5z}{20} \\
&= \frac{10x - 4y + 5z}{20}
\end{aligned}$$

This line would often be left out.

EXAMPLE 1.9

Simplify $\dfrac{x^2}{y} - \dfrac{y^2}{x}$.

SOLUTION

$$\begin{aligned}
\text{Expression} &= \frac{x^3}{xy} - \frac{y^3}{xy} \\
&= \frac{x^3 - y^3}{xy}
\end{aligned}$$

The common denominator is xy.

EXAMPLE 1.10 Simplify $\dfrac{3x^2}{5y} \times \dfrac{5yz}{6x}$.

SOLUTION

Since the two parts of the expression are multiplied, terms may be cancelled top and bottom as in arithmetic. In this case 3, 5, x and y may all be cancelled.

$$\text{Expression} = \frac{\cancel{3}x^{\cancel{2}}}{\cancel{5}\cancel{y}} \times \frac{\cancel{5}\cancel{y}z}{\cancel{6}_2\cancel{x}}$$

$$= \frac{xz}{2}$$

EXAMPLE 1.11 Simplify $\dfrac{(x-1)^3}{4x(x-1)}$.

SOLUTION

$(x-1)$ is a common factor of both top and bottom, so may be cancelled. However, x is not a factor of the top (the numerator), so may not be cancelled.

$$\text{Expression} = \frac{(x-1)^2}{4x}$$

EXAMPLE 1.12 Simplify $\dfrac{24x+6}{3(4x+1)}$.

SOLUTION

When the numerator (top) and/or the denominator (bottom) are not factorised, first factorise them as much as possible. Then you can see whether there are any common factors which can be cancelled.

$$\text{Expression} = \frac{6(4x+1)}{3(4x+1)}$$

$$= 2$$

EXERCISE 1A

1 Simplify the following expressions by collecting like terms.

(i) $8x + 3x + 4x - 6x$

(ii) $3p + 3 + 5p - 7 - 7p - 9$

(iii) $2k + 3m + 8n - 3k - 6m - 5n + 2k - m + n$

(iv) $2a + 3b - 4c + 4a - 5b - 8c - 6a + 2b + 12c$

(v) $r - 2s - t + 2r - 5t - 6r - 7t - s + 5s - 2t + 4r$

2 Factorise the following expressions.

(i) $4x + 8y$

(ii) $12a + 15b - 18c$

(iii) $72f - 36g - 48h$

(iv) $p^2 - pq + pr$

(v) $12k^2 + 144km - 72kn$

3 Simplify the following expressions, factorising the answers where possible.

(i) $8(3x + 2y) + 4(x + 3y)$

(ii) $2(3a - 4b + 5c) - 3(2a - 5b - c)$

(iii) $6(2p - 3q + 4r) - 5(2p - 6q - 3r) - 3(p - 4q + 2r)$

(iv) $4(l + w + h) + 3(2l - w - 2h) + 5w$

(v) $5u - 6(w - v) + 2(3u + 4w - v) - 11u$

4 Simplify the following expressions, factorising the answers where possible.

(i) $a(b + c) + a(b - c)$

(ii) $k(m + n) - m(k + n)$

(iii) $p(2q + r + 3s) - pr - s(3p + q)$

(iv) $x(x - 2) - x(x - 6) + 8$

(v) $x(x - 1) + 2(x - 1) - x(x + 1)$

5 Perform the following multiplications, simplifying your answers.

(i) $2xy \times 3x^2y$

(ii) $5a^2bc^3 \times 2ab^2 \times 3c$

(iii) $km \times mn \times nk$

(iv) $3pq^2r \times 6p^2qr \times 9pqr^2$

(v) $rs \times 2st \times 3tu \times 4ur$

6 Simplify the following fractions as much as possible.

(i) $\dfrac{ab}{ac}$

(ii) $\dfrac{2e}{4f}$

(iii) $\dfrac{x^2}{5x}$

(iv) $\dfrac{4a^2b}{2ab}$

(v) $\dfrac{6p^2q^3r}{3p^3q^3r^2}$

7 Simplify the following as much as possible.

(i) $\dfrac{a}{b} \times \dfrac{b}{c} \times \dfrac{c}{a}$

(ii) $\dfrac{3x}{2y} \times \dfrac{8y}{3z} \times \dfrac{5z}{4x}$

(iii) $\dfrac{p^2}{q} \times \dfrac{q^2}{p}$

(iv) $\dfrac{2fg}{16h} \times \dfrac{4gh^2}{4fh} \times \dfrac{32fh^3}{12f^3}$

(v) $\dfrac{kmn}{3n^3} \times \dfrac{6k^2m^3}{2k^3m}$

8 Write the following as single fractions.

(i) $\dfrac{x}{2} + \dfrac{x}{3}$

(ii) $\dfrac{2x}{5} - \dfrac{x}{3} + \dfrac{3x}{4}$

(iii) $\dfrac{3z}{8} + \dfrac{2z}{12} - \dfrac{5z}{24}$

(iv) $\dfrac{2x}{3} - \dfrac{x}{4}$

(v) $\dfrac{y}{2} - \dfrac{5y}{8} + \dfrac{4y}{5}$

9 Write the following as single fractions.

(i) $\dfrac{3}{x} + \dfrac{5}{x}$

(ii) $\dfrac{1}{x} + \dfrac{1}{y}$

(iii) $\dfrac{4}{x} + \dfrac{x}{y}$

(iv) $\dfrac{p}{q} + \dfrac{q}{p}$

(v) $\dfrac{1}{a} - \dfrac{1}{b} + \dfrac{1}{c}$

10 Write the following as single fractions.

    (i) $\dfrac{x+1}{4} + \dfrac{x-1}{2}$ **(ii)** $\dfrac{2x}{3} - \dfrac{x-1}{5}$ **(iii)** $\dfrac{3x-5}{4} + \dfrac{x-7}{6}$

    (iv) $\dfrac{3(2x+1)}{5} - \dfrac{7(x-2)}{2}$ **(v)** $\dfrac{4x+1}{8} + \dfrac{7x-3}{12}$

11 Simplify the following expressions.

    (i) $\dfrac{x+3}{2x+6}$ **(ii)** $\dfrac{6(2x+1)^2}{3(2x+1)^5}$ **(iii)** $\dfrac{2x(y-3)^4}{8x^2(y-3)}$

    (iv) $\dfrac{6x-12}{x-2}$ **(v)** $\dfrac{(3x+2)^2}{6x} \times \dfrac{x^4}{6x+4}$

ⓑ Linear equations

 What is a variable?

You will often need to find the value of the variable in an expression in a particular case, as in the following example.

EXAMPLE 1.13   A polygon is a closed figure whose sides are straight lines. Figure 1.1 shows a seven-sided polygon (a heptagon).

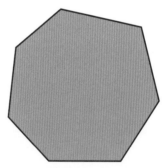

Figure 1.1

An expression for $S°$, the sum of the angles of a polygon with n sides, is

$$S = 180(n-2).$$

❓ How is this expression obtained?

    Try dividing a polygon into triangles, starting from one vertex.

Find the number of sides in a polygon with an angle sum of **(i)** 180° **(ii)** 1080°.

SOLUTION

(i) Substituting 180 for S gives $\qquad$ $180 = 180(n-2)$ ← This is an equation which can be solved to find n.

Dividing both sides by 180 $\quad \Rightarrow \quad 1 = n - 2$

Adding 2 to both sides $\quad \Rightarrow \quad 3 = n$

The polygon has three sides: it is a triangle.

(ii) Substituting 1080 for S gives $\qquad$ $1080 = 180(n-2)$

Dividing both sides by 180 $\quad \Rightarrow \quad 6 = n - 2$

Adding 2 to both sides $\quad \Rightarrow \quad 8 = n$

The polygon has eight sides: it is an octagon.

Example 1.13 illustrates the process of solving an equation. An *equation* is formed when an expression, in this case $180(n-2)$, is set equal to a value, in this case 180 or 1080, or to another expression. *Solving* means finding the value(s) of the variable(s) in the equation.

Since both sides of an equation are equal, you may do what you wish to an equation provided that you do exactly the same thing to both sides. If there is only one variable involved (like n in the above examples), you aim to get that on one side of the equation, and everything else on the other. The two examples which follow illustrate this.

In both of these examples the working is given in full, step by step. In practice you would expect to omit some of these lines by tidying up as you went along.

 Look at the statement $5(x-1) = 5x - 5$.

What happens when you try to solve it as an equation?

This is an *identity* and not an equation. It is true for *all* values of x.

For example, try $x = 11$: $5(x-1) = 5 \times (11-1) = 50$; $5x - 5 = 55 - 5 = 50$ ✓,
or try $x = 46$: $5(x-1) = 5 \times (46-1) = 225$; $5x - 5 = 230 - 5 = 225$ ✓,
or try $x =$ anything else and it will still be true.

To distinguish an identity from an equation, the symbol $\equiv$ is sometimes used.

Thus $5(x-1) \equiv 5x - 5$.

EXAMPLE 1.14   Solve the equation $5(x-3) = 2(x+6)$.

SOLUTION

Open the brackets	$\Rightarrow$	$5x - 15 = 2x + 12$
Subtract $2x$ from both sides	$\Rightarrow$	$5x - 2x - 15 = 2x - 2x + 12$
Tidy up	$\Rightarrow$	$3x - 15 = 12$
Add 15 to both sides	$\Rightarrow$	$3x - 15 + 15 = 12 + 15$
Tidy up	$\Rightarrow$	$3x = 27$
Divide both sides by 3	$\Rightarrow$	$\dfrac{3x}{3} = \dfrac{27}{3}$
	$\Rightarrow$	$x = 9$

CHECK

When the answer is substituted in the original equation both sides should come out to be equal. If they are different, you have made a mistake.

Left-hand side	**Right-hand side**
$5(x-3)$	$2(x+6)$
$5(9-3)$	$2(9+6)$
5×6	2×15
30	30 (as required).

EXAMPLE 1.15   Solve the equation $\frac{1}{2}(x+6) = x + \frac{1}{3}(2x-5)$.

SOLUTION

Start by clearing the fractions. Since the numbers 2 and 3 appear on the bottom line, multiply through by 6 which cancels both of them.

Multiply both sides by 6	$\Rightarrow$	$6 \times \frac{1}{2}(x+6) = 6 \times x + 6 \times \frac{1}{3}(2x-5)$
Tidy up	$\Rightarrow$	$3(x+6) = 6x + 2(2x-5)$
Open the brackets	$\Rightarrow$	$3x + 18 = 6x + 4x - 10$
Subtract $6x$, $4x$, and 18 from both sides	$\Rightarrow$	$3x - 6x - 4x = -10 - 18$
Tidy up	$\Rightarrow$	$-7x = -28$
Divide both sides by (-7)	$\Rightarrow$	$\dfrac{-7x}{-7} = \dfrac{-28}{-7}$
	$\Rightarrow$	$x = 4$

CHECK

Substituting $x = 4$ in $\frac{1}{2}(x+6) = x + \frac{1}{3}(2x-5)$ gives:

Left-hand side	**Right-hand side**
$\frac{1}{2}(4+6)$	$4 + \frac{1}{3}(8-5)$
$\dfrac{10}{2}$	$4 + \dfrac{3}{3}$
5	5 (as required).

1 Solve the following equations.

(i) $5a - 32 = 68$

(ii) $4b - 6 = 3b + 2$

(iii) $2c + 12 = 5c + 12$

(iv) $5(2d + 8) = 2(3d + 24)$

(v) $3(2e - 1) = 6(e + 2) + 3e$

(vi) $7(2 - f) - 3(f - 4) = 10f - 4$

(vii) $5g + 2(g - 9) = 3(2g - 5) + 11$

(viii) $3(2h - 6) - 6(h + 5) = 2(4h - 4) - 10(h + 4)$

(ix) $\frac{1}{2}k + \frac{1}{4}k = 36$

(x) $\frac{1}{2}(l - 5) + l = 11$

(xi) $\frac{1}{2}(3m + 5) + 1\frac{1}{2}(2m - 1) = 5\frac{1}{2}$

(xii) $n + \frac{1}{3}(n + 1) + \frac{1}{4}(n + 2) = \frac{5}{6}$

2 The largest angle of a triangle is six times as big as the smallest. The third angle is 75°.

(i) Write this information in the form of an equation for a, the size in degrees of the smallest angle.

(ii) Solve the equation and so find the sizes of the three angles.

3 Miriam and Saloma are twins and their sister Rohana is 2 years older than them.
The total of their ages is 32 years.

(i) Write this information in the form of an equation for r, Rohana's age in years.

(ii) What are the ages of the three girls?

4 The length, d m, of a rectangular field is 40 m greater than the width.
The perimeter of the field is 400 m.

(i) Write this information in the form of an equation for d.

(ii) Solve the equation and so find the area of the field.

5 Yash can buy three pencils and have 49c change, or he can buy five pencils and have 15c change.

(i) Write this information as an equation for x, the cost in cents of one pencil.

(ii) How much money did Yash have to start with?

6 In a multiple-choice examination of 25 questions, four marks are given for each correct answer and two marks are deducted for each wrong answer. One mark is deducted for any question which is not attempted. A candidate attempts q questions and gets c correct.

    (i) Write down an expression for the candidate's total mark in terms of q and c.

    (ii) James attempts 22 questions and scores 55 marks. Write down and solve an equation for the number of questions which James gets right.

7 Joe buys 18 kg of potatoes. Some of these are old potatoes at 22c per kilogram, the rest are new ones at 36c per kilogram.

    (i) Denoting the mass of old potatoes he buys by m kg, write down an expression for the total cost of Joe's potatoes.

    (ii) Joe pays with a \$5 note and receives 20c change. What mass of new potatoes does he buy?

8 In 18 years' time Hussein will be five times as old as he was 2 years ago.

    (i) Write this information in the form of an equation involving Hussein's present age, a years.

    (ii) How old is Hussein now?

ⓑ Changing the subject of a formula

The area of a trapezium is given by

$$A = \tfrac{1}{2}(a + b)h$$

where a and b are the lengths of the parallel sides and h is the distance between them (see figure 1.2). An equation like this is often called a *formula*.

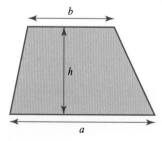

Figure 1.2

The variable A is called the subject of this formula because it only appears once on its own on the left-hand side. You often need to make one of the other variables the subject of a formula. In that case, the steps involved are just the same as those in solving an equation, as the following examples show.

EXAMPLE 1.16   Make a the subject in $A = \frac{1}{2}(a+b)h$.

SOLUTION

It is usually easiest if you start by arranging the equation so that the variable you want to be its subject is on the left-hand side.

$$\frac{1}{2}(a+b)h = A$$

Multiply both sides by 2 $\Rightarrow$ $(a+b)h = 2A$

Divide both sides by h $\Rightarrow$ $a+b = \dfrac{2A}{h}$

Subtract b from both sides $\Rightarrow$ $a = \dfrac{2A}{h} - b$

EXAMPLE 1.17   Make T the subject in the simple interest formula $I = \dfrac{PRT}{100}$.

SOLUTION

Arrange with T on the left-hand side $\dfrac{PRT}{100} = I$

Multiply both sides by 100 $\Rightarrow$ $PRT = 100I$

Divide both sides by P and R $\Rightarrow$ $T = \dfrac{100I}{PR}$

EXAMPLE 1.18   Make x the subject in the formula $v = \omega\sqrt{a^2 - x^2}$. (This formula gives the speed of an oscillating point.)

SOLUTION

Square both sides $\Rightarrow$ $v^2 = \omega^2(a^2 - x^2)$

Divide both sides by ω^2 $\Rightarrow$ $\dfrac{v^2}{\omega^2} = a^2 - x^2$

Add x^2 to both sides $\Rightarrow$ $\dfrac{v^2}{\omega^2} + x^2 = a^2$

Subtract $\dfrac{v^2}{\omega^2}$ from both sides $\Rightarrow$ $x^2 = a^2 - \dfrac{v^2}{\omega^2}$

Take the square root of both sides $\Rightarrow$ $x = \pm\sqrt{a^2 - \dfrac{v^2}{\omega^2}}$

EXAMPLE 1.19   Make m the subject of the formula $mv = I + mu$. (This formula gives the momentum after an impulse.)

SOLUTION

Collect terms in m on the left-hand side
and terms without m on the other. $\Rightarrow$ $mv - mu = I$

Factorise the left-hand side $\Rightarrow$ $m(v - u) = I$

Divide both sides by $(v - u)$ $\Rightarrow$ $m = \dfrac{I}{v - u}$

EXERCISE 1C

1 Make **(i)** a **(ii)** t the subject in $v = u + at$.

2 Make h the subject in $V = lwh$.

3 Make r the subject in $A = \pi r^2$.

4 Make **(i)** s **(ii)** u the subject in $v^2 - u^2 = 2as$.

5 Make h the subject in $A = 2\pi rh + 2\pi r^2$.

6 Make a the subject in $s = ut + \frac{1}{2}at^2$.

7 Make b the subject in $h = \sqrt{a^2 + b^2}$.

8 Make g the subject in $T = 2\pi \sqrt{\dfrac{l}{g}}$.

9 Make m the subject in $E = mgh + \frac{1}{2}mv^2$.

10 Make R the subject in $\dfrac{1}{R} = \dfrac{1}{R_1} + \dfrac{1}{R_2}$.

11 Make h the subject in $bh = 2A - ah$.

12 Make u the subject in $f = \dfrac{uv}{u + v}$.

13 Make d the subject in $u^2 - du + fd = 0$.

14 Make V the subject in $p_1 VM = mRT + p_2 VM$.

? All the formulae in Exercise 1C refer to real situations. Can you recognise them?

Quadratic equations

EXAMPLE 1.20

The length of a rectangular field is 40 m greater than its width, and its area is $6000\,\text{m}^2$. Form an equation involving the length, x m, of the field.

SOLUTION

Since the length of the field is 40 m greater than the width,

the width in m must be $x - 40$

and the area in m^2 is $x(x - 40)$.

So the required equation is $x(x - 40) = 6000$

or $\qquad\qquad x^2 - 40x - 6000 = 0$.

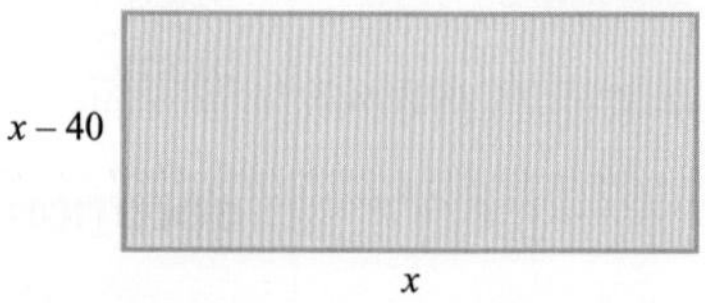

$x - 40$

x

Figure 1.3

This equation, involving terms in x^2 and x as well as a constant term (i.e. a number, in this case 6000), is an example of a *quadratic equation*. This is in contrast to a linear equation. A linear equation in the variable x involves only terms in x and constant terms.

It is usual to write a quadratic equation with the right-hand side equal to zero. To solve it, you first factorise the left-hand side if possible, and this requires a particular technique.

Quadratic factorisation

EXAMPLE 1.21

Factorise $xa + xb + ya + yb$.

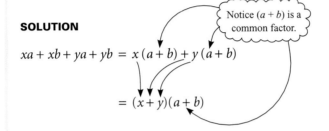

SOLUTION

Notice $(a + b)$ is a common factor.

$$xa + xb + ya + yb = x(a + b) + y(a + b)$$

$$= (x + y)(a + b)$$

The expression is now in the form of two factors, $(x + y)$ and $(a + b)$, so this is the answer.

You can see this result in terms of the area of the rectangle in figure 1.4. This can be written as the product of its length $(x + y)$ and its width $(a + b)$, or as the sum of the areas of the four smaller rectangles, xa, xb, ya and yb.

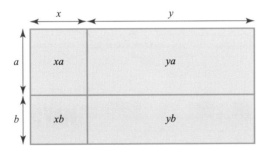

Figure 1.4

The same pattern is used for quadratic factorisation, but first you need to split the middle term into two parts. This gives you four terms, which correspond to the areas of the four regions in a diagram like figure 1.4.

EXAMPLE 1.22

Factorise $x^2 + 7x + 12$.

SOLUTION

Splitting the middle term, $7x$, as $4x + 3x$ you have

$$x^2 + 7x + 12 = x^2 + 4x + 3x + 12$$
$$= x(x+4) + 3(x+4)$$
$$= (x+3)(x+4).$$

How do you know to split the middle term, $7x$, into $4x + 3x$, rather than say $5x + 2x$ or $9x - 2x$?

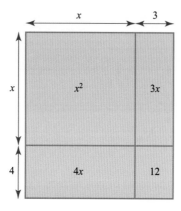

Figure 1.5

The numbers 4 and 3 can be added to give 7 (the middle coefficient) and multiplied to give 12 (the constant term), so these are the numbers chosen.

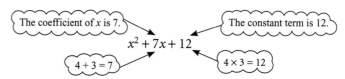

EXAMPLE 1.23

Factorise $x^2 - 2x - 24$.

SOLUTION

First you look for two numbers that can be added to give -2 and multiplied to give -24:

$$-6 + 4 = -2 \qquad -6 \times (+4) = -24.$$

The numbers are -6 and $+4$ and so the middle term, $-2x$, is split into $-6x + 4x$.

$$x^2 - 2x - 24 = x^2 - 6x + 4x - 24$$
$$= x(x-6) + 4(x-6)$$
$$= (x+4)(x-6).$$

This example raises a number of important points.

1   It makes no difference if you write $+4x - 6x$ instead of $-6x + 4x$. In that case the factorisation reads:

$$x^2 - 2x - 24 = x^2 + 4x - 6x - 24$$
$$= x(x + 4) - 6(x + 4)$$
$$= (x - 6)(x + 4) \qquad \text{(clearly the same answer).}$$

2   There are other methods of quadratic factorisation. If you have already learned another way, and consistently get your answers right, then continue to use it. This method has one major advantage: it is self-checking. In the last line but one of the solution to the example, you will see that $(x + 4)$ appears twice. If at this point the contents of the two brackets are different, for example $(x + 4)$ and $(x - 4)$, then something is wrong. You may have chosen the wrong numbers, or made a careless mistake, or perhaps the expression cannot be factorised. There is no point in proceeding until you have sorted out why they are different.

3   You may check your final answer by multiplying it out to get back to the original expression. There are two common ways of setting this out.

(i)   Long multiplication

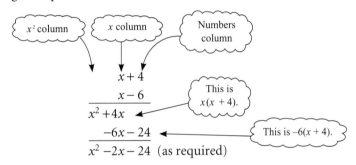

(ii)   Multiplying term by term

$$(x + 4)(x - 6) = x^2 - 6x + 4x - 24$$
$$= x^2 - 2x - 24 \quad \text{(as required)}$$

You would not expect to draw the lines and arrows in your answers. They have been put in to help you understand where the terms have come from.

EXAMPLE 1.24   Factorise $x^2 - 20x + 100$.

SOLUTION

$$x^2 - 20x + 100 = x^2 - 10x - 10x + 100$$
$$= x(x - 10) - 10(x - 10)$$
$$= (x - 10)(x - 10)$$
$$= (x - 10)^2$$

Notice:
$(-10) + (-10) = -20$
$(-10) \times (-10) = +100$

Note

The expression in Example 1.24 was a *perfect square*. It is helpful to be able to recognise the form of such expressions.

$$(x + a)^2 = x^2 + 2ax + a^2 \quad \text{(in this case } a = 10\text{)}$$
$$(x - a)^2 = x^2 - 2ax + a^2$$

EXAMPLE 1.25

Factorise $x^2 - 49$.

SOLUTION

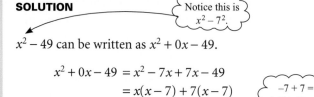

Notice this is $x^2 - 7^2$.

$x^2 - 49$ can be written as $x^2 + 0x - 49$.

$$x^2 + 0x - 49 = x^2 - 7x + 7x - 49$$
$$= x(x - 7) + 7(x - 7)$$
$$= (x + 7)(x - 7)$$

$-7 + 7 = 0$
$(-7) \times 7 = -49$

Note

The expression in Example 1.25 was an example of *the difference of two squares* which may be written in more general form as

$$a^2 - b^2 = (a + b)(a - b).$$

? What would help you to remember the general results from Examples 1.24 and 1.25?

The previous examples have all started with the term x^2, that is the coefficient of x^2 has been 1. This is not the case in the next example.

EXAMPLE 1.26

Factorise $6x^2 + x - 12$.

SOLUTION

The technique for finding how to split the middle term is now adjusted. Start by multiplying the two outside numbers together:

$$6 \times (-12) = -72.$$

Now look for two numbers which add to give $+1$ (the coefficient of x) and multiply to give -72 (the number found above).

$$(+9) + (-8) = +1 \qquad\qquad (+9) \times (-8) = -72$$

Splitting the middle term gives

$3x$ is a factor of both $6x^2$ and $9x$.

$$6x^2 + 9x - 8x - 12 = 3x(2x + 3) - 4(2x + 3)$$
$$= (3x - 4)(2x + 3)$$

-4 is a factor of both $-8x$ and -12.

Note

The method used in the earlier examples is really the same as this. It is just that in those cases the coefficient of x^2 was 1 and so multiplying the constant term by it had no effect.

 Before starting the procedure for factorising a quadratic, you should always check that the terms do not have a common factor as for example in

$$2x^2 - 8x + 6.$$

This can be written as $2(x^2 - 4x + 3)$ and factorised to give $2(x - 3)(x - 1)$.

Solving quadratic equations

It is a simple matter to solve a quadratic equation once the quadratic expression has been factorised. Since the product of the two factors is zero, it follows that one or other of them must equal zero, and this gives the solution.

EXAMPLE 1.27

Solve $x^2 - 40x - 6000 = 0$.

SOLUTION

$$
\begin{aligned}
x^2 - 40x - 6000 &= x^2 - 100x + 60x - 6000 \\
&= x(x - 100) + 60(x - 100) \\
&= (x + 60)(x - 100)
\end{aligned}
$$

$\Rightarrow \qquad (x + 60)(x - 100) = 0$

$\Rightarrow \qquad$ either $x + 60 = 0 \quad \Rightarrow \quad x = -60$

$\Rightarrow \qquad$ or $x - 100 = 0 \quad \Rightarrow \quad x = 100$

The solution is $x = -60$ or 100. ◄───

? Look back to page 12. What is the length of the field?

Note

The *solution* of the equation in the example is $x = -60$ or 100.

The *roots* of the equation are the values of x which satisfy the equation, in this case one root is $x = -60$ and the other root is $x = 100$.

Sometimes an equation can be rewritten as a quadratic and then solved.

EXAMPLE 1.28

Solve $x^4 - 13x^2 + 36 = 0$

SOLUTION

This is a quartic equation (its highest power of x is 4) and it isn't easy to factorise this directly. However, you can rewrite the equation as a quadratic in x^2.

Let $y = x^2$

$$x^4 - 13x^2 + 36 = 0$$
$$\Rightarrow (x^2)^2 - 13x^2 + 36 = 0$$
$$\Rightarrow \quad y^2 - 13y + 36 = 0$$

You can replace x^2 with y to get a quadratic equation.

Now you have a quadratic equation which you can factorise.

$$(y - 4)(y - 9) = 0$$

Don't stop here. You are asked to find x, not y.

So $\quad y = 4$ or $y = 9$

Since $y = x^2$ then $x^2 = 4 \Rightarrow x = \pm 2$

or $x^2 = 9 \Rightarrow x = \pm 3$

Remember the negative square root.

You may have to do some work rearranging the equation before you can solve it.

EXAMPLE 1.29

Find the real roots of the equation $x^2 - 2 = \dfrac{8}{x^2}$.

SOLUTION

You need to rearrange the equation before you can solve it.

$$x^2 - 2 = \frac{8}{x^2}$$

Multiply by x^2: $\quad x^4 - 2x^2 = 8$

Rearrange: $\quad x^4 - 2x^2 - 8 = 0$

This is a quadratic in x^2. You can factorise it directly, without substituting in for x^2.

$\Rightarrow (x^2 + 2)(x^2 - 4) = 0$

So $x^2 = -2$ which has no real solutions.

or $x^2 = 4 \Rightarrow x = \pm 2$

So this quartic equation only has two real roots. You can find out more about roots which are not real in P3.

EXERCISE 1D

1 Factorise the following expressions.

(i) $al + am + bl + bm$

(ii) $px + py - qx - qy$

(iii) $ur - vr + us - vs$

(iv) $m^2 + mn + pm + pn$

(v) $x^2 - 3x + 2x - 6$

(vi) $y^2 + 3y + 7y + 21$

(vii) $z^2 - 5z + 5z - 25$

(viii) $q^2 - 3q - 3q + 9$

(ix) $2x^2 + 2x + 3x + 3$

(x) $6v^2 + 3v - 20v - 10$

2 Multiply out the following expressions and collect like terms.

(i) $(a + 2)(a + 3)$

(ii) $(b + 5)(b + 7)$

(iii) $(c - 4)(c - 2)$

(iv) $(d - 5)(d - 4)$

(v) $(e + 6)(e - 1)$

(vi) $(g - 3)(g + 3)$

(vii) $(h + 5)^2$

(viii) $(2i - 3)^2$

(ix) $(a + b)(c + d)$

(x) $(x + y)(x - y)$

3 Factorise the following quadratic expressions.

    (i) $x^2 + 6x + 8$ (ii) $x^2 - 6x + 8$

    (iii) $y^2 + 9y + 20$ (iv) $r^2 + 2r - 15$

    (v) $r^2 - 2r - 15$ (vi) $s^2 - 4s + 4$

    (vii) $x^2 - 5x - 6$ (viii) $x^2 + 2x + 1$

    (ix) $a^2 - 9$ (x) $(x + 3)^2 - 9$

4 Factorise the following expressions.

    (i) $2x^2 + 5x + 2$ (ii) $2x^2 - 5x + 2$

    (iii) $5x^2 + 11x + 2$ (iv) $5x^2 - 11x + 2$

    (v) $2x^2 + 14x + 24$ (vi) $4x^2 - 49$

    (vii) $6x^2 - 5x - 6$ (viii) $9x^2 - 6x + 1$

    (ix) $t_1^{\,2} - t_2^{\,2}$ (x) $2x^2 - 11xy + 5y^2$

5 Solve the following equations.

    (i) $x^2 - 11x + 24 = 0$ (ii) $x^2 + 11x + 24 = 0$

    (iii) $x^2 - 11x + 18 = 0$ (iv) $x^2 - 6x + 9 = 0$

    (v) $x^2 - 64 = 0$

6 Solve the following equations.

    (i) $3x^2 - 5x + 2 = 0$ (ii) $3x^2 + 5x + 2 = 0$

    (iii) $3x^2 - 5x - 2 = 0$ (iv) $25x^2 - 16 = 0$

    (v) $9x^2 - 12x + 4 = 0$

7 Solve the following equations.

    (i) $x^2 - x = 20$ (ii) $\dfrac{3x^2 + 5x}{3} = 4$

    (iii) $x^2 + 4 = 4x$ (iv) $2x + 1 = \dfrac{15}{x}$

    (v) $x - 1 = \dfrac{6}{x}$ (vi) $3x + \dfrac{8}{x} = 14$

8 Solve the following equations.

    (i) $x^4 - 5x^2 + 4 = 0$ (ii) $x^4 - 10x^2 + 9 = 0$

    (iii) $9x^4 - 13x^2 + 4 = 0$ (iv) $4x^4 - 25x^2 + 36 = 0$

    (v) $25x^4 - 4x^2 = 0$ (vi) $x - 6\sqrt{x} + 5 = 0$

    (vii) $x^6 - 9x^3 + 8 = 0$ (viii) $x - \sqrt{x} - 6 = 0$

9 Find the real roots of the following equations.

    (i) $x^2 + 1 = \dfrac{2}{x^2}$ (ii) $x^2 = 1 + \dfrac{12}{x^2}$

    (iii) $x^2 - 6 = \dfrac{27}{x^2}$ (iv) $1 + \dfrac{1}{x^2} - \dfrac{20}{x^4} = 0$

    (v) $\dfrac{9}{x^4} + 4 = \dfrac{13}{x^2}$ (vi) $x^3 + \dfrac{2}{x^3} = 3$

    (vii) $\sqrt{x} + \dfrac{8}{\sqrt{x}} = 6$ (viii) $2 + \dfrac{3}{x} = \dfrac{7}{\sqrt{x}}$

10 Find the real roots of the equation $\dfrac{9}{x^4} + \dfrac{8}{x^2} = 1$.

11 The length of a rectangular field is 30 m greater than its width, w metres.

    (i) Write down an expression for the area $A\,\mathrm{m}^2$ of the field, in terms of w.

    (ii) The area of the field is $8800\,\mathrm{m}^2$. Find its width and perimeter.

12 A cylindrical tin of height h cm and radius r cm, has surface area, including its top and bottom, $A\,\mathrm{cm}^2$.

    (i) Write down an expression for A in terms of r, h and π.

    (ii) A tin of height 6 cm has surface area $54\pi\,\mathrm{cm}^2$. What is the radius of the tin?

    (iii) Another tin has the same diameter as height. Its surface area is $150\pi\,\mathrm{cm}^2$. What is its radius?

13 When the first n positive integers are added together, their sum is given by

$$\tfrac{1}{2}n(n+1).$$

    (i) Demonstrate that this result holds for the case $n = 5$.

    (ii) Find the value of n for which the sum is 105.

    (iii) What is the smallest value of n for which the sum exceeds 1000?

14 The shortest side AB of a right-angled triangle is x cm long. The side BC is 1 cm longer than AB and the hypotenuse, AC, is 29 cm long. Form an equation for x and solve it to find the lengths of the three sides of the triangle.

Equations that cannot be factorised

The method of quadratic factorisation is fine so long as the quadratic expression can be factorised, but not all of them can. In the case of $x^2 - 6x + 2$, for example, it is not possible to find two whole numbers which add to give -6 and multiply to give $+2$.

There are other techniques available for such situations, as you will see in the next few pages.

Graphical solution

If an equation has a solution, you can always find an approximate value for it by drawing a graph. In the case of

$$x^2 - 6x + 2 = 0$$

you draw the graph of

$$y = x^2 - 6x + 2$$

and find where it cuts the x axis.

x	0	1	2	3	4	5	6
x^2	0	1	4	9	16	25	36
$-6x$	0	-6	-12	-18	-24	-30	-36
$+2$	$+2$	$+2$	$+2$	$+2$	$+2$	$+2$	$+2$
y	$+2$	-3	-6	-7	-6	-3	$+2$

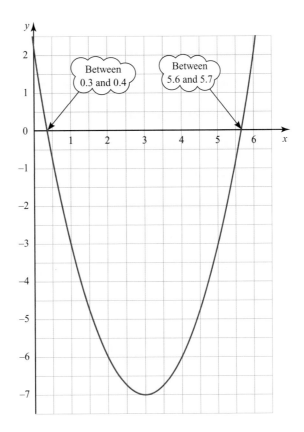

Figure 1.6

From figure 1.6, x is between 0.3 and 0.4 so approximately 0.35, or between 5.6 and 5.7 so approximately 5.65.

Clearly the accuracy of the answer is dependent on the scale of the graph but, however large a scale you use, your answer will never be completely accurate.

Completing the square

If a quadratic equation has a solution, this method will give it accurately. It involves adjusting the left-hand side of the equation to make it a perfect square. The steps involved are shown in the following example.

EXAMPLE 1.30

Solve the equation $x^2 - 6x + 2 = 0$ by completing the square.

SOLUTION

Subtract the constant term from both sides of the equation:

$$\Rightarrow \quad x^2 - 6x \quad = -2$$

Take the coefficient of x: −6
Halve it: −3
Square the answer: +9

Explain why this makes the left-hand side a perfect square.

Add it to both sides of the equation:

$$\Rightarrow \quad x^2 - 6x + 9 = -2 + 9$$

Factorise the left-hand side. It will be found to be a perfect square:

$$\Rightarrow \quad (x - 3)^2 = 7$$

Take the square root of both sides:

$$\Rightarrow \quad x - 3 = \pm \sqrt{7}$$

$$\Rightarrow \quad x = 3 \pm \sqrt{7}$$ *This is an exact answer.*

Using your calculator to find the value of $\sqrt{7}$ *This is an approximate answer.*

$$\Rightarrow \quad x = 5.646 \text{ or } 0.354, \text{ to 3 decimal places.}$$

The graphs of quadratic functions

Look at the curve in figure 1.7. It is the graph of $y = x^2 - 4x + 5$ and it has the characteristic shape of a quadratic; it is a parabola.

Notice that:

● it has a minimum point (or *vertex*) at (2, 1)

● it has a line of symmetry, $x = 2$.

It is possible to find the vertex and the line of symmetry without plotting the points by using the technique of completing the square.

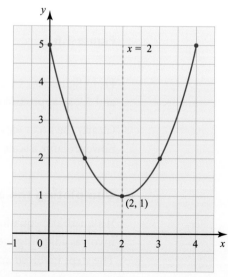

Figure 1.7

Rewrite the expression with the constant term moved to the right

$$x^2 - 4x \qquad + 5.$$

Take the coefficient of x: -4
Divide it by 2: -2
Square the answer: $+4$

Add this to the left-hand part and compensate by subtracting it from the constant term on the right

$$x^2 - 4x + 4 \qquad + 5 - 4.$$

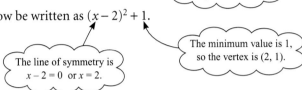

This is the completed square form.

This can now be written as $(x - 2)^2 + 1$.

The minimum value is 1, so the vertex is $(2, 1)$.

The line of symmetry is $x - 2 = 0$ or $x = 2$.

EXAMPLE 1.31

Write $x^2 + 5x + 4$ in completed square form.

Hence state the equation of the line of symmetry and the co-ordinates of the vertex of the curve $y = x^2 + 5x + 4$.

SOLUTION

$$x^2 + 5x \qquad + 4$$
$$x^2 + 5x + 6.25 \quad + 4 - 6.25$$
$$(x + 2.5)^2 - 2.25 \quad \text{(This is the completed square form.)}$$

$5 \div 2 = 2.5; \ 2.5^2 = 6.25$

The line of symmetry is $x + 2.5 = 0$, or $x = -2.5$.

The vertex is $(-2.5, -2.25)$.

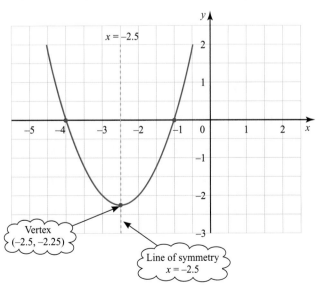

$x = -2.5$

Vertex $(-2.5, -2.25)$

Line of symmetry $x = -2.5$

Figure 1.8

⚠ For this method, the coefficient of x^2 must be 1. To use it on, say, $2x^2 + 6x + 5$, you must write it as $2(x^2 + 3x + 2.5)$ and then work with $x^2 + 3x + 2.5$. In completed square form, it is $2(x + 1.5)^2 + 0.5$. Similarly treat $-x^2 + 6x + 5$ as $-1(x^2 - 6x - 5)$ and work with $x^2 - 6x - 5$. In completed square form it is $-1(x - 3)^2 + 14$.

Completing the square is an important technique. Knowing the symmetry and least (or greatest) value of a quadratic function will often give you valuable information about the situation it is modelling.

EXERCISE 1E

1 For each of the following equations:

(a) write it in completed square form

(b) hence write down the equation of the line of symmetry and the co-ordinates of the vertex

(c) sketch the curve.

(i) $y = x^2 + 4x + 9$ (ii) $y = x^2 - 4x + 9$

(iii) $y = x^2 + 4x + 3$ (iv) $y = x^2 - 4x + 3$

(v) $y = x^2 + 6x - 1$ (vi) $y = x^2 - 10x$

(vii) $y = x^2 + x + 2$ (viii) $y = x^2 - 3x - 7$

(ix) $y = x^2 - \frac{1}{2}x + 1$ (x) $y = x^2 + 0.1x + 0.03$

2 Write the following as quadratic expressions in descending powers of x.

(i) $(x + 2)^2 - 3$ (ii) $(x + 4)^2 - 4$

(iii) $(x - 1)^2 + 2$ (iv) $(x - 10)^2 + 12$

(v) $\left(x - \frac{1}{2}\right)^2 + \frac{3}{4}$ (vi) $(x + 0.1)^2 + 0.99$

3 Write the following in completed square form.

(i) $2x^2 + 4x + 6$ (ii) $3x^2 - 18x - 27$

(iii) $-x^2 - 2x + 5$ (iv) $-2x^2 - 2x - 2$

(v) $5x^2 - 10x + 7$ (vi) $4x^2 - 4x - 4$

(vii) $-3x^2 - 12x$ (viii) $8x^2 + 24x - 2$

4 The curves below all have equations of the form $y = x^2 + bx + c$.
In each case find the values of b and c.

(i)

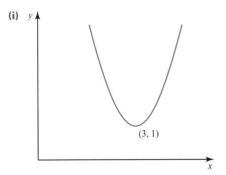

$(3, 1)$

(ii)

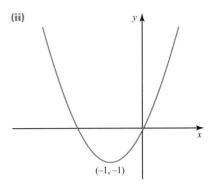

$(-1, -1)$

(iii)

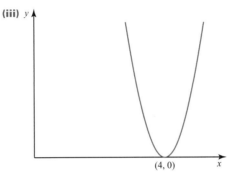

$(4, 0)$

(iv)

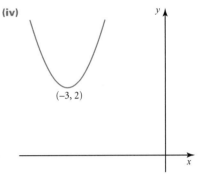

$(-3, 2)$

5 Solve the following equations by completing the square.

(i) $x^2 - 6x + 3 = 0$ **(ii)** $x^2 - 8x - 1 = 0$

(iii) $x^2 - 3x + 1 = 0$ **(iv)** $2x^2 - 6x + 1 = 0$

(v) $5x^2 + 4x - 2 = 0$

The quadratic formula

Completing the square is a powerful method because it can be used on any quadratic equation. However it is seldom used to solve an equation in practice because it can be generalised to give a formula which is used instead. The derivation of this follows exactly the same steps.

To solve a general quadratic equation $ax^2 + bx + c = 0$ by completing the square:

First divide both sides by a: $\Rightarrow x^2 + \dfrac{bx}{a} + \dfrac{c}{a} = 0$.

Subtract the constant term from both sides of the equation:

$$\Rightarrow x^2 + \frac{bx}{a} = -\frac{c}{a}$$

Take the coefficient of x: $+\dfrac{b}{a}$

Halve it: $\qquad\qquad +\dfrac{b}{2a}$

Square the answer: $\qquad +\dfrac{b^2}{4a^2}$

Add it to both sides of the equation:

$$\Rightarrow x^2 + \frac{bx}{a} + \frac{b^2}{4a^2} = \frac{b^2}{4a^2} - \frac{c}{a}$$

Factorise the left-hand side and tidy up the right-hand side:

$$\Rightarrow \left(x + \frac{b}{2a}\right)^2 = \frac{b^2 - 4ac}{4a^2}$$

Take the square root of both sides:

$$\Rightarrow x + \frac{b}{2a} = \pm\frac{\sqrt{b^2 - 4ac}}{2a}$$

$$\Rightarrow x = \frac{-b \pm \sqrt{b^2 - 4ac}}{2a}$$

This important result, known as the quadratic formula, has significance beyond the solution of awkward quadratic equations, as you will see later. The next two examples, however, demonstrate its use as a tool for solving equations.

EXAMPLE 1.32

Use the quadratic formula to solve $3x^2 - 6x + 2 = 0$.

SOLUTION

Comparing this to the form $ax^2 + bx + c = 0$

gives $a = 3$, $b = -6$ and $c = 2$.

Substituting these values in the formula $x = \dfrac{-b \pm \sqrt{b^2 - 4ac}}{2a}$

gives $x = \dfrac{6 \pm \sqrt{36 - 24}}{6}$

$\qquad = 0.423$ or 1.577 (to 3 d.p.).

EXAMPLE 1.33

Solve $x^2 - 2x + 2 = 0$.

SOLUTION

The first thing to notice is that this cannot be factorised. The only two whole numbers which multiply to give 2 are 2 and 1 (or −2 and −1) and they cannot be added to get −2.

Comparing $x^2 - 2x + 2$ to the form $ax^2 + bx + c = 0$
gives $a = 1$, $b = -2$ and $c = 2$.

Substituting these values in $x = \dfrac{-b \pm \sqrt{b^2 - 4ac}}{2a}$

gives $\dfrac{2 \pm \sqrt{4 - 8}}{2}$

$= \dfrac{2 \pm \sqrt{-4}}{2}$

Trying to find the square root of a negative number creates problems.
A positive number multiplied by itself is positive: $+2 \times +2 = +4$.
A negative number multiplied by itself is also positive: $-2 \times -2 = +4$.
Since $\sqrt{-4}$ can be neither positive nor negative, no such number exists, and so you can find no real solution.

Note

It is not quite true to say that a negative number has no square root. Certainly it has none among the real numbers but mathematicians have invented an imaginary number, denoted by i, with the property that $i^2 = -1$. Numbers like $1 + i$ and $-1 - i$ (which are in fact the solutions of the equation above) are called complex numbers. Complex numbers are extremely useful in both pure and applied mathematics; they are covered in P3.

To return to the problem of solving the equation $x^2 - 2x + 2 = 0$, look what happens if you draw the graph of $y = x^2 - 2x + 2$. The table of values is given below and the graph is shown in figure 1.9. As you can see, the graph does not cut the x axis and so there is indeed no real solution to this equation.

x	−1	0	1	2	3
x^2	+1	0	+1	+4	+9
$-2x$	+2	0	−2	−4	−6
$+2$	+2	+2	+2	+2	+2
y	+5	+2	+1	+2	+5

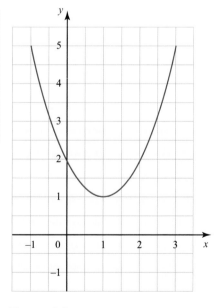

Figure 1.9

The part of the quadratic formula which determines whether or not there are real roots is the part under the square root sign. This is called the *discriminant*.

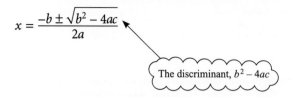

The discriminant, $b^2 - 4ac$

If $b^2 - 4ac > 0$, the equation has two real roots (see figure 1.10).

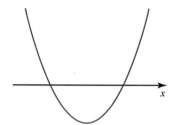

Figure 1.10

If $b^2 - 4ac < 0$, the equation has no real roots (see figure 1.11).

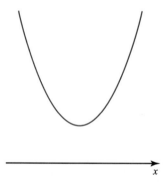

Figure 1.11

If $b^2 - 4ac = 0$, the equation has one repeated root (see figure 1.12).

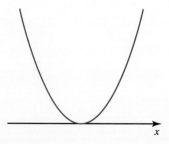

Figure 1.12

1 Use the quadratic formula to solve the following equations, where possible.

(i) $x^2 + 8x + 5 = 0$

(ii) $x^2 + 2x + 4 = 0$

(iii) $x^2 - 5x - 19 = 0$

(iv) $5x^2 - 3x + 4 = 0$

(v) $3x^2 + 2x - 4 = 0$

(vi) $x^2 - 12 = 0$

2 Find the value of the discriminant and use it to find the number of real roots for each of the following equations.

(i) $x^2 - 3x + 4 = 0$

(ii) $x^2 - 3x - 4 = 0$

(iii) $4x^2 - 3x = 0$

(iv) $3x^2 + 8 = 0$

(v) $3x^2 + 4x + 1 = 0$

(vi) $x^2 + 10x + 25 = 0$

3 Show that the equation $ax^2 + bx - a = 0$ has real roots for all values of a and b.

4 Find the value(s) of k for which these equations have one repeated root.

(i) $x^2 - 2x + k = 0$

(ii) $3x^2 - 6x + k = 0$

(iii) $kx^2 + 3x - 4 = 0$

(iv) $2x^2 + kx + 8 = 0$

(v) $3x^2 + 2kx - 3k = 0$

5 The height h metres of a ball at time t seconds after it is thrown up in the air is given by the expression

$$h = 1 + 15t - 5t^2.$$

(i) Find the times at which the height is $11\,\text{m}$.

(ii) Use your calculator to find the time at which the ball hits the ground.

(iii) What is the greatest height the ball reaches?

Simultaneous equations

There are many situations which can only be described mathematically in terms of more than one variable. When you need to find the values of the variables in such situations, you need to solve two or more equations simultaneously (i.e. at the same time). Such equations are called *simultaneous equations*. If you need to find values of two variables, you will need to solve two simultaneous equations; if three variables, then three equations, and so on. The work here is confined to solving two equations to find the values of two variables, but most of the methods can be extended to more variables if required.

ⓑ Linear simultaneous equations

EXAMPLE 1.34

At a poultry farm, six hens and one duck cost $40, while four hens and three ducks cost $36. What is the cost of each type of bird?

SOLUTION

Let the cost of one hen be $\$h$ and the cost of one duck be $\$d$.

Then the information given can be written as:

$$6h + d = 40 \quad ①$$
$$4h + 3d = 36. \quad ②$$

There are several methods of solving this pair of equations.

Method 1: Elimination

Multiplying equation ① by 3	$\Rightarrow$	$18h + 3d = 120$
Leaving equation ②	$\Rightarrow$	$4h + 3d = 36$
Subtracting	$\Rightarrow$	$14h = 84$
Dividing both sides by 14	$\Rightarrow$	$h = 6$
Substituting $h = 6$ in equation ① gives		$36 + d = 40$
	$\Rightarrow$	$d = 4$

Therefore a hen costs $6 and a duck $4.

Note

1 The first step was to multiply equation ① by 3 so that there would be a term $3d$ in both equations. This meant that when equation ② was subtracted, the variable d was eliminated and so it was possible to find the value of h.

2 The value $h = 6$ was substituted in equation ① but it could equally well have been substituted in the other equation. Check for yourself that this too gives the answer $d = 4$.

Before looking at other methods for solving this pair of equations, here is another example.

EXAMPLE 1.35

Solve
$$3x + 5y = 12 \quad ①$$
$$2x - 6y = -20 \quad ②$$

SOLUTION

① × 6	$\Rightarrow$	$18x + 30y = 72$
② × 5	$\Rightarrow$	$10x - 30y = -100$
Adding	$\Rightarrow$	$28x = -28$
Giving		$x = -1$

Substituting $x = -1$ in equation ①	$\Rightarrow$	$-3 + 5y = 12$
Adding 3 to each side	$\Rightarrow$	$5y = 15$
Dividing by 5	$\Rightarrow$	$y = 3$

Therefore $x = -1$, $y = 3$.

Note

In this example, both equations were multiplied, the first by 6 to give $+30y$ and the second by 5 to give $-30y$. Because one of these terms was positive and the other negative, it was necessary to add rather than subtract in order to eliminate y.

Returning now to the pair of equations giving the prices of hens and ducks,

$$6h + d = 40 \qquad ①$$
$$4h + 3d = 36 \qquad ②$$

here are two alternative methods of solving them.

Method 2: Substitution

The equation $6h + d = 40$ is rearranged to make d its subject:

$$d = 40 - 6h.$$

This expression for d is now substituted in the other equation, $4h + 3d = 36$, giving

$$
\begin{aligned}
4h + 3(40 - 6h) &= 36 \\
\Rightarrow \quad 4h + 120 - 18h &= 36 \\
\Rightarrow \quad -14h &= -84 \\
\Rightarrow \quad h &= 6
\end{aligned}
$$

Substituting for h in $d = 40 - 6h$ gives $d = 40 - 36 = 4$.

Therefore a hen costs \$6 and a duck \$4 (the same answer as before, of course).

Method 3: Intersection of the graphs of the equations

Figure 1.13 shows the graphs of the two equations, $6h + d = 40$ and $4h + 3d = 36$. As you can see, they intersect at the solution, $h = 6$ and $d = 4$.

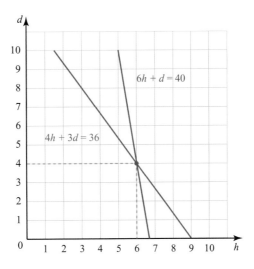

Figure 1.13

Non-linear simultaneous equations

The simultaneous equations in the examples so far have all been *linear*, that is their graphs have been straight lines. A linear equation in, say, x and y contains only terms in x and y and a constant term. So $7x + 2y = 11$ is linear but $7x^2 + 2y = 11$ is not linear, since it contains a term in x^2.

You can solve a pair of simultaneous equations, one of which is linear and the other not, using the substitution method. This is shown in the next example.

EXAMPLE 1.36

Solve
$$x + 2y = 7 \qquad ①$$
$$x^2 + y^2 = 10 \qquad ②$$

SOLUTION

Rearranging equation ① gives $x = 7 - 2y$.
Substituting for x in equation ②:

$$(7 - 2y)^2 + y^2 = 10$$

Multiplying out the $(7 - 2y) \times (7 - 2y)$

gives $49 - 14y - 14y + 4y^2 = 49 - 28y + 4y^2$,

so the equation is

$$49 - 28y + 4y^2 + y^2 = 10.$$

This is rearranged to give

$$5y^2 - 28y + 39 = 0$$
$$\Rightarrow \quad 5y^2 - 15y - 13y + 39 = 0$$
$$\Rightarrow \quad 5y(y - 3) - 13(y - 3) = 0$$
$$\Rightarrow \quad (5y - 13)(y - 3) = 0$$

> A quadratic in y which you can now solve using factorisation or the formula.

Either $\quad 5y - 13 = 0 \quad \Rightarrow \quad y = 2.6$
Or $\quad\quad\quad y - 3 = 0 \quad \Rightarrow \quad y = 3$

Substituting in equation ①, $x + 2y = 7$:

$$y = 2.6 \quad \Rightarrow \quad x = 1.8$$
$$y = 3 \quad \Rightarrow \quad x = 1$$

The solution is either $x = 1.8$, $y = 2.6$ or $x = 1$, $y = 3$.

 Always substitute into the linear equation. Substituting in the quadratic will give you extra answers which are not correct.

1 Solve the following pairs of simultaneous equations.

(i) $2x + 3y = 8$
$3x + 2y = 7$

(ii) $x + 4y = 16$
$3x + 5y = 20$

(iii) $7x + y = 15$
$4x + 3y = 11$

(iv) $5x - 2y = 3$
$x + 4y = 5$

(v) $8x - 3y = 21$
$5x + y = 16$

(vi) $8x + y = 32$
$7x - 9y = 28$

(vii) $4x + 3y = 5$
$2x - 6y = -5$

(viii) $3u - 2v = 17$
$5u - 3v = 28$

(ix) $4l - 3m = 2$
$5l - 7m = 9$

2 A student wishes to spend exactly \$10 at a second-hand bookshop. All the paperbacks are one price, all the hardbacks another. She can buy five paperbacks and eight hardbacks. Alternatively she can buy ten paperbacks and six hardbacks.

(i) Write this information as a pair of simultaneous equations.

(ii) Solve your equations to find the cost of each type of book.

3 The cost of a pear is 5c greater than that of an apple. Eight apples and nine pears cost \$1.64.

(i) Write this information as a pair of simultaneous equations.

(ii) Solve your equations to find the cost of each type of fruit.

4 A car journey of 380 km lasts 4 hours. Part of this is on a motorway at an average speed of 110 $km\,h^{-1}$, the rest on country roads at an average speed of 70 $km\,h^{-1}$.

(i) Write this information as a pair of simultaneous equations.

(ii) Solve your equations to find how many kilometres of the journey is spent on each type of road.

5 Solve the following pairs of simultaneous equations.

(i) $x^2 + y^2 = 10$
$x + y = 4$

(ii) $x^2 - 2y^2 = 8$
$x + 2y = 8$

(iii) $2x^2 + 3y = 12$
$x - y = -1$

(iv) $k^2 + km = 8$
$m = k - 6$

(v) $t_1^2 - t_2^2 = 75$
$t_1 = 2t_2$

(vi) $p + q + 5 = 0$
$p^2 = q^2 + 5$

(vii) $k(k - m) = 12$
$k(k + m) = 60$

(viii) $p_1^2 - p_2^2 = 0$
$p_1 + p_2 = 2$

6 The diagram shows the net of a cylindrical container of radius r cm and height h cm. The full width of the metal sheet from which the container is made is 1 m, and the shaded area is waste. The surface area of the container is 1400π cm².

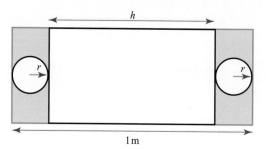

(i) Write down a pair of simultaneous equations for r and h.

(ii) Find the volume of the container, giving your answers in terms of π. (There are two possible answers.)

7 A large window consists of six square panes of glass as shown. Each pane is x m by x m, and all the dividing wood is y m wide.

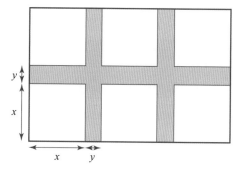

(i) Write down the total area of the whole window in terms of x and y.

(ii) Show that the total area of the dividing wood is $7xy + 2y^2$.

(iii) The total area of glass is 1.5 m², and the total area of dividing wood is 1 m². Find x, and hence find an equation for y and solve it.

[MEI]

Inequalities

Not all algebraic statements involve the equals sign and it is just as important to be able to handle algebraic inequalities as it is to solve algebraic equations. The solution to an inequality is a range of possible values, not specific value(s) as in the case of an equation.

Linear inequalities

 The methods for linear inequalities are much the same as those for equations but you must be careful when multiplying or dividing through an inequality by a negative number.

Take for example the following statement:

$$5 > 3 \text{ is true}$$

Multiply both sides by -1 $-5 > -3$ is false.

 It is actually the case that multiplying or dividing by a negative number reverses the inequality, but you may prefer to avoid the difficulty, as shown in the examples below.

EXAMPLE 1.37

Solve $5x - 3 \leqslant 2x - 15$.

SOLUTION

Add 3 to, and subtract $2x$ from, both sides $\Rightarrow 5x - 2x \leqslant -15 + 3$
Tidy up $\Rightarrow \qquad 3x \leqslant -12$
Divide both sides by 3 $\Rightarrow \qquad x \leqslant -4$

Note

Since there was no need to multiply or divide both sides by a negative number, no problems arose in this example.

EXAMPLE 1.38

Solve $2y + 6 > 7y + 11$.

SOLUTION

Subtract 6 and $7y$ from both sides $\Rightarrow \quad 2y - 7y > 11 - 6$
Tidy up $\Rightarrow \qquad -5y > +5$

> Beware: do not divide both sides by -5.

Add $5y$ to both sides and subtract 5 $\Rightarrow \qquad -5 > +5y$

> This now allows you to divide both sides by $+5$.

Divide both sides by $+5$ $\Rightarrow \qquad -1 > y$

Note that logically $-1 > y$ is the same as $y < -1$, so the solution is $y < -1$.

Quadratic inequalities

EXAMPLE 1.39

Solve (i) $x^2 - 4x + 3 > 0$ (ii) $x^2 - 4x + 3 \leqslant 0$.

SOLUTION

The graph of $y = x^2 - 4x + 3$ is shown in figure 1.14 with the green parts of the x axis corresponding to the solutions to the two parts of the question.

(i) You want the values of x for which $y > 0$, which that is where the curve is above the x axis.

(ii) You want the values of x for which $y \leqslant 0$, that is where the curve crosses or is below the x axis.

Here the end points *are not* included in the inequality so you draw open circles: ○

Here the end points *are* included in the inequality so you draw solid circles: ●

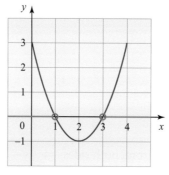

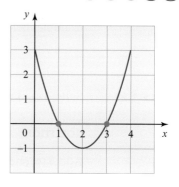

Figure 1.14

The solution is $x < 1$ or $x > 3$.

The solution is $x \geqslant 1$ and $x \leqslant 3$, usually witten $1 \leqslant x \leqslant 3$.

EXAMPLE 1.40

Find the set of values of k for which $x^2 + kx + 4 = 0$ has real roots.

SOLUTION

A quadratic equation, $ax^2 + bx + c = 0$, has real roots if $b^2 - 4ac \geqslant 0$.

So $x^2 + kx + 4 = 0$ has real roots if $k^2 - 4 \times 4 \times 1 \geqslant 0$.

$\Rightarrow k^2 - 16 \geqslant 0$
$\Rightarrow k^2 \geqslant 16$

Take the square root of both sides.

So the set of values is $k \geqslant 4$ and $k \leqslant -4$.

Take care: $(-5)^2 = 25$ and $(-3)^2 = 9$, so k must be less than or equal to -4.

EXERCISE 1H

1 Solve the following inequalities.

(i) $5a + 6 > 2a + 24$

(ii) $3b - 5 \leqslant b - 1$

(iii) $4(c - 1) > 3(c - 2)$

(iv) $d - 3(d + 2) \geqslant 2(1 + 2d)$

(v) $\frac{1}{2}e + 3\frac{1}{2} < e$

(vi) $-f - 2f - 3 < 4(1 + f)$

(vii) $5(2 - 3g) + g \geqslant 8(2g - 4)$

(viii) $3(h + 2) - 2(h - 4) > 7(h + 2)$

2 Solve the following inequalities by sketching the curves of the functions involved.

(i) $p^2 - 5p + 4 < 0$

(ii) $p^2 - 5p + 4 \geqslant 0$

(iii) $x^2 + 3x + 2 \leqslant 0$

(iv) $x^2 + 3x > -2$

(v) $y^2 - 2y - 3 > 0$

(vi) $z(z - 1) \leqslant 20$

(vii) $q^2 - 4q + 4 > 0$

(viii) $y(y - 2) > 8$

(ix) $3x^2 + 5x - 2 < 0$

(x) $2y^2 - 11y - 6 \geqslant 0$

(xi) $4x - 3 \geqslant x^2$

(xii) $10y^2 > y + 3$

3 Find the set of values of k for which each of these equations has two real roots.

(i) $2x^2 - 3x + k = 0$

(ii) $kx^2 + 4x - 1 = 0$

(iii) $5x^2 + kx + 5 = 0$

(iv) $3x^2 + 2kx + k = 0$

4 Find the set of values of k for which each of these equations has no real roots.

(i) $x^2 - 6x + k = 0$

(ii) $kx^2 + x - 2 = 0$

(iii) $4x^2 - kx + 4 = 0$

(iv) $2kx^2 - kx + 1 = 0$

KEY POINTS

1 The quadratic formula for solving $ax^2 + bx + c = 0$ is

$$x = \frac{-b \pm \sqrt{b^2 - 4ac}}{2a}$$

where $b^2 - 4ac$ is called the discriminant.

If $b^2 - 4ac > 0$, the equation has two real roots.
If $b^2 - 4ac = 0$, the equation has one repeated root.
If $b^2 - 4ac < 0$, the equation has no real roots.

2 To solve a pair of simultaneous equations where one equation is non-linear:

● first make x or y the subject of the *linear* equation
● then substitute this rearranged equation for x or y in the *non-linear* equation
● solve to find y or x
● substitute back into the linear equation to find pairs of solutions.

3 Linear inequalities are dealt with like equations *but* if you multiply or divide by a negative number you must reverse the inequality sign.

4 When solving a quadratic inequality it is advisable to sketch the graph.

2 Co-ordinate geometry

A place for everything, and everything in its place

Samuel Smiles

Co-ordinates

Co-ordinates are a means of describing a position relative to some fixed point, or origin. In two dimensions you need two pieces of information; in three dimensions, you need three pieces of information.

In the Cartesian system (named after René Descartes), position is given in perpendicular directions: x, y in two dimensions; x, y, z in three dimensions (see figure 2.1). This chapter concentrates exclusively on two dimensions.

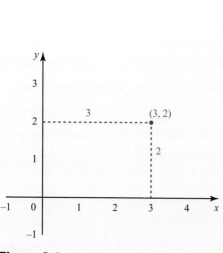

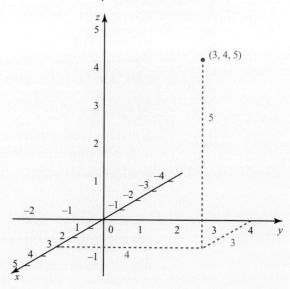

Figure 2.1

Plotting, sketching and drawing

In two dimensions, the co-ordinates of points are often marked on paper and joined up to form lines or curves. A number of words are used to describe this process.

Plot (a line or curve) means mark the points and join them up as accurately as you can. You would expect to do this on graph paper and be prepared to read information from the graph.

Sketch means mark points in approximately the right positions and join them up in the right general shape. You would not expect to use graph paper for a sketch and would not read precise information from one. You would however mark on the co-ordinates of important points, like intersections with the x and y axes and points at which the curve changes direction.

Draw means that you are to use a level of accuracy appropriate to the circumstances, and this could be anything between a rough sketch and a very accurately plotted graph.

The gradient of a line

In everyday English, the word *line* is used to mean a straight line or a curve. In mathematics, it is usually understood to mean a straight line. If you know the co-ordinates of any two points on a line, then you can draw the line.

The slope of a line is measured by its *gradient*. It is often denoted by the letter m.

In figure 2.2, A and B are two points on the line. The gradient of the line AB is given by the increase in the y co-ordinate from A to B divided by the increase in the x co-ordinate from A to B.

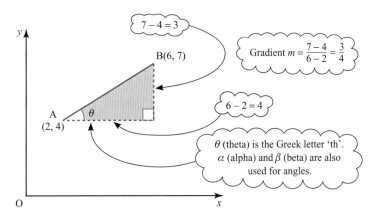

$7 - 4 = 3$

B(6, 7)

Gradient $m = \dfrac{7-4}{6-2} = \dfrac{3}{4}$

$6 - 2 = 4$

A
(2, 4)

θ (theta) is the Greek letter 'th'. α (alpha) and β (beta) are also used for angles.

Figure 2.2

In general, when A is the point (x_1, y_1) and B is the point (x_2, y_2), the gradient is

$$m = \frac{y_2 - y_1}{x_2 - x_1}.$$

When the same scale is used on both axes, $m = \tan \theta$ (see figure 2.2). Figure 2.3 shows four lines. Looking at each one from left to right: line A goes uphill and its gradient is positive; line B goes downhill and its gradient is negative. Line C is horizontal and its gradient is 0; the vertical line D has an infinite gradient.

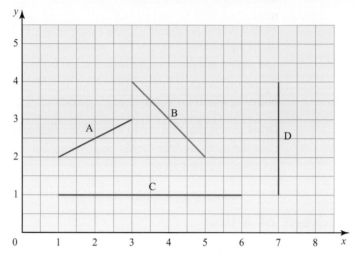

Figure 2.3

ACTIVITY 2.1

On each line in figure 2.3, take any two points and call them (x_1, y_1) and (x_2, y_2). Substitute the values of x_1, y_1, x_2 and y_2 in the formula

$$m = \frac{y_2 - y_1}{x_2 - x_1}$$

and so find the gradient.

❓ Does it matter which point you call (x_1, y_1) and which (x_2, y_2)?

Parallel and perpendicular lines

If you know the gradients m_1 and m_2 of two lines, you can tell at once if they are either parallel or perpendicular – see figure 2.4.

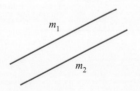

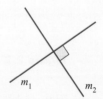

Figure 2.4   parallel lines: $m_1 = m_2$ perpendicular lines: $m_1 m_2 = -1$

Lines which are parallel have the same slope and so $m_1 = m_2$. If the lines are perpendicular, $m_1 m_2 = -1$. You can see why this is so in the activities below.

ACTIVITY 2.2   Draw the line L_1 joining $(0, 2)$ to $(4, 4)$, and draw another line L_2 perpendicular to L_1. Find the gradients m_1 and m_2 of these two lines and show that $m_1 m_2 = -1$.

ACTIVITY 2.3   The lines AB and BC in figure 2.5 are equal in length and perpendicular. By showing that triangles ABE and BCD are congruent prove that the gradients m_1 and m_2 must satisfy $m_1 m_2 = -1$.

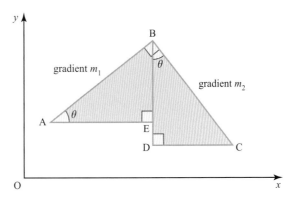

Figure 2.5

⚠ Lines for which $m_1 m_2 = -1$ will only look perpendicular if the same scale has been used for both axes.

The distance between two points

When the co-ordinates of two points are known, the distance between them can be calculated using Pythagoras' theorem, as shown in figure 2.6.

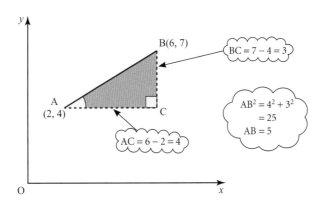

B(6, 7)

BC = 7 − 4 = 3

A
(2, 4)

C

$AB^2 = 4^2 + 3^2$
$= 25$
$AB = 5$

AC = 6 − 2 = 4

Figure 2.6

This method can be generalised to find the distance between any two points, $A(x_1, y_1)$ and $B(x_2, y_2)$, as in figure 2.7.

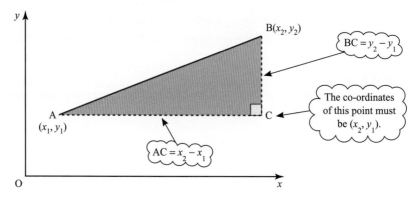

Figure 2.7

The length of the line AB is $\sqrt{(x_2 - x_1)^2 + (y_2 - y_1)^2}$.

The mid-point of a line joining two points

Look at the line joining the points A(2, 1) and B(8, 5) in figure 2.8. The point M(5, 3) is the mid-point of AB.

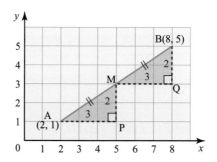

Figure 2.8

Notice that the co-ordinates of M are the means of the co-ordinates of A and B.

$$5 = \tfrac{1}{2}(2 + 8); \quad 3 = \tfrac{1}{2}(1 + 5).$$

This result can be generalised as follows. For any two points $A(x_1, y_1)$ and $B(x_2, y_2)$, the co-ordinates of the mid-point of AB are the means of the co-ordinates of A and B so the mid-point is

$$\left(\frac{x_1 + x_2}{2}, \frac{y_1 + y_2}{2} \right).$$

EXAMPLE 2.1

A and B are the points (2, 5) and (6, 3) respectively (see figure 2.9). Find:

(i)   the gradient of AB
(ii) the length of AB
(iii) the mid-point of AB
(iv) the gradient of a line perpendicular to AB.

SOLUTION

Taking A(2, 5) as the point (x_1, y_1), and B(6, 3) as the point (x_2, y_2) gives $x_1 = 2$, $y_1 = 5$, $x_2 = 6$, $y_2 = 3$.

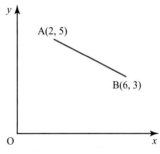

(i)   Gradient $= \dfrac{y_2 - y_1}{x_2 - x_1}$

$= \dfrac{3 - 5}{6 - 2} = -\dfrac{1}{2}$

(ii) Length AB $= \sqrt{(x_2 - x_1)^2 + (y_2 - y_1)^2}$

$= \sqrt{(6 - 2)^2 + (3 - 5)^2}$

$= \sqrt{16 + 4} = \sqrt{20}$

Figure 2.9

(iii) Mid-point $= \left(\dfrac{x_1 + x_2}{2}, \dfrac{y_1 + y_2}{2} \right)$

$= \left(\dfrac{2 + 6}{2}, \dfrac{5 + 3}{2} \right) = (4, 4)$

(iv) Gradient of AB $= m_1 = -\dfrac{1}{2}$.

If m_2 is the gradient of a line perpendicular to AB, then $m_1 m_2 = -1$

$\Rightarrow -\dfrac{1}{2} m_2 = -1$

$m_2 = 2$.

EXAMPLE 2.2

Using two different methods, show that the lines joining P(2, 7), Q(3, 2) and R(0, 5) form a right-angled triangle (see figure 2.10).

SOLUTION

Method 1

Gradient of RP $= \dfrac{7 - 5}{2 - 0} = 1$

Gradient of RQ $= \dfrac{2 - 5}{3 - 0} = -1$

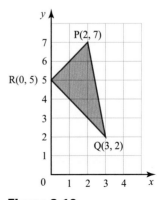

$\Rightarrow$ Product of gradients $= 1 \times (-1) = -1$

Figure 2.10

$\Rightarrow$ Sides RP and RQ are at right angles.

Method 2

Pythagoras' theorem states that for a right-angled triangle whose hypotenuse has length a and whose other sides have lengths b and c, $a^2 = b^2 + c^2$.

Conversely, if you can show that $a^2 = b^2 + c^2$ for a triangle with sides of lengths a, b, and c, then the triangle has a right angle and the side of length a is the hypotenuse.

This is the basis for the alternative proof, in which you use

$$\text{length}^2 = (x_2 - x_1)^2 + (y_2 - y_1)^2.$$

$$PQ^2 = (3 - 2)^2 + (2 - 7)^2 = 1 + 25 = 26$$

$$RP^2 = (2 - 0)^2 + (7 - 5)^2 = 4 + 4 = 8$$

$$RQ^2 = (3 - 0)^2 + (2 - 5)^2 = 9 + 9 = 18$$

Since $26 = 8 + 18$, $\qquad PQ^2 = RP^2 + RQ^2$

$\Rightarrow$ Sides RP and RQ are at right angles.

EXERCISE 2A

1 For the following pairs of points A and B, calculate:

  (a) the gradient of the line AB

  (b) the mid-point of the line joining A to B

  (c) the distance AB

  (d) the gradient of the line perpendicular to AB.

  (i) A(0, 1)   B(2, −3)   **(ii)** A(3, 2)   B(4, −1)

  (iii) A(−6, 3)   B(6, 3)   **(iv)** A(5, 2)   B(2, −8)

  (v) A(4, 3)   B(2, 0)   **(vi)** A(1, 4)   B(1, −2)

2 The line joining the point P(3, −4) to Q(q, 0) has a gradient of 2. Find the value of q.

3 The three points X(2, −1), Y(8, y) and Z(11, 2) are collinear (i.e. they lie on the same straight line). Find the value of y.

4 The points A, B, C and D have co-ordinates (1, 2), (7, 5), (9, 8) and (3, 5).

  (i) Find the gradients of the lines AB, BC, CD and DA.

  (ii) What do these gradients tell you about the quadrilateral ABCD?

  (iii) Draw a diagram to check your answer to part **(ii)**.

5 The points A, B and C have co-ordinates (2, 1), (b, 3) and (5, 5), where $b > 3$ and $\angle ABC = 90°$. Find:

  (i) the value of b

  (ii) the lengths of AB and BC

  (iii) the area of triangle ABC.

6 The triangle PQR has vertices P(8, 6), Q(0, 2) and R(2, r). Find the values of r when the triangle:

   (i) has a right angle at P

   (ii) has a right angle at Q

   (iii) has a right angle at R

   (iv) is isosceles with RQ = RP.

7 The points A, B, and C have co-ordinates (−4, 2), (7, 4) and (−3, −1).

   (i) Draw the triangle ABC.

   (ii) Show by calculation that the triangle ABC is isosceles and name the two equal sides.

   (iii) Find the mid-point of the third side.

   (iv) By calculating appropriate lengths, calculate the area of the triangle ABC.

8 For the points P(x, y), and Q($3x$, $5y$), find in terms of x and y:

   (i) the gradient of the line PQ

   (ii) the mid-point of the line PQ

   (iii) the length of the line PQ.

9 A quadrilateral has vertices A(0, 0), B(0, 3), C(6, 6) and D(12, 6).

   (i) Draw the quadrilateral.

   (ii) Show by calculation that it is a trapezium.

   (iii) Find the co-ordinates of E when EBCD is a parallelogram.

10 Three points A, B and C have co-ordinates (1, 3), (3, 5) and (−1, y). Find the values of y when:

   (i) AB = AC

   (ii) AC = BC

   (iii) AB is perpendicular to BC

   (iv) A, B and C are collinear.

11 The diagonals of a rhombus bisect each other at 90°, and conversely, when two lines bisect each other at 90°, the quadrilateral formed by joining the end points of the lines is a rhombus.

   Use the converse result to show that the points with co-ordinates (1, 2), (8, −2), (7, 6) and (0, 10) are the vertices of a rhombus, and find its area.

The equation of a straight line

The word *straight* means going in a constant direction, that is with fixed gradient. This fact allows you to find the equation of a straight line from first principles.

EXAMPLE 2.3

Find the equation of the straight line with gradient 2 through the point $(0, -5)$.

SOLUTION

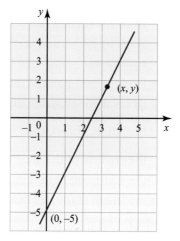

Figure 2.11

Take a general point (x, y) on the line, as shown in figure 2.11. The gradient of the line joining $(0, -5)$ to (x, y) is given by

$$\text{gradient} = \frac{y - (-5)}{x - 0} = \frac{y + 5}{x}.$$

Since we are told that the gradient of the line is 2, this gives

$$\frac{y + 5}{x} = 2$$

$$\Rightarrow \qquad y = 2x - 5.$$

Since (x, y) is a general point on the line, this holds for any point on the line and is therefore the equation of the line.

The example above can easily be generalised (see page 50) to give the result that the equation of the line with gradient m cutting the y axis at the point $(0, c)$ is

$$y = mx + c.$$

(In the example above, m is 2 and c is -5.)

This is a well-known standard form for the equation of a straight line.

Drawing a line, given its equation

There are several standard forms for the equation of a straight line, as shown in figure 2.12.

When you need to draw the graph of a straight line, given its equation, the first thing to do is to look carefully at the form of the equation and see if you can recognise it.

(a) Equations of the form $x = a$

(b) Equations of the form $y = b$

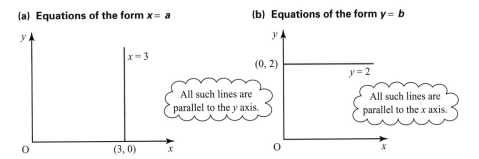

(c) Equations of the form $y = mx$

(d) Equations of the form $y = mx + c$

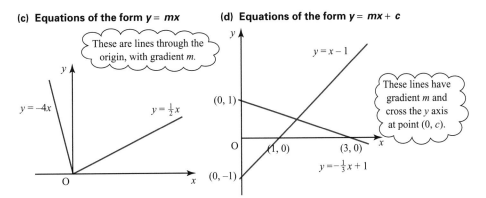

(e) Equations of the form $px + qy + r = 0$

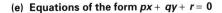

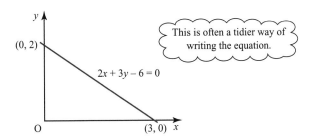

Figure 2.12

(a), (b): *Lines parallel to the axes*

Lines parallel to the x axis have the form $y =$ constant, those parallel to the y axis the form $x =$ constant. Such lines are easily recognised and drawn.

(c), (d): *Equations of the form* $y = mx + c$

The line $y = mx + c$ crosses the y axis at the point $(0, c)$ and has gradient m. If $c = 0$, it goes through the origin. In either case you know one point and can complete the line either by finding one more point, for example by substituting $x = 1$, or by following the gradient (e.g. 1 along and 2 up for gradient 2).

(e): *Equations of the form* $px + qy + r = 0$

In the case of a line given in this form, like $2x + 3y - 6 = 0$, you can either rearrange it in the form $y = mx + c$ (in this example $y = -\frac{2}{3}x + 2$), or you can find the co-ordinates of two points that lie on it. Putting $x = 0$ gives the point where it crosses the y axis, $(0, 2)$, and putting $y = 0$ gives its intersection with the x axis, $(3, 0)$.

EXAMPLE 2.4

Sketch the lines $x = 5$, $y = 0$ and $y = x$ on the same axes.
Describe the triangle formed by these lines.

SOLUTION

The line $x = 5$ is parallel to the y axis and passes through $(5, 0)$.
The line $y = 0$ is the x axis.
The line $y = x$ has gradient 1 and goes through the origin.

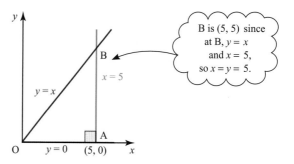

B is $(5, 5)$ since at B, $y = x$ and $x = 5$, so $x = y = 5$.

Figure 2.13

The triangle obtained is an isosceles right-angled triangle, since OA = AB = 5 units, and $\angle OAB = 90°$.

EXAMPLE 2.5

Draw $y = x - 1$ and $3x + 4y = 24$ on the same axes.

SOLUTION

The line $y = x - 1$ has gradient 1 and passes through the point $(0, -1)$.
Substituting $y = 0$ gives $x = 1$, so the line also passes through $(1, 0)$.

Find two points on the line $3x + 4y = 24$.

Substituting $x = 0$	gives	$4y = 24$	so	$y = 6$.
Substituting $y = 0$	gives	$3x = 24$	so	$x = 8$.

The line passes through $(0, 6)$ and $(8, 0)$.

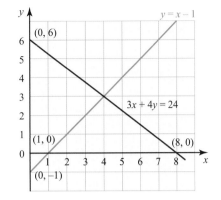

Figure 2.14

EXERCISE 2B

1 Sketch the following lines.

(i) $y = -2$ **(ii)** $x = 5$ **(iii)** $y = 2x$

(iv) $y = -3x$ **(v)** $y = 3x + 5$ **(vi)** $y = x - 4$

(vii) $y = x + 4$ **(viii)** $y = \frac{1}{2}x + 2$ **(ix)** $y = 2x + \frac{1}{2}$

(x) $y = -4x + 8$ **(xi)** $y = 4x - 8$ **(xii)** $y = -x + 1$

(xiii) $y = -\frac{1}{2}x - 2$ **(xiv)** $y = 1 - 2x$ **(xv)** $3x - 2y = 6$

(xvi) $2x + 5y = 10$ **(xvii)** $2x + y - 3 = 0$ **(xviii)** $2y = 5x - 4$

(xix) $x + 3y - 6 = 0$ **(xx)** $y = 2 - x$

2 By calculating the gradients of the following pairs of lines, state whether they are parallel, perpendicular or neither.

(i) $y = -4$ $x = 2$ **(ii)** $y = 3x$ $x = 3y$

(iii) $2x + y = 1$ $x - 2y = 1$ **(iv)** $y = 2x + 3$ $4x - y + 1 = 0$

(v) $3x - y + 2 = 0$ $3x + y = 0$ **(vi)** $2x + 3y = 4$ $2y = 3x - 2$

(vii) $x + 2y - 1 = 0$ $x + 2y + 1 = 0$ **(viii)** $y = 2x - 1$ $2x - y + 3 = 0$

(ix) $y = x - 2$ $x + y = 6$ **(x)** $y = 4 - 2x$ $x + 2y = 8$

(xi) $x + 3y - 2 = 0$ $y = 3x + 2$ **(xii)** $y = 2x$ $4x + 2y = 5$

Finding the equation of a line

The simplest way to find the equation of a straight line depends on what information you have been given.

(i) ***Given the gradient, m, and the co-ordinates (x_1, y_1) of one point on the line***

Take a general point (x, y) on the line, as shown in figure 2.15.

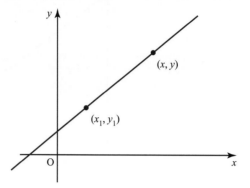

Figure 2.15

The gradient, m, of the line joining (x_1, y_1) to (x, y) is given by

$$m = \frac{y - y_1}{x - x_1}$$

$$\Rightarrow \quad y - y_1 = m(x - x_1).$$

This is a very useful form of the equation of a straight line. Two positions of the point (x_1, y_1) lead to particularly important forms of the equation.

(a) When the given point (x_1, y_1) is the point $(0, c)$, where the line crosses the y axis, the equation takes the familiar form

$$y = mx + c$$

as shown in figure 2.16.

(b) When the given point (x_1, y_1) is the origin, the equation takes the form

$$y = mx$$

as shown in figure 2.17.

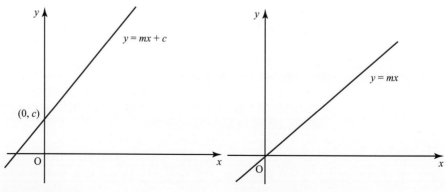

Figure 2.16   **Figure 2.17**

EXAMPLE 2.6

Find the equation of the line with gradient 3 which passes through the point $(2, -4)$.

SOLUTION

Using $y - y_1 = m(x - x_1)$
$\Rightarrow y - (-4) = 3(x - 2)$
$\Rightarrow \quad y + 4 = 3x - 6$
$\Rightarrow \quad\quad y = 3x - 10$.

(ii) Given two points, (x_1, y_1) and (x_2, y_2)

The two points are used to find the gradient:

$$m = \frac{y_2 - y_1}{x_2 - x_1}.$$

This value of m is then substituted in the equation

$$y - y_1 = m(x - x_1).$$

This gives

$$y - y_1 = \left(\frac{y_2 - y_1}{x_2 - x_1}\right)(x - x_1).$$

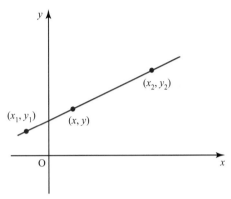

Figure 2.18

Rearranging the equation gives

$$\frac{y - y_1}{y_2 - y_1} = \frac{x - x_1}{x_2 - x_1} \quad \text{or} \quad \frac{y - y_1}{x - x_1} = \frac{y_2 - y_1}{x_2 - x_1}$$

EXAMPLE 2.7

Find the equation of the line joining $(2, 4)$ to $(5, 3)$.

SOLUTION

Taking (x_1, y_1) to be $(2, 4)$ and (x_2, y_2) to be $(5, 3)$, and substituting the values in

$$\frac{y - y_1}{y_2 - y_1} = \frac{x - x_1}{x_2 - x_1}$$

gives $\dfrac{y - 4}{3 - 4} = \dfrac{x - 2}{5 - 2}.$

This can be simplified to $x + 3y - 14 = 0$.

❓ Show that the equation of the line in figure 2.19 can be written

$$\frac{x}{a} + \frac{y}{b} = 1.$$

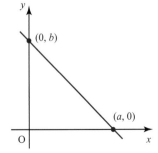

Figure 2.19

Different techniques to solve problems

The following examples illustrate the different techniques and show how these can be used to solve a problem.

EXAMPLE 2.8

Find the equations of the lines (a) – (e) in figure 2.20.

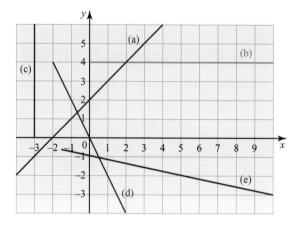

Figure 2.20

SOLUTION

Line (a) passes through (0, 2) and has gradient 1
$\Rightarrow$ equation of (a) is $y = x + 2$.

Line (b) is parallel to the x axis and passes through (0, 4)
$\Rightarrow$ equation of (b) is $y = 4$.

Line (c) is parallel to the y axis and passes through (−3, 0)
$\Rightarrow$ equation of (c) is $x = -3$.

Line (d) passes through (0, 0) and has gradient −2
$\Rightarrow$ equation of (d) is $y = -2x$.

Line (e) passes through (0, −1) and has gradient $-\frac{1}{5}$
$\Rightarrow$ equation of (e) is $y = -\frac{1}{5}x - 1$.

This can be rearranged to give $x + 5y + 5 = 0$.

EXAMPLE 2.9

Two sides of a parallelogram are the lines $2y = x + 12$ and $y = 4x - 10$. Sketch these lines on the same diagram.

The origin is a vertex of the parallelogram. Complete the sketch of the parallelogram and find the equations of the other two sides.

SOLUTION

The line $2y = x + 12$ has gradient $\frac{1}{2}$ and passes through the point $(0, 6)$

(since dividing by 2 gives $y = \frac{1}{2}x + 6$).

The line $y = 4x - 10$ has gradient 4 and passes through the point $(0, -10)$.

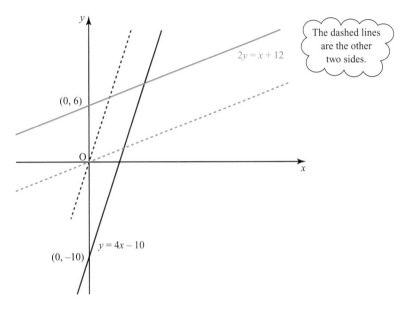

The dashed lines are the other two sides.

Figure 2.21

The other two sides are lines with gradients $\frac{1}{2}$ and 4 which pass through $(0, 0)$,

i.e. $y = \frac{1}{2}x$ and $y = 4x$.

EXAMPLE 2.10   Find the equation of the perpendicular bisector of the line joining P(−4, 5) to Q(2, 3).

SOLUTION

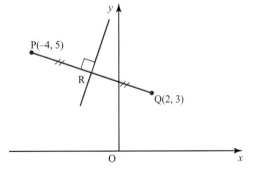

Figure 2.22

The gradient of the line PQ is

$$\frac{3-5}{2-(-4)} = \frac{-2}{6} = -\frac{1}{3}$$

and so the gradient of the perpendicular bisector is +3.

The perpendicular bisector passes throught the mid-point, R, of the line PQ. The co-ordinates of R are

$$\left(\frac{2+(-4)}{2}, \frac{3+5}{2}\right) \text{ i.e.} (-1, 4).$$

Using $y - y_1 = m(x - x_1)$, the equation of the perpendicular bisector is

$$y - 4 = 3(x - (-1))$$
$$y - 4 = 3x + 3$$
$$y = 3x + 7.$$

EXERCISE 2C

1 Find the equations of the lines (i) – (x) in the diagrams below.

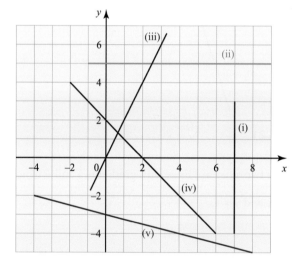

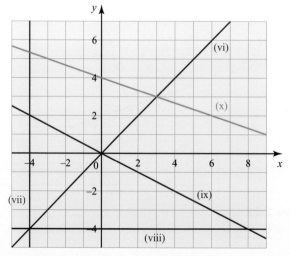

2 Find the equations of the following lines.

   (i) parallel to $y = 2x$ and passing through $(1, 5)$

   (ii) parallel to $y = 3x - 1$ and passing through $(0, 0)$

   (iii) parallel to $2x + y - 3 = 0$ and passing through $(-4, 5)$

   (iv) parallel to $3x - y - 1 = 0$ and passing through $(4, -2)$

   (v) parallel to $2x + 3y = 4$ and passing through $(2, 2)$

   (vi) parallel to $2x - y - 8 = 0$ and passing through $(-1, -5)$

3 Find the equations of the following lines.

   (i) perpendicular to $y = 3x$ and passing through $(0, 0)$

   (ii) perpendicular to $y = 2x + 3$ and passing through $(2, -1)$

   (iii) perpendicular to $2x + y = 4$ and passing through $(3, 1)$

   (iv) perpendicular to $2y = x + 5$ and passing through $(-1, 4)$

   (v) perpendicular to $2x + 3y = 4$ and passing through $(5, -1)$

   (vi) perpendicular to $4x - y + 1 = 0$ and passing through $(0, 6)$

4 Find the equations of the line AB in each of the following cases.

   (i) A$(0, 0)$ B$(4, 3)$ **(ii)** A$(2, -1)$ B$(3, 0)$

   (iii) A$(2, 7)$ B$(2, -3)$ **(iv)** A$(3, 5)$ B$(5, -1)$

   (v) A$(-2, 4)$ B$(5, 3)$ **(vi)** A$(-4, -2)$ B$(3, -2)$

5 Triangle ABC has an angle of 90° at B. Point A is on the y axis, AB is part of the line $x - 2y + 8 = 0$ and C is the point $(6, 2)$.

   (i) Sketch the triangle.

   (ii) Find the equations of AC and BC.

   (iii) Find the lengths of AB and BC and hence find the area of the triangle.

   (iv) Using your answer to part **(iii)**, find the length of the perpendicular from B to AC.

6 A median of a triangle is a line joining one of the vertices to the mid-point of the opposite side.

   In a triangle OAB, O is at the origin, A is the point $(0, 6)$ and B is the point $(6, 0)$.

   (i) Sketch the triangle.

   (ii) Find the equations of the three medians of the triangle.

   (iii) Show that the point $(2, 2)$ lies on all three medians. (This shows that the medians of this triangle are concurrent.)

7 A quadrilateral ABCD has its vertices at the points $(0, 0)$, $(12, 5)$, $(0, 10)$ and $(-6, 8)$ respectively.

   (i) Sketch the quadrilateral.

   (ii) Find the gradient of each side.

   (iii) Find the length of each side.

   (iv) Find the equation of each side.

   (v) Find the area of the quadrilateral.

The intersection of two lines

The intersection of any two curves (or lines) can be found by solving their equations simultaneously. In the case of two distinct lines, there are two possibilities:

(i) they are parallel

(ii) they intersect at a single point.

EXAMPLE 2.11

Sketch the lines $x + 2y = 1$ and $2x + 3y = 4$ on the same axes, and find the co-ordinates of the point where they intersect.

SOLUTION

The line $x + 2y = 1$ passes through $\left(0, \frac{1}{2}\right)$ and $(1, 0)$.

The line $2x + 3y = 4$ passes through $\left(0, \frac{4}{3}\right)$ and $(2, 0)$.

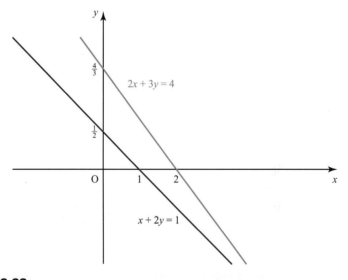

Figure 2.23

①: $x + 2y = 1$ ①: × 2: $2x + 4y = 2$
②: $2x + 3y = 4$ ②: $2x + 3y = 4$
                  Subtract: $y = -2$.

Substituting $y = -2$ in ①: $x - 4 = 1$
                           $\Rightarrow$ $x = 5$.

The co-ordinates of the point of intersection are $(5, -2)$.

EXAMPLE 2.12

Find the co-ordinates of the vertices of the triangle whose sides have the equations $x + y = 4$, $2x - y = 8$ and $x + 2y = -1$.

SOLUTION

A sketch will be helpful, so first find where each line crosses the axes.

① $x + y = 4$ crosses the axes at $(0, 4)$ and $(4, 0)$.

② $2x - y = 8$ crosses the axes at $(0, -8)$ and $(4, 0)$.

③ $x + 2y = -1$ crosses the axes at $\left(0, -\frac{1}{2}\right)$ and $(-1, 0)$.

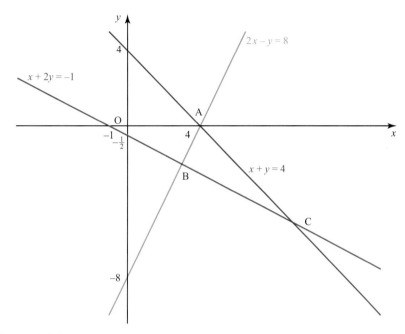

Figure 2.24

Since two lines pass through the point $(4, 0)$ this is clearly one of the vertices. It has been labelled A on figure 2.24.

Point B is found by solving ② and ③ simultaneously:

$$\begin{array}{ll} ② \times 2: & 4x - 2y = 16 \\ ③: & \underline{x + 2y = -1} \\ \text{Add} & 5x \qquad = 15 \quad \text{so} \quad x = 3. \end{array}$$

Substituting $x = 3$ in ② gives $y = -2$, so B is the point $(3, -2)$.

Point C is found by solving ① and ③ simultaneously:

$$\begin{array}{ll} ①: & x + \ y = 4 \\ ③: & \underline{x + 2y = -1} \\ \text{Subtract} & -y = 5 \quad \text{so} \quad y = -5. \end{array}$$

Substituting $y = -5$ in ① gives $x = 9$, so C is the point $(9, -5)$.

❓ The line l has equation $2x - y = 4$ and the line m has equation $y = 2x - 3$.

What can you say about the intersection of these two lines?

Historical note

René Descartes was born near Tours in France in 1596. At the age of eight he was sent to a Jesuit boarding school where, because of his frail health, he was allowed to stay in bed until late in the morning. This habit stayed with him for the rest of his life and he claimed that he was at his most productive before getting up.

After leaving school he studied mathematics in Paris before becoming in turn a soldier, traveller and optical instrument maker. Eventually he settled in Holland where he devoted his time to mathematics, science and philosophy, and wrote a number of books on these subjects.

In an appendix, entitled *La Géométrie*, to one of his books, Descartes made the contribution to co-ordinate geometry for which he is particularly remembered.

In 1649 he left Holland for Sweden at the invitation of Queen Christina but died there, of a lung infection, the following year.

EXERCISE 2D

1 **(i)** Find the vertices of the triangle ABC whose sides are given by the lines
   AB: $x - 2y = -1$, BC: $7x + 6y = 53$ and AC: $9x + 2y = 11$.
   (ii) Show that the triangle is isosceles.

2 Two sides of a parallelogram are formed by parts of the lines $2x - y = -9$ and $x - 2y = -9$.

   (i) Show these two lines on a graph.
   (ii) Find the co-ordinates of the vertex where they intersect.

   Another vertex of the parallelogram is the point $(2, 1)$.

   (iii) Find the equations of the other two sides of the parallelogram.
   (iv) Find the co-ordinates of the other two vertices.

3 A$(0, 1)$, B$(1, 4)$, C$(4, 3)$ and D$(3, 0)$ are the vertices of a quadrilateral ABCD.

   (i) Find the equations of the diagonals AC and BD.
   (ii) Show that the diagonals AC and BD bisect each other at right angles.
   (iii) Find the lengths of AC and BD.
   (iv) What type of quadrilateral is ABCD?

4 The line with equation $5x + y = 20$ meets the x axis at A and the line with equation $x + 2y = 22$ meets the y axis at B. The two lines intersect at a point C.

   (i) Sketch the two lines on the same diagram.
   (ii) Calculate the co-ordinates of A, B and C.
   (iii) Calculate the area of triangle OBC where O is the origin.
   (iv) Find the co-ordinates of the point E such that ABEC is a parallelogram.

5 A median of a triangle is a line joining a vertex to the mid-point of the opposite side. In any triangle, the three medians meet at a point.

The centroid of a triangle is at the point of intersection of the medians.

Find the co-ordinates of the centroid for each triangle shown.

(i)　　　　　　　　　　　　　**(ii)**

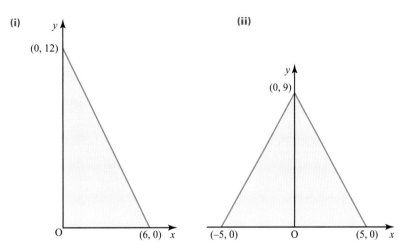

6 You are given the co-ordinates of the four points A(6, 2), B(2, 4), C(−6, −2) and D(−2, −4).

(i)   Calculate the gradients of the lines AB, CB, DC and DA.
     Hence describe the shape of the figure ABCD.

(ii) Show that the equation of the line DA is $4y − 3x = −10$ and find the length DA.

(iii) Calculate the gradient of a line which is perpendicular to DA and hence find the equation of the line *l* through B which is perpendicular to DA.

(iv) Calculate the co-ordinates of the point P where *l* meets DA.

(v) Calculate the area of the figure ABCD.

[MEI]

7 The diagram shows a triangle whose vertices are A(−2, 1), B(1, 7) and C(3, 1). The point L is the foot of the perpendicular from A to BC, and M is the foot of the perpendicular from B to AC.

(i)   Find the gradient of the line BC.

(ii) Find the equation of the line AL.

(iii) Write down the equation of the line BM.

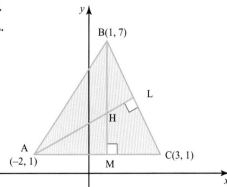

The lines AL and BM meet at H.

(iv) Find the co-ordinates of H.

(v) Show that CH is perpendicular to AB.

(vi) Find the area of the triangle BLH.

[MEI]

8 The diagram shows a rectangle ABCD. The point A is (0, −2) and C is (12, 14). The diagonal BD is parallel to the x axis.

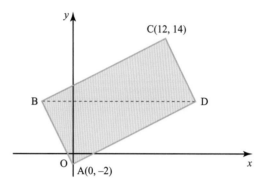

(i) Explain why the y co-ordinate of D is 6.

The x co-ordinate of D is h.

(ii) Express the gradients of AD and CD in terms of h.

(iii) Calculate the x co-ordinates of D and B.

(iv) Calculate the area of the rectangle ABCD.

[Cambridge AS & A Level Mathematics 9709, Paper 12 Q9 November 2009]

9 The diagram shows a rhombus ABCD. The points B and D have co-ordinates (2, 10) and (6, 2) respectively, and A lies on the x axis. The mid-point of BD is M. Find, by calculation, the co-ordinates of each of M, A and C.

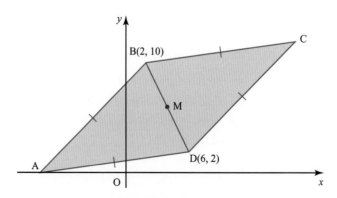

[Cambridge AS & A Level Mathematics 9709, Paper 1 Q5 June 2005]

10 Three points have co-ordinates A(2, 6), B(8, 10) and C(6, 0). The perpendicular bisector of AB meets the line BC at D. Find

(i) the equation of the perpendicular bisector of AB in the form $ax + by = c$

(ii) the co-ordinates of D.

[Cambridge AS & A Level Mathematics 9709, Paper 1 Q7 November 2005]

11 The diagram shows a rectangle ABCD. The point A is (2, 14), B is (−2, 8) and C lies on the x axis.

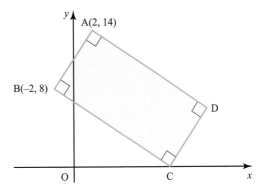

Find

(i) the equation of BC.

(ii) the co-ordinates of C and D.

[Cambridge AS & A Level Mathematics 9709, Paper 1 Q6 June 2007]

12 The three points A(3, 8), B(6, 2) and C(10, 2) are shown in the diagram. The point D is such that the line DA is perpendicular to AB and DC is parallel to AB. Calculate the co-ordinates of D.

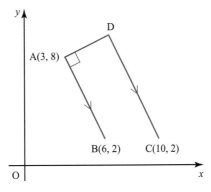

[Cambridge AS & A Level Mathematics 9709, Paper 1 Q6 November 2007]

13 In the diagram, the points A and C lie on the x and y axes respectively and the equation of AC is $2y + x = 16$. The point B has co-ordinates (2, 2). The perpendicular from B to AC meets AC at the point X.

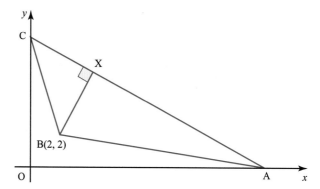

(i)   Find the co-ordinates of X.

The point D is such that the quadrilateral ABCD has AC as a line of symmetry.

(ii) Find the co-ordinates of D.

(iii) Find, correct to 1 decimal place, the perimeter of ABCD.

[Cambridge AS & A Level Mathematics 9709, Paper 1 Q11 June 2008]

14 The diagram shows points A, B and C lying on the line $2y = x + 4$. The point A lies on the y axis and AB = BC. The line from D(10, −3) to B is perpendicular to AC. Calculate the co-ordinates of B and C.

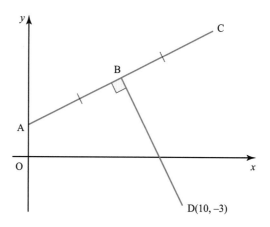

[Cambridge AS & A Level Mathematics 9709, Paper 1 Q8 June 2009]

You can always plot a curve, point by point, if you know its equation. Often, however, all you need is a general idea of its shape and a sketch is quite sufficient.

Figures 2.25 and 2.26 show some common curves of the form $y = x^n$ for $n = 1, 2, 3$ and 4 and $y = \dfrac{1}{x^n}$ for $n = 1$ and 2.

Curves of the form $y = x^n$ for $n = 1, 2, 3$ and 4

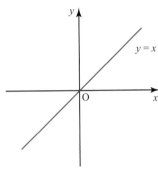

(a) $n = 1, y = x$

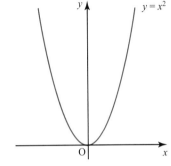

(b) $n = 2, y = x^2$

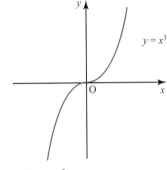

(c) $n = 3, y = x^3$

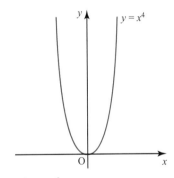

(d) $n = 4, y = x^4$

Figure 2.25

? How are the curves for even values of n different from those for odd values of n?

Stationary points

A turning point is a place where a curve changes from increasing (curve going up) to decreasing (curve going down), or vice versa. A *turning point* may be described as a *maximum* (change from increasing to decreasing) or a *minimum* (change from decreasing to increasing). Turning points are examples of *stationary points*, where the gradient is zero. In general, the curve of a polynomial of order n has up to $n - 1$ turning points as shown in figure 2.26.

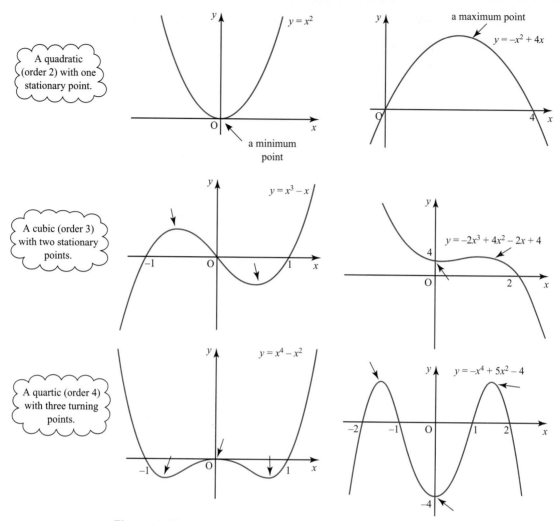

A quadratic (order 2) with one stationary point.

A cubic (order 3) with two stationary points.

A quartic (order 4) with three turning points.

Figure 2.26

There are some polynomials for which not all the stationary points materialise, as in the case of $y = x^4 - 4x^3 + 5x^2$ (whose curve is shown in figure 2.27). To be accurate, you say that the curve of a polynomial of order n has *at most* $n-1$ stationary points.

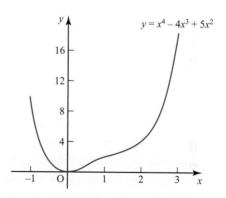

Figure 2.27

Behaviour for large x (positive and negative)

What can you say about the value of a polynomial for large positive values and large negative values of x? As an example, look at

$$f(x) = x^3 + 2x^2 + 3x + 9,$$

and take 1000 as a large number.

$$f(1000) = 1\,000\,000\,000 + 2\,000\,000 + 3000 + 9$$
$$= 1\,002\,003\,009$$

Similarly,

$$f(-1000) = -1\,000\,000\,000 + 2\,000\,000 - 3000 + 9$$
$$= -998\,002\,991.$$

Note

1 The term x^3 makes by far the largest contribution to the answers. It is the *dominant* term.
   For a polynomial of order n, the term in x^n is dominant as $x \to \pm\infty$.

2 In both cases the answers are extremely large numbers. You will probably have noticed already that away from their turning points, polynomial curves quickly disappear off the top or bottom of the page.
   For all polynomials as $x \to \pm\infty$, either $f(x) \to +\infty$ or $f(x) \to -\infty$.

When investigating the behaviour of a polynomial of order n as $x \to \pm\infty$, you need to look at the term in x^n and ask two questions.

(i)   Is n even or odd?
(ii) Is the coefficient of x^n positive or negative?

According to the answers, the curve will have one of the four types of shape illustrated in figure 2.28.

Intersections with the x and y axes

The constant term in the polynomial gives the value of y where the curve intersects the y axis. So $y = x^8 + 5x^6 + 17x^3 + 23$ crosses the y axis at the point $(0, 23)$. Similarly, $y = x^3 + x$ crosses the y axis at $(0, 0)$, the origin, since the constant term is zero.

When the polynomial is given, or known, in factorised form you can see at once where it crosses the x axis. The curve $y = (x - 2)(x - 8)(x - 9)$, for example, crosses the x axis at $x = 2$, $x = 8$ and $x = 9$. Each of these values makes one of the brackets equal to zero, and so $y = 0$.

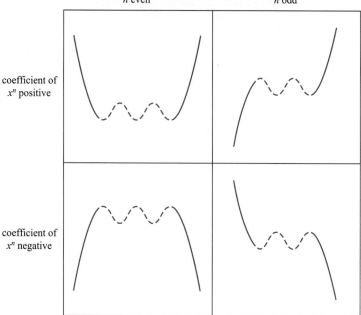

n even   *n* odd

coefficient of
x^n positive

coefficient of
x^n negative

Figure 2.28

EXAMPLE 2.13

Sketch the curve $y = x^3 - 3x^2 - x + 3 = (x+1)(x-1)(x-3)$.

SOLUTION

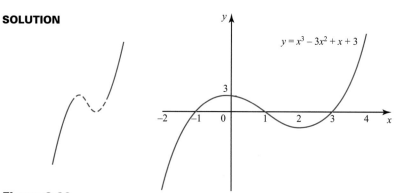

Figure 2.29

Since the polynomial is of order 3, the curve has up to two stationary points. The term in x^3 has a positive coefficient (+1) and 3 is an odd number, so the general shape is as shown on the left of figure 2.29.

The actual equation

$$y = x^3 - 3x^2 - x + 3 = (x+1)(x-1)(x-3)$$

tells you that the curve:

– crosses the y axis at $(0, 3)$
– crosses the x axis at $(-1, 0)$, $(1, 0)$ and $(3, 0)$.

This is enough information to sketch the curve (see the right of figure 2.29).

In this example the polynomial $x^3 - 3x^2 - x + 3$ has three factors, $(x + 1)$, $(x - 1)$ and $(x - 3)$. Each of these corresponds to an intersection with the x axis, and to a root of the equation $x^3 - 3x^2 - x + 3 = 0$. Clearly a cubic polynomial cannot have more than three factors of this type, since the highest power of x is 3. A cubic polynomial may, however, cross the x axis fewer than three times, as in the case of $f(x) = x^3 - x^2 - 4x + 6$ (see figure 2.30).

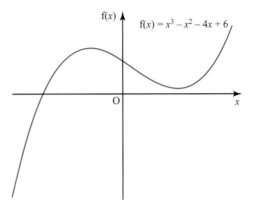

Figure 2.30

Note

This illustrates an important result. If $f(x)$ is a polynomial of degree n, the curve with equation $y = f(x)$ crosses the x axis at most n times, and the equation $f(x) = 0$ has at most n roots.

An important case occurs when the polynomial function has one or more repeated factors, as in figure 2.31. In such cases the curves touch the x axis at points corresponding to the repeated roots.

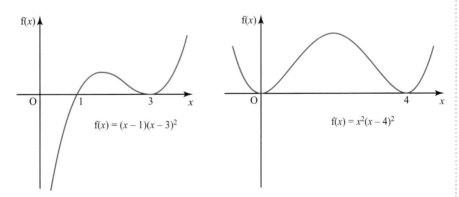

Figure 2.31

Sketch the following curves, marking clearly the values of x and y where they cross the co-ordinate axes.

1 $y = x(x-3)(x+4)$

2 $y = (x+1)(2x-5)(x-4)$

3 $y = (5-x)(x-1)(x+3)$

4 $y = x^2(x-3)$

5 $y = (x+1)^2(2-x)$

6 $y = (3x-4)(4x-3)^2$

7 $y = (x+2)^2(x-4)^2$

8 $y = (x-3)^2(4+x)^2$

9 Suggest an equation for this curve.

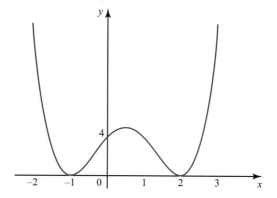

❓ What happens to the curve of a polynomial if it has a factor of the form $(x-a)^3$? Or $(x-a)^4$?

Curves of the form $y = \frac{1}{x^n}$ (for $x \neq 0$)

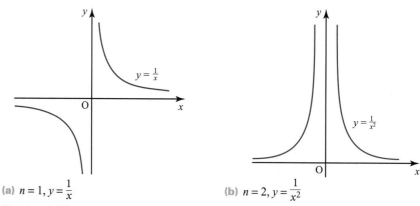

(a) $n = 1, y = \frac{1}{x}$ (b) $n = 2, y = \frac{1}{x^2}$

Figure 2.32

The curves for $n = 3, 5, \ldots$ are not unlike that for $n = 1$, those for $n = 4, 6, \ldots$ are like that for $n = 2$. In all cases the point $x = 0$ is excluded because $\frac{1}{0}$ is undefined.

An important feature of these curves is that they approach both the x and the y axes ever more closely but never actually reach them. These lines are described as *asymptotes* to the curves. Asymptotes may be vertical (e.g. the y axis), horizontal, or lie at an angle, when they are called oblique.

Asymptotes are usually marked on graphs as dotted lines but in the cases above the lines are already there, being co-ordinate axes. The curves have different branches which never meet. A curve with different branches is said to be *discontinuous*, whereas one with no breaks, like $y = x^2$, is *continuous*.

The circle

You are of course familiar with the circle, and have probably done calculations involving its area and circumference. In this section you are introduced to the *equation* of a circle.

The circle is defined as the *locus* of all the points in a plane which are at a fixed distance (the radius) from a given point (the centre). (Locus means path.)

As you have seen, the length of a line joining (x_1, y_1) to (x_2, y_2) is given by

$$\text{length} = \sqrt{(x_2 - x_1)^2 + (y_2 - y_1)^2}.$$

This is used to derive the equation of a circle.

In the case of a circle of radius 3, with its centre at the origin, any point (x, y) on the circumference is distance 3 from the origin. Since the distance of (x, y) from $(0, 0)$ is given by $\sqrt{(x - 0)^2 + (y - 0)^2}$, this means that $\sqrt{(x - 0)^2 + (y - 0)^2} = 3$ or $x^2 + y^2 = 9$ and this is the equation of the circle.

This circle is shown in figure 2.33.

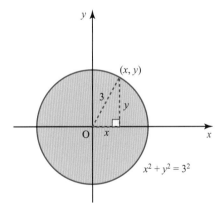

Figure 2.33

These results can be generalised to give the equation of a circle centre $(0, 0)$, radius r as follows:

$$x^2 + y^2 = r^2$$

The intersection of a line and a curve

When a line and a curve are in the same plane, there are three possible situations.

(i) *All points of intersection are distinct* (see figure 2.34).

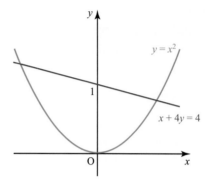

Figure 2.34

(ii) *The line is a tangent to the curve at one (or more) point(s)* (see figure 2.35).

In this case, each point of contact corresponds to two (or more) co-incident points of intersection. It is possible that the tangent will also intersect the curve somewhere else.

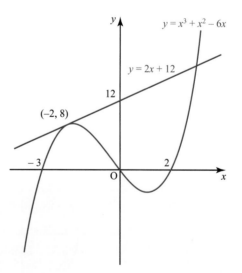

Figure 2.35

(iii) *The line and the curve do not meet* (see figure 2.36).

The co-ordinates of the point of intersection can be found by solving the two equations simultaneously. If you obtain an equation with no real roots, the conclusion is that there is no point of intersection.

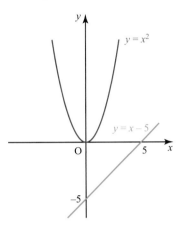

Figure 2.36

The equation of the straight line is, of course, linear and that of the curve non-linear. The examples which follow remind you how to solve such pairs of equations.

EXAMPLE 2.14

Find the co-ordinates of the two points where the line $y - 3x = 2$ intersects the curve $y = 2x^2$.

SOLUTION

First sketch the line and the curve.

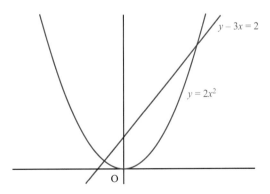

Figure 2.37

You can find where the line and curve intersect by solving the simultaneous equations:

$$y - 3x = 2 \qquad \text{①}$$
$$\text{and} \qquad y = 2x^2 \qquad \text{②}$$

Make y the subject of ①: $\quad y = 3x + 2 \qquad \text{③}$

Substitute ③ into ②: $\qquad y = 2x^2$

$$\Rightarrow \qquad 3x + 2 = 2x^2$$
$$\Rightarrow \qquad 2x^2 - 3x - 2 = 0$$
$$\Rightarrow \qquad (2x + 1)(x - 2) = 0$$
$$\Rightarrow \quad x = 2 \text{ or } x = -\tfrac{1}{2}$$

These are the x co-ordinates of the points of intersection.

Substitute into the linear equation, $y = 3x + 2$, to find the corresponding y co-ordinates.

$$x = 2 \Rightarrow y = 8$$
$$x = -\tfrac{1}{2} \Rightarrow y = \tfrac{1}{2}$$

So the co-ordinates of the points of intersection are $(2, 8)$ and $\left(-\tfrac{1}{2}, \tfrac{1}{2}\right)$

EXAMPLE 2.15

(i) Find the value of k for which the line $2y = x + k$ forms a tangent to the curve $y^2 = 2x$.

(ii) Hence, for this value of k, find the co-ordinates of the point where the line $2y = x + k$ meets the curve.

SOLUTION

(i) You can find where the line forms a tangent to the curve by solving the simultaneous equations:

$$2y = x + k \qquad \text{①}$$
$$\text{and} \qquad y^2 = 2x \qquad \text{②}$$

When you eliminate either x or y between the equations you will be left with a quadratic equation. A tangent meets the curve at just one point and so you need to find the value of k which gives you just one repeated root for the quadratic equation.

Make x the subject of ①: $\quad x = 2y - k \qquad \text{③}$

Substitute ③ into ②: $\qquad y^2 = 2x$

$$\Rightarrow \qquad y^2 = 2(2y - k)$$
$$\Rightarrow \qquad y^2 = 4y - 2k$$
$$\Rightarrow \quad y^2 - 4y + 2k = 0 \qquad \text{④}$$

You can use the discriminant, $b^2 - 4ac$, to find the value of k such that the equation has one repeated root. The condition is $b^2 - 4ac = 0$

$$y^2 - 4y + 2k = 0 \implies a = 1, b = -4 \text{ and } c = 2k$$
$$b^2 - 4ac = 0 \implies (-4)^2 - 4 \times 1 \times 2k = 0$$
$$\implies 16 - 8k = 0$$
$$\implies k = 2$$

So the line $2y = x + 2$ forms a tangent to the curve $y^2 = 2x$.

(ii) You have already started to solve the equations $2y = x + 2$ and $y^2 = 2x$ in part (i). Look at equation ④: $y^2 - 4y + 2k = 0$

You know from part (i) that $k = 2$ so you can solve the quadratic to find y.

$$y^2 - 4y + 4 = 0$$
$$\implies (y - 2)(y - 2) = 0$$
$$\implies y = 2$$

Notice that this is a repeated root so the line is a tangent to the curve.

Now substitute $y = 2$ into the equation of the line to find the x co-ordinate.

When $y = 2$: $2y = x + 2 \implies 4 = x + 2$
$$x = 2$$

So the tangent meets the curve at the point $(2, 2)$.

EXERCISE 2F

1 Show that the line $y = 3x + 1$ crosses the curve $y = x^2 + 3$ at $(1, 4)$ and find the co-ordinates of the other point of intersection.

2 (i) Find the co-ordinates of the points A and B where the line $y = 2x - 1$ cuts the curve $y = x^2 - 4$.
   (ii) Find the distance AB.

3 (i) Find the co-ordinates of the points of intersection of the line $y = 2x$ and the curve $y = x^2 + 6x - 5$.
   (ii) Show also that the line $y = 2x$ does not cross the curve $y = x^2 + 6x + 5$.

4 The line $3y = 5 - x$ intersects the curve $2y^2 = x$ at two points. Find the distance between the two points.

5 The equation of a curve is $xy = 8$ and the equation of a line is $2x + y = k$, where k is a constant. Find the values of k for which the line forms a tangent to the curve.

6 Find the value of the constant c for which the line $y = 4x + c$ is a tangent to the curve $y^2 = 4x$.

7 The equation of a curve is $xy = 10$ and the equation of a line l is $2x + y = q$, where q is a number.

   (i) In the case where $q = 9$, find the co-ordinates of the points of intersection of l and the curve.

   (ii) Find the set of values of q for which l does not intersect the curve.

8 The curve $y^2 = 12x$ intersects the line $3y = 4x + 6$ at two points. Find the distance between the two points.

[Cambridge AS & A Level Mathematics 9709, Paper 1 Q5 June 2006]

9 Determine the set of values of the constant k for which the line $y = 4x + k$ does not intersect the curve $y = x^2$.

[Cambridge AS & A Level Mathematics 9709, Paper 1 Q1 November 2007]

10 Find the set of values of k for which the line $y = kx - 4$ intersects the curve $y = x^2 - 2x$ at two distinct points.

[Cambridge AS & A Level Mathematics 9709, Paper 1 Q2 June 2009]

KEY POINTS

1 The gradient of the straight line joining the points (x_1, y_1) and (x_2, y_2) is given by

$$\text{gradient} = \frac{y_2 - y_1}{x_2 - x_1}.$$

when the same scale is used on both axes, $m = \tan\theta$.

2 Two lines are parallel when their gradients are equal.

3 Two lines are perpendicular when the product of their gradients is -1.

4 When the points A and B have co-ordinates (x_1, y_1) and (x_2, y_2) respectively, then

the distance AB is $\sqrt{(x_2 - x_1)^2 + (y_2 - y_1)^2}$

the mid-point of the line AB is $\left(\dfrac{x_1 + x_2}{2}, \dfrac{y_1 + y_2}{2} \right)$.

5 The equation of a straight line may take any of the following forms:

   • line parallel to the y axis: $x = a$
   • line parallel to the x axis: $y = b$
   • line through the origin with gradient m: $y = mx$
   • line through $(0, c)$ with gradient m: $y = mx + c$
   • line through (x_1, y_1) with gradient m: $y - y_1 = m(x - x_1)$
   • line through (x_1, y_1) and (x_2, y_2):

$$\frac{y - y_1}{y_2 - y_1} = \frac{x - x_1}{x_2 - x_1} \quad \text{or} \quad \frac{y - y_1}{x - x_1} = \frac{y_2 - y_1}{x_2 - x_1}.$$

Sequences and series

Population, when unchecked, increases in a geometrical ratio.
Subsistence increases only in an arithmetical ratio. A slight
acquaintance with numbers will show the immensity of the first
power in comparison with the second.

Thomas Malthus (1798)

❓ Each of the following sequences is related to one of the pictures above.

(i) 5000, 10 000, 20 000, 40 000, ...

(ii) 8, 0, 10, 10, 10, 10, 12, 8, 0, ...

(iii) 5, 3.5, 0, –3.5, –5, –3.5, 0, 3.5, 5, 3.5, ...

(iv) 20, 40, 60, 80, 100, ...

(a) Identify which sequence goes with which picture.

(b) Give the next few numbers in each sequence.

(c) Describe the pattern of the numbers in each case.

(d) Decide whether the sequence will go on for ever, or come to a stop.

Definitions and notation

A *sequence* is a set of numbers in a given order, like

$$\frac{1}{2}, \frac{1}{4}, \frac{1}{8}, \frac{1}{16}, \ldots$$

Each of these numbers is called a *term* of the sequence. When writing the terms of a sequence algebraically, it is usual to denote the position of any term in the sequence by a subscript, so that a general sequence might be written:

$$u_1, u_2, u_3, \ldots, \text{ with general term } u_k.$$

For the sequence above, the first term is $u_1 = \frac{1}{2}$, the second term is $u_2 = \frac{1}{4}$, and so on.

When the terms of a sequence are added together, like

$$\frac{1}{2} + \frac{1}{4} + \frac{1}{8} + \frac{1}{16} + \ldots$$

the resulting sum is called a *series*. The process of adding the terms together is called *summation* and indicated by the symbol $\sum$ (the Greek letter sigma), with the position of the first and last terms involved given as *limits*.

So $u_1 + u_2 + u_3 + u_4 + u_5$ is written $\sum_{k=1}^{k=5} u_k$ or $\sum_{k=1}^{5} u_k$.

In cases like this one, where there is no possibility of confusion, the sum would normally be written more simply as $\sum_{1}^{5} u_k$.

If all the terms were to be summed, it would usually be denoted even more simply, as $\sum_{k} u_k$, or even $\sum u_k$.

A sequence may have an infinite number of terms, in which case it is called an *infinite sequence*. The corresponding series is called an *infinite series*.

In mathematics, although the word *series* can describe the sum of the terms of any sequence, it is usually used only when summing the sequence provides some useful or interesting overall result.

For example:

$$(1 + x)^5 = 1 + 5x + 10x^2 + 10x^3 + 5x^4 + x^5$$

> This series has a finite number of terms (6).

$$\pi = 2\sqrt{3}\left[1 + \left(\frac{-1}{3}\right) + 5\left(\frac{-1}{3}\right)^2 + 7\left(\frac{-1}{3}\right)^3 + \ldots\right]$$

> This series has an infinite number of terms.

The phrase 'sum of a sequence' is often used to mean the sum of the terms of a sequence (i.e. the series).

Arithmetic progressions

SCORECARD · J. GREEN

OUT	4	4	5	10	3	2	4	8	6
HOME	3	5	7	1	4	5	4	5	7

Figure 3.1

Any ordered set of numbers, like the scores of this golfer on an 18-hole round (see figure 3.1) form a sequence. In mathematics, we are particularly interested in those which have a well-defined pattern, often in the form of an algebraic formula linking the terms. The sequences you met at the start of this chapter show various types of pattern.

A sequence in which the terms increase by the addition of a fixed amount (or decrease by the subtraction of a fixed amount), is described as *arithmetic*. The increase from one term to the next is called the *common difference*.

Thus the sequence 5 $\quad$ 8 $\quad$ 11 $\quad$ 14... is arithmetic with

$$+3 \quad +3 \quad +3$$

common difference 3.

This sequence can be written algebraically as

$u_k = 2 + 3k$ for $k = 1, 2, 3, \ldots$

When $\quad k = 1, u_1 = 2 + 3 = 5$
$\qquad k = 2, u_2 = 2 + 6 = 8$
$\qquad k = 3, u_3 = 2 + 9 = 11$

> This version has the advantage that the right-hand side begins with the first term of the sequence.

and so on.

(An equivalent way of writing this is $u_k = 5 + 3(k - 1)$ for $k = 1, 2, 3, \ldots$.)

As successive terms of an arithmetic sequence increase (or decrease) by a fixed amount called the common difference, d, you can define each term in the sequence in relation to the previous term:

$$u_{k+1} = u_k + d.$$

When the terms of an arithmetic sequence are added together, the sum is called an *arithmetic progression*, often abbreviated to A.P. An alternative name is an arithmetic series.

Notation

When describing arithmetic progressions and sequences in this book, the following conventions will be used:

- first term, $u_1 = a$
- number of terms $= n$
- last term, $u_n = l$
- common difference $= d$
- the general term, u_k, is that in position k (i.e. the kth term).

Thus in the arithmetic sequence 5, 7, 9, 11, 13, 15, 17,

$a = 5$, $l = 17$, $d = 2$ and $n = 7$.

The terms are formed as follows.

$u_1 = a \quad = 5$
$u_2 = a + d \quad = 5 + 2 \quad = 7$
$u_3 = a + 2d = 5 + 2 \times 2 = 9$
$u_4 = a + 3d = 5 + 3 \times 2 = 11$
$u_5 = a + 4d = 5 + 4 \times 2 = 13$
$u_6 = a + 5d = 5 + 5 \times 2 = 15$
$u_7 = a + 6d = 5 + 6 \times 2 = 17$

The 7th term is the 1st term (5) plus six times the common difference (2).

You can see that any term is given by the first term plus a number of differences. The number of differences is, in each case, one less than the number of the term. You can express this mathematically as

$$u_k = a + (k-1)d.$$

For the last term, this becomes

$$l = a + (n-1)d.$$

These are both general formulae which apply to any arithmetic sequence.

EXAMPLE 3.1 Find the 17th term in the arithmetic sequence 12, 9, 6, … .

SOLUTION

In this case $a = 12$ and $d = -3$.

Using $\quad u_k = a + (k-1)d$, you obtain
$$u_{17} = 12 + (17-1) \times (-3)$$
$$= 12 - 48$$
$$= -36.$$

The 17th term is -36.

EXAMPLE 3.2

How many terms are there in the sequence 11, 15, 19, …, 643?

SOLUTION

This is an arithmetic sequence with first term $a = 11$, last term $l = 643$ and common difference $d = 4$.

Using the result $\quad l = a + (n - 1)d$, you have

$$643 = 11 + 4(n - 1)$$
$$\Rightarrow \quad 4n = 643 - 11 + 4$$
$$\Rightarrow \quad n = 159.$$

There are 159 terms.

> *Note*
>
> The relationship $l = a + (n - 1)d$ may be rearranged to give
>
> $$n = \frac{l - a}{d} + 1$$
>
> This gives the number of terms in an A.P. directly if you know the first term, the last term and the common difference.

The sum of the terms of an arithmetic progression

When Carl Friederich Gauss (1777–1855) was at school he was always quick to answer mathematics questions. One day his teacher, hoping for half an hour of peace and quiet, told his class to add up all the whole numbers from 1 to 100. Almost at once the 10-year-old Gauss announced that he had done it and that the answer was 5050.

Gauss had not of course added the terms one by one. Instead he wrote the series down twice, once in the given order and once backwards, and added the two together:

$$S = \quad 1 + \quad 2 + \quad 3 + \ldots + \quad 98 + \quad 99 + 100$$
$$S = 100 + \quad 99 + \quad 98 + \ldots + \quad 3 + \quad 2 + \quad 1.$$

Adding, $2S = 101 + 101 + 101 + \ldots + 101 + 101 + 101.$

Since there are 100 terms in the series,

$$2S = 101 \times 100$$
$$S = 5050.$$

The numbers 1, 2, 3, … , 100 form an arithmetic sequence with common difference 1. Gauss' method can be used for finding the sum of any arithmetic series.

It is common to use the letter S to denote the sum of a series. When there is any doubt as to the number of terms that are being summed, this is indicated by a subscript: S_5 indicates five terms, S_n indicates n terms.

EXAMPLE 3.3

Find the value of $8 + 6 + 4 + \ldots + (-32)$.

SOLUTION

This is an arithmetic progression, with common difference -2. The number of terms, n, may be calculated using

$$n = \frac{l-a}{d} + 1$$

$$n = \frac{-32-8}{-2} + 1$$

$$= 21.$$

The sum S of the progression is then found as follows.

$$
\begin{aligned}
S &= 8 + 6 + \ldots - 30 - 32 \\
S &= -32 - 30 - \ldots + 6 + 8 \\
\hline
2S &= -24 - 24 - \ldots - 24 - 24
\end{aligned}
$$

Since there are 21 terms, this gives $2S = -24 \times 21$, so $S = -12 \times 21 = -252$.

Generalising this method by writing the series in the conventional notation gives:

$$
\begin{aligned}
S_n &= [a] + [a+d] + \ldots + [a+(n-2)d] + [a+(n-1)d] \\
S_n &= [a+(n-1)d] + [a+(n-2)d] + \ldots + [a+d] + [a] \\
\hline
2S_n &= [2a+(n-1)d] + [2a+(n-1)d] + \ldots + [2a+(n-1)d] + [2a+(n-1)d]
\end{aligned}
$$

Since there are n terms, it follows that

$$S_n = \frac{1}{2}n[2a+(n-1)d]$$

This result may also be written as

$$S_n = \frac{1}{2}n(a+l).$$

EXAMPLE 3.4

Find the sum of the first 100 terms of the progression

$$1, 1\tfrac{1}{4}, 1\tfrac{1}{2}, 1\tfrac{3}{4}, \ldots.$$

SOLUTION

In this arithmetic progression

$a = 1$, $d = \frac{1}{4}$ and $n = 100$.

Using $S_n = \frac{1}{2}n[2a+(n-1)d]$, you have

$$S_n = \frac{1}{2} \times 100\left(2 + 99 \times \tfrac{1}{4}\right)$$

$$= 1337\tfrac{1}{2}.$$

EXAMPLE 3.5

Jamila starts a part-time job on a salary of $9000 per year, and this increases by an annual increment of $1000. Assuming that, apart from the increment, Jamila's salary does not increase, find

(i) her salary in the 12th year

(ii) the length of time she has been working when her total earnings are $100 000.

SOLUTION

Jamila's annual salaries (in dollars) form the arithmetic sequence

$$9000, 10\,000, 11\,000, \dots .$$

with first term $a = 9000$, and common difference $d = 1000$.

(i) Her salary in the 12th year is calculated using:

$$u_k = a + (k-1)d$$
$$\Rightarrow \quad u_{12} = 9000 + (12-1) \times 1000$$
$$= 20\,000.$$

(ii) The number of years that have elapsed when her total earnings are $100\,000$ is given by:

$$S = \tfrac{1}{2}n\big[2a + (n-1)d\big]$$

where $S = 100\,000$, $a = 9000$ and $d = 1000$.

This gives $\quad 100\,000 = \tfrac{1}{2}n\big[2 \times 9000 + 1000(n-1)\big].$

This simplifies to the quadratic equation:

$$n^2 + 17n - 200 = 0.$$

Factorising,

$$(n-8)(n+25) = 0$$
$$\Rightarrow \quad n = 8 \text{ or } n = -25.$$

The root $n = -25$ is irrelevant, so the answer is $n = 8$.

Jamila has earned a total of $100 000 after eight years.

1 Are the following sequences arithmetic?
   If so, state the common difference and the seventh term.

   (i) 27, 29, 31, 33, …   **(ii)** 1, 2, 3, 5, 8, …   **(iii)** 2, 4, 8, 16, …
   (iv) 3, 7, 11, 15, …   **(v)** 8, 6, 4, 2, …

2 The first term of an arithmetic sequence is −8 and the common difference is 3.

   (i) Find the seventh term of the sequence.
   (ii) The last term of the sequence is 100.
   How many terms are there in the sequence?

3 The first term of an arithmetic sequence is 12, the seventh term is 36 and the last term is 144.

   (i) Find the common difference.

   (ii) Find how many terms there are in the sequence.

4 There are 20 terms in an arithmetic progression.
The first term is −5 and the last term is 90.

   (i) Find the common difference.

   (ii) Find the sum of the terms in the progression.

5 The kth term of an arithmetic progression is given by

$$u_k = 14 + 2k.$$

   (i) Write down the first three terms of the progression.

   (ii) Calculate the sum of the first 12 terms of this progression.

6 Below is an arithmetic progression.

$$120 + 114 + \ldots + 36$$

   (i) How many terms are there in the progression?

   (ii) What is the sum of the terms in the progression?

7 The fifth term of an arithmetic progression is 28 and the tenth term is 58.

   (i) Find the first term and the common difference.

   (ii) The sum of all the terms in this progression is 444.
How many terms are there?

8 The sixth term of an arithmetic progression is twice the third term, and the first term is 3. The sequence has ten terms.

   (i) Find the common difference.

   (ii) Find the sum of all the terms in the progression.

9 **(i)** Find the sum of all the odd numbers between 50 and 150.

   (ii) Find the sum of all the even numbers from 50 to 150, inclusive.

   (iii) Find the sum of the terms of the arithmetic sequence with first term 50, common difference 1 and 101 terms.

   (iv) Explain the relationship between your answers to parts **(i)**, **(ii)** and **(iii)**.

10 The first term of an arithmetic progression is 3000 and the tenth term is 1200.

   (i) Find the sum of the first 20 terms of the progression.

   (ii) After how many terms does the sum of the progression become negative?

11 An arithmetic progression has first term 7 and common difference 3.

   (i) Write down a formula for the kth term of the progression.
Which term of the progression equals 73?

   (ii) Write down a formula for the sum of the first n terms of the progression.
How many terms of the progression are required to give a sum equal to 6300?

[MEI]

12 Paul's starting salary in a company is $14 000 and during the time he stays with the company it increases by $500 each year.

(i) What is his salary in his sixth year?
(ii) How many years has Paul been working for the company when his total earnings for all his years there are $126 000?

13 A jogger is training for a 10 km charity run. He starts with a run of 400 m; then he increases the distance he runs by 200 m each day.

(i) How many days does it take the jogger to reach a distance of 10 km in training?
(ii) What total distance will he have run in training by then?

14 A piece of string 10 m long is to be cut into pieces, so that the lengths of the pieces form an arithmetic sequence.

(i) The lengths of the longest and shortest pieces are 1 m and 25 cm respectively; how many pieces are there?
(ii) If the same string had been cut into 20 pieces with lengths that formed an arithmetic sequence, and if the length of the second longest had been 92.5 cm, how long would the shortest piece have been?

15 The 11th term of an arithmetic progression is 25 and the sum of the first 4 terms is 49.

(i) Find the first term of the progression and the common difference.

The nth term of the progression is 49.

(ii) Find the value of n.

16 The first term of an arithmetic progression is 6 and the fifth term is 12. The progression has n terms and the sum of all the terms is 90. Find the value of n.

[Cambridge AS & A Level Mathematics 9709, Paper 1 Q3 November 2008]

17 The training programme of a pilot requires him to fly 'circuits' of an airfield. Each day he flies 3 more circuits than the day before. On the fifth day he flew 14 circuits.

Calculate how many circuits he flew:
(i) on the first day
(ii) in total by the end of the fifth day
(iii) in total by the end of the nth day
(iv) in total from the end of the nth day to the end of the $2n$th day. Simplify your answer.

[MEI]

18 As part of a fund-raising campaign, I have been given some books of raffle tickets to sell. Each book has the same number of tickets and all the tickets I have been given are numbered in sequence. The number of the ticket on the front of the 5th book is 205 and that on the front of the 19th book is 373.

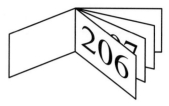

(i) By writing the number of the ticket on the front of the first book as *a* and the number of tickets in each book as *d*, write down two equations involving *a* and *d*.

(ii) From these two equations find how many tickets are in each book and the number on the front of the first book I have been given.

(iii) The last ticket I have been given is numbered 492. How many books have I been given?

[MEI]

Geometric progressions

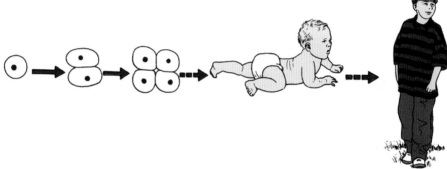

Figure 3.2

A human being begins life as one cell, which divides into two, then four... .

The terms of a geometric sequence are formed by multiplying one term by a fixed number, the common ratio, to obtain the next. This can be written inductively as:

$$u_{k+1} = ru_k \text{ with first term } u_1.$$

The sum of the terms of a geometric sequence is called a *geometric progression*, shortened to G.P. An alternative name is a *geometric series*.

Notation

When describing geometric sequences in this book, the following conventions are used:

● first term $u_1 = a$

● common ratio $= r$

- number of terms $= n$

- the general term u_k is that in position k (i.e. the kth term).

Thus in the geometric sequence 3, 6, 12, 24, 48,

$$a = 3, r = 2 \text{ and } n = 5.$$

The terms of this sequence are formed as follows.

$$\begin{aligned}
u_1 &= a && = 3 \\
u_2 &= a \times r && = 3 \times 2 && = 6 \\
u_3 &= a \times r^2 && = 3 \times 2^2 && = 12 \\
u_4 &= a \times r^3 && = 3 \times 2^3 && = 24 \\
u_5 &= a \times r^4 && = 3 \times 2^4 && = 48
\end{aligned}$$

You will see that in each case the power of r is one less than the number of the term: $u_5 = ar^4$ and 4 is one less than 5. This can be written deductively as

$$u_k = ar^{k-1},$$

and the last term is

$$u_n = ar^{n-1}.$$

These are both general formulae which apply to any geometric sequence.

Given two consecutive terms of a geometric sequence, you can always find the common ratio by dividing the later term by the earlier. For example, the geometric sequence ... 5, 8, ... has common ratio $r = \frac{8}{5}$.

EXAMPLE 3.6

Find the seventh term in the geometric sequence 8, 24, 72, 216, ...

SOLUTION

In the sequence, the first term $a = 8$ and the common ratio $r = 3$.

The kth term of a geometric sequence is given by $u_k = ar^{k-1}$,

and so $u_7 = 8 \times 3^6$
$$= 5832.$$

EXAMPLE 3.7

How many terms are there in the geometric sequence 4, 12, 36, ... , 708 588?

SOLUTION

Since it is a geometric sequence and the first two terms are 4 and 12, you can immediately write down

First term: $\qquad a = 4$
Common ratio: $\qquad r = 3 \longleftarrow \enclose{roundedbox}{\frac{12}{4} = 3}$

The third term allows you to check you are right.

$$12 \times 3 = 36 \quad \checkmark$$

The nth term of a geometric sequence is ar^{n-1}, so in this case

$$4 \times 3^{n-1} = 708\,588$$

Dividing through by 4 gives

> You will learn about these in P2 and P3.

$$3^{n-1} = 177\,147$$

You can use logarithms to solve an equation like this, but since you know that n is a whole number it is just as easy to work out the powers of 3 until you come to 177 147.

They go $3^1 = 3$, $3^2 = 9$, $3^3 = 27$, $3^4 = 81$, ...

> You can do this by hand or you can use your calculator.

and before long you come to $3^{11} = 177\,147$.

So $n - 1 = 11$ and $n = 12$.

There are 12 terms in the sequence.

 How would you use a spreadsheet to solve the equation $3^{n-1} = 177\,147$?

The sum of the terms of a geometric progression

The origins of chess are obscure, with several countries claiming the credit for its invention. One story is that it came from China. It is said that its inventor presented the game to the Emperor, who was so impressed that he asked the inventor what he would like as a reward.

'One grain of rice for the first square on the board, two for the second, four for the third, eight for the fourth, and so on up to the last square', came the answer.

The Emperor agreed, but it soon became clear that there was not enough rice in the whole of China to give the inventor his reward.

How many grains of rice was the inventor actually asking for?

The answer is the geometric series with 64 terms and common ratio 2:

$$1 + 2 + 4 + 8 + \ldots + 2^{63}.$$

This can be summed as follows.

Call the series S:

$$S = 1 + 2 + 4 + 8 + \ldots + 2^{63}. \qquad ①$$

Now multiply it by the common ratio, 2:

$$2S = 2 + 4 + 8 + 16 + \ldots + 2^{64}. \qquad ②$$

Then subtract ① from ②

$$② \quad 2S = \qquad 2 + 4 + 8 + 16 + \ldots + 2^{63} + 2^{64}$$

$$① \quad S = \quad 1 + 2 + 4 + 8 \qquad + \ldots + 2^{63}$$

$$\text{subtracting:} \quad S = -1 + 0 + 0 + 0 \qquad + \ldots + 2^{64}.$$

The total number of rice grains requested was therefore $2^{64} - 1$ (which is about 1.85×10^{19}).

❓ How many tonnes of rice is this, and how many tonnes would you expect there to be in China at any time?

(One hundred grains of rice weigh about 2 grammes. The world annual production of all cereals is about 1.8×10^9 tonnes.)

Note

The method shown above can be used to sum any geometric progression.

Find the value of $0.2 + 1 + 5 + \ldots + 390\,625$.

SOLUTION

This is a geometric progression with common ratio 5.

$$\text{Let} \quad S = 0.2 + 1 + 5 + \ldots + 390\,625. \qquad ①$$

Multiplying by the common ratio, 5, gives:

$$5S = 1 + 5 + 25 + \ldots + 390\,625 + 1\,953\,125. \qquad ②$$

Subtracting ① from ②:

$$5S = \qquad 1 + 5 + 25 + \ldots + 390\,625 + 1\,953\,125$$
$$S = \quad 0.2 + 1 + 5 + 25 + \ldots + 390\,625$$
$$\overline{4S = -0.2 + 0 + \ldots \qquad\qquad + 0 \qquad + 1\,953\,125}$$

This gives $\quad 4S = 1\,953\,124.8$

$\Rightarrow \qquad S = 488\,281.2.$

The same method can be applied to the general geometric progression to give a formula for its value:

$$S_n = a + ar + ar^2 + \ldots + ar^{n-1}.$$ ①

Multiplying by the common ratio, r, gives:

$$rS_n = ar + ar^2 + ar^3 + \ldots + ar^n.$$ ②

Subtracting ① from ②, as before, gives:

$$(r-1)S_n = -a + ar^n$$
$$= a(r^n - 1)$$

so $$S_n = \frac{a(r^n - 1)}{(r-1)}.$$

This can also be written as:

$$S_n = \frac{a(1 - r^n)}{(1-r)}.$$

Infinite geometric progressions

The progression $1 + \frac{1}{2} + \frac{1}{4} + \frac{1}{8} + \frac{1}{16} + \ldots$ is geometric, with common ratio $\frac{1}{2}$.

Summing the terms one by one gives $1, 1\frac{1}{2}, 1\frac{3}{4}, 1\frac{7}{8}, 1\frac{15}{16} \ldots$.

Clearly the more terms you take, the nearer the sum gets to 2. In the limit, as the number of terms tends to infinity, the sum tends to 2.

As $n \to \infty$, $S_n \to 2$.

This is an example of a *convergent* series. The sum to infinity is a finite number.

You can see this by substituting $a = 1$ and $r = \frac{1}{2}$ in the formula for the sum of the series:

$$S_n = \frac{a\left(1 - r^n\right)}{1 - r}$$

giving $$S_n = \frac{1 \times \left(1 - \left(\frac{1}{2}\right)^n\right)}{\left(1 - \frac{1}{2}\right)}$$

$$= 2 \times \left(1 - \left(\frac{1}{2}\right)^n\right).$$

The larger the number of terms, n, the smaller $\left(\frac{1}{2}\right)^n$ becomes and so the nearer S_n is to the limiting value of 2 (see figure 3.3). Notice that $\left(\frac{1}{2}\right)^n$ can never be negative, however large n becomes; so S_n can never exceed 2.

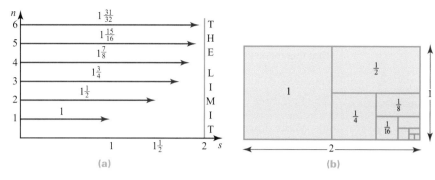

Figure 3.3

In the general geometric series $a + ar + ar^2 + \ldots$ the terms become progressively smaller in size if the common ratio r is between -1 and 1. This was the case above: r had the value $\frac{1}{2}$. In such cases, the geometric series is *convergent*.

If, on the other hand, the value of r is greater than 1 (or less than -1) the terms in the series become larger and larger in size and so the series is described as *divergent*.

A series corresponding to a value of r of exactly $+1$ consists of the first term a repeated over and over again. A sequence corresponding to a value of r of exactly -1 oscillates between $+a$ and $-a$. Neither of these is convergent.

It only makes sense to talk about the sum of an infinite series if it is convergent. Otherwise the sum is undefined.

The condition for a geometric series to converge, $-1 < r < 1$, ensures that as $n \to \infty$, $r^n \to 0$, and so the formula for the sum of a geometric series:

$$S_n = \frac{a(1 - r^n)}{(1 - r)}$$

may be rewritten for an infinite series as:

$$S_\infty = \frac{a}{1 - r}.$$

EXAMPLE 3.9

Find the sum of the terms of the infinite progression $0.2, 0.02, 0.002, \ldots$.

SOLUTION

This is a geometric progression with $a = 0.2$ and $r = 0.1$.

Its sum is given by

$$S_\infty = \frac{a}{1 - r}$$

$$= \frac{0.2}{1 - 0.1}$$

$$= \frac{0.2}{0.9}$$

$$= \frac{2}{9}.$$

Note

You may have noticed that the sum of the series 0.2 + 0.02 + 0.002 + ... is $0.\dot{2}$, and that this recurring decimal is indeed the same as $\frac{2}{9}$.

EXAMPLE 3.10

The first three terms of an infinite geometric progression are 16, 12 and 9.

(i) Write down the common ratio.

(ii) Find the sum of the terms of the progression.

SOLUTION

(i) The common ratio is $\frac{3}{4}$.

(ii) The sum of the terms of an infinite geometric progression is given by:

$$S_\infty = \frac{a}{1-r}.$$

In this case $a = 16$ and $r = \frac{3}{4}$, so:

$$S_\infty = \frac{16}{1-\frac{3}{4}} = 64.$$

? A paradox

Consider the following arguments.

(i) $S = 1 - 2 + 4 - 8 + 16 - 32 + 64 - ...$
    $\Rightarrow S = 1 - 2(1 - 2 + 4 - 8 + 16 - 32 + ...)$
        $= 1 - 2S$
    $\Rightarrow 3S = 1$
    $\Rightarrow S = \frac{1}{3}.$

(ii) $S = 1 + (-2 + 4) + (-8 + 16) + (-32 + 64) + ...$
    $\Rightarrow S = 1 + 2 + 8 + 32 + ...$

So S diverges towards $+\infty$.

(iii) $S = (1 - 2) + (4 - 8) + (16 - 32) + ...$
    $\Rightarrow S = -1 - 4 - 8 - 16 ...$

So S diverges towards $-\infty$.

What is the sum of the series: $\frac{1}{3}$, $+\infty$, $-\infty$, or something else?

1 Are the following sequences geometric?
If so, state the common ratio and calculate the seventh term.

(i) 5, 10, 20, 40, …

(ii) 2, 4, 6, 8, …

(iii) 1, −1, 1, −1, …

(iv) 5, 5, 5, 5, …

(v) 6, 3, 0, −3, …

(vi) $6, 3, 1\frac{1}{2}, \frac{3}{4}, \ldots$

(vii) 1, 1.1, 1.11, 1.111, …

2 A geometric sequence has first term 3 and common ratio 2.
The sequence has eight terms.

(i) Find the last term.

(ii) Find the sum of the terms in the sequence.

3 The first term of a geometric sequence of positive terms is 5 and the fifth term
is 1280.

(i) Find the common ratio of the sequence.

(ii) Find the eighth term of the sequence.

4 A geometric sequence has first term $\frac{1}{9}$ and common ratio 3.

(i) Find the fifth term.

(ii) Which is the first term of the sequence which exceeds 1000?

5 (i) Find how many terms there are in the geometric sequence 8, 16, …, 2048.

(ii) Find the sum of the terms in this sequence.

6 (i) Find how many terms there are in the geometric sequence
200, 50, …, 0.195 312 5.

(ii) Find the sum of the terms in this sequence.

7 The fifth term of a geometric progression is 48 and the ninth term is 768.
All the terms are positive.

(i) Find the common ratio.

(ii) Find the first term.

(iii) Find the sum of the first ten terms.

8 The first three terms of an infinite geometric progression are 4, 2 and 1.

(i) State the common ratio of this progression.

(ii) Calculate the sum to infinity of its terms.

9 The first three terms of an infinite geometric progression are 0.7, 0.07, 0.007.

(i) Write down the common ratio for this progression.

(ii) Find, as a fraction, the sum to infinity of the terms of this progression.

(iii) Find the sum to infinity of the geometric progression 0.7 − 0.07 + 0.007 − …,
and hence show that $\frac{7}{11} = 0.\dot{6}\dot{3}$.

10 The first three terms of a geometric sequence are 100, 90 and 81.

    (i) Write down the common ratio of the sequence.

    (ii) Which is the position of the first term in the sequence that has a value less than 1?

    (iii) Find the sum to infinity of the terms of this sequence.

    (iv) After how many terms is the sum of the sequence greater than 99% of the sum to infinity?

11 A geometric progression has first term 4 and its sum to infinity is 5.

    (i) Find the common ratio.

    (ii) Find the sum to infinity if the first term is excluded from the progression.

12 (i) The third term of a geometric progression is 16 and the fourth term is 12.8. Find the common ratio and the first term.

    (ii) The sum of the first n terms of a geometric progression is $2^{(2n+1)} - 2$. Find the first term and the common ratio.   **[MEI]**

13 (i) The first two terms of a geometric series are 3 and 4. Find the third term.

    (ii) Given that x, 4, $x+6$ are consecutive terms of a geometric series, find:

        (a) the possible values of x

        (b) the corresponding values of the common ratio of the geometric series.

    (iii) Given that x, 4, $x+6$ are the sixth, seventh and eighth terms of a geometric series and that the sum to infinity of the series exists, find:

        (a) the first term

        (b) the sum to infinity.   **[MEI]**

14 The first four terms in an infinite geometric series are 54, 18, 6, 2.

    (i) What is the common ratio r?

    (ii) Write down an expression for the nth term of the series.

    (iii) Find the sum of the first n terms of the series.

    (iv) Find the sum to infinity.

    (v) How many terms are needed for the sum to be greater than 80.999?

15 A tank is filled with 20 litres of water. Half the water is removed and replaced with anti-freeze and thoroughly mixed. Half this mixture is then removed and replaced with anti-freeze. The process continues.

    (i) Find the first five terms in the sequence of amounts of water in the tank at each stage.

    (ii) Find the first five terms in the sequence of amounts of anti-freeze in the tank at each stage.

    (iii) Is either of these sequences geometric? Explain.

16 A pendulum is set swinging. Its first oscillation is through an angle of 30°, and each succeeding oscillation is through 95% of the angle of the one before it.

(i) After how many swings is the angle through which it swings less than 1°?

(ii) What is the total angle it has swung through at the end of its tenth oscillation?

17 A ball is thrown vertically upwards from the ground. It rises to a height of 10 m and then falls and bounces. After each bounce it rises vertically to $\frac{2}{3}$ of the height from which it fell.

(i) Find the height to which the ball bounces after the nth impact with the ground.

(ii) Find the total distance travelled by the ball from the first throw to the tenth impact with the ground.

18 The first three terms of an arithmetic sequence, a, $a + d$ and $a + 2d$, are the same as the first three terms, a, ar, ar^2, of a geometric sequence $(a \neq 0)$.

Show that this is only possible if $r = 1$ and $d = 0$.

19 The first term of a geometric progression is 81 and the fourth term is 24. Find

(i) the common ratio of the progression

(ii) the sum to infinity of the progression.

The second and third terms of this geometric progression are the first and fourth terms respectively of an arithmetic progression.

(iii) Find the sum of the first ten terms of the arithmetic progression.

[Cambridge AS & A Level Mathematics 9709, Paper 1 Q7 June 2008]

20 A progression has a second term of 96 and a fourth term of 54. Find the first term of the progression in each of the following cases:

(i) the progression is arithmetic

(ii) the progression is geometric with a positive common ratio.

[Cambridge AS & A Level Mathematics 9709, Paper 12 Q3 November 2009]

21 (i) Find the sum to infinity of the geometric progression with first three terms 0.5, 0.5^3 and 0.5^5.

(ii) The first two terms in an arithmetic progression are 5 and 9. The last term in the progression is the only term which is greater than 200. Find the sum of all the terms in the progression.

[Cambridge AS & A Level Mathematics 9709, Paper 1 Q7 June 2009]

22 The 1st term of an arithmetic progression is a and the common difference is d, where $d \neq 0$.

(i) Write down expressions, in terms of a and d, for the 5th term and the 15th term.

The 1st term, the 5th term and the 15th term of the arithmetic progression are the first three terms of a geometric progression.

(ii) Show that $3a = 8d$.

(iii) Find the common ratio of the geometric progression.

[Cambridge AS & A Level Mathematics 9709, Paper 1 Q4 November 2007]

INVESTIGATIONS

Snowflakes

Draw an equilateral triangle with sides 9 cm long.
Trisect each side and construct equilateral triangles on the middle section of each side as shown in diagram **(b)**.

Repeat the procedure for each of the small triangles as shown in **(c)** and **(d)** so that you have the first four stages in an infinite sequence.

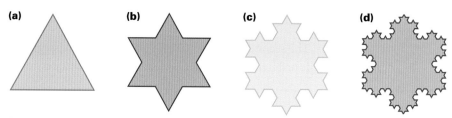

(a)　　　　**(b)**　　　　**(c)**　　　　**(d)**

Figure 3.4

Calculate the length of the perimeter of the figure for each of the first six steps, starting with the original equilateral triangle.

What happens to the length of the perimeter as the number of steps increases?

Does the area of the figure increase without limit?

Achilles and the tortoise

Achilles (it is said) once had a race with a tortoise. The tortoise started 100 m ahead of Achilles and moved at $\frac{1}{10}$ ms^{-1} compared to Achilles' speed of 10 ms^{-1}.

Achilles ran to where the tortoise started only to see that it had moved 1 m further on. So he ran on to that spot but again the tortoise had moved further on, this time by 0.01 m. This happened again and again: whenever Achilles got to the spot where the tortoise was, it had moved on. Did Achilles ever manage to catch the tortoise?

Binomial expansions

A special type of series is produced when a binomial (i.e. two-part) expression like $(x + 1)$ is raised to a power. The resulting expression is often called a *binomial expansion*.

The simplest binomial expansion is $(x + 1)$ itself. This and other powers of $(x + 1)$ are given below.

$$(x+1)^1 = \qquad\qquad\qquad 1x \;+\; 1$$
$$(x+1)^2 = \qquad\qquad 1x^2 \;+\; 2x \;+\; 1$$
$$(x+1)^3 = \qquad 1x^3 \;+\; 3x^2 \;+\; 3x \;+\; 1$$
$$(x+1)^4 = \quad 1x^4 \;+\; 4x^3 \;+\; 6x^2 \;+\; 4x \;+\; 1$$
$$(x+1)^5 = 1x^5 \;+\; 5x^4 \;+\; 10x^3 \;+\; 10x^2 \;+\; 5x \;+\; 1$$

> Expressions like these, consisting of integer powers of x and constants are called *polynomials*.

If you look at the coefficients on the right-hand side above you will see that they form a pattern.

> These numbers are called *binomial* coefficients.

$$
\begin{array}{ccccccccccc}
 & & & & & (1) & & & & & \\
 & & & & 1 & & 1 & & & & \\
 & & & 1 & & 2 & & 1 & & & \\
 & & 1 & & 3 & & 3 & & 1 & & \\
 & 1 & & 4 & & 6 & & 4 & & 1 & \\
1 & & 5 & & 10 & & 10 & & 5 & & 1
\end{array}
$$

This is called *Pascal's triangle*, or the *Chinese triangle*. Each number is obtained by adding the two above it, for example

$$4 \quad + \quad 6$$

gives $\qquad\quad 10$

This pattern of coefficients is very useful. It enables you to write down the expansions of other binomial expressions. For example,

$$(x + y) = \qquad\qquad\quad 1x \;+\; 1y$$
$$(x + y)^2 = \qquad\quad 1x^2 \;+\; 2xy \;+\; 1y^2$$
$$(x + y)^3 = \quad 1x^3 \;+\; 3x^2y \;+\; 3xy^2 \;+\; 1y^3$$

> Notice how in each term the sum of the powers of x and y is the same as the power of $(x + y)$.

> This is a binomial expression.

> These numbers are called *binomial* coefficients.

EXAMPLE 3.11

Write out the binomial expansion of $(x + 2)^4$.

SOLUTION

The binomial coefficients for power 4 are $\quad 1 \quad 4 \quad 6 \quad 4 \quad 1$.

In each term, the sum of the powers of x and 2 must equal 4.

So the expansion is

$$1 \times x^4 \quad + \quad 4 \times x^3 \times 2 \quad + \quad 6 \times x^2 \times 2^2 \quad + \quad 4 \times x \times 2^3 \quad + \quad 1 \times 2^4$$

i.e. $\quad x^4 \quad + \quad 8x^3 \quad + \quad 24x^2 \quad + \quad 32x \quad + \quad 16.$

EXAMPLE 3.12   Write out the binomial expansion of $(2a - 3b)^5$.

SOLUTION

The binomial coefficients for power 5 are   1   5   10   10   5   1.

The expression $(2a - 3b)$ is treated as $(2a + (-3b))$.

So the expansion is

$$1 \times (2a)^5 + 5 \times (2a)^4 \times (-3b) + 10 \times (2a)^3 \times (-3b)^2 + 10 \times (2a)^2 \times (-3b)^3$$
$$+ 5 \times (2a) \times (-3b)^4 + 1 \times (-3b)^5$$

i.e. $32a^5 - 240a^4b + 720a^3b^2 - 1080a^2b^3 + 810ab^4 - 243b^5.$

Historical note

Blaise Pascal has been described as the greatest might-have-been in the history of mathematics. Born in France in 1623, he was making discoveries in geometry by the age of 16 and had developed the first computing machine before he was 20.

Pascal suffered from poor health and religious anxiety, so that for periods of his life he gave up mathematics in favour of religious contemplation. The second of these periods was brought on when he was riding in his carriage: his runaway horses dashed over the parapet of a bridge, and he was only saved by the miraculous breaking of the traces. He took this to be a sign of God's disapproval of his mathematical work. A few years later a toothache subsided when he was thinking about geometry and this, he decided, was God's way of telling him to return to mathematics.

Pascal's triangle (and the binomial theorem) had actually been discovered by Chinese mathematicians several centuries earlier, and can be found in the works of Yang Hui (around 1270 A.D.) and Chu Shi-kie (in 1303 A.D.). Pascal is remembered for his application of the triangle to elementary probability, and for his study of the relationships between binomial coefficients.

Pascal died at the early age of 39.

Tables of binomial coefficients

Values of binomial coefficients can be found in books of tables. It is helpful to use these when the power becomes large, since writing out Pascal's triangle becomes progressively longer and more tedious, row by row.

EXAMPLE 3.13   Write out the full expansion of $(x + y)^{10}$.

SOLUTION

The binomial coefficients for the power 10 can be found from tables to be

1   10   45   120   210   252   210   120   45   10   1

and so the expansion is

$$x^{10} + 10x^9y + 45x^8y^2 + 120x^7y^3 + 210x^6y^4 + 252x^5y^5 + 210x^4y^6 + 120x^3y^7$$
$$+ 45x^2y^8 + 10xy^9 + y^{10}.$$

There are 10 + 1 = 11 terms.

 As the numbers are symmetrical about the middle number, tables do not always give the complete row of numbers.

The formula for a binomial coefficient

There will be times when you need to find binomial coefficients that are outside the range of your tables. The tables may, for example, list the binomial coefficients for powers up to 20. What happens if you need to find the coefficient of x^{17} in the expansion of $(x + 2)^{25}$? Clearly you need a formula that gives binomial coefficients.

The first thing you need is a notation for identifying binomial coefficients. It is usual to denote the power of the binomial expression by n, and the position in the row of binomial coefficients by r, where r can take any value from 0 to n. So for row 5 of Pascal's triangle

$n = 5$:	1	5	10	10	5	1
	$r = 0$	$r = 1$	$r = 2$	$r = 3$	$r = 4$	$r = 5$

The general binomial coefficient corresponding to values of n and r is written as $\binom{n}{r}$. An alternative notation is ^nC_r, which is said as 'N C R'.

Thus $\binom{5}{3} = {}^5C_3 = 10$.

The next step is to find a formula for the general binomial coefficient $\binom{n}{r}$. However, to do this you must be familiar with the term *factorial*.

The quantity '8 factorial', written 8!, is

$$8! = 8 \times 7 \times 6 \times 5 \times 4 \times 3 \times 2 \times 1 = 40\ 320.$$

Similarly, $12! = 12 \times 11 \times 10 \times 9 \times 8 \times 7 \times 6 \times 5 \times 4 \times 3 \times 2 \times 1 = 479\ 001\ 600$,

and $n! = n \times (n - 1) \times (n - 2) \times \ldots \times 1$, where n is a positive integer.

 Note that 0! is defined to be 1. You will see the need for this when you use the formula for $\binom{n}{r}$.

ACTIVITY 3.1

The table shows an alternative way of laying out Pascal's triangle.

		Column (r)								
		0	**1**	**2**	**3**	**4**	**5**	**6**	**...**	**r**
	1	1	1							
Row	**2**	1	2	1						
(n)	**3**	1	3	3	1					
	4	1	4	6	4	1				
	5	1	5	10	10	5	1			
	6	1	6	15	20	15	6	1		
	...	...	...	...	...	...	...	...	...	
	...	...	...	...	...	...	...	...	...	...
	n	1	n	?	?	?	?	?	?	?

Show that $\binom{n}{r} = \dfrac{n!}{r!(n-r)!}$, by following the procedure below.

The numbers in column 0 are all 1.

To find each number in column 1 you multiply the 1 in column 0 by the row number, n.

(i) Find, in terms of n, what you must multiply each number in column 1 by to find the corresponding number in column 2.

(ii) Repeat the process to find the relationship between each number in column 2 and the corresponding one in column 3.

(iii) Show that repeating the process leads to

$$\binom{n}{r} = \frac{n(n-1)(n-2)...(n-r+1)}{1 \times 2 \times 3 \times ... \times r} \text{ for } r \geqslant 1.$$

(iv) Show that this can also be written as

$$\binom{n}{r} = \frac{n!}{r!(n-r)!}$$

and that it is also true for $r = 0$.

EXAMPLE 3.14

Use the formula $\binom{n}{r} = \dfrac{n!}{r!(n-r)!}$ to calculate these.

(i) $\binom{5}{0}$ (ii) $\binom{5}{1}$ (iii) $\binom{5}{2}$

(iv) $\binom{5}{3}$ (v) $\binom{5}{4}$ (vi) $\binom{5}{5}$

SOLUTION

(i) $\begin{pmatrix} 5 \\ 0 \end{pmatrix} = \dfrac{5!}{0!(5-0)!} = \dfrac{120}{1 \times 120} = 1$

(ii) $\begin{pmatrix} 5 \\ 1 \end{pmatrix} = \dfrac{5!}{1!4!} = \dfrac{120}{1 \times 24} = 5$

(iii) $\begin{pmatrix} 5 \\ 2 \end{pmatrix} = \dfrac{5!}{2!3!} = \dfrac{120}{2 \times 6} = 10$

(iv) $\begin{pmatrix} 5 \\ 3 \end{pmatrix} = \dfrac{5!}{3!2!} = \dfrac{120}{6 \times 2} = 10$

(v) $\begin{pmatrix} 5 \\ 4 \end{pmatrix} = \dfrac{5!}{4!1!} = \dfrac{120}{24 \times 1} = 5$

(vi) $\begin{pmatrix} 5 \\ 5 \end{pmatrix} = \dfrac{5!}{5!0!} = \dfrac{120}{120 \times 1} = 1$

Note

You can see that these numbers, 1, 5, 10, 10, 5, 1, are row 5 of Pascal's triangle.

 Most scientific calculators have factorial buttons, e.g. $\boxed{x!}$. Many also have $\boxed{{}^nC_r}$ buttons. Find out how best to use your calculator to find binomial coefficients, as well as practising non-calculator methods.

EXAMPLE 3.15   Find the coefficient of x^{17} in the expansion of $(x+2)^{25}$.

SOLUTION

$(x+2)^{25} = \begin{pmatrix} 25 \\ 0 \end{pmatrix} x^{25} + \begin{pmatrix} 25 \\ 1 \end{pmatrix} x^{24} 2^1 + \begin{pmatrix} 25 \\ 2 \end{pmatrix} x^{23} 2^2 + \ldots + \begin{pmatrix} 25 \\ 8 \end{pmatrix} x^{17} 2^8 + \ldots \begin{pmatrix} 25 \\ 25 \end{pmatrix} 2^{25}$

So the required term is $\begin{pmatrix} 25 \\ 8 \end{pmatrix} \times 2^8 \times x^{17}$

$\begin{pmatrix} 25 \\ 8 \end{pmatrix} = \dfrac{25!}{8!17!} = \dfrac{25 \times 24 \times 23 \times 22 \times 21 \times 20 \times 19 \times 18 \times \cancel{17!}}{8! \times \cancel{17!}}$

$= 1\,081\,575.$

So the coefficient of x^{17} is $1\,081\,575 \times 2^8 = 276\,883\,200$.

Note

Notice how 17! was cancelled in working out $\begin{pmatrix} 25 \\ 8 \end{pmatrix}$. Factorials become large numbers very quickly and you should keep a look-out for such opportunities to simplify calculations.

The expansion of $(1 + x)^n$

When deriving the result for $\binom{n}{r}$ you found the binomial coefficients in the form

$$1 \quad n \quad \frac{n(n-1)}{2!} \quad \frac{n(n-1)(n-2)}{3!} \quad \frac{n(n-1)(n-2)(n-3)}{4!} \quad \ldots$$

This form is commonly used in the expansion of expressions of the type $(1 + x)^n$.

$$(1+x)^n = 1 + nx + \frac{n(n-1)x^2}{1 \times 2} + \frac{n(n-1)(n-2)x^3}{1 \times 2 \times 3} + \frac{n(n-1)(n-2)(n-3)x^4}{1 \times 2 \times 3 \times 4} + \ldots$$

$$+ \frac{n(n-1)}{1 \times 2}x^{n-2} + nx^{n-1} + 1x^n$$

EXAMPLE 3.16

Use the binomial expansion to write down the first four terms, in ascending powers of x, of $(1 + x)^9$.

SOLUTION

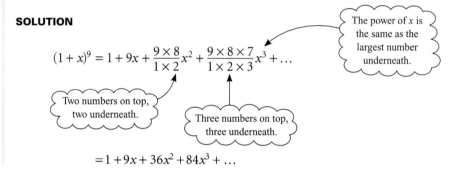

The power of x is the same as the largest number underneath.

$$(1 + x)^9 = 1 + 9x + \frac{9 \times 8}{1 \times 2}x^2 + \frac{9 \times 8 \times 7}{1 \times 2 \times 3}x^3 + \ldots$$

Two numbers on top, two underneath.

Three numbers on top, three underneath.

$$= 1 + 9x + 36x^2 + 84x^3 + \ldots$$

The expression $1 + 9x + 36x^2 + 84x^3 \ldots$ is said to be in *ascending* powers of x, because the powers of x are increasing from one term to the next.

An expression like $x^9 + 9x^8 + 36x^7 + 84x^6 \ldots$ is in *descending* powers of x, because the powers of x are decreasing from one term to the next.

EXAMPLE 3.17

Use the binomial expansion to write down the first four terms, in ascending powers of x, of $(1 - 3x)^7$. Simplify the terms.

SOLUTION

Think of $(1 - 3x)^7$ as $(1 + (-3x))^7$. Keep the brackets while you write out the terms.

$$(1 + (-3x))^7 = 1 + 7(-3x) + \frac{7 \times 6}{1 \times 2}(-3x)^2 + \frac{7 \times 6 \times 5}{1 \times 2 \times 3}(-3x)^3 + \ldots$$

$$= 1 - 21x + 189x^2 - 945x^3 + \ldots$$

Note how the signs alternate.

EXAMPLE 3.18

The first three terms in the expansion of $\left(ax + \dfrac{b}{x}\right)^6$ where $a > 0$, in descending powers of x, are $64x^6 - 576x^4 + cx^2$. Find the values of a, b and c.

SOLUTION

Find the first three terms in the expansion in terms of a and b:

$$\left(ax + \frac{b}{x}\right)^6 = \binom{6}{0}(ax)^6 + \binom{6}{1}(ax)^5\left(\frac{b}{x}\right) + \binom{6}{2}(ax)^4\left(\frac{b}{x}\right)^2$$

$$x^4 \times \frac{1}{x^2} = x^2$$

$$= a^6x^6 + 6a^5bx^4 + 15a^4b^2x^2$$

So $a^6x^6 + 6a^5bx^4 + 15a^4b^2x^2 = 64x^6 - 576x^4 + cx^2$

Compare the coefficients of x^6: $a^6 = 64 \Rightarrow a = 2$

Remember both $2^6 = 64$ and $(-2)^6 = 64$, but as $a > 0$ then $a = 2$.

Compare the coefficients of x^4: $6a^5b = -576$

Since $a = 2$ then $192b = -576 \Rightarrow b = -3$

Compare the coefficients of x^2: $15a^4b^2 = c$

Since $a = 2$ and $b = -3$ then $c = 15 \times 2^4 \times (-3)^2 \Rightarrow c = 2160$

? A Pascal puzzle

$1.1^2 = 1.21 \qquad 1.1^3 = 1.331 \qquad 1.1^4 = 1.4641$

What is 1.1^5?
What is the connection between your results and the coefficients in Pascal's triangle?

---

e Relationships between binomial coefficients

There are several useful relationships between binomial coefficients.

Symmetry

Because Pascal's triangle is symmetrical about its middle, it follows that

$$\binom{n}{r} = \binom{n}{n-r}.$$

Adding terms

You have seen that each term in Pascal's triangle is formed by adding the two above it. This is written formally as

$$\binom{n}{r} + \binom{n}{r+1} = \binom{n+1}{r+1}.$$

Sum of terms

You have seen that

$$(x+y)^n = \binom{n}{0}x^n + \binom{n}{1}x^{n-1}y + \binom{n}{2}x^{n-2}y^2 + \ldots + \binom{n}{n}y^n$$

Substituting $x = y = 1$ gives

$$2^n = \binom{n}{0} + \binom{n}{1} + \binom{n}{2} + \ldots + \binom{n}{n}.$$

Thus the sum of the binomial coefficients for power n is 2^n.

The binomial theorem and its applications

The binomial expansions covered in the last few pages can be stated formally as the binomial theorem for positive integer powers:

$$(a+b)^n = \sum_{r=0}^{n} \binom{n}{r} a^{n-r} b^r \quad \text{for } n \in \mathbb{Z}^+, \quad \text{where} \binom{n}{r} = \frac{n!}{r!(n-r)!} \quad \text{and } 0! = 1.$$

Note

Notice the use of the summation symbol, Σ. The right-hand side of the statement reads 'the sum of $\binom{n}{r}$ $a^{n-r}b^r$ for values of r from 0 to n'.

It therefore means

$$\binom{n}{0}a^n + \binom{n}{1}a^{n-1}b + \binom{n}{2}a^{n-2}b^2 + \ldots + \binom{n}{k}a^{n-k}b^k + \ldots + \binom{n}{n}b^n.$$
$$\;\; r=0 \qquad\;\; r=1 \qquad\;\;\; r=2 \qquad\qquad\;\; r=k \qquad\qquad\; r=n$$

The binomial theorem is used on other types of expansion and it has applications in many areas of mathematics.

The binomial distribution

In some situations involving repetitions of trials with two possible outcomes, the probabilities of the various possible results are given by the terms of a binomial expansion. This is covered in *Probability and Statistics 1*.

Selections

The number of ways of selecting r objects from n (all different) is given by $\binom{n}{r}$. This is also covered in *Probability and Statistics 1*.

1 Write out the following binomial expansions.

(i) $(x+1)^4$

(ii) $(1+x)^7$

(iii) $(x+2)^5$

(iv) $(2x+1)^6$

(v) $(2x-3)^4$

(vi) $(2x+3y)^3$

(vii) $\left(x-\dfrac{2}{x}\right)^3$

(viii) $\left(x+\dfrac{2}{x^2}\right)^4$

(ix) $\left(3x^2-\dfrac{2}{x}\right)^5$

2 Use a non-calculator method to calculate the following binomial coefficients. Check your answers using your calculator's shortest method.

(i) $\begin{pmatrix} 4 \\ 2 \end{pmatrix}$

(ii) $\begin{pmatrix} 6 \\ 2 \end{pmatrix}$

(iii) $\begin{pmatrix} 6 \\ 3 \end{pmatrix}$

(iv) $\begin{pmatrix} 6 \\ 4 \end{pmatrix}$

(v) $\begin{pmatrix} 6 \\ 0 \end{pmatrix}$

(vi) $\begin{pmatrix} 12 \\ 9 \end{pmatrix}$

3 In these expansions, find the coefficient of these terms.

(i) x^5 in $(1+x)^8$

(ii) x^4 in $(1-x)^{10}$

(iii) x^6 in $(1+3x)^{12}$

(iv) x^7 in $(1-2x)^{15}$

(v) x^2 in $\left(x^2+\dfrac{2}{x}\right)^{10}$

4 (i) Simplify $(1+x)^3-(1-x)^3$.

(ii) Show that $a^3-b^3=(a-b)(a^2+ab+b^2)$.

(iii) Substitute $a=1+x$ and $b=1-x$ in the result in part (ii) and show that your answer is the same as that for part (i).

5 Find the first three terms, in descending powers of x, in the expansion of $\left(2x-\dfrac{2}{x}\right)^4$.

6 Find the first three terms, in ascending powers of x, in the expansion $(2+kx)^6$.

7 (i) Find the first three terms, in ascending powers of x, in the expansion $(1-2x)^6$.

(ii) Hence find the coefficients of x and x^2 in the expansion of $(4-x)(2-4x)^6$.

8 (i) Find the first three terms, in descending powers of x, in the expansion $\left(4x-\dfrac{k}{x^2}\right)^6$.

(ii) Given that the value of the term in the expansion which is independent of x is 240, find possible values of k.

9 (i) Find the first three terms, in descending powers of x, in the expansion of $\left(x^2-\dfrac{1}{x}\right)^6$.

(ii) Find the coefficient of x^3 in the expansion of $\left(x^2-\dfrac{1}{x}\right)^6$.

10 (i) Find the first three terms, in descending powers of x, in the expansion of $\left(x - \dfrac{2}{x}\right)^5$.

(ii) Hence find the coefficient of x in the expansion of $\left(4 + \dfrac{1}{x^2}\right)\left(x - \dfrac{2}{x}\right)^5$.

11 (i) Show that $(2 + x)^4 = 16 + 32x + 24x^2 + 8x^3 + x^4$ for all x.

(ii) Find the values of x for which $(2 + x)^4 = 16 + 16x + x^4$.

[MEI]

12 The first three terms in the expansion of $(2 + ax)^n$, in ascending powers of x, are $32 - 40x + bx^2$. Find the values of the constants n, a and b.

[Cambridge AS & A Level Mathematics 9709, Paper 1 Q4 June 2006]

13 (i) Find the first three terms in the expansion of $(2 - x)^6$ in ascending powers of x.

(ii) Find the value of k for which there is no term in x^2 in the expansion of $(1 + kx)(2 - x)^6$.

[Cambridge AS & A Level Mathematics 9709, Paper 1 Q4 June 2005]

14 (i) Find the first three terms in the expansion of $(1 + ax)^5$ in ascending powers of x.

(ii) Given that there is no term in x in the expansion of $(1 - 2x)(1 + ax)^5$, find the value of the constant a.

(iii) For this value of a, find the coefficient of x^2 in the expansion of $(1 - 2x)(1 + ax)^5$.

[Cambridge AS & A Level Mathematics 9709, Paper 12 Q6 June 2010]

INVESTIGATIONS

Routes to victory

In a recent soccer match, Juventus beat Manchester United 2–1.
What could the half-time score have been?

(i) How many different possible half-time scores are there if the final score is 2–1? How many if the final score is 4–3?

(ii) How many different 'routes' are there to any final score? For example, for the above match, putting Juventus' score first, the sequence could be:

$$0\text{–}0 \rightarrow 0\text{–}1 \rightarrow 1\text{–}1 \rightarrow 2\text{–}1$$
$$\text{or } 0\text{–}0 \rightarrow 1\text{–}0 \rightarrow 1\text{–}1 \rightarrow 2\text{–}1$$
$$\text{or } 0\text{–}0 \rightarrow 1\text{–}0 \rightarrow 2\text{–}0 \rightarrow 2\text{–}1.$$

So in this case there are three routes.

Investigate the number of routes that exist to any final score (up to a maximum of five goals for either team).
Draw up a table of your results. Is there a pattern?

Cubes

A cube is painted red. It is then cut up into a number of identical cubes, as in figure 3.5.

How many of the cubes have the following numbers of faces painted red?

(i) 3   **(ii)** 2   **(iii)** 1   **(iv)** 0

In figure 3.5 there are 125 cubes but your answer should cover all possible cases.

Figure 3.5

KEY POINTS

1 A sequence is an ordered set of numbers, u_1, u_2, u_3, ..., u_k, ... u_n, where u_k is the general term.

2 In an arithmetic sequence, $u_{k+1} = u_k + d$ where d is a fixed number called the common difference.

3 In a geometric sequence, $u_{k+1} = ru_k$ where r is a fixed number called the common ratio.

4 For an arithmetic progression with first term a, common difference d and n terms:
   - the kth term $u_k = a + (k-1)d$
   - the last term $l = a + (n-1)d$
   - the sum of the terms $= \frac{1}{2}n(a+l) = \frac{1}{2}n[2a + (n-1)d]$.

5 For a geometric progression with first term a, common ratio r and n terms:
   - the kth term $u_k = ar^{k-1}$
   - the last term $a_n = ar^{n-1}$
   - the sum of the terms $= \dfrac{a(r^n - 1)}{(r-1)} = \dfrac{a(1 - r^n)}{(1-r)}$.

6 For an infinite geometric series to converge, $-1 < r < 1$.

   In this case the sum of all the terms is given by $\dfrac{a}{(1-r)}$.

7 Binomial coefficients, denoted by $\begin{pmatrix} n \\ r \end{pmatrix}$ or ^nC_r, can be found
   - using Pascal's triangle
   - using tables
   - using the formula $\begin{pmatrix} n \\ r \end{pmatrix} = \dfrac{n!}{r!(n-r)!}$.

8 The binomial expansion of $(1 + x)^n$ may also be written

$$(1 + x)^n = 1 + nx + \frac{n(n-1)}{2!}x^2 + \frac{n(n-1)(n-2)}{3!}x^3 + \ldots + nx^{n-1} + x^n.$$

Functions

Still glides the stream and shall forever glide;
The form remains, the function never dies.

William Wordsworth

Why fly to Geneva in January?

Several people arriving at Geneva airport from London were asked the main purpose of their visit. Their answers were recorded.

This is an example of a *mapping*.

The language of functions

A mapping is any rule which associates two sets of items. In this example, each of the names on the left is an *object*, or *input*, and each of the reasons on the right is an *image*, or *output*.

For a mapping to make sense or to have any practical application, the inputs and outputs must each form a natural collection or set. The set of possible inputs (in this case, all of the people who flew to Geneva from London in January) is called the *domain* of the mapping.

The seven people questioned in this example gave a set of four reasons, or outputs. These form the *range* of the mapping for this particular set of inputs.

Notice that Jonathan, Louise and Karen are all visiting Geneva on business: each person gave only one reason for the trip, but the same reason was given by several people. This mapping is said to be *many-to-one*. A mapping can also be *one-to-one, one-to-many* or *many-to-many*. The relationship between the people from any country and their passport numbers will be one-to-one. The relationship between the people and their items of luggage is likely to be one-to-many, and that between the people and the countries they have visited in the last 10 years will be many-to-many.

Mappings

In mathematics, many (but not all) mappings can be expressed using algebra. Here are some examples of mathematical mappings.

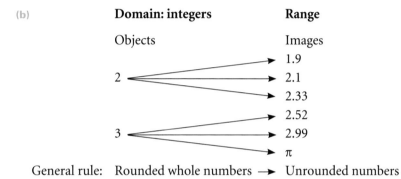

(a)

Domain: integers　　　　**Range**

Objects　　　　　　　　　　　Images

-1 ⟶ 3

0 ⟶ 5

1 ⟶ 7

2 ⟶ 9

3 ⟶ 11

General rule:　x ⟶ $2x + 5$

(b)

Domain: integers　　　　**Range**

Objects　　　　　　　　　　　Images

2 ⟶ 1.9

⟶ 2.1

⟶ 2.33

3 ⟶ 2.52

⟶ 2.99

⟶ π

General rule:　Rounded whole numbers ⟶ Unrounded numbers

(c)

Domain: real numbers　　**Range**

Objects　　　　　　　　　　　Images

0

45 ⟶ 0

90 ⟶ 0.707

135 ⟶ 1

180

General rule:　$x°$ ⟶ $\sin x°$

(d)

Domain: quadratic equations with real roots　　**Range**

Objects　　　　　　　　　　　Images

$x^2 - 4x + 3 = 0$ ⟶ 0

$x^2 - x = 0$ ⟶ 1

$x^2 - 3x + 2 = 0$ ⟶ 2

⟶ 3

General rule:　$ax^2 + bx + c = 0$ ⟶ $x = \dfrac{-b - \sqrt{b^2 - 4ac}}{2a}$

$x = \dfrac{-b + \sqrt{b^2 - 4ac}}{2a}$

❷ For each of the examples above:

(i) decide whether the mapping is one-to-one, many-to-many, one-to-many or many-to-one

(ii) take a different set of inputs and identify the corresponding range.

Functions

Mappings which are one-to-one or many-to-one are of particular importance, since in these cases there is only one possible image for any object. Mappings of these types are called *functions*. For example, $x \mapsto x^2$ and $x \mapsto \cos x$ are both functions, because in each case for any value of x there is only one possible answer. By contrast, the mapping of rounded whole numbers (objects) on to unrounded numbers (images) is not a function, since, for example, the rounded number 5 could map on to any unrounded number between 4.5 and 5.5.

There are several different but equivalent ways of writing a function. For example, the function which maps the real numbers, x, on to x^2 can be written in any of the following ways.

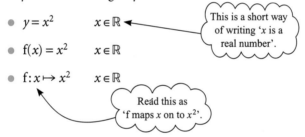

- $y = x^2$ $x \in \mathbb{R}$ ← This is a short way of writing 'x is a real number'.

- $f(x) = x^2$ $x \in \mathbb{R}$

- $f: x \mapsto x^2$ $x \in \mathbb{R}$ Read this as 'f maps x on to x^2'.

To define a function you need to specify a suitable domain. For example, you cannot choose a domain of $x \in \mathbb{R}$ (all the real numbers) for the function $f: x \mapsto \sqrt{x-5}$ because when, say, $x = 3$, you would be trying to take the square root of a negative number; so you need to define the function as $f: x \mapsto \sqrt{x-5}$ for $x \geqslant 5$, so that the function is valid for all values in its domain.

Likewise, when choosing a suitable domain for the function $g: x \mapsto \dfrac{1}{x-5}$, you need to remember that division by 0 is undefined and therefore you cannot input $x = 5$. So the function g is defined as $g: x \mapsto \dfrac{1}{x-5}$, $x \neq 5$.

It is often helpful to represent a function graphically, as in the following example, which also illustrates the importance of knowing the domain.

EXAMPLE 4.1   Sketch the graph of $y = 3x + 2$ when the domain of x is

(i) $x \in \mathbb{R}$

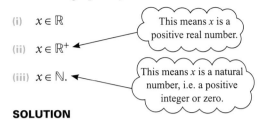

This means x is a positive real number.

(ii) $x \in \mathbb{R}^+$

(iii) $x \in \mathbb{N}$.

This means x is a natural number, i.e. a positive integer or zero.

SOLUTION

(i)   When the domain is $\mathbb{R}$, all values of y are possible. The range is therefore $\mathbb{R}$, also.

(ii)   When x is restricted to positive values, all the values of y are greater than 2, so the range is $y > 2$.

(iii)   In this case the range is the set of points $\{2, 5, 8, \ldots\}$. These are clearly all of the form $3x + 2$ where x is a natural number $(0, 1, 2, \ldots)$. This set can be written neatly as $\{3x + 2 : x \in \mathbb{N}\}$.

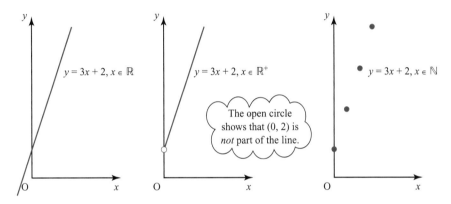

The open circle shows that $(0, 2)$ is *not* part of the line.

Figure 4.1

When you draw the graph of a mapping, the x co-ordinate of each point is an input value, the y co-ordinate is the corresponding output value. The table below shows this for the mapping $x \mapsto x^2$, or $y = x^2$, and figure 4.2 shows the resulting points on a graph.

Input (x)	Output (y)	Point plotted
−2	4	(−2, 4)
−1	1	(−1, 1)
0	0	(0, 0)
1	1	(1, 1)
2	4	(2, 4)

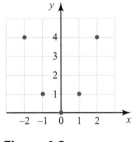

Figure 4.2

If the mapping is a function, there is one and only one value of y for every value of x in the domain. Consequently the graph of a function is a simple curve or line going from left to right, with no doubling back.

Figure 4.3 illustrates some different types of mapping. The graphs in (a) and (b) illustrate functions, those in (c) and (d) do not.

(a) One-to-one

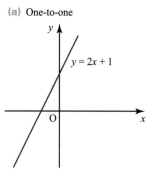

(b) Many-to-one

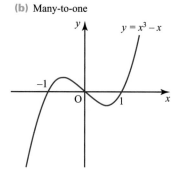

(c) One-to-many

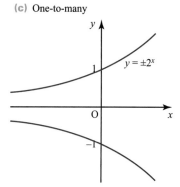

(d) Many-to-many

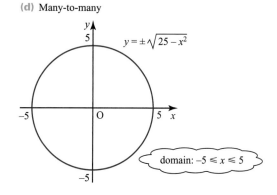

Figure 4.3

1 Describe each of the following mappings as either one-to-one, many-to-one, one-to-many or many-to-many, and say whether it represents a function.

(i)

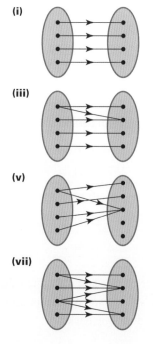

(ii)

(iii)

(iv)

(v)

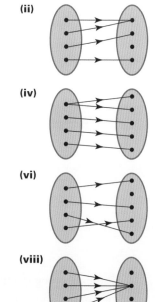

(vi)

(vii)

(viii)

2 For each of the following mappings:

    (a) write down a few examples of inputs and corresponding outputs

    (b) state the type of mapping (one-to-one, many-to-one, etc.)

    (c) suggest a suitable domain.

    (i)   Words $\mapsto$ number of letters they contain

    (ii)   Side of a square in cm $\mapsto$ its perimeter in cm

    (iii) Natural numbers $\mapsto$ the number of factors (including 1 and the number itself)

    (iv) $x \mapsto 2x - 5$

    (v) $x \mapsto \sqrt{x}$

    (vi) The volume of a sphere in cm^3 $\mapsto$ its radius in cm

    (vii) The volume of a cylinder in cm^3 $\mapsto$ its height in cm

    (viii) The length of a side of a regular hexagon in cm $\mapsto$ its area in cm^2

    (ix) $x \mapsto x^2$

3 **(i)** A function is defined by $f(x) = 2x - 5$, $x \in \mathbb{R}$. Write down the values of

      (a) $f(0)$ **(b)** $f(7)$ **(c)** $f(-3)$.

   (ii) A function is defined by g:(polygons) $\mapsto$ (number of sides). What are

      (a) g(triangle)   **(b)** g(pentagon)   **(c)** g(decagon)?

  (iii) The function t maps Celsius temperatures on to Fahrenheit temperatures. It is defined by t: $C \mapsto \dfrac{9C}{5} + 32$, $C \in \mathbb{R}$. Find

      (a) t(0)   **(b)** t(28)   **(c)** t(−10)

      (d) the value of C when t$(C) = C$.

4 Find the range of each of the following functions. (You may find it helpful to draw the graph first.)

    (i) $f(x) = 2 - 3x$ $x \geqslant 0$

    (ii) $f(\theta) = \sin\theta$ $0° \leqslant \theta \leqslant 180°$

    (iii) $y = x^2 + 2$ $x \in \{0, 1, 2, 3, 4\}$

    (iv) $y = \tan\theta$ $0° < \theta < 90°$

    (v)   f: $x \mapsto 3x - 5$ $x \in \mathbb{R}$

    (vi) f: $x \mapsto 2^x$ $x \in \{-1, 0, 1, 2\}$

    (vii) $y = \cos x$ $-90° \leqslant x \leqslant 90°$

    (viii) f: $x \mapsto x^3 - 4$ $x \in \mathbb{R}$

    (ix) $f(x) = \dfrac{1}{1 + x^2}$ $x \in \mathbb{R}$

    (x) $f(x) = \sqrt{x - 3} + 3$ $x \geqslant 3$

5 The mapping f is defined by $f(x) = x^2$ $0 \leqslant x \leqslant 3$
                               $f(x) = 3x$ $3 \leqslant x \leqslant 10$.

  The mapping g is defined by $g(x) = x^2$ $0 \leqslant x \leqslant 2$
                               $g(x) = 3x$ $2 \leqslant x \leqslant 10$.

  Explain why f is a function and g is not.

Composite functions

It is possible to combine functions in several different ways, and you have already met some of these. For example, if $f(x) = x^2$ and $g(x) = 2x$, then you could write

$$f(x) + g(x) = x^2 + 2x.$$

In this example, two functions are added.

Similarly if $f(x) = x$ and $g(x) = \sin x$, then

$$f(x).g(x) = x\sin x.$$

In this example, two functions are multiplied.

Sometimes you need to apply one function and then apply another to the answer. You are then creating a *composite function* or a *function of a function*.

EXAMPLE 4.2

A new mother is bathing her baby for the first time. She takes the temperature of the bath water with a thermometer which reads in Celsius, but then has to convert the temperature to degrees Fahrenheit to apply the rule that her own mother taught her:

> At one o five
> He'll cook alive
> But ninety four
> is rather raw.

Write down the two functions that are involved, and apply them to readings of

(i) 30°C   (ii) 38°C   (iii) 45°C.

SOLUTION

The first function converts the Celsius temperature C into a Fahrenheit temperature, F.

$$F = \frac{9C}{5} + 32$$

The second function maps Fahrenheit temperatures on to the state of the bath.

$F \leqslant 94$	too cold
$94 < F < 105$	all right
$F \geqslant 105$	too hot

This gives

(i) $30°C \mapsto 86°F \quad \mapsto \quad$ too cold
(ii) $38°C \mapsto 100.4°F \mapsto$ all right
(iii) $45°C \mapsto 113°C \quad \mapsto \quad$ too hot.

In this case the composite function would be (to the nearest degree)

$$C \leqslant 34°C \quad \text{too cold}$$
$$35°C \leqslant C \leqslant 40°C \quad \text{all right}$$
$$C \geqslant 41°C \quad \text{too hot}.$$

In algebraic terms, a composite function is constructed as

Input $x \xmapsto{\text{f}}$ Output $f(x)$

Input $f(x) \xmapsto{\text{g}}$ Output $g[f(x)]$ ← (or $gf(x)$).

Read this as 'g of f of x'.

Thus the composite function $gf(x)$ should be performed from right to left: start with x then apply f and then g.

Notation

To indicate that f is being applied twice in succession, you could write $ff(x)$ but you would usually use $f^2(x)$ instead. Similarly $g^3(x)$ means three applications of g.

In order to apply a function repeatedly its range must be completely contained within its domain.

Order of functions

If f is the rule 'square the input value' and g is the rule 'add 1', then

$$x \underset{\text{square}}{\xmapsto{\text{f}}} x^2 \underset{\text{add 1}}{\xmapsto{\text{g}}} x^2 + 1.$$

So $gf(x) = x^2 + 1$.

Notice that $gf(x)$ is not the same as $fg(x)$, since for $fg(x)$ you must apply g first. In the example above, this would give:

$$x \underset{\text{add 1}}{\xmapsto{\text{g}}} (x+1) \underset{\text{square}}{\xmapsto{\text{f}}} (x+1)^2$$

and so $fg(x) = (x+1)^2$.

Clearly this is *not* the same result.

Figure 4.4 illustrates the relationship between the domains and ranges of the functions f and g, and the range of the composite function gf.

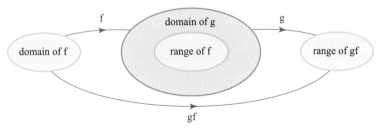

Figure 4.4

Notice the range of f must be completely contained within the domain of g. If this wasn't the case you wouldn't be able to form the composite function gf because you would be trying to input values into g that weren't in its domain.

For example, consider these functions f and g.

$$f : x \mapsto 2x, x > 0$$

$$g : x \mapsto \sqrt{x}, x > 0$$

You need this restriction so you are not taking the square root of a negative number.

The composite function gf can be formed:

$$x \xrightarrow[\times 2]{f} 2x \xrightarrow[\text{square root}]{g} \sqrt{2x}$$

and so $gf : x \mapsto \sqrt{2x}, x > 0$

Now think about a different function h.

$$h : x \mapsto 2x, x \in \mathbb{R}$$

This function looks like f but h has a different domain; it is all the real numbers whereas f was restricted to positive numbers. The range of h is also all real numbers and so it includes negative numbers, which are not in the domain of g.

So you cannot form the composite function gh. If you tried, h would input negative numbers into g and you cannot take the square root of a negative number.

EXAMPLE 4.3

The functions f, g and h are defined by:

$$f(x) = 2x \text{ for } x \in \mathbb{R}, g(x) = x^2 \text{ for } x \in \mathbb{R}, h(x) = \frac{1}{x} \text{ for } x \in \mathbb{R}, x \neq 0.$$

Find the following.

(i) $fg(x)$ (ii) $gf(x)$ (iii) $gh(x)$

(iv) $f^2(x)$ (v) $fgh(x)$

SOLUTION

(i) $fg(x) = f[g(x)]$
$$= f(x^2)$$
$$= 2x^2$$

(ii) $gf(x) = g[f(x)]$
$$= g(2x)$$
$$= (2x)^2$$
$$= 4x^2$$

(iii) $gh(x) = g[h(x)]$
$$= g\left(\frac{1}{x}\right)$$
$$= \frac{1}{x^2}$$

(iv) $f^2(x) = f[f(x)]$
$$= f(2x)$$
$$= 2(2x)$$
$$= 4x$$

(v) $fgh(x) = f[gh(x)]$
$$= f\left(\frac{1}{x^2}\right) \text{ using (iii)}$$
$$= \frac{2}{x^2}$$

Inverse functions

Look at the mapping $x \mapsto x + 2$ with domain the set of integers.

The mapping is clearly a function, since for every input there is one and only one output, the number that is two greater than that input.

This mapping can also be seen in reverse. In that case, each number maps on to the number two less than itself: $x \mapsto x - 2$. The reverse mapping is also a function because for any input there is one and only one output. The reverse mapping is called the *inverse function*, f^{-1}.

Function: $f : x \mapsto x + 2$ $x \in \mathbb{Z}$.

> This is a short way of writing x is an integer.

Inverse function: $f^{-1} : x \mapsto x - 2$ $x \in \mathbb{Z}$.

For a mapping to be a function which also has an inverse function, every object in the domain must have one and only one image in the range, and vice versa. This can only be the case if the mapping is one-to-one.

So the condition for a function f to have an inverse function is that, over the given domain, f represents a one-to-one mapping. This is a common situation, and many inverse functions are self-evident as in the following examples, for all of which the domain is the real numbers.

$f : x \mapsto x - 1;$ $f^{-1} : x \mapsto x + 1$

$g : x \mapsto 2x;$ $g^{-1} : x \mapsto \frac{1}{2}x$

$h : x \mapsto x^3;$ $h^{-1} : x \mapsto \sqrt[3]{x}$

? Some of the following mappings are functions which have inverse functions, and others are not.

(a) Decide which mappings fall into each category, and for those which do not have inverse functions, explain why.

(b) For those which have inverse functions, how can the functions and their inverses be written down algebraically?

(i)   Temperature measured in Celsius $\mapsto$ temperature measured in Fahrenheit.
(ii) Marks in an examination $\mapsto$ grade awarded.
(iii) Distance measured in light years $\mapsto$ distance measured in metres.
(iv) Number of stops travelled on the London Underground $\mapsto$ fare.

You can decide whether an algebraic mapping is a function, and whether it has an inverse function, by looking at its graph. The curve or line representing a one-to-one function does not double back on itself and has no turning points. The x values cover the full domain and the y values give the range. Figure 4.5 illustrates the functions f, g and h given on the previous page.

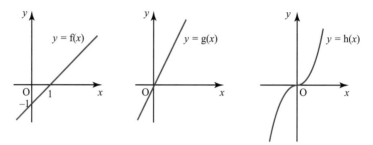

Figure 4.5

Now look at $f(x) = x^2$ for $x \in \mathbb{R}$ (figure 4.6). You can see that there are two distinct input values giving the same output: for example $f(2) = f(-2) = 4$. When you want to reverse the effect of the function, you have a mapping which for a single input of 4 gives two outputs, -2 and $+2$. Such a mapping is not a function.

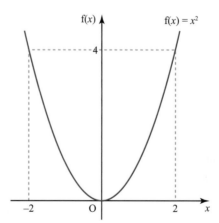

Figure 4.6

You can make a new function, $g(x) = x^2$ by restricting the domain to $\mathbb{R}^+$ (the set of positive real numbers). This is shown in figure 4.7. The function $g(x)$ is a one-to-one function and its inverse is given by $g^{-1}(x) = \sqrt{x}$ since the sign $\sqrt{}$ means 'the positive square root of'.

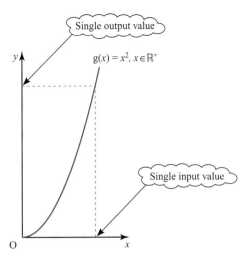

Figure 4.7

It is often helpful to define a function with a restricted domain so that its inverse is also a function. When you use the inv sin (i.e. $\sin^{-1}$ or arcsin) key on your calculator the answer is restricted to the range $-90°$ to $90°$, and is described as the *principal value*. Although there are infinitely many roots of the equation $\sin x = 0.5$ ($\ldots, -330°, -210°, 30°, 150°, \ldots$), only one of these, $30°$, lies in the restricted range and this is the value your calculator will give you.

The graph of a function and its inverse

ACTIVITY 4.1

For each of the following functions, work out the inverse function, and draw the graphs of both the original and the inverse on the same axes, using the same scale on both axes.

(i) $f(x) = x^2$, $x \in \mathbb{R}^+$ (ii) $f(x) = 2x$, $x \in \mathbb{R}$

(iii) $f(x) = x + 2$, $x \in \mathbb{R}$ (iv) $f(x) = x^3 + 2$, $x \in \mathbb{R}$

Look at your graphs and see if there is any pattern emerging.

Try out a few more functions of your own to check your ideas.

Make a conjecture about the relationship between the graph of a function and its inverse.

You have probably realised by now that the graph of the inverse function is the same shape as that of the function, but reflected in the line $y = x$. To see why this is so, think of a function $f(x)$ mapping a on to b; (a, b) is clearly a point on the graph of $f(x)$. The inverse function $f^{-1}(x)$, maps b on to a and so (b, a) is a point on the graph of $f^{-1}(x)$.

The point (b, a) is the reflection of the point (a, b) in the line $y = x$. This is shown for a number of points in figure 4.8.

This result can be used to obtain a sketch of the inverse function without having to find its equation, provided that the sketch of the original function uses the same scale on both axes.

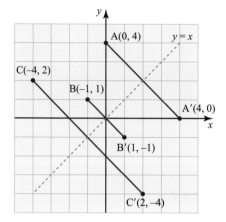

Figure 4.8

Finding the algebraic form of the inverse function

To find the algebraic form of the inverse of a function f(x), you should start by changing notation and writing it in the form $y = \ldots$.

Since the graph of the inverse function is the reflection of the graph of the original function in the line $y = x$, it follows that you may find its equation by interchanging y and x in the equation of the original function. You will then need to make y the subject of your new equation. This procedure is illustrated in Example 4.4.

EXAMPLE 4.4

Find $f^{-1}(x)$ when $f(x) = 2x + 1$, $x \in \mathbb{R}$.

SOLUTION

The function f(x) is given by $y = 2x + 1$

Interchanging x and y gives $x = 2y + 1$

Rearranging to make y the subject: $y = \dfrac{x - 1}{2}$

So $f^{-1}(x) = \dfrac{x - 1}{2}$, $x \in \mathbb{R}$

Sometimes the domain of the function f will not include the whole of $\mathbb{R}$. When any real numbers are excluded from the domain of f, it follows that they will be excluded from the range of f^{-1}, and vice versa.

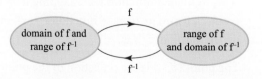

Figure 4.9

EXAMPLE 4.5

Find $f^{-1}(x)$ when $f(x) = 2x - 3$ and the domain of f is $x \geqslant 4$.

SOLUTION

	Domain	Range
Function: $y = 2x - 3$	$x \geqslant 4$	$y \geqslant 5$
Inverse function: $x = 2y - 3$	$x \geqslant 5$	$y \geqslant 4$

Rearranging the inverse function to make y the subject: $y = \dfrac{x + 3}{2}$.

The full definition of the inverse function is therefore:

$$f^{-1}(x) = \frac{x + 3}{2} \text{ for } x \geqslant 5.$$

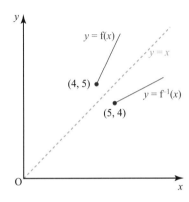

Figure 4.10

You can see in figure 4.10 that the inverse function is the reflection of a restricted part of the line $y = 2x - 3$.

EXAMPLE 4.6

(i)   Find $f^{-1}(x)$ when $f(x) = x^2 + 2,\ x \geqslant 0$.

(ii) Find $f(7)$ and $f^{-1}f(7)$. What do you notice?

SOLUTION

(i)

	Domain	Range
Function: $y = x^2 + 2$	$x \geqslant 0$	$y \geqslant 2$
Inverse function: $x = y^2 + 2$	$x \geqslant 2$	$y \geqslant 0$

Rearranging the inverse function to make y its subject: $y^2 = x - 2$.

This gives $y = \pm \sqrt{x - 2}$, but since you know the range of the inverse function to be $y \geqslant 0$ you can write:

$$y = +\sqrt{x - 2} \text{ or just } y = \sqrt{x - 2}.$$

The full definition of the inverse function is therefore:

$$f^{-1}(x) = \sqrt{x-2} \text{ for } x \geqslant 2.$$

The function and its inverse function are shown in figure 4.11.

(ii) $f(7) = 7^2 + 2 = 51$

$$f^{-1}f(7) = f^{-1}(51) = \sqrt{51-2} = 7$$

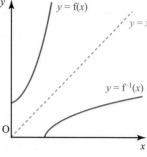

Figure 4.11

Applying the function followed by its inverse brings you back to the original input value.

Note

Part (ii) of Example 4.6 illustrates an important general result. For any function f(x) with an inverse $f^{-1}(x)$, $f^{-1}f(x) = x$. Similarly $ff^{-1}(x) = x$. The effects of a function and its inverse can be thought of as cancelling each other out.

EXERCISE 4B

1 The functions f, g and h are defined for $x \in \mathbb{R}$ by $f(x) = x^3$, $g(x) = 2x$ and $h(x) = x + 2$. Find each of the following, in terms of x.

(i) fg (ii) gf (iii) fh (iv) hf (v) fgh

(vi) ghf (vii) g^2 (viii) $(fh)^2$ (ix) h^2

2 Find the inverses of the following functions.

(i) $f(x) = 2x + 7, x \in \mathbb{R}$ (ii) $f(x) = 4 - x, x \in \mathbb{R}$

(iii) $f(x) = \dfrac{4}{2-x}, x \neq 2$ (iv) $f(x) = x^2 - 3, x \geqslant 0$

3 The function f is defined by $f(x) = (x-2)^2 + 3$ for $x \geqslant 2$.

(i) Sketch the graph of $f(x)$.

(ii) On the same axes, sketch the graph of $f^{-1}(x)$ without finding its equation.

4 Express the following in terms of the functions f: $x \mapsto \sqrt{x}$ and g: $x \mapsto x + 4$ for $x > 0$.

(i) $x \mapsto \sqrt{x+4}$ (ii) $x \mapsto x + 8$

(iii) $x \mapsto \sqrt{x+8}$ (iv) $x \mapsto \sqrt{x} + 4$

5 A function f is defined by:

$$f: x \mapsto \frac{1}{x} \qquad x \in \mathbb{R}, x \neq 0.$$

Find (i) $f^2(x)$ (ii) $f^3(x)$ (iii) $f^{-1}(x)$ (iv) $f^{999}(x)$.

6 (i) Show that $x^2 + 4x + 7 = (x + 2)^2 + a$, where a is to be determined.

(ii) Sketch the graph of $y = x^2 + 4x + 7$, giving the equation of its axis of symmetry and the co-ordinates of its vertex.

The function f is defined by f: $x \mapsto x^2 + 4x + 7$ with domain the set of all real numbers.

(iii) Find the range of f.

(iv) Explain, with reference to your sketch, why f has no inverse with its given domain. Suggest a domain for f for which it has an inverse.

[MEI]

7 The function f is defined by f: $x \mapsto 4x^3 + 3$, $x \in \mathbb{R}$.
Give the corresponding definition of f^{-1}.
State the relationship between the graphs of f and f^{-1}.

[UCLES]

8 Two functions are defined for $x \in \mathbb{R}$ as f$(x) = x^2$ and g$(x) = x^2 + 4x - 1$.

(i) Find a and b so that g$(x) = f(x + a) + b$.

(ii) Show how the graph of $y = g(x)$ is related to the graph of $y = f(x)$ and sketch the graph of $y = g(x)$.

(iii) State the range of the function g(x).

(iv) State the least value of c so that g(x) is one-to-one for $x \geqslant c$.

(v) With this restriction, sketch g(x) and g$^{-1}(x)$ on the same axes.

9 The functions f and g are defined for $x \in \mathbb{R}$ by

$$f: x \mapsto 4x - 2x^2;$$
$$g: x \mapsto 5x + 3.$$

(i) Find the range of f.

(ii) Find the value of the constant k for which the equation gf$(x) = k$ has equal roots.

[Cambridge AS & A Level Mathematics 9709, Paper 12 Q3 June 2010]

10 Functions f and g are defined by

$$f: x \mapsto k - x \qquad \text{for } x \in \mathbb{R}, \text{ where } k \text{ is a constant,}$$
$$g: x \mapsto \frac{9}{x + 2} \qquad \text{for } x \in \mathbb{R}, x \neq -2.$$

(i) Find the values of k for which the equation f$(x) = g(x)$ has two equal roots and solve the equation f$(x) = g(x)$ in these cases.

(ii) Solve the equation fg$(x) = 5$ when $k = 6$.

(iii) Express g$^{-1}(x)$ in terms of x.

[Cambridge AS & A Level Mathematics 9709, Paper 1 Q11 June 2006]

11 The function f is defined by $f: x \mapsto 2x^2 - 8x + 11$ for $x \in \mathbb{R}$.

 (i) Express $f(x)$ in the form $a(x + b)^2 + c$, where a, b and c are constants.

 (ii) State the range of f.

 (iii) Explain why f does not have an inverse.

 The function g is defined by $g: x \mapsto 2x^2 - 8x + 11$ for $x \leqslant A$, where A is a constant.

 (iv) State the largest value of A for which g has an inverse.

 (v) When A has this value, obtain an expression, in terms of x, for $g^{-1}(x)$ and state the range of g^{-1}.

[Cambridge AS & A Level Mathematics 9709, Paper 1 Q11 November 2007]

12 The function f is defined by $f: x \mapsto 3x - 2$ for $x \in \mathbb{R}$.

 (i) Sketch, in a single diagram, the graphs of $y = f(x)$ and $y = f^{-1}(x)$, making clear the relationship between the two graphs.

 The function g is defined by $g: x \mapsto 6x - x^2$ for $x \in \mathbb{R}$.

 (ii) Express $gf(x)$ in terms of x, and hence show that the maximum value of $gf(x)$ is 9.

 The function h is defined by $h: x \mapsto 6x - x^2$ for $x \geqslant 3$.

 (iii) Express $6x - x^2$ in the form $a - (x - b)^2$, where a and b are positive constants.

 (iv) Express $h^{-1}(x)$ in terms of x.

[Cambridge AS & A Level Mathematics 9709, Paper 1 Q10 November 2008]

KEY POINTS

1 A mapping is any rule connecting input values (objects) and output values (images). It can be many-to-one, one-to-many, one-to-one or many-to-many.

2 A many-to-one or one-to-one mapping is called a function. It is a mapping for which each input value gives exactly one output value.

3 The domain of a mapping or function is the set of possible input values (values of x).

4 The range of a mapping or function is the set of output values.

5 A composite function is obtained when one function (say g) is applied after another (say f). The notation used is $g[f(x)]$ or $gf(x)$.

6 For any one-to-one function $f(x)$, there is an inverse function $f^{-1}(x)$.

7 The curves of a function and its inverse are reflections of each other in the line $y = x$.

5

Differentiation

Hold infinity in the palm of your hand.

William Blake

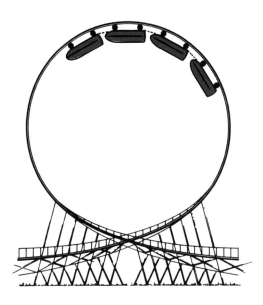

This picture illustrates one of the more frightening rides at an amusement park. To ensure that the ride is absolutely safe, its designers need to know the gradient of the curve at any point. What do we mean by the gradient of a curve?

The gradient of a curve

To understand what this means, think of a log on a log-flume, as in figure 5.1. If you draw the straight line $y = mx + c$ passing along the bottom of the log, then this line is a tangent to the curve at the point of contact. The gradient m of the tangent is the gradient of the curve at the point of contact.

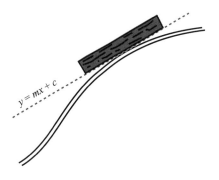

$y = mx + c$

Figure 5.1

One method of finding the gradient of a curve is shown for point A in figure 5.2.

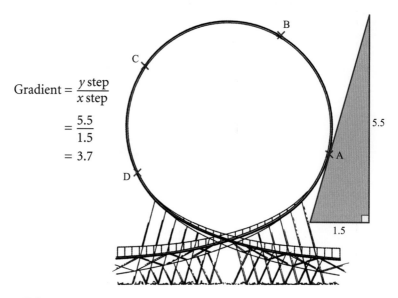

$$\text{Gradient} = \frac{y \text{ step}}{x \text{ step}}$$

$$= \frac{5.5}{1.5}$$

$$= 3.7$$

Figure 5.2

ACTIVITY 5.1   Find the gradient at the points B, C and D using the method shown in figure 5.2. (Use a piece of tracing paper to avoid drawing directly on the book!) Repeat the process for each point, using different triangles, and see whether you get the same answers.

You probably found that your answers were slightly different each time, because they depended on the accuracy of your drawing and measuring. Clearly you need a more accurate method of finding the gradient at a point. As you will see in this chapter, a method is available which can be used on many types of curve, and which does not involve any drawing at all.

Finding the gradient of a curve

Figure 5.3 shows the part of the graph $y = x^2$ which lies between $x = -1$ and $x = 3$. What is the value of the gradient at the point P(3, 9)?

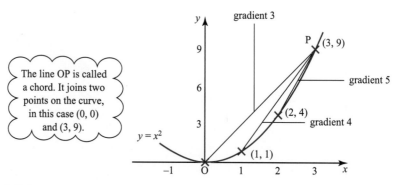

The line OP is called a chord. It joins two points on the curve, in this case (0, 0) and (3, 9).

Figure 5.3

You have already seen that drawing the tangent at the point by hand provides only an approximate answer. A different approach is to calculate the gradients of chords to the curve. These will also give only approximate answers for the gradient of the curve, but they will be based entirely on calculation and not depend on your drawing skill. Three chords are marked on figure 5.3.

Chord $(0, 0)$ to $(3, 9)$:   gradient $= \dfrac{9 - 0}{3 - 0} = 3$

Chord $(1, 1)$ to $(3, 9)$:   gradient $= \dfrac{9 - 1}{3 - 1} = 4$

Chord $(2, 4)$ to $(3, 9)$:   gradient $= \dfrac{9 - 4}{3 - 2} = 5$

Clearly none of these three answers is exact, but which of them is the most accurate?

Of the three chords, the one closest to being a tangent is that joining $(2, 4)$ to $(3, 9)$, the two points that are closest together.

You can take this process further by 'zooming in' on the point $(3, 9)$ and using points which are much closer to it, as in figure 5.4.

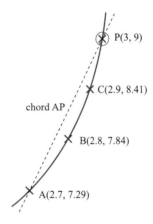

Figure 5.4

The x co-ordinate of point A is 2.7, the y co-ordinate 2.7^2, or 7.29 (since the point lies on the curve $y = x^2$). Similarly B and C are $(2.8, 7.84)$ and $(2.9, 8.41)$. The gradients of the chords joining each point to $(3, 9)$ are as follows.

Chord $(2.7, 7.29)$ to $(3, 9)$: gradient $= \dfrac{9 - 7.29}{3 - 2.7} = 5.7$

Chord $(2.8, 7.84)$ to $(3, 9)$: gradient $= \dfrac{9 - 7.84}{3 - 2.8} = 5.8$

Chord $(2.9, 8.41)$ to $(3, 9)$: gradient $= \dfrac{9 - 8.41}{3 - 2.9} = 5.9$

These results are getting closer to the gradient of the tangent. What happens if you take points much closer to $(3, 9)$, for example $(2.99, 8.9401)$ and $(2.999, 8.994001)$?

The gradients of the chords joining these to $(3, 9)$ work out to be 5.99 and 5.999 respectively.

ACTIVITY 5.2   Take points X, Y, Z on the curve $y = x^2$ with x co-ordinates 3.1, 3.01 and 3.001 respectively, and find the gradients of the chords joining each of these points to (3, 9).

It looks as if the gradients are approaching the value 6, and if so this is the gradient of the tangent at (3, 9).

Taking this method to its logical conclusion, you might try to calculate the gradient of the 'chord' from (3, 9) to (3, 9), but this is undefined because there is a zero in the denominator. So although you can find the gradient of a chord which is as close as you like to the tangent, it can never be exactly that of the tangent. What you need is a way of making that final step from a chord to a tangent.

The concept of a *limit* enables us to do this, as you will see in the next section. It allows us to confirm that in the limit as point Q tends to point P(3, 9), the chord QP tends to the tangent of the curve at P, and the gradient of QP tends to 6 (see figure 5.5).

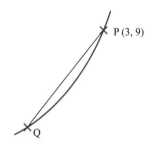

Figure 5.5

The idea of a limit is central to calculus, which is sometimes described as the study of limits.

Historical note | This method of using chords approaching the tangent at P to *calculate* the gradient of the tangent was first described clearly by Pierre de Fermat (*c.*1608–65). He spent his working life as a civil servant in Toulouse and produced an astonishing amount of original mathematics in his spare time.

ⓔ Finding the gradient from first principles

Although the work in the previous section was more formal than the method of drawing a tangent and measuring its gradient, it was still somewhat experimental. The result that the gradient of $y = x^2$ at (3, 9) is 6 was a sensible conclusion, rather than a proved fact.

In this section the method is formalised and extended.

Take the point P(3, 9) and another point Q close to (3, 9) on the curve $y = x^2$. Let the x co-ordinate of Q be $3 + h$ where h is small. Since $y = x^2$ at Q, the y co-ordinate of Q will be $(3 + h)^2$.

⚠ Figure 5.6 shows Q in a position where *h* is positive, but negative values of *h* would put Q to the left of P.

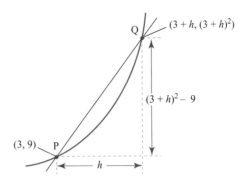

Figure 5.6

From figure 5.6, the gradient of PQ is $\dfrac{(3+h)^2 - 9}{h}$

$$= \frac{9 + 6h + h^2 - 9}{h}$$

$$= \frac{6h + h^2}{h}$$

$$= \frac{h(6+h)}{h}$$

$$= 6 + h.$$

For example, when $h = 0.001$, the gradient of PQ is 6.001, and when $h = -0.001$, the gradient of PQ is 5.999. The gradient of the tangent at P is between these two values. Similarly the gradient of the tangent would be between $6 - h$ and $6 + h$ for all small non-zero values of *h*.

For this to be true the gradient of the tangent at (3, 9) must be *exactly* 6.

ACTIVITY 5.3 Using a similar method, find the gradient of the tangent to the curve at

(i) (1, 1)
(ii) (−2, 4)
(iii) (4, 16).

What do you notice?

The gradient function

The work so far has involved finding the gradient of the curve $y = x^2$ at a particular point (3, 9), but this is not the way in which you would normally find the gradient at a point. Rather you would consider the general point, (x, y), and then substitute the value(s) of *x* (and/or *y*) corresponding to the point of interest.

EXAMPLE 5.1

Find the gradient of the curve $y = x^3$ at the general point (x, y).

SOLUTION

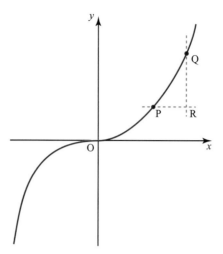

Figure 5.7

Let P have the general value x as its x co-ordinate, so P is the point (x, x^3) (since it is on the curve $y = x^3$). Let the x co-ordinate of Q be $(x + h)$ so Q is $((x+h), (x+h)^3)$. The gradient of the chord PQ is given by

$$\frac{QR}{PR} = \frac{(x+h)^3 - x^3}{(x+h) - x}$$

$$= \frac{x^3 + 3x^2h + 3xh^2 + h^3 - x^3}{h}$$

$$= \frac{3x^2h + 3xh^2 + h^3}{h}$$

$$= \frac{h(3x^2 + 3xh + h^2)}{h}$$

$$= 3x^2 + 3xh + h^2$$

As Q takes values closer to P, h takes smaller and smaller values and the gradient approaches the value of $3x^2$ which is the gradient of the tangent at P. The gradient of the curve $y = x^3$ at the point (x, y) is equal to $3x^2$.

Note

If the equation of the curve is written as $y = f(x)$, then the *gradient function* (i.e. the gradient at the general point (x, y)) is written as $f'(x)$. Using this notation the result above can be written as $f(x) = x^3 \Longrightarrow f'(x) = 3x^2$.

1 Use the method in Example 5.1 to prove that the gradient of the curve $y = x^2$ at the point (x, y) is equal to $2x$.

2 Use the binomial theorem to expand $(x + h)^4$ and hence find the gradient of the curve $y = x^4$ at the point (x, y).

3 Copy the table below, enter your answer to question **2**, and suggest how the gradient pattern should continue when $f(x) = x^5$, $f(x) = x^6$ and $f(x) = x^n$ (where n is a positive whole number).

f(x)	f'(x) (gradient at (x, y))
x^2	$2x$
x^3	$3x^2$
x^4	
x^5	
x^6	
$\vdots$	
x^n	

4 Prove the result when $f(x) = x^5$.

Note

The result you should have obtained from question 3 is known as *Wallis's rule* and can be used as a formula.

? How can you use the binomial theorem to prove this general result for integer values of n?

An alternative notation

So far h has been used to denote the difference between the x co-ordinates of our points P and Q, where Q is close to P.

h is sometimes replaced by δx. The Greek letter δ (delta) is shorthand for 'a small change in' and so δx represents a small change in x and δy a corresponding small change in y.

In figure 5.8 the gradient of the chord PQ is $\dfrac{\delta y}{\delta x}$.

In the limit as $\delta x \rightarrow 0$, δx and δy both become infinitesimally small and the value obtained for $\dfrac{\delta y}{\delta x}$ approaches the gradient of the tangent at P.

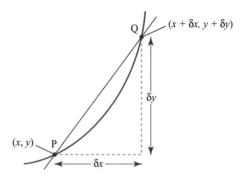

Figure 5.8

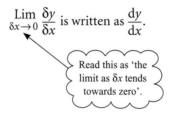

$$\lim_{\delta x \to 0} \frac{\delta y}{\delta x} \text{ is written as } \frac{dy}{dx}.$$

Read this as 'the limit as δx tends towards zero'.

Using this notation, Wallis's rule becomes

$$y = x^n \Rightarrow \frac{dy}{dx} = nx^{n-1}.$$

The gradient function, $\frac{dy}{dx}$ or $f'(x)$ is sometimes called the *derivative* of y with respect to x, and when you find it you have *differentiated* y with respect to x.

Note

There is nothing special about the letters x, y and f.

If, for example, your curve represented time (t) on the horizontal axis and velocity (v) on the vertical axis, then the relationship may be referred to as $v = g(t)$, i.e. v is a function of t, and the gradient function is given by $\frac{dv}{dt} = g'(t)$.

ACTIVITY 5.4   Plot the curve with equation $y = x^3 + 2$, for values of x from -2 to $+2$. On the same axes and for the same range of values of x, plot the curves $y = x^3 - 1$, $y = x^3$ and $y = x^3 + 1$.

What do you notice about the gradients of this family of curves when $x = 0$?

What about when $x = 1$ or $x = -1$?

ACTIVITY 5.5   Differentiate the equation $y = x^3 + c$, where c is a constant. How does this result help you to explain your findings in Activity 5.4?

Historical note The notation $\frac{dy}{dx}$ was first used by the German mathematician and philosopher Gottfried Leibniz (1646–1716) in 1675. Leibniz was a child prodigy and a self-taught mathematician. The terms 'function' and 'co-ordinates' are due to him and, because of his influence, the sign '=' is used for equality and '×' for multiplication. In 1684 he published his work on calculus (which deals with the way in which quantities change) in a six-page article in the periodical *Acta Eruditorum*.

Sir Isaac Newton (1642–1727) worked independently on calculus but Leibniz published his work first. Newton always hesitated to publish his discoveries. Newton used different notation (introducing 'fluxions' and 'moments of fluxions') and his expressions were thought to be rather vague. Over the years the best aspects of the two approaches have been combined, but at the time the dispute as to who 'discovered' calculus first was the subject of many articles and reports, and indeed nearly caused a war between England and Germany.

Differentiating by using standard results

The method of differentiation from first principles will always give the gradient function, but it is rather tedious and, in practice, it is hardly ever used. Its value is in establishing a formal basis for differentiation rather than as a working tool.

If you look at the results of differentiating $y = x^n$ for different values of n a pattern is immediately apparent, particularly when you include the result that the line $y = x$ has constant gradient 1.

y	$\dfrac{dy}{dx}$
x^1	1
x^2	$2x^1$
x^3	$3x^2$

This pattern continues and, in general

$$y = x^n \implies \frac{dy}{dx} = nx^{n-1}.$$

This can be extended to functions of the type $y = kx^n$ for any constant k, to give

$$y = kx^n \implies \frac{dy}{dx} = knx^{n-1}.$$

> The power n can be any real number and this includes positive and negative integers and fractions, i.e. all rational numbers.

Another important result is that

$$y = c \implies \frac{dy}{dx} = 0 \quad \text{where } c \text{ is any constant.}$$

This follows from the fact that the graph of $y = c$ is a horizontal line with gradient zero (see figure 5.9).

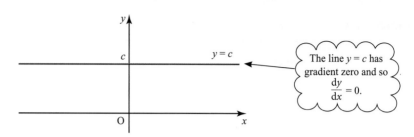

Figure 5.9

EXAMPLE 5.2

For each of these functions of x, find the gradient function.

(i) $y = x^5$ (ii) $z = 7x^6$ (iii) $p = 11$ (iv) $f(x) = \dfrac{3}{x}$

SOLUTION

(i) $\dfrac{dy}{dx} = 5x^4$

(ii) $\dfrac{dz}{dx} = 6 \times 7x^5 = 42x^5$

(iii) $\dfrac{dp}{dx} = 0$

(iv) $f(x) = 3x^{-1}$ ← You many find it easier to write $\dfrac{1}{x}$ as x^{-1}.

$\Rightarrow f'(x) = (-1) \times 3x^{-2}$

$= -\dfrac{3}{x^2}$

Sums and differences of functions

Many of the functions you will meet are sums or differences of simpler ones. For example, the function $(3x^2 + 4x^3)$ is the sum of the functions $3x^2$ and $4x^3$.

To differentiate a function such as this you differentiate each part separately and then add the results together.

EXAMPLE 5.3

Differentiate $y = 3x^2 + 4x^3$.

SOLUTION

$\dfrac{dy}{dx} = 6x + 12x^2$

Note

This may be written in general form as:

$$y = f(x) + g(x) \quad \Rightarrow \quad \dfrac{dy}{dx} = f'(x) + g'(x).$$

EXAMPLE 5.4

Differentiate $f(x) = \dfrac{(x^2+1)(x-5)}{x}$

SOLUTION

You cannot differentiate $f(x)$ as it stands, so you need to start by rewriting it.

Expanding the brackets: $f(x) = \dfrac{x^3 - 5x^2 + x - 5}{x}$

$$= \dfrac{x^3}{x} - \dfrac{5x^2}{x} + \dfrac{x}{x} - \dfrac{5}{x}$$

$$= x^2 - 5x + 1 - 5x^{-1}$$

Now you can differentiate $f(x)$ to give $f'(x) = 2x - 5 + 5x^{-2}$

$$= 2x + \dfrac{5}{x^2} - 5$$

EXERCISE 5B

Differentiate the following functions using the rules

$$y = kx^n \implies \dfrac{\mathrm{d}y}{\mathrm{d}x} = knx^{n-1}$$

and $y = f(x) + g(x) \implies \dfrac{\mathrm{d}y}{\mathrm{d}x} = f'(x) + g'(x).$

1 $y = x^5$ **2** $y = 4x^2$ **3** $y = 2x^3$

4 $y = x^{11}$ **5** $y = 4x^{10}$ **6** $y = 3x^5$

7 $y = 7$ **8** $y = 7x$ **9** $y = 2x^3 + 3x^5$

10 $y = x^7 - x^4$ **11** $y = x^2 + 1$ **12** $y = x^3 + 3x^2 + 3x + 1$

13 $y = x^3 - 9$ **14** $y = \frac{1}{2}x^2 + x + 1$ **15** $y = 3x^2 + 6x + 6$

16 $A = 4\pi r^2$ **17** $A = \frac{4}{3}\pi r^3$ **18** $d = \frac{1}{4}t^2$

19 $C = 2\pi r$ **20** $V = l^3$ **21** $f(x) = x^{\frac{3}{2}}$

22 $y = \dfrac{1}{x}$ **23** $y = \sqrt{x}$ **24** $y = \frac{1}{5}x^{\frac{5}{2}}$

25 $f(x) = \dfrac{1}{x^2}$ **26** $f(x) = \dfrac{5}{x^3}$ **27** $y = \dfrac{2}{\sqrt{x}}$

28 $f(x) = 4\sqrt{x} - \dfrac{8}{\sqrt{x}}$ **29** $f(x) = x^{\frac{3}{2}} + x^{-\frac{3}{2}}$ **30** $f(x) = x^{\frac{5}{3}} - x^{-\frac{2}{3}}$

31 $y = x(4x - 1)$ **32** $f(x) = (2x-1)(x+3)$ **33** $y = \dfrac{x^2 + 6x}{x}$

34 $y = \dfrac{4x^6 - 5x^4}{x^2}$ **35** $y = x\sqrt{x}$ **36** $f(x) = \dfrac{2x}{\sqrt{x}}$

37 $g(x) = \dfrac{3x^2 - 2x}{\sqrt{x}}$ **38** $y = \left(\dfrac{x}{4} + \dfrac{4}{x}\right)(x^2 - x)$ **39** $h(x) = \left(\sqrt{x}\right)^3$

40 $y = \dfrac{(x^2 + 2x)(x - 4)}{2\sqrt{x}}$

Using differentiation

EXAMPLE 5.5

Given that $y = \sqrt{x} - \dfrac{8}{x^2}$, find

(i) $\dfrac{dy}{dx}$

(ii) the gradient of the curve at the point $\left(4, 1\frac{1}{2}\right)$.

SOLUTION

(i) Rewrite $y = \sqrt{x} - \dfrac{8}{x^2}$ as $y = x^{\frac{1}{2}} - 8x^{-2}$.

Now you can differentiate using the rule $y = kx^n \Rightarrow \dfrac{dy}{dx} = knx^{n-1}$.

$$\frac{dy}{dx} = \frac{1}{2}x^{-\frac{1}{2}} + 16x^{-3}$$

$$= \frac{1}{2\sqrt{x}} + \frac{16}{x^3}$$

(ii) At $\left(4, 1\frac{1}{2}\right)$, $x = 4$

Substituting $x = 4$ into the expression for $\dfrac{dy}{dx}$ gives

$$\frac{dy}{dx} = \frac{1}{2\sqrt{4}} + \frac{16}{4^3}$$

$$= \tfrac{1}{4} + \tfrac{16}{64}$$

$$= \tfrac{1}{2}$$

EXAMPLE 5.6

Figure 5.10 shows the graph of

$$y = x^2(x - 6) = x^3 - 6x^2.$$

Find the gradient of the curve at the points A and B where it meets the x axis.

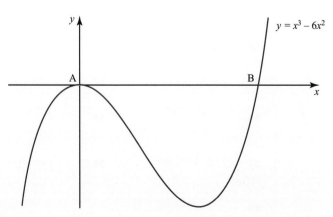

Figure 5.10

SOLUTION

The curve cuts the x axis when $y = 0$, and so at these points

$$x^2(x - 6) = 0$$
$$\Rightarrow \quad x = 0 \text{ (twice) or } x = 6.$$

Differentiating $y = x^3 - 6x^2$ gives

$$\frac{dy}{dx} = 3x^2 - 12x.$$

At the point $(0, 0)$, $\dfrac{dy}{dx} = 0$

and at $(6, 0)$, $\quad \dfrac{dy}{dx} = 3 \times 6^2 - 12 \times 6 = 36.$

At $A(0, 0)$ the gradient of the curve is 0 and at $B(6, 0)$ the gradient of the curve is 36.

Note

This curve goes through the origin. You can see from the graph and from the value of $\frac{dy}{dx}$ that the x axis is a tangent to the curve at this point. You could also have deduced this from the fact that $x = 0$ is a repeated root of the equation $x^3 - 6x^2 = 0$.

EXAMPLE 5.7

Find the points on the curve with equation $y = x^3 + 6x^2 + 5$ where the value of the gradient is -9.

SOLUTION

The gradient at any point on the curve is given by

$$\frac{dy}{dx} = 3x^2 + 12x.$$

Therefore you need to find points at which $\dfrac{dy}{dx} = -9$, i.e.

$$3x^2 + 12x = -9$$
$$3x^2 + 12x + 9 = 0$$
$$3(x^2 + 4x + 3) = 0$$
$$3(x + 1)(x + 3) = 0$$
$$\Rightarrow \quad x = -1 \text{ or } x = -3.$$

When $x = -1$, $y = (-1)^3 + 6(-1)^2 + 5 = 10$.

When $x = -3$, $y = (-3)^3 + 6(-3)^2 + 5 = 32$.

Therefore the gradient is -9 at the points $(-1, 10)$ and $(-3, 32)$ (see figure 5.11).

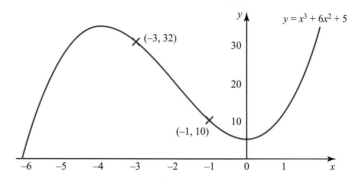

Figure 5.11

1 For each part of this question,

   (a) find $\dfrac{dy}{dx}$

   (b) find the gradient of the curve at the given point.

   (i) $y = x^{-2}$; (0.25, 16)

   (ii) $y = x^{-1} + x^{-4}$; (−1, 0)

   (iii) $y = 4x^{-3} + 2x^{-5}$; (1, 6)

   (iv) $y = 3x^4 - 4 - 8x^{-3}$; (2, 43)

   (v) $y = \sqrt{x} + 3x$; (4, 14)

   (vi) $y = 4x^{-\frac{1}{2}}$; $\left(9, 1\frac{1}{3}\right)$

2 **(i)** Sketch the curve $y = x^2 - 4$.

   (ii) Write down the co-ordinates of the points where the curve crosses the x axis.

   (iii) Differentiate $y = x^2 - 4$.

   (iv) Find the gradient of the curve at the points where it crosses the x axis.

3 **(i)** Sketch the curve $y = x^2 - 6x$.

   (ii) Differentiate $y = x^2 - 6x$.

   (iii) Show that the point (3, −9) lies on the curve $y = x^2 - 6x$ and find the gradient of the curve at this point.

   (iv) Relate your answer to the shape of the curve.

4 **(i)** Sketch, on the same axes, the graphs with equations

$$y = 2x + 5 \quad \text{and} \quad y = 4 - x^2 \quad \text{for } -3 \leqslant x \leqslant 3.$$

   (ii) Show that the point (−1, 3) lies on both graphs.

   (iii) Differentiate $y = 4 - x^2$ and so find its gradient at (−1, 3).

   (iv) Do you have sufficient evidence to decide whether the line $y = 2x + 5$ is a tangent to the curve $y = 4 - x^2$?

   (v) Is the line joining $\left(2\frac{1}{2}, 0\right)$ to (0, 5) a tangent to the curve $y = 4 - x^2$?

5 The curve $y = x^3 - 6x^2 + 11x - 6$ cuts the x axis at $x = 1$, $x = 2$ and $x = 3$.

(i) Sketch the curve.

(ii) Differentiate $y = x^3 - 6x^2 + 11x - 6$.

(iii) Show that the tangents to the curve at two of the points at which it cuts the x axis are parallel.

6 (i) Sketch the curve $y = x^2 + 3x - 1$.

(ii) Differentiate $y = x^2 + 3x - 1$.

(iii) Find the co-ordinates of the point on the curve $y = x^2 + 3x - 1$ at which it is parallel to the line $y = 5x - 1$.

(iv) Is the line $y = 5x - 1$ a tangent to the curve $y = x^2 + 3x - 1$?
Give reasons for your answer.

7 (i) Sketch, on the same axes, the curves with equations

$$y = x^2 - 9 \quad \text{and} \quad y = 9 - x^2 \quad \text{for } -4 \leqslant x \leqslant 4.$$

(ii) Differentiate $y = x^2 - 9$.

(iii) Find the gradient of $y = x^2 - 9$ at the points $(2, -5)$ and $(-2, -5)$.

(iv) Find the gradient of the curve $y = 9 - x^2$ at the points $(2, 5)$ and $(-2, 5)$.

(v) The tangents to $y = x^2 - 9$ at $(2, -5)$ and $(-2, -5)$, and those to $y = 9 - x^2$ at $(2, 5)$ and $(-2, 5)$ are drawn to form a quadrilateral.
Describe this quadrilateral and give reasons for your answer.

8 (i) Sketch, on the same axes, the curves with equations

$$y = x^2 - 1 \quad \text{and} \quad y = x^2 + 3 \quad \text{for } -3 \leqslant x \leqslant 3.$$

(ii) Find the gradient of the curve $y = x^2 - 1$ at the point $(2, 3)$.

(iii) Give two explanations, one involving geometry and the other involving calculus, as to why the gradient at the point $(2, 7)$ on the curve $y = x^2 + 3$ should have the same value as your answer to part (ii).

(iv) Give the equation of another curve with the same gradient function as $y = x^2 - 1$.

9 The function $f(x) = ax^3 + bx + 4$, where a and b are constants, goes through the point $(2, 14)$ with gradient 21.

(i) Using the fact that $(2, 14)$ lies on the curve, find an equation involving a and b.

(ii) Differentiate $f(x)$ and, using the fact that the gradient is 21 when $x = 2$, form another equation involving a and b.

(iii) By solving these two equations simultaneously find the values of a and b.

10 In his book *Mathematician's Delight*, W.W. Sawyer observes that the arch of Victoria Falls Bridge appears to agree with the curve

$$y = \frac{116 - 21x^2}{120}$$

taking the origin as the point mid-way between the feet of the arch, and taking the distance between its feet as 4.7 units.

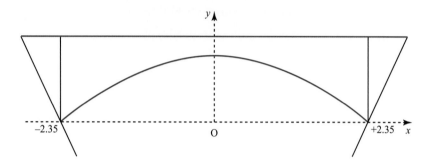

(i) Find $\dfrac{dy}{dx}$.

(ii) Evaluate $\dfrac{dy}{dx}$ when $x = -2.35$ and when $x = 2.35$.

(iii) Find the value of x for which $\dfrac{dy}{dx} = -0.5$.

11 (i) Use your knowledge of the shape of the curve $y = \dfrac{1}{x}$ to sketch the curve $y = \dfrac{1}{x} + 2$.

(ii) Write down the co-ordinates of the point where the curve crosses the x axis.

(iii) Differentiate $y = \dfrac{1}{x} + 2$.

(iv) Find the gradient of the curve at the point where it crosses the x axis.

12 The sketch shows the graph of $y = \dfrac{4}{x^2} + x$.

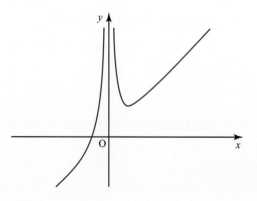

(i) Differentiate $y = \dfrac{4}{x^2} + x.$

(ii) Show that the point $(-2, -1)$ lies on the curve.

(iii) Find the gradient of the curve at $(-2, -1)$.

(iv) Show that the point $(2, 3)$ lies on the curve.

(v) Find the gradient of the curve at $(2, 3)$.

(vi) Relate your answer to part (v) to the shape of the curve.

13 (i) Sketch, on the same axes, the graphs with equations

$$y = \frac{1}{x^2} + 1 \quad \text{and} \quad y = -16x + 13 \quad \text{for} \quad -3 \leqslant x \leqslant 3.$$

(ii) Show that the point $(0.5, 5)$ lies on both graphs.

(iii) Differentiate $y = \dfrac{1}{x^2} + 1$ and find its gradient at $(0.5, 5)$.

(iv) What can you deduce about the two graphs?

14 (i) Sketch the curve $y = \sqrt{x}$ for $0 \leqslant x \leqslant 10$.

(ii) Differentiate $y = \sqrt{x}$.

(iii) Find the gradient of the curve at the point $(9, 3)$.

15 (i) Sketch the curve $y = \dfrac{4}{x^2}$ for $-3 \leqslant x \leqslant 3$.

(ii) Differentiate $y = \dfrac{4}{x^2}$.

(iii) Find the gradient of the curve at the point $(-2, 1)$.

(iv) Write down the gradient of the curve at the point $(2, 1)$.

Explain why your answer is $-1 \times$ your answer to part (iii).

16 The sketch shows the curve $y = \dfrac{x}{2} - \dfrac{2}{x}$.

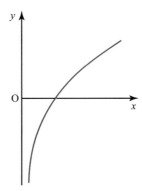

(i) Differentiate $y = \dfrac{x}{2} - \dfrac{2}{x}$.

(ii) Find the gradient of the curve at the point where it crosses the x axis.

17 The gradient of the curve $y = kx^{\frac{3}{2}}$ at the point $x = 9$ is 18. Find the value of k.

18 Find the gradient of the curve $y = \dfrac{x-2}{\sqrt{x}}$ at the point where $x = 4$.

Tangents and normals

Now that you know how to find the gradient of a curve at any point you can use this to find the equation of the tangent at any specified point on the curve.

EXAMPLE 5.8 Find the equation of the tangent to the curve $y = x^2 + 3x + 2$ at the point (2, 12).

SOLUTION

Calculating $\dfrac{dy}{dx}$: $\dfrac{dy}{dx} = 2x + 3$.

Substituting $x = 2$ into the expression $\dfrac{dy}{dx}$ to find the gradient m of the tangent at that point:

$$m = 2 \times 2 + 3$$
$$= 7.$$

The equation of the tangent is given by

$$y - y_1 = m(x - x_1).$$

In this case $x_1 = 2$, $y_1 = 12$ so

$$y - 12 = 7(x - 2)$$
$$\Rightarrow \qquad y = 7x - 2.$$

This is the equation of the tangent.

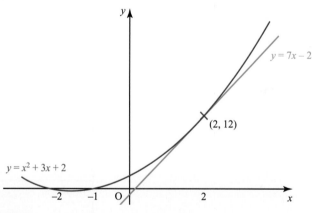

Figure 5.12

The *normal* to a curve at a particular point is the straight line which is at right angles to the tangent at that point (see figure 5.13). Remember that for perpendicular lines, $m_1 m_2 = -1$.

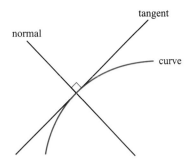

normal

tangent

curve

Figure 5.13

If the gradient of the tangent is m_1, the gradient, m_2, of the normal is given by

$$m_2 = -\frac{1}{m_1}.$$

This enables you to find the equation of the normal at any specified point on a curve.

EXAMPLE 5.9

A curve has equation $y = \frac{16}{x} - 4\sqrt{x}$. The normal to the curve at the point $(4, -4)$ meets the y axis at the point P. Find the co-ordinates of P.

SOLUTION

You may find it easier to write $y = \frac{16}{x} - 4\sqrt{x}$ as $y = 16x^{-1} - 4x^{\frac{1}{2}}$.

Differentiating gives $\dfrac{dy}{dx} = -16x^{-2} - \frac{1}{2} \times 4x^{-\frac{1}{2}}$

$$= -\frac{16}{x^2} - \frac{2}{\sqrt{x}}$$

At the point $(4, -4)$, $x = 4$ and

$$\frac{dy}{dx} = -\frac{16}{4^2} - \frac{2}{\sqrt{4}}$$

$$= -1 - 1 = -2$$

So at the point $(4, -4)$ the gradient of the tangent is -2.

$$\text{Gradient of normal} = \frac{-1}{\text{gradient of tangent}} = \frac{1}{2}$$

The equation of the normal is given by

$$y - y_1 = m(x - x_1)$$
$$y - (-4) = \frac{1}{2}(x - 4)$$
$$y = \frac{1}{2}x - 6$$

P is the point where the normal meets the y axis and so where $x = 0$.

Substituting $x = 0$ into $y = \frac{1}{2}x - 6$ gives $y = -6$.

So P is the point $(0, -6)$.

EXERCISE 5D

1 The graph of $y = 6x - x^2$ is shown below.

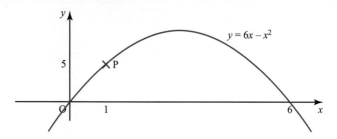

The marked point, P, is (1, 5).

   (i)   Find the gradient function $\dfrac{dy}{dx}$.

   (ii) Find the gradient of the curve at P.

   (iii) Find the equation of the tangent at P.

2 **(i)**   Sketch the curve $y = 4x - x^2$.

   (i)   Differentiate $y = 4x - x^2$.

   (iii) Find the gradient of $y = 4x - x^2$ at the point (1, 3).

   (iv) Find the equation of the tangent to the curve $y = 4x - x^2$ at the point (1, 3).

3 **(i)**   Differentiate $y = x^3 - 4x^2$.

   (ii) Find the gradient of $y = x^3 - 4x^2$ at the point (2, –8).

   (iii) Find the equation of the tangent to the curve $y = x^3 - 4x^2$ at the point (2, –8).

   (iv) Find the co-ordinates of the other point at which this tangent meets the curve.

4 **(i)**   Sketch the curve $y = 6 - x^2$.

   (ii) Find the gradient of the curve at the points (–1, 5) and (1, 5).

   (iii) Find the equations of the tangents to the curve at these points.

   (iv) Find the co-ordinates of the point of intersection of these two tangents.

5 **(i)**   Sketch the curve $y = x^2 + 4$ and the straight line $y = 4x$ on the same axes.

   (ii) Show that both $y = x^2 + 4$ and $y = 4x$ pass through the point (2, 8).

   (iii) Show that $y = x^2 + 4$ and $y = 4x$ have the same gradient at (2, 8), and state what you conclude from this result and that in part **(ii)**.

6 **(i)**   Find the equation of the tangent to the curve $y = 2x^3 - 15x^2 + 42x$ at (2, 40).

   (ii) Using your expression for $\dfrac{dy}{dx}$, find the co-ordinates of another point on the curve at which the tangent is parallel to the one at (2, 40).

   (iii) Find the equation of the normal at this point.

7 **(i)** Given that $y = x^3 - 4x^2 + 5x - 2$, find $\dfrac{dy}{dx}$.

The point P is on the curve and its x co-ordinate is 3.

    (ii) Calculate the y co-ordinate of P.

    (iii) Calculate the gradient at P.

    (iv) Find the equation of the tangent at P.

    (v) Find the equation of the normal at P.

    (vi) Find the values of x for which the curve has a gradient of 5.

                                                          [MEI]

8 **(i)** Sketch the curve whose equation is $y = x^2 - 3x + 2$ and state the co-ordinates of the points A and B where it crosses the x axis.

    (ii) Find the gradient of the curve at A and at B.

    (iii) Find the equations of the tangent and normal to the curve at both A and B.

    (iv) The tangent at A meets the tangent at B at the point P. The normal at A meets the normal at B at the point Q. What shape is the figure APBQ?

9 **(i)** Find the points of intersection of $y = 2x^2 - 9x$ and $y = x - 8$.

    (ii) Find $\dfrac{dy}{dx}$ for the curve and hence find the equation of the tangent to the curve at each of the points in part **(i)**.

    (iii) Find the point of intersection of the two tangents.

    (iv) The two tangents from a point to a circle are always equal in length. Are the two tangents to the curve $y = 2x^2 - 9x$ (a parabola) from the point you found in part **(iii)** equal in length?

10 The equation of a curve is $y = \sqrt{x}$.

    (i) Find the equation of the tangent to the curve at the point $(1, 1)$.

    (ii) Find the equation of the normal to the curve at the point $(1, 1)$.

    (iii) The tangent cuts the x axis at A and the normal cuts the x axis at B. Find the length of AB.

11 The equation of a curve is $y = \dfrac{1}{x}$.

    (i) Find the equation of the tangent to the curve at the point $\left(2, \tfrac{1}{2}\right)$.

    (ii) Find the equation of the normal to the curve at the point $\left(2, \tfrac{1}{2}\right)$.

    (iii) Find the area of the triangle formed by the tangent, the normal and the y axis.

12 The sketch shows the graph of $y = \sqrt{x} - 1$.

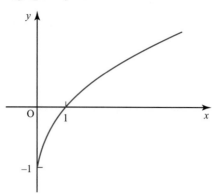

(i) Differentiate $y = \sqrt{x} - 1$.

(ii) Find the co-ordinates of the point on the curve $y = \sqrt{x} - 1$ at which the tangent is parallel to the line $y = 2x - 1$.

(iii) Is the line $y = 2x - 1$ a tangent to the curve $y = \sqrt{x} - 1$?
Give reasons for your answer.

13 The equation of a curve is $y = \sqrt{x} - \dfrac{1}{4x}$.

(i) Find the equation of the tangent to the curve at the point where $x = \frac{1}{4}$.

(ii) Find the equation of the normal to the curve at the point where $x = \frac{1}{4}$.

(iii) Find the area of the triangle formed by the tangent, the normal and the x axis.

14 The equation of a curve is $y = \dfrac{9}{\sqrt{x}}$.

The tangent to the curve at the point $(9, 3)$ meets the x axis at A and the y axis at B.

Find the length of AB.

15 The equation of a curve is $y = 2 + \dfrac{8}{x^2}$.

(i) Find the equation of the normal to the curve at the point $(2, 4)$.

(ii) Find the area of the triangle formed by the normal and the axes.

16 The graph of $y = 3x - \dfrac{1}{x^2}$ is shown below.

The point marked P is $(1, 2)$.

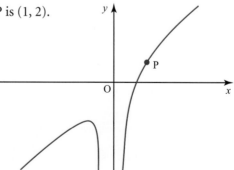

(i) Find the gradient function $\dfrac{dy}{dx}$.

(ii) Use your answer from part (i) to find the gradient of the curve at P.

(iii) Use your answer from part (ii), and the fact that the gradient of the curve at P is the same as that of the tangent at P, to find the equation of the tangent at P in the form $y = mx + c$.

17 The graph of $y = x^2 + \dfrac{1}{x}$ is shown below. The point marked Q is $(1, 2)$.

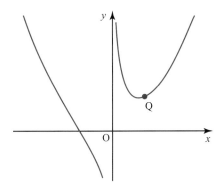

(i) Find the gradient function $\dfrac{dy}{dx}$.

(ii) Find the gradient of the tangent at Q.

(iii) Show that the equation of the normal to the curve at Q can be written as $x + y = 3$.

(iv) At what other points does the normal cut the curve?

18 The equation of a curve is $y = x^{\frac{3}{2}}$.

The tangent and normal to the curve at the point $x = 4$ intersect the x axis at A and B respectively.

Calculate the length of AB.

19 (i) The diagram shows the line $2y = x + 5$ and the curve $y = x^2 - 4x + 7$, which intersect at the points A and B.

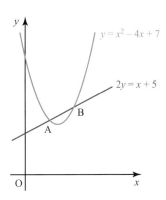

Find

(a) the x co-ordinates of A and B,

(b) the equation of the tangent to the curve at B,

(c) the acute angle, in degrees correct to 1 decimal place, between this tangent and the line $2y = x + 5$.

(ii) Determine the set of values of k for which the line $2y = x + k$ does not intersect the curve $y = x^2 - 4x + 7$.

[Cambridge AS & A Level Mathematics 9709, Paper 12 Q10 November 2009]

20 The equation of a curve is $y = 5 - \dfrac{8}{x}$.

(i) Show that the equation of the normal to the curve at the point P(2, 1) is $2y + x = 4$.

This normal meets the curve again at the point Q.

(ii) Find the co-ordinates of Q.

(iii) Find the length of PQ.

[Cambridge AS & A Level Mathematics 9709, Paper 1 Q8 November 2008]

Maximum and minimum points

ACTIVITY 5.6   Plot the graph of $y = x^4 - x^3 - 2x^2$, taking values of x from -2.5 to $+2.5$ in steps of 0.5, and answer these questions.

(i) How many stationary points has the graph?

(ii) What is the gradient at a stationary point?

(iii) One of the stationary points is a maximum and the others are minima. Which are of each type?

(iv) Is the maximum the highest point of the graph?

(v) Do the two minima occur exactly at the points you plotted?

(vi) Estimate the lowest value that y takes.

Gradient at a maximum or minimum point

Figure 5.14 shows the graph of $y = -x^2 + 16$. It has a *maximum point* at (0, 16).

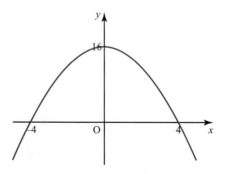

Figure 5.14

You will see that

- at the maximum point the gradient $\dfrac{\mathrm{d}y}{\mathrm{d}x}$ is zero
- the gradient is positive to the left of the maximum and negative to the right of it.

This is true for any maximum point (see figure 5.15).

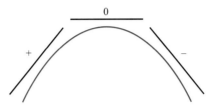

Figure 5.15

In the same way, for any minimum point (see figure 5.16):

- the gradient is zero at the minimum
- the gradient goes from negative to zero to positive.

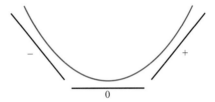

Figure 5.16

Maximum and minimum points are also known as stationary points as the gradient function is zero and so is neither increasing nor decreasing.

EXAMPLE 5.10

Find the stationary points on the curve of $y = x^3 - 3x + 1$, and sketch the curve.

SOLUTION

The gradient function for this curve is

$$\frac{\mathrm{d}y}{\mathrm{d}x} = 3x^2 - 3.$$

The x values for which $\dfrac{\mathrm{d}y}{\mathrm{d}x} = 0$ are given by

$$3x^2 - 3 = 0$$
$$3(x^2 - 1) = 0$$
$$3(x + 1)(x - 1) = 0$$
$$\Rightarrow \qquad x = -1 \text{ or } x = 1.$$

The signs of the gradient function just either side of these values tell you the nature of each stationary point.

For $x = -1$: $x = -2 \Rightarrow \dfrac{dy}{dx} = 3(-2)^2 - 3 = +9$

$x = 0 \Rightarrow \dfrac{dy}{dx} = 3(0)^2 - 3 = -3.$

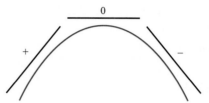

Figure 5.17

For $x = 1$: $x = 0 \Rightarrow \dfrac{dy}{dx} = -3$

$x = 2 \Rightarrow \dfrac{dy}{dx} = 3(2)^2 - 3 = +9.$

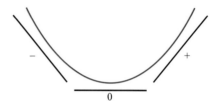

Figure 5.18

Thus the stationary point at $x = -1$ is a maximum and the one at $x = 1$ is a minimum.

Substituting the x values of the stationary points into the original equation, $y = x^3 - 3x + 1$, gives

when $x = -1$, $y = (-1)^3 - 3(-1) + 1 = 3$
when $x = 1$, $y = (1)^3 - 3(1) + 1 = -1.$

There is a maximum at $(-1, 3)$ and a minimum at $(1, -1)$. The sketch can now be drawn (see figure 5.19).

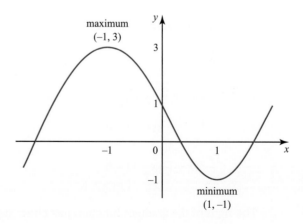

Figure 5.19

In this case you knew the general shape of the cubic curve and the positions of all of the maximum and minimum points, so it was easy to select values of x for which to test the sign of $\frac{dy}{dx}$. The curve of a more complicated function may have several maxima and minima close together, and even some points at which the gradient is undefined. To decide in such cases whether a particular stationary point is a maximum or a minimum, you must look at points which are *just* either side of it.

EXAMPLE 5.11

Find all the stationary points on the curve of $y = 2t^4 - t^2 + 1$ and sketch the curve.

SOLUTION

$$\frac{dy}{dt} = 8t^3 - 2t$$

At a stationary point, $\frac{dy}{dt} = 0$, so

$$8t^3 - 2t = 0$$
$$2t(4t^2 - 1) = 0$$
$$2t(2t - 1)(2t + 1) = 0$$

$$\Rightarrow \frac{dy}{dt} = 0 \text{ when } t = -0.5, 0 \text{ or } 0.5.$$

You may find it helpful to summarise your working in a table like the one below. You can find the various signs, + or −, by taking a test point in each interval, for example $t = 0.25$ in the interval $0 < t < 0.5$.

	$t < -0.5$	-0.5	$-0.5 < t < 0$	0	$0 < t < 0.5$	0.5	$t > 0.5$
Sign of $\frac{dy}{dt}$	−	0	+	0	−	0	+
Stationary point		min		max		min	

There is a maximum point when $t = 0$ and there are minimum points when $t = -0.5$ and $+0.5$.

When $t = 0$: $\quad y = 2(0)^4 - (0)^2 + 1 = 1.$
When $t = -0.5$: $\quad y = 2(-0.5)^4 - (-0.5)^2 + 1 = 0.875.$
When $t = 0.5$: $\quad y = 2(0.5)^4 - (0.5)^2 + 1 = 0.875.$

Therefore $(0, 1)$ is a maximum point and $(-0.5, 0.875)$ and $(0.5, 0.875)$ are minima.

The graph of this function is shown in figure 5.20.

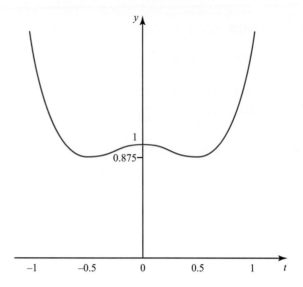

Figure 5.20

Increasing and decreasing functions

When the gradient is positive, the function is described as an increasing function. Similarly, when the gradient is negative, it is a decreasing function. These terms are often used for functions that are increasing or decreasing for all values of x.

EXAMPLE 5.12

Show that $y = x^3 + x$ is an increasing function.

SOLUTION

$y = x^3 + x \Rightarrow \dfrac{dy}{dx} = 3x^2 + 1.$

Since $x^2 \geqslant 0$ for all real values of x, $\dfrac{dy}{dx} \geqslant 1$

$\Rightarrow y = x^3 + x$ is an increasing function.

Figure 5.21 shows its graph.

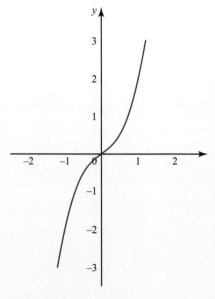

Figure 5.21

EXAMPLE 5.13

Find the range of values of x for which the function $y = x^2 - 6x$ is a decreasing function.

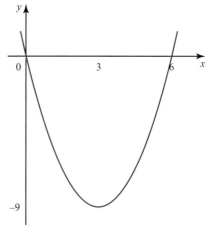

Figure 5.22

SOLUTION

$y = x^2 - 6x \Rightarrow \dfrac{dy}{dx} = 2x - 6.$

y decreasing $\Rightarrow \dfrac{dy}{dx} < 0$

$\Rightarrow \quad 2x - 6 < 0$

$\Rightarrow \qquad x < 3.$

Figure 5.22 shows the graph of $y = x^2 - 6x$.

EXERCISE 5E

1 Given that $y = x^2 + 8x + 13$

    (i) find $\dfrac{dy}{dx}$, and the value of x for which $\dfrac{dy}{dx} = 0$

    (ii) showing your working clearly, decide whether the point corresponding to this x value is a maximum or a minimum by considering the gradient either side of it

    (iii) show that the corresponding y value is -3

    (iv) sketch the curve.

2 Given that $y = x^2 + 5x + 2$

    (i) find $\dfrac{dy}{dx}$, and the value of x for which $\dfrac{dy}{dx} = 0$

    (ii) classify the point that corresponds to this x value as a maximum or a minimum

    (iii) find the corresponding y value

    (iv) sketch the curve.

3 Given that $y = x^3 - 12x + 2$

    (i) find $\dfrac{dy}{dx}$, and the values of x for which $\dfrac{dy}{dx} = 0$

    (ii) classify the points that correspond to these x values

    (iii) find the corresponding y values

    (iv) sketch the curve.

4 (i) Find the co-ordinates of the stationary points of the curve $y = x^3 - 6x^2$, and determine whether each one is a maximum or a minimum.

    (ii) Use this information to sketch the graph of $y = x^3 - 6x^2$.

5 Find $\dfrac{dy}{dx}$ when $y = x^3 - x$ and show that $y = x^3 - x$ is an increasing function

for $x < -\dfrac{1}{\sqrt{3}}$ and $x > \dfrac{1}{\sqrt{3}}$.

6 Given that $y = x^3 + 4x$

(i) find $\dfrac{dy}{dx}$

(ii) show that $y = x^3 + 4x$ is an increasing function for all values of x.

7 Given that $y = x^3 + 3x^2 - 9x + 6$

(i) find $\dfrac{dy}{dx}$ and factorise the quadratic expression you obtain

(ii) write down the values of x for which $\dfrac{dy}{dx} = 0$

(iii) show that one of the points corresponding to these x values is a minimum and the other a maximum

(iv) show that the corresponding y values are 1 and 33 respectively

(v) sketch the curve.

8 Given that $y = 9x + 3x^2 - x^3$

(i) find $\dfrac{dy}{dx}$ and factorise the quadratic expression you obtain

(ii) find the values of x for which the curve has stationary points, and classify these stationary points

(iii) find the corresponding y values

(iv) sketch the curve.

9 (i) Find the co-ordinates and nature of each of the stationary points of $y = x^3 - 2x^2 - 4x + 3$.

(ii) Sketch the curve.

10 (i) Find the co-ordinates and nature of each of the stationary points of the curve with equation $y = x^4 + 4x^3 - 36x^2 + 300$.

(ii) Sketch the curve.

11 (i) Differentiate $y = x^3 + 3x$.

(ii) What does this tell you about the number of stationary points of the curve with equation $y = x^3 + 3x$?

(iii) Find the values of y corresponding to $x = -3, -2, -1, 0, 1, 2$ and 3.

(iv) Hence sketch the curve and explain your answer to part (ii).

12 You are given that $y = 2x^3 + 3x^2 - 72x + 130$.

(i) Find $\dfrac{dy}{dx}$.

P is the point on the curve where $x = 4$.

(ii) Calculate the y co-ordinate of P.

(iii) Calculate the gradient at P and hence find the equation of the tangent to the curve at P.

(iv) There are two stationary points on the curve. Find their co-ordinates.

[MEI]

13 (i) Find the co-ordinates of the stationary points of the curve $f(x) = 4x + \dfrac{1}{x}$.

    (ii) Find the set of values of x for which $f(x)$ is an increasing function.

14 The equation of a curve is $y = \dfrac{1}{6}(2x - 3)^3 - 4x$.

    (i) Find $\dfrac{\mathrm{d}y}{\mathrm{d}x}$.

    (ii) Find the equation of the tangent to the curve at the point where the curve intersects the y axis.

    (iii) Find the set of values of x for which $\dfrac{1}{6}(2x - 3)^3 - 4x$ is an increasing function of x.

[Cambridge AS & A Level Mathematics 9709, Paper 12 Q10 June 2010]

15 The equation of a curve is $y = x^2 - 3x + 4$.

    (i) Show that the whole of the curve lies above the x axis.

    (ii) Find the set of values of x for which $x^2 - 3x + 4$ is a decreasing function of x.

The equation of a line is $y + 2x = k$, where k is a constant.

    (iii) In the case where $k = 6$, find the co-ordinates of the points of intersection of the line and the curve.

    (iv) Find the value of k for which the line is a tangent to the curve.

[Cambridge AS & A Level Mathematics 9709, Paper 1 Q10 June 2005]

16 The equation of a curve C is $y = 2x^2 - 8x + 9$ and the equation of a line L is $x + y = 3$.

    (i) Find the x co-ordinates of the points of intersection of L and C.

    (ii) Show that one of these points is also the stationary point of C.

[Cambridge AS & A Level Mathematics 9709, Paper 1 Q4 June 2008]

e Points of inflection

It is possible for the value of $\dfrac{\mathrm{d}y}{\mathrm{d}x}$ to be zero at a point on a curve without it being a maximum or minimum. This is the case with the curve $y = x^3$, at the point $(0, 0)$ (see figure 5.23).

$$y = x^3 \quad \Rightarrow \quad \frac{\mathrm{d}y}{\mathrm{d}x} = 3x^2$$

and when $x = 0$, $\dfrac{\mathrm{d}y}{\mathrm{d}x} = 0$.

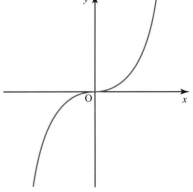

Figure 5.23

This is an example of a *point of inflection*. In general, a point of inflection occurs where the tangent to a curve crosses the curve. This can happen also when $\frac{dy}{dx} \neq 0$, as shown in figure 5.24.

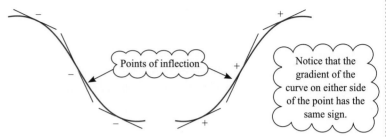

Points of inflection

Notice that the gradient of the curve on either side of the point has the same sign.

Figure 5.24

If you are a driver you may find it helpful to think of a point of inflection as the point at which you change from left lock to right lock, or vice versa. Another way of thinking about a point of inflection is to view the curve from one side and see it as the point where the curve changes from being concave to convex.

The second derivative

Figure 5.25 shows a sketch of a function $y = f(x)$, and beneath it a sketch of the corresponding gradient function $\frac{dy}{dx} = f'(x)$.

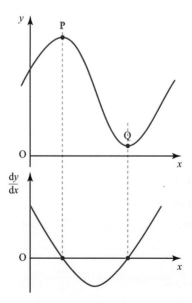

Figure 5.25

ACTIVITY 5.7   Sketch the graph of the gradient of $\dfrac{dy}{dx}$ against x for the function illustrated in figure 5.25. Do this by tracing the two graphs shown in figure 5.25, and extending the dashed lines downwards on to a third set of axes.

You can see that P is a maximum point and Q is a minimum point. What can you say about the gradient of $\dfrac{dy}{dx}$ at these points: is it positive, negative or zero?

The gradient of any point on the curve of $\dfrac{dy}{dx}$ is given by $\dfrac{d}{dx}\left(\dfrac{dy}{dx}\right)$. This is written as $\dfrac{d^2y}{dx^2}$ or $f''(x)$, and is called the *second derivative*. It is found by differentiating the function a second time.

 The second derivative, $\dfrac{d^2y}{dx^2}$, is not the same as $\left(\dfrac{dy}{dx}\right)^2$.

EXAMPLE 5.14   Given that $y = x^5 + 2x$, find $\dfrac{d^2y}{dx^2}$.

SOLUTION

$$\dfrac{dy}{dx} = 5x^4 + 2$$

$$\dfrac{d^2y}{dx^2} = 20x^3.$$

Using the second derivative

You can use the second derivative to identify the nature of a stationary point, instead of looking at the sign of $\dfrac{dy}{dx}$ just either side of it.

Stationary points

Notice that at P, $\dfrac{dy}{dx} = 0$ and $\dfrac{d^2y}{dx^2} < 0$. This tells you that the gradient, $\dfrac{dy}{dx}$, is zero and decreasing. It must be going from positive to negative, so P is a maximum point (see figure 5.26).

At Q, $\dfrac{dy}{dx} = 0$ and $\dfrac{d^2y}{dx^2} > 0$. This tells you that the gradient, $\dfrac{dy}{dx}$, is zero and increasing. It must be going from negative to positive, so Q is a minimum point (see figure 5.27).

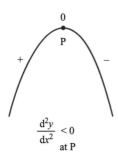

$$\frac{d^2y}{dx^2} < 0$$ at P

$$\frac{d^2y}{dx^2} > 0$$ at Q

Figure 5.26   **Figure 5.27**

The next example illustrates the use of the second derivative to identify the nature of stationary points.

EXAMPLE 5.15   Given that $y = 2x^3 + 3x^2 - 12x$

(i)   find $\frac{dy}{dx}$, and find the values of x for which $\frac{dy}{dx} = 0$

(ii) find the value of $\frac{d^2y}{dx^2}$ at each stationary point and hence determine its nature

(iii) find the y values of each of the stationary points

(iv) sketch the curve given by $y = 2x^3 + 3x^2 - 12x$.

SOLUTION

(i) $\dfrac{dy}{dx} = 6x^2 + 6x - 12$

$\qquad = 6(x^2 + x - 2)$

$\qquad = 6(x + 2)(x - 1)$

$\dfrac{dy}{dx} = 0$ when $x = -2$ or $x = 1$.

(ii) $\dfrac{d^2y}{dx^2} = 12x + 6.$

When $x = -2$, $\dfrac{d^2y}{dx^2} = 12 \times (-2) + 6 = -18.$

$\qquad\qquad\qquad \dfrac{d^2y}{dx^2} < 0 \Rightarrow$ a maximum.

When $x = 1$, $\dfrac{d^2y}{dx^2} = 6(2 \times 1 + 1) = 18.$

$\qquad\qquad\qquad \dfrac{d^2y}{dx^2} > 0 \Rightarrow$ a minimum.

(iii) When $x = -2$, $y = 2(-2)^3 + 3(-2)^2 - 12(-2)$

$\qquad\qquad\qquad\qquad = 20$

so $(-2, 20)$ is a maximum point.

When $x = 1$, $y = 2 + 3 - 12$

$\qquad\qquad\qquad\quad = -7$

so $(1, -7)$ is a minimum point.

(iv)

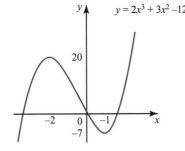

Figure 5.28

⚠ Remember that you are looking for the value of $\dfrac{d^2y}{dx^2}$ at the stationary point.

Note

On occasions when it is difficult or laborious to find $\dfrac{d^2y}{dx^2}$, remember that you can always determine the nature of a stationary point by looking at the sign of $\dfrac{dy}{dx}$ for points just either side of it.

⚠ Take care when $\dfrac{d^2y}{dx^2} = 0$. Look at these three graphs to see why.

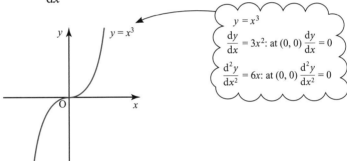

Figure 5.29

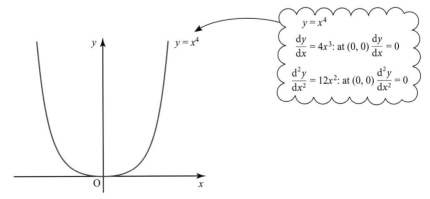

Figure 5.30

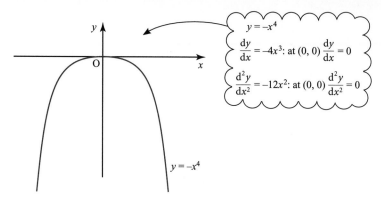

Figure 5.31

You can see that for all three of these functions both $\dfrac{dy}{dx}$ and $\dfrac{d^2y}{dx^2}$ are zero at the origin.

Consequently, if both $\dfrac{dy}{dx}$ and $\dfrac{d^2y}{dx^2}$ are zero at a point, you still need to check the values of $\dfrac{dy}{dx}$ either side of the point in order to determine its nature.

EXERCISE 5F

1 For each of the following functions, find $\dfrac{dy}{dx}$ and $\dfrac{d^2y}{dx^2}$.

(i) $y = x^3$ **(ii)** $y = x^5$ **(iii)** $y = 4x^2$

(iv) $y = x^{-2}$ **(v)** $y = x^{\frac{3}{2}}$ **(vi)** $y = x^4 - \dfrac{2}{x^3}$

2 Find any stationary points on the curves of the following functions and identify their nature.

(i) $y = x^2 + 2x + 4$ **(ii)** $y = 6x - x^2$

(iii) $y = x^3 - 3x$ **(iv)** $y = 4x^5 - 5x^4$

(v) $y = x^4 + x^3 - 2x^2 - 3x + 1$ **(vi)** $y = x + \dfrac{1}{x}$

(vii) $y = 16x + \dfrac{1}{x^2}$ **(viii)** $y = x^3 + \dfrac{12}{x}$

(ix) $y = 6x - x^{\frac{3}{2}}$

3 You are given that $y = x^4 - 8x^2$.

(i) Find $\dfrac{dy}{dx}$.

(ii) Find $\dfrac{d^2y}{dx^2}$.

(iii) Find any stationary points and identify their nature.

(iv) Hence sketch the curve.

4 Given that $y = (x-1)^2(x-3)$

    (i) multiply out the right-hand side and find $\dfrac{dy}{dx}$

    (ii) find the position and nature of any stationary points

    (iii) sketch the curve.

5 Given that $y = x^2(x-2)^2$

    (i) multiply out the right-hand side and find $\dfrac{dy}{dx}$

    (ii) find the position and nature of any stationary points

    (iii) sketch the curve.

6 The function $y = px^3 + qx^2$, where p and q are constants, has a stationary point at $(1, -1)$.

    (i) Using the fact that $(1, -1)$ lies on the curve, form an equation involving p and q.

    (ii) Differentiate y and, using the fact that $(1, -1)$ is a stationary point, form another equation involving p and q.

    (iii) Solve these two equations simultaneously to find the values of p and q.

7 You are given $f(x) = 4x^2 + \dfrac{1}{x}$.

    (i) Find $f'(x)$ and $f''(x)$.

    (ii) Find the position and nature of any stationary points.

8 For the function $y = x - 4\sqrt{x}$,

    (i) find $\dfrac{dy}{dx}$ and $\dfrac{d^2y}{dx^2}$

    (ii) find the co-ordinates of the stationary point and determine its nature.

9 The equation of a curve is $y = 6\sqrt{x} - x\sqrt{x}$.

    Find the x co-ordinate of the stationary point and show that the turning point is a maximum.

10 For the curve $x^{\frac{5}{2}} - 10x^{\frac{3}{2}}$,

    (i) find the values of x for which $y = 0$

    (ii) show that there is a minimum turning point of the curve when $x = 6$ and calculate the y value of this minimum, giving the answer correct to 1 decimal place.

Applications

There are many situations in which you need to find the maximum or minimum value of an expression. The examples which follow, and those in Exercise 5G, illustrate a few of these.

EXAMPLE 5.16

Kelly's father has agreed to let her have part of his garden as a vegetable plot. He says that she can have a rectangular plot with one side against an old wall. He hands her a piece of rope 5 m long, and invites her to mark out the part she wants. Kelly wants to enclose the largest area possible.

What dimensions would you advise her to use?

SOLUTION

Let the dimensions of the bed be x m $\times$ y m as shown in figure 5.32.

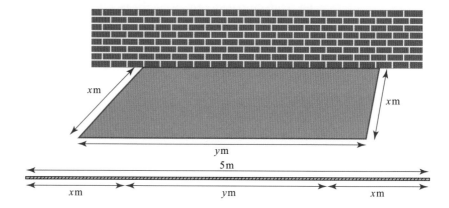

Figure 5.32

The area, A m^2, to be enclosed is given by $A = xy$.

Since the rope is 5 m long, $2x + y = 5$ or $y = 5 - 2x$.

Writing A in terms of x only $A = x(5 - 2x) = 5x - 2x^2$.

To maximise A, which is now written as a function of x, you differentiate A with respect to x

$$\frac{dA}{dx} = 5 - 4x.$$

At a stationary point, $\frac{dA}{dx} = 0$, so

$$5 - 4x = 0$$

$$x = \tfrac{5}{4} = 1.25.$$

$$\frac{d^2A}{dx^2} = -4 \Rightarrow \text{the turning point is a maximum.}$$

The corresponding value of y is $5 - 2(1.25) = 2.5$. Kelly should mark out a rectangle 1.25 m wide and 2.5 m long.

EXAMPLE 5.17

A stone is projected vertically upwards with a speed of $30\,\text{m}\,\text{s}^{-1}$. Its height, h m, above the ground after t seconds $(t < 6)$ is given by:

$$h = 30t - 5t^2.$$

(i) Find $\dfrac{\mathrm{d}h}{\mathrm{d}t}$ and $\dfrac{\mathrm{d}^2h}{\mathrm{d}t^2}$.

(ii) Find the maximum height reached.

(iii) Sketch the graph of h against t.

SOLUTION

(i) $\dfrac{\mathrm{d}h}{\mathrm{d}t} = 30 - 10t.$

$\dfrac{\mathrm{d}^2h}{\mathrm{d}t^2} = -10.$

(ii) For a stationary point, $\dfrac{\mathrm{d}h}{\mathrm{d}t} = 0$

$$30 - 10t = 0$$
$$\Rightarrow \qquad 10(3 - t) = 0$$
$$\Rightarrow \qquad t = 3.$$

$\dfrac{\mathrm{d}^2h}{\mathrm{d}t^2} < 0 \Rightarrow$ the stationary point is a maximum.

The maximum height is
$$h = 30(3) - 5(3)^2 = 45\,\text{m}.$$

(iii)

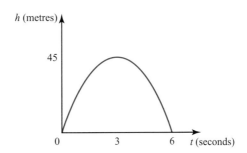

Figure 5.33

Note

For a position–time graph, such as this one, the gradient, $\dfrac{\mathrm{d}h}{\mathrm{d}t}$, is the velocity and $\dfrac{\mathrm{d}^2h}{\mathrm{d}t^2}$ is the acceleration.

1 A farmer wants to construct a temporary rectangular enclosure of length x m and width y m for his prize bull while he works in the field. He has 120 m of fencing and wants to give the bull as much room to graze as possible.

(i) Write down an expression for y in terms of x.

(ii) Write down an expression in terms of x for the area, A, to be enclosed.

(iii) Find $\dfrac{dA}{dx}$ and $\dfrac{d^2A}{dx^2}$, and so find the dimensions of the enclosure that give the bull the maximum area in which to graze. State this maximum area.

2 A square sheet of card of side 12 cm has four equal squares of side x cm cut from the corners. The sides are then turned up to make an open rectangular box to hold drawing pins as shown in the diagram.

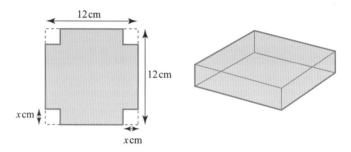

(i) Form an expression for the volume, V, of the box in terms of x.

(ii) Find $\dfrac{dV}{dx}$ and $\dfrac{d^2V}{dx^2}$, and show that the volume is a maximum when the depth is 2 cm.

3 The sum of two numbers, x and y, is 8.

(i) Write down an expression for y in terms of x.

(ii) Write down an expression for S, the sum of the squares of these two numbers, in terms of x.

(iii) By considering $\dfrac{dS}{dx}$ and $\dfrac{d^2S}{dx^2}$, find the least value of the sum of their squares.

4 A new children's slide is to be built with a cross-section as shown in the diagram. A long strip of metal 80 cm wide is available for the shute and will be bent to form the base and two sides.
The designer thinks that for maximum safety the area of the cross-section should be as large as possible.

cross-section

x cm $\qquad$ x cm

y cm

(i)   Write down an equation linking x and y.

(ii) Using your answer to part (i), form an expression for the cross-sectional area, A, in terms of x.

(iii) By considering $\dfrac{\mathrm{d}A}{\mathrm{d}x}$ and $\dfrac{\mathrm{d}^2A}{\mathrm{d}x^2}$, find the dimensions which make the slide as safe as possible.

5   A carpenter wants to make a box to hold toys. The box is to be made so that its volume is as large as possible. A rectangular sheet of thin plywood measuring 1.5 m by 1 m is available to cut into pieces as shown.

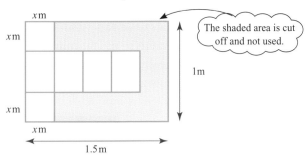

x m

x m

The shaded area is cut off and not used.

1 m

x m

x m

1.5 m

(i)   Write down the dimensions of one of the four rectangular faces in terms of x.

(ii) Form an expression for the volume, V, of the made-up box, in terms of x.

(iii) Find $\dfrac{\mathrm{d}V}{\mathrm{d}x}$ and $\dfrac{\mathrm{d}^2V}{\mathrm{d}x^2}$.

(iv) Hence find the dimensions of a box with maximum volume, and the corresponding volume.

6   A piece of wire 16 cm long is cut into two pieces. One piece is $8x$ cm long and is bent to form a rectangle measuring $3x$ cm by x cm. The other piece is bent to form a square.

(i)   Find in terms of x:
   (a) the length of a side of the square
   (b) the area of the square.

(ii) Show that the combined area of the rectangle and the square is A cm^2 where $A = 7x^2 - 16x + 16$.

(iii) Find the value of x for which A has its minimum value.

(iv) Find the minimum value of A.

[MEI]

7 A piece of wire 30 cm long is going to be made into two frames for blowing bubbles. The wire is to be cut into two parts. One part is bent into a circle of radius r cm and the other part is bent into a square of side x cm.

   (i) Write down an expression for the perimeter of the circle in terms of r, and hence write down an expression for r in terms of x.

   (ii) Show that the combined area, A, of the two shapes can be written as

$$A = \frac{(4 + \pi)x^2 - 60x + 225}{\pi}.$$

   (iii) Find the lengths that must be cut if the area is to be a minimum.

8 A cylindrical can with a lid is to be made from a thin sheet of metal. Its height is to be h cm and its radius r cm. The surface area is to be 250π cm^2.

   (i) Find h in terms of r.

   (ii) Write down an expression for the volume, V, of the can in terms of r.

   (iii) Find $\dfrac{dV}{dr}$ and $\dfrac{d^2V}{dr^2}$.

   (iv) Use your answers to part **(iii)** to show that the can's maximum possible volume is 1690 cm^3 (to 3 significant figures), and find the corresponding dimensions of the can.

9 Charlie wants to add an extension with a floor area of 18 m^2 to the back of his house. He wants to use the minimum possible number of bricks, so he wants to know the smallest perimeter he can use. The dimensions, in metres, are x and y as shown.

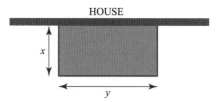

   (i) Write down an expression for the area in terms of x and y.

   (ii) Write down an expression, in terms of x and y, for the total length, T, of the outside walls.

   (iii) Show that

$$T = 2x + \frac{18}{x}.$$

   (iv) Find $\dfrac{dT}{dx}$ and $\dfrac{d^2T}{dx^2}$.

   (v) Find the dimensions of the extension that give a minimum value of T, and confirm that it is a minimum.

10 A fish tank with a square base and no top is to be made from a thin sheet of toughened glass. The dimensions are as shown.

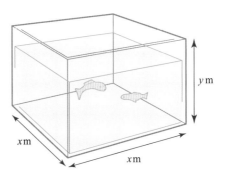

(i) Write down an expression for the volume V in terms of x and y.

(ii) Write down an expression for the total surface area A in terms of x and y.

The tank needs a capacity of $0.5\,\mathrm{m}^3$ and the manufacturer wishes to use the minimum possible amount of glass.

(iii) Deduce an expression for A in terms of x only.

(iv) Find $\dfrac{\mathrm{d}A}{\mathrm{d}x}$ and $\dfrac{\mathrm{d}^2A}{\mathrm{d}x^2}$.

(v) Find the values of x and y that use the smallest amount of glass and confirm that these give the minimum value.

11 A closed rectangular box is made of thin card, and its length is three times its width. The height is $h\,\mathrm{cm}$ and the width is $x\,\mathrm{cm}$.

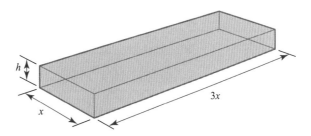

(i) The volume of the box is $972\,\mathrm{cm}^3$.
Use this to write down an expression for h in terms of x.

(ii) Show that the surface area, A, can be written as $A = 6x^2 + \dfrac{2592}{x}$.

(iii) Find $\dfrac{\mathrm{d}A}{\mathrm{d}x}$ and use it to find a stationary point.

Find $\dfrac{\mathrm{d}^2A}{\mathrm{d}x^2}$ and use it to verify that the stationary point gives the minimum value of A.

(iv) Hence find the minimum surface area and the corresponding dimensions of the box.

12 A garden is planned with a lawn area of $24\,\text{m}^2$ and a path around the edge. The dimensions of the lawn and path are as shown in the diagram.

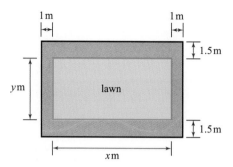

(i) Write down an expression for y in terms of x.

(ii) Find an expression for the overall area of the garden, A, in terms of x.

(iii) Find the smallest possible overall area for the garden.

13 The diagram shows the cross-section of a hollow cone and a circular cylinder. The cone has radius $6\,\text{cm}$ and height $12\,\text{cm}$, and the cylinder has radius $r\,\text{cm}$ and height $h\,\text{cm}$. The cylinder just fits inside the cone with all of its upper edge touching the surface of the cone.

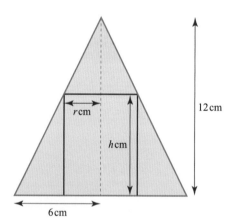

(i) Express h in terms of r and hence show that the volume, $V\,\text{cm}^3$, of the cylinder is given by
$$V = 12\pi r^2 - 2\pi r^3$$

(ii) Given that r varies, find the stationary value of V.

[Cambridge AS & A Level Mathematics 9709, Paper 1 Q5 November 2005]

The chain rule

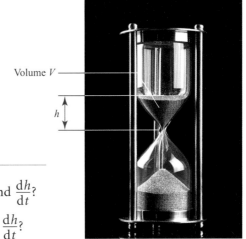

Volume V

h

?
What information is given by $\dfrac{\mathrm{d}V}{\mathrm{d}h}$ and $\dfrac{\mathrm{d}h}{\mathrm{d}t}$?

What information is given by $\dfrac{\mathrm{d}V}{\mathrm{d}h} \times \dfrac{\mathrm{d}h}{\mathrm{d}t}$?

How would you differentiate an expression like

$$y = \sqrt{x^2 + 1}?$$

Your first thought may be to write it as $y = (x^2 + 1)^{\frac{1}{2}}$ and then get rid of the brackets, but that is not possible in this case because the power $\frac{1}{2}$ is not a positive integer. Instead you need to think of the expression as a composite function, a 'function of a function'.

You have already met composite functions in Chapter 4, using the notation $g[f(x)]$ or $gf(x)$.

In this chapter we call the first function to be applied $u(x)$, or just u, rather than $f(x)$.

In this case, $u = x^2 + 1$
and $y = \sqrt{u} = u^{\frac{1}{2}}$.

This is now in a form which you can differentiate using the *chain rule*.

Differentiating a composite function

To find $\dfrac{\mathrm{d}y}{\mathrm{d}x}$ for a function of a function, you consider the effect of a small change in x on the two variables, y and u, as follows. A small change δx in x leads to a small change δu in u and a corresponding small change δy in y, and by simple algebra,

$$\frac{\delta y}{\delta x} = \frac{\delta y}{\delta u} \times \frac{\delta u}{\delta x}.$$

In the limit, as $\delta x \to 0$,

$$\frac{\delta y}{\delta x} \to \frac{dy}{dx}, \frac{\delta y}{\delta u} \to \frac{dy}{du} \text{ and } \frac{\delta u}{\delta x} \to \frac{du}{dx}$$

and so the relationship above becomes

$$\frac{dy}{dx} = \frac{dy}{du} \times \frac{du}{dx}.$$

This is known as the chain rule.

EXAMPLE 5.18

Differentiate $y = (x^2 + 1)^{\frac{1}{2}}$.

SOLUTION

As you saw earlier, you can break down this expression as follows.

$$y = u^{\frac{1}{2}}, \quad u = x^2 + 1$$

Differentiating these gives

$$\frac{dy}{du} = \frac{1}{2}u^{-\frac{1}{2}} = \frac{1}{2\sqrt{x^2 + 1}}$$

and

$$\frac{du}{dx} = 2x.$$

By the chain rule

$$\frac{dy}{dx} = \frac{dy}{du} \times \frac{du}{dx}$$

$$= \frac{1}{2\sqrt{x^2 + 1}} \times 2x$$

$$= \frac{x}{\sqrt{x^2 + 1}}$$

 Notice that the answer must be given in terms of the same variables as the question, in this case x and y. The variable u was your invention and so should not appear in the answer.

You can see that effectively you have made a substitution, in this case $u = x^2 + 1$. This transformed the problem into one that could easily be solved.

Note

Notice that the substitution gave you two functions that you could differentiate. Some substitutions would not have worked. For example, the substitution $u = x^2$, would give you

$$y = (u + 1)^{\frac{1}{2}} \text{ and } u = x^2.$$

You would still not be able to differentiate y, so you would have gained nothing.

EXAMPLE 5.19

Use the chain rule to find $\dfrac{dy}{dx}$ when $y = (x^2 - 2)^4$.

SOLUTION

Let $u = x^2 - 2$, then $y = u^4$.

$$\frac{du}{dx} = 2x$$

and

$$\frac{dy}{du} = 4u^3$$

$$= 4(x^2 - 2)^3$$

$$\frac{dy}{dx} = \frac{dy}{du} \times \frac{du}{dx}$$

$$= 4(x^2 - 2)^3 \times 2x$$

$$= 8x\,(x^2 - 2)^3.$$

(P) A student does this question by first multiplying out $(x^2 - 2)^4$ to get a polynomial of order 8. Prove that this heavy-handed method gives the same result.

(!) With practice you may find that you can do some stages of questions like this in your head, and just write down the answer. If you have any doubt, however, you should write down the full method.

Differentiation with respect to different variables

The chain rule makes it possible to differentiate with respect to a variable which does not feature in the original expression. For example, the volume V of a sphere of radius r is given by $V = \frac{4}{3}\pi r^3$. Differentiating this with respect to r gives the rate of change of volume with radius, $\dfrac{dV}{dr} = 4\pi r^2$. However you might be more interested in finding $\dfrac{dV}{dt}$, the rate of change of volume with time, t.

To find this, you would use the chain rule:

$$\frac{dV}{dt} = \frac{dV}{dr} \times \frac{dr}{dt}$$

$$\frac{dV}{dt} = 4\pi r^2 \frac{dr}{dt}$$

> Notice that the expression for $\dfrac{dV}{dt}$ includes $\dfrac{dr}{dt}$, the rate of increase of radius with time.

You have now differentiated V with respect to t.

The use of the chain rule in this way widens the scope of differentiation and this means that you have to be careful how you describe the process.

⚠ 'Differentiate $y = x^2$' could mean differentiation with respect to x, or t, or any other variable. In this book, and others in this series, we have adopted the convention that, unless otherwise stated, differentiation is with respect to the variable on the right-hand side of the expression. So when we write 'differentiate $y = x^2$' or simply 'differentiate x^2', it is to be understood that the differentiation is with respect to x.

⚠ The expression 'increasing at a rate of' is generally understood to imply differentation with respect to time, t.

EXAMPLE 5.20

The radius r cm of a circular ripple made by dropping a stone into a pond is increasing at a rate of $8\,\text{cm}\,\text{s}^{-1}$. At what rate is the area $A\,\text{cm}^2$ enclosed by the ripple increasing when the radius is 25 cm?

SOLUTION

$$A \ = \pi r^2$$
$$\frac{\mathrm{d}A}{\mathrm{d}r} = 2\pi r$$

The question is asking for $\dfrac{\mathrm{d}A}{\mathrm{d}t}$, the rate of change of area with respect to time.

Now $\dfrac{\mathrm{d}A}{\mathrm{d}t} = \dfrac{\mathrm{d}A}{\mathrm{d}r} \times \dfrac{\mathrm{d}r}{\mathrm{d}t}$

$\qquad\quad = 2\pi r \dfrac{\mathrm{d}r}{\mathrm{d}t}.$

When $r = 25$ and $\dfrac{\mathrm{d}r}{\mathrm{d}t} = 8$

$\qquad \dfrac{\mathrm{d}A}{\mathrm{d}t} = 2\pi \times 25 \times 8$

$\qquad\qquad \approx 1260\,\text{cm}^2\,\text{s}^{-1}.$

1 Use the chain rule to differentiate the following functions.

(i) $y = (x+2)^3$

(ii) $y = (2x+3)^4$

(iii) $y = (x^2-5)^3$

(iv) $y = (x^3+4)^5$

(v) $y = (3x+2)^{-1}$

(vi) $y = \dfrac{1}{(x^2-3)^3}$

(vii) $y = (x^2-1)^{\frac{3}{2}}$

(viii) $y = \left(\dfrac{1}{x}+x\right)^3$

(ix) $y = \left(\sqrt{x}-1\right)^4$

2 Given that $y = (3x-5)^3$

(i) find $\dfrac{dy}{dx}$

(ii) find the equation of the tangent to the curve at $(2, 1)$

(iii) show that the equation of the normal to the curve at $(1, -8)$ can be written in the form
$$36y + x + 287 = 0.$$

3 Given that $y = (2x-1)^4$

(i) find $\dfrac{dy}{dx}$

(ii) find the co-ordinates of any stationary points and determine their nature

(iii) sketch the curve.

4 Given that $y = (x^2-x-2)^4$

(i) find $\dfrac{dy}{dx}$

(ii) find the co-ordinates of any stationary points and determine their nature

(iii) sketch the curve.

5 The length of a side of a square is increasing at a rate of $0.2\,\text{cm}\,\text{s}^{-1}$.
At what rate is the area increasing when the length of the side is $10\,\text{cm}$?

6 The force F newtons between two magnetic poles is given by the formula
$F = \dfrac{1}{500r^2}$, where r m is their distance apart.
Find the rate of change of the force when the poles are $0.2\,\text{m}$ apart and the distance between them is increasing at a rate of $0.03\,\text{m}\,\text{s}^{-1}$.

7 The radius of a circular fungus is increasing at a uniform rate of $5\,\text{cm}$ per day.
At what rate is the area increasing when the radius is $1\,\text{m}$?

KEY POINTS

1 $y = kx^n \implies \dfrac{dy}{dx} = knx^{n-1}$ ⎫

   $y = c \implies \dfrac{dy}{dx} = 0$ ⎬ Where k, n and c are constants.

2 $y = f(x) + g(x) \implies \dfrac{dy}{dx} = f'(x) + g'(x)$.

3 Tangent and normal at (x_1, y_1)

   Gradient of tangent, $m_1 = $ value of $\dfrac{dy}{dx}$ when $x = x_1$.

   Gradient of normal, $m_2 = -\dfrac{1}{m_1}$.

   Equation of tangent is

   $$y - y_1 = m_1(x - x_1).$$

   Equation of normal is

   $$y - y_1 = m_2(x - x_1).$$

4 At a stationary point, $\dfrac{dy}{dx} = 0$.

   The nature of a stationary point can be determined by looking at the sign of the gradient just either side of it.

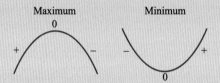

5 The nature of a stationary point can also be determined by considering the sign of $\dfrac{d^2y}{dx^2}$.

   - If $\dfrac{d^2y}{dx^2} < 0$, the point is a maximum.

   - If $\dfrac{d^2y}{dx^2} > 0$, the point is a minimum.

6 If $\dfrac{d^2y}{dx^2} = 0$, check the values of $\dfrac{dy}{dx}$ on either side of the point to determine its nature.

7 Chain rule: $\dfrac{dy}{dx} = \dfrac{dy}{du} \times \dfrac{du}{dx}$.

6

Integration

Many small make a great.

Chaucer

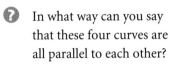

In what way can you say that these four curves are all parallel to each other?

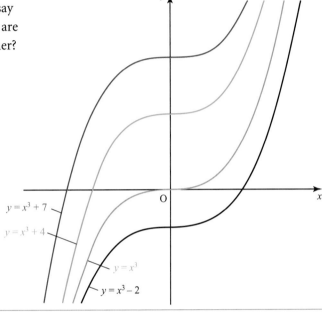

$y = x^3 + 7$

$y = x^3 + 4$

$y = x^3$

$y = x^3 - 2$

Reversing differentiation

In some situations you know the gradient function, $\dfrac{dy}{dx}$, and want to find the function itself, y. For example, you might know that $\dfrac{dy}{dx} = 2x$ and want to find y.

You know from the previous chapter that if $y = x^2$ then $\dfrac{dy}{dx} = 2x$, but

$y = x^2 + 1$, $y = x^2 - 2$ and many other functions also give $\dfrac{dy}{dx} = 2x$.

Suppose that $f(x)$ is a function with $f'(x) = 2x$. Let $g(x) = f(x) - x^2$.
Then $g'(x) = f'(x) - 2x = 2x - 2x = 0$ for all x. So the graph of $y = g(x)$ has zero gradient everywhere, i.e. the graph is a horizontal straight line.
Thus $g(x) = c$ (a constant). Therefore $f(x) = x^2 + c$.

All that you can say at this point is that if $\dfrac{dy}{dx} = 2x$ then $y = x^2 + c$ where c is described as an *arbitrary constant*. An arbitrary constant may take any value.

The equation $\dfrac{dy}{dx} = 2x$ is an example of a *differential equation* and the process of solving this equation to find y is called *integration*.

So the solution of the differential equation $\dfrac{dy}{dx} = 2x$ is $y = x^2 + c$.

Such a solution is often referred to as the *general solution* of the differential equation. It may be drawn as a family of curves as in figure 6.1. Each curve corresponds to a particular value of c.

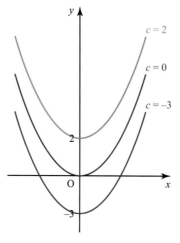

Recall from Activity 5.4 on page 130 that for each member of a family of curves, the gradient is the same for any particular value of x.

Figure 6.1 $y = x^2 + c$ for different values of c

Particular solutions

Sometimes you are given more information about a problem and this enables you to find just one solution, called the *particular solution*.

Suppose that in the previous example, in which

$$\frac{dy}{dx} = 2x \quad \Rightarrow \quad y = x^2 + c$$

you were also told that when $x = 2$, $y = 1$.

Substituting these values in $y = x^2 + c$ gives

$$1 = 2^2 + c$$
$$c = -3$$

and so the particular solution is

$$y = x^2 - 3.$$

This is the red curve shown in figure 6.1.

The rule for integrating x^n

Recall the rule for differentiation:

$$y = x^n \qquad \Rightarrow \frac{dy}{dx} = nx^{n-1}.$$

Similarly $\quad y = x^{n+1} \qquad \Rightarrow \frac{dy}{dx} = (n+1)x^n$

or $\quad y = \frac{1}{(n+1)}x^{n+1} \Rightarrow \frac{dy}{dx} = x^n.$

Reversing this, integrating x^n gives $\frac{x^{n+1}}{n+1}.$

This rule holds for all real values of the power n except -1.

> *Note*
>
> In words: to integrate a power of x, add 1 to the power and divide by the new power.
>
> This works even when n is negative or a fraction.

 Differentiating x gives 1, so integrating 1 gives x. This follows the pattern if you remember that $1 = x^0$.

EXAMPLE 6.1

Given that $\frac{dy}{dx} = 3x^2 + 4x + 3$

(i) find the general solution of this differential equation

(ii) find the equation of the curve with this gradient function which passes through $(1, 10)$.

SOLUTION

(i) By integration, $y = \frac{3x^3}{3} + \frac{4x^2}{2} + 3x + c$

$\qquad\qquad\qquad = x^3 + 2x^2 + 3x + c$, where c is a constant.

(ii) Since the curve passes through $(1, 10)$,

$$10 = 1^3 + 2(1)^2 + 3(1) + c$$
$$c = 4$$
$$\Rightarrow \qquad y = x^3 + 2x^2 + 3x + 4.$$

EXAMPLE 6.2

A curve is such that $\dfrac{dy}{dx} = 3\sqrt{x} + \dfrac{8}{x^2}$. Given that the point (4, 20) lies on the curve, find the equation of the curve.

SOLUTION

Rewrite the gradient function as $\dfrac{dy}{dx} = 3x^{\frac{1}{2}} + 8x^{-2}$.

> Dividing by $\frac{3}{2}$ is the same as multiplying by $\frac{2}{3}$.

By integration, $\quad y = 3 \times \dfrac{2}{3}x^{\frac{3}{2}} + \dfrac{8x^{-1}}{-1} + c$

$$y = 2x^{\frac{3}{2}} - \dfrac{8}{x} + c$$

Since the curve passes through the point (4, 20),

$$20 = 2(4)^{\frac{3}{2}} - \dfrac{8}{4} + c$$

$$\Rightarrow 20 = 16 - 2 + c$$

$$\Rightarrow \quad c = 6$$

So the equation of the curve is $y = 2x^{\frac{3}{2}} - \dfrac{8}{x} + 6$.

EXAMPLE 6.3

The gradient function of a curve is $\dfrac{dy}{dx} = 4x - 12$.

(i) The minimum y value is 16. By considering the gradient function, find the corresponding x value.

(ii) Use the gradient function and your answer from part (i) to find the equation of the curve.

SOLUTION

(i) At the minimum, the gradient of the curve must be zero,

$$4x - 12 = 0 \quad \Rightarrow \quad x = 3.$$

(ii) $\dfrac{dy}{dx} = 4x - 12$

$\Rightarrow y = 2x^2 - 12x + c.$

At the minimum point, $x = 3$ and $y = 16$

$$\Rightarrow 16 = 2 \times 3^2 - 12 \times 3 + c$$

$$\Rightarrow \quad c = 34$$

So the equation of the curve is $y = 2x^2 - 12x + 34$.

1 Given that $\dfrac{dy}{dx} = 6x^2 + 5$

   (i) find the general solution of the differential equation

   (ii) find the equation of the curve with gradient function $\dfrac{dy}{dx}$ and which passes through $(1, 9)$

   (iii) hence show that $(-1, -5)$ also lies on the curve.

2 The gradient function of a curve is $\dfrac{dy}{dx} = 4x$ and the curve passes through the point $(1, 5)$.

   (i) Find the equation of the curve.

   (ii) Find the value of y when $x = -1$.

3 The curve C passes through the point $(2, 10)$ and its gradient at any point is given by $\dfrac{dy}{dx} = 6x^2$.

   (i) Find the equation of the curve C.

   (ii) Show that the point $(1, -4)$ lies on the curve.

4 A stone is thrown upwards out of a window, and the rate of change of its height (h metres) is given by $\dfrac{dh}{dt} = 15 - 10t$ where t is the time (in seconds). When $t = 0$, $h = 20$.

   (i) Show that the solution of the differential equation, under the given conditions, is $h = 20 + 15t - 5t^2$.

   (ii) For what value of t does $h = 0$? (Assume $t \geqslant 0$.)

5 **(i)** Find the general solution of the differential equation $\dfrac{dy}{dx} = 5$.

   (ii) Find the particular solution which passes through the point $(1, 8)$.

   (iii) Sketch the graph of this particular solution.

6 The gradient function of a curve is $3x^2 - 3$. The curve has two stationary points. One is a maximum with a y value of 5 and the other is a minimum with a y value of 1.

   (i) Find the value of x at each stationary point. Make it clear in your solution how you know which corresponds to the maximum and which to the minimum.

   (ii) Use the gradient function and one of your points from part **(i)** to find the equation of the curve.

   (iii) Sketch the curve.

7 A curve passes through the point (4, 1) and its gradient at any point is given by $\frac{dy}{dx} = 2x - 6$.

  (i) Find the equation of the curve.

  (ii) Draw a sketch of the curve and state whether it passes under, over or through the point (1, 4).

8 A curve passes through the point (2, 3). The gradient of the curve is given by $\frac{dy}{dx} = 3x^2 - 2x - 1$.

  (i) Find y in terms of x.

  (ii) Find the co-ordinates of any stationary points of the graph of y.

  (iii) Sketch the graph of y against x, marking the co-ordinates of any stationary points and the point where the curve cuts the y axis.

  [MEI]

9 The gradient of a curve is given by $\frac{dy}{dx} = 3x^2 - 8x + 5$. The curve passes through the point (0, 3).

  (i) Find the equation of the curve.

  (ii) Find the co-ordinates of the two stationary points on the curve. State, with a reason, the nature of each stationary point.

  (iii) State the range of values of k for which the curve has three distinct intersections with the line $y = k$.

  (iv) State the range of values of x for which the curve has a negative gradient. Find the x co-ordinate of the point within this range where the curve is steepest.

  [MEI]

10 A curve is such that $\frac{dy}{dx} = \sqrt{x}$. Given that the point (9, 20) lies on the curve, find the equation of the curve.

11 A curve is such that $\frac{dy}{dx} = \frac{2}{x^2} - 3$. Given that the point (2, 10) lies on the curve, find the equation of the curve.

12 A curve is such that $\frac{dy}{dx} = \sqrt{x} + \frac{1}{x^2}$. Given that the point (1, 5) lies on the curve, find the equation of the curve.

13 A curve is such that $\frac{dy}{dx} = 3x^2 + 5$. Given that the point (1, 8) lies on the curve, find the equation of the curve.

14 A curve is such that $\frac{dy}{dx} = 3\sqrt{x} - 9$ and the point (4, 0) lies on the curve.

  (i) Find the equation of the curve.

  (ii) Find the x co-ordinate of the stationary point on the curve and determine the nature of the stationary point.

15 The equation of a curve is such that $\dfrac{dy}{dx} = \dfrac{3}{\sqrt{x}} - x$. Given that the curve passes

through the point (4, 6), find the equation of the curve.

[Cambridge AS & A Level Mathematics 9709, Paper 12 Q1 November 2009]

16 A curve is such that $\dfrac{dy}{dx} = 4 - x$ and the point P(2, 9) lies on the curve. The

normal to the curve at P meets the curve again at Q. Find

   (i) the equation of the curve,

  (ii) the equation of the normal to the curve at P,

 (iii) the co-ordinates of Q.

[Cambridge AS & A Level Mathematics 9709, Paper 1 Q9 November 2007]

Finding the area under a curve

Figure 6.2 shows a curve $y = f(x)$ and the area required is shaded.

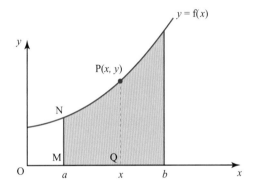

Figure 6.2

P is a point on the curve with an x co-ordinate between a and b. Let A denote the area bounded by MNPQ. As P moves, the values of A and x change, so you can see that the area A depends on the value of x. Figure 6.3 enlarges part of figure 6.2 and introduces T to the right of P.

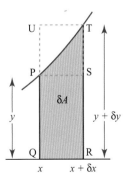

Figure 6.3

If T is close to P it is appropriate to use the notation δx (a small change in x) for the difference in their x co-ordinates and δy for the difference in their y co-ordinates. The area shaded in figure 6.3 is then referred to as δA (a small change in A).

This area δA will lie between the areas of the rectangles PQRS and UQRT

$$y\delta x < \delta A < (y + \delta y)\delta x.$$

Dividing by δx

$$y < \frac{\delta A}{\delta x} < y + \delta y.$$

In the limit as $\delta x \to 0$, δy also approaches zero so δA is sandwiched between y and something which tends to y.

But $\displaystyle\lim_{\delta x \to 0} \frac{\delta A}{\delta x} = \frac{dA}{dx}.$

This gives $\dfrac{dA}{dx} = y.$

Note

This important result is known as the fundamental theorem of calculus: the rate of change of the area under a curve is equal to the length of the moving boundary.

EXAMPLE 6.4

Find the area under the curve $y = 6x^5 + 6$ between $x = -1$ and $x = 2$.

SOLUTION

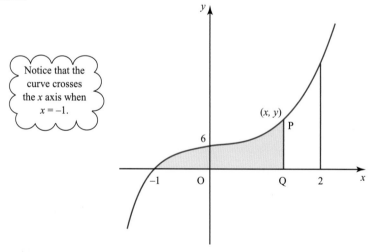

Notice that the curve crosses the x axis when $x = -1$.

Figure 6.4

Let A be the shaded area which is bounded by the curve, the x axis, and the moving boundary PQ (see figure 6.4).

Then $\dfrac{dA}{dx} = y = 6x^5 + 6.$

Integrating, $A = x^6 + 6x + c$.

When $x = -1$, the line PQ coincides with the left-hand boundary so $A = 0$

$$\Rightarrow \quad 0 = 1 - 6 + c$$
$$\Rightarrow \quad c = 5.$$

So $A = x^6 + 6x + 5$.

The required area is found by substituting $x = 2$

$$A = 64 + 12 + 5$$
$$= 81 \text{ square units.}$$

Note

The term 'square units' is used since area is a square measure and the units are unknown.

Standardising the procedure

Suppose that you want to find the area between the curve $y = f(x)$, the x axis, and the lines $x = a$ and $x = b$. This is shown shaded in figure 6.5.

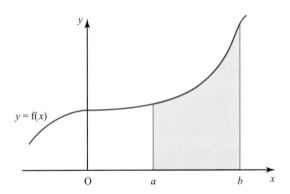

Figure 6.5

- $\dfrac{\mathrm{d}A}{\mathrm{d}x} = y = f(x)$.

- Integrate $f(x)$ to give $A = F(x) + c$.

- $A = 0$ when $x = a \Rightarrow \quad 0 = F(a) + c$
$$\Rightarrow \quad c = -F(a)$$
$$\Rightarrow \quad A = F(x) - F(a).$$

- The value of A when $x = b$ is $F(b) - F(a)$.

Notation

$F(b) - F(a)$ is written as $[F(x)]_a^b$.

EXAMPLE 6.5   Find the area between the curve $y = 20 - 3x^2$, the x axis and the lines $x = 1$ and $x = 2$.

SOLUTION

$f(x) = 20 - 3x^2 \Rightarrow F(x) = 20x - x^3$

$a = 1$ and $b = 2$

$\Rightarrow \quad$ Area $= [20x - x^3]_1^2$

$\qquad = (40 - 8) - (20 - 1)$

$\qquad = 13$ square units.

Area as the limit of a sum

Suppose you want to find the area between the curve $y = x^2 + 1$, the x axis and the lines $x = 1$ and $x = 5$. This area is shaded in figure 6.6.

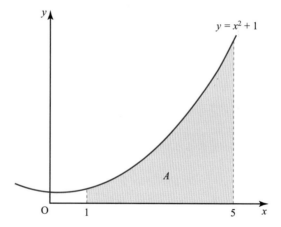

Figure 6.6

You can find an estimate of the shaded area, A, by considering the area of four rectangles of equal width, as shown in figure 6.7.

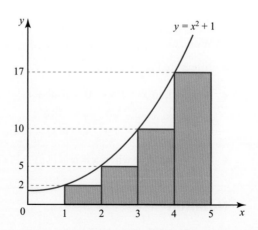

Figure 6.7

The estimated value of A is

$$2 + 5 + 10 + 17 = 34 \text{ square units.}$$

This is an underestimate.

To get an overestimate, you take the four rectangles in figure 6.8.

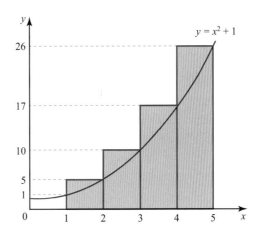

Figure 6.8

The corresponding estimate for A is

$$5 + 10 + 17 + 26 = 58 \text{ square units.}$$

This means that the true value of A satisfies the inequality

$$34 < A < 58.$$

If you increase the number of rectangles, your bounds for A become closer. The equivalent calculation using eight rectangles gives

$$1 + \tfrac{13}{8} + \tfrac{5}{2} + \tfrac{29}{8} + 5 + \tfrac{53}{8} + \tfrac{17}{2} + \tfrac{85}{8} < A < \tfrac{13}{8} + \tfrac{5}{2} + \tfrac{29}{8} + 5 + \tfrac{53}{8} + \tfrac{17}{2} + \tfrac{85}{8} + 13$$

$$39.5 < A < 51.5.$$

Similarly with 16 rectangles

$$42.375 < A < 48.375$$

and so on. With enough rectangles, the bounds for A can be brought as close together as you wish.

ACTIVITY 6.1   Use ICT to get the bounds closer.

Notation

This process can be expressed more formally. Suppose you have n rectangles, each of width δx. Notice that n and δx are related by

$$n\delta x = \text{width of required area.}$$

So in the example above,

$$n\delta x = 5 - 1 = 4.$$

In the limit, as $n \to \infty$, $\delta x \to 0$, the lower estimate $\to A$ and the higher estimate $\to A$.

$$\delta A_i = y_i\,\delta x \qquad y_i$$

The area δA of a typical rectangle may be written $y_i\,\delta x$ where y_i is the appropriate y value (see figure 6.9).

$$\delta x$$

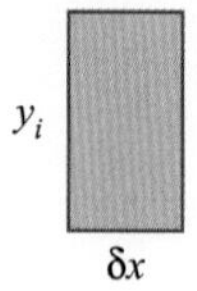

Figure 6.9

So for a finite number of strips, n, as shown in figure 6.10, the area A is given approximately by

$$A \approx \delta A_1 + \delta A_2 + \ldots + \delta A_n$$

$$\text{or} \qquad A \approx y_1\delta x + y_2\delta x + \ldots + y_n\delta x.$$

This can be written as $A \approx \sum\limits_{i=1}^{i=n} \delta A_i$

> Σ means 'the sum of' so all the δA_i are added from δA_1 (given by $i = 1$) to δA_n (when $i = n$).

$$\text{or} \qquad A \approx \sum_{i=1}^{i=n} y_i\,\delta x.$$

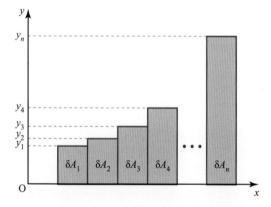

Figure 6.10

In the limit, as $n \to \infty$ and $\delta x \to 0$, the result is no longer an approximation; it is exact. At this point, $A \approx \sum y_i\,\delta x$ is written $A = \int y\,dx$, which you read as 'the integral of y with respect to x'. In this case $y = x^2 + 1$, and you require the area for values of x from 1 to 5, so you can write

$$A = \int_1^5 (x^2 + 1)dx.$$

Notice that in the limit:

- $\approx$ is replaced by $=$
- δx is replaced by $\mathrm{d}x$
- $\sum$ is replaced by $\int$, the integral sign (the symbol is the Old English letter S)
- instead of summing for $i = 1$ to n the process is now carried out over a range of values of x (in this case 1 to 5), and these are called the *limits* of the integral. (Note that this is a different meaning of the word limit.)

This method must give the same results as the previous one which used $\dfrac{\mathrm{d}A}{\mathrm{d}x} = y$, and at this stage the notation $\left[\mathrm{F}(x) \right]_a^b$ is used again.

In this case $\displaystyle\int_1^5 (x^2 + 1)\,\mathrm{d}x = \left[\dfrac{x^3}{3} + x \right]_1^5.$

> The limits have now moved to the right of the square brackets.

Recall that this notation means: find the value of $\dfrac{x^3}{3} + x$ when $x = 5$ (the upper limit) and subtract the value of $\dfrac{x^3}{3} + x$ when $x = 1$ (the lower limit).

$$\left[\dfrac{x^3}{3} + x \right]_1^5 = \left(\dfrac{5^3}{3} + 5 \right) - \left(\dfrac{1^3}{3} + 1 \right) = 45\tfrac{1}{3}.$$

So the area A is $45\tfrac{1}{3}$ square units.

EXAMPLE 6.6

Find the area under the curve $y = 4x^3 + 4$ between $x = -1$ and $x = 2$.

SOLUTION

The graph is shown in figure 6.11.
The shaded part, A

$= \displaystyle\int_{-1}^2 (4x^3 + 4)\,\mathrm{d}x$

$= [x^4 + 4x]_{-1}^2$

$= (2^4 + 4(2)) - ((-1)^4 + 4(-1))$

$= 27$ square units.

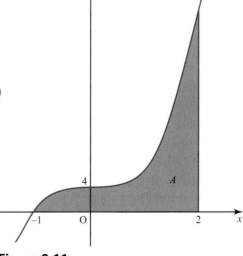

Figure 6.11

EXAMPLE 6.7

Evaluate the definite integral $\int_4^9 x^{\frac{3}{2}}\,dx$

SOLUTION

$$\int_4^9 x^{\frac{3}{2}}\,dx = \left[\frac{x^{\frac{5}{2}}}{\frac{5}{2}}\right]_4^9 \qquad \left(\frac{3}{2}+1=\frac{5}{2}\right)$$

$$= \frac{2}{5}\left[x^{\frac{5}{2}}\right]_4^9 \qquad \text{To divide by a fraction, invert it and multiply.}$$

$$= \frac{2}{5}\left(9^{\frac{5}{2}} - 4^{\frac{5}{2}}\right)$$

$$= \frac{2}{5}(243 - 32)$$

$$= 84\frac{2}{5}.$$

This gives the shaded area in figure 6.12.

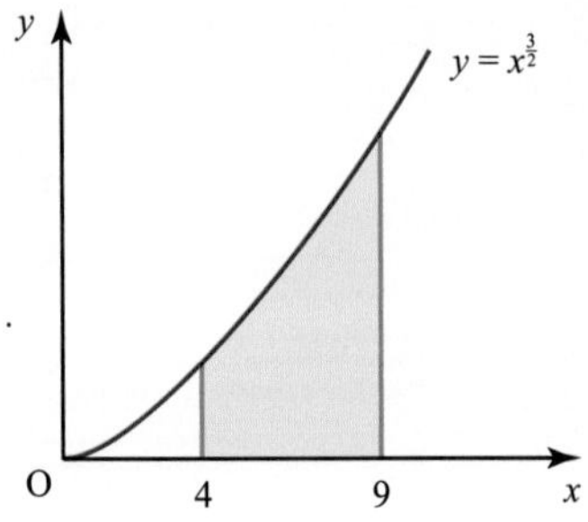

Figure 6.12

Definite integrals

Expressions like $\int_{-1}^2 (4x^3 + 4)\,dx$ and $\int_4^9 x^{\frac{3}{2}}\,dx$ in Examples 6.6 and 6.7 are called *definite integrals*. A definite integral has an upper limit and a lower limit and can be evaluated as a number. In the case of Example 6.6 the definite integral is 27.

Note

In Example 6.6 you found that the value of $\int_{-1}^2 (4x^3 + 4)\,dx$ was 27. If you evaluate $\int_2^{-1} (4x^3 + 4)\,dx$ you will find its value is –27.

Consider $\int_a^b f(x)\,dx = F(b) - F(a),$

So $\int_b^a f(x)\,dx = F(a) - F(b)$

$$= -(F(b) - F(a))$$

$$= -\int_a^b f(x)\,dx$$

In general, interchanging the limits of a definite integral has the effect of reversing the sign of the answer.

Figure 6.13 shows the region bounded by the graph of $y = x + 3$, the x axis and the lines $x = a$ and $x = b$.

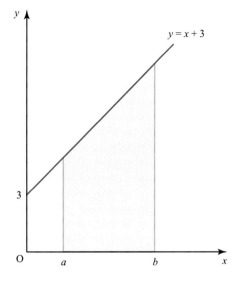

Figure 6.13

(i) Find the shaded area, A, by considering it as the difference between the two trapezia shown in figure 6.14.

(ii) Show that the expression for A you obtained in part (i) may be written as

$$\left[\frac{x^2}{2} + 3x \right]_a^b .$$

(iii) Show that you obtain the same answer for A by integration.

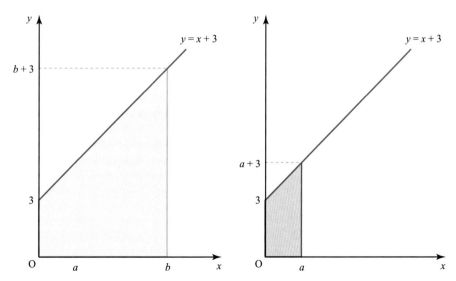

Figure 6.14

EXAMPLE 6.8

Evaluate $\int_1^2 \left(\frac{3}{x^4} - \frac{1}{x^2} + 4 \right) dx.$

SOLUTION

$$\int_1^2 \left(\frac{3}{x^4} - \frac{1}{x^2} + 4 \right) dx = \int_1^2 \left(3x^{-4} - x^{-2} + 4 \right) dx$$

$$= \left[\frac{3x^{-3}}{-3} - \frac{x^{-1}}{-1} + 4x \right]_1^2$$

$$= \left[-\frac{1}{x^3} + \frac{1}{x} + 4x \right]_1^2$$

$$= \left(-\frac{1}{8} + \frac{1}{2} + 8 \right) - \left(-1 + 1 + 4 \right)$$

$$= 4\frac{3}{8}$$

Indefinite integrals

The integral symbol can be used without the limits to denote that a function is to be integrated. Earlier in the chapter, you saw $\frac{dy}{dx} = 2x \Rightarrow y = x^2 + c.$

An alternative way of expressing this is

$$\int 2x \, dx = x^2 + c.$$

Read as 'the integral of $2x$ with respect to x'.

EXAMPLE 6.9

Find $\int (2x^3 - 3x + 4) \, dx.$

SOLUTION

$$\int (2x^3 - 3x + 4) \, dx = 2\frac{x^4}{4} - 3\frac{x^2}{2} + 4x + c$$

$$= \frac{x^4}{2} - \frac{3x^2}{2} + 4x + c.$$

EXAMPLE 6.10

Find the indefinite integral $\int \left(x^{\frac{3}{2}} + \sqrt{x} \right) dx.$

SOLUTION

$$\int \left(x^{\frac{3}{2}} + \sqrt{x} \right) dx = \int \left(x^{\frac{3}{2}} + x^{\frac{1}{2}} \right) dx$$

$$= \frac{2}{5} x^{\frac{5}{2}} + \frac{2}{3} x^{\frac{3}{2}} + c$$

$\frac{3}{2} + 1 = \frac{5}{2}$, and dividing by $\frac{5}{2}$ is the same as multiplying by $\frac{2}{5}$.

1 Find the following indefinite integrals.

(i) $\int 3x^2 \, dx$

(ii) $\int (5x^4 + 7x^6) \, dx$

(iii) $\int (6x^2 + 5) \, dx$

(iv) $\int (x^3 + x^2 + x + 1) \, dx$

(v) $\int (11x^{10} + 10x^9) \, dx$

(vi) $\int (3x^2 + 2x + 1) \, dx$

(vii) $\int (x^2 + 5) \, dx$

(viii) $\int 5 \, dx$

(ix) $\int (6x^2 + 4x) \, dx$

(x) $\int (x^4 + 3x^2 + 2x + 1) \, dx$

2 Find the following indefinite integrals.

(i) $\int 10x^{-4} \, dx$

(ii) $\int (2x - 3x^{-4}) \, dx$

(iii) $\int (2 + x^3 + 5x^{-3}) \, dx$

(iv) $\int (6x^2 - 7x^{-2}) \, dx$

(v) $\int 5x^{\frac{1}{4}} \, dx$

(vi) $\int \frac{1}{x^4} \, dx$

(vii) $\int \sqrt{x} \, dx$

(viii) $\int \left(2x^4 - \frac{4}{x^2} \right) \, dx$

3 Evaluate the following definite integrals.

(i) $\int_1^2 2x \, dx$

(ii) $\int_0^3 2x \, dx$

(iii) $\int_0^3 3x^2 \, dx$

(iv) $\int_1^5 x \, dx$

(v) $\int_5^6 (2x + 1) \, dx$

(vi) $\int_{-1}^2 (2x + 4) \, dx$

(vii) $\int_3^5 (3x^2 + 2x) \, dx$

(viii) $\int_0^1 x^5 \, dx$

(ix) $\int_{-2}^{-1} (x^4 + x^3) \, dx$

(x) $\int_{-1}^1 x^3 \, dx$

(xi) $\int_{-5}^4 (x^3 + 3x) \, dx$

(xii) $\int_{-3}^{-2} 5 \, dx$

4 Evaluate the following definite integrals.

(i) $\int_1^4 3x^{-2} \, dx$

(ii) $\int_2^4 8x^{-3} \, dx$

(iii) $\int_1^4 12x^{\frac{1}{2}} \, dx$

(iv) $\int_{-3}^{-1} \frac{6}{x^3} \, dx$

(v) $\int_{0.5}^2 \left(\frac{x^2 + 3x + 4}{x^4} \right) \, dx$

(vi) $\int_4^9 \left(\sqrt{x} - \frac{1}{\sqrt{x}} \right) \, dx$

5 The graph of $y = 2x$ is shown here.

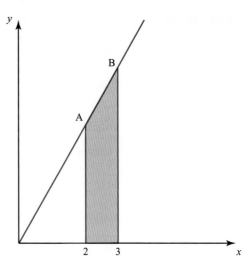

The shaded region is bounded by $y = 2x$, the x axis and the lines $x = 2$ and $x = 3$.

  (i) Find the co-ordinates of the points A and B in the diagram.

  (ii) Use the formula for the area of a trapezium to find the area of the shaded region.

  (iii) Find the area of the shaded region as $\int_2^3 2x\,dx$, and confirm that your answer is the same as that for part **(ii)**.

  (iv) The method of part **(ii)** cannot be used to find the area under the curve $y = x^2$ bounded by the lines $x = 2$ and $x = 3$. Why?

6 **(i)** Sketch the curve $y = x^2$ for $-1 \leqslant x \leqslant 3$ and shade the area bounded by the curve, the lines $x = 1$ and $x = 2$ and the x axis.

  (ii) Find, by integration, the area of the region you have shaded.

7 **(i)** Sketch the curve $y = 4 - x^2$ for $-3 \leqslant x \leqslant 3$.

  (ii) For what values of x is the curve above the x axis?

  (iii) Find the area between the curve and the x axis when the curve is above the x axis.

8 **(i)** Sketch the graph of $y = (x - 2)^2$ for values of x between $x = -1$ and $x = +5$. Shade the area under the curve, between $x = 0$ and $x = 2$.

  (ii) Calculate the area you have shaded.   **[MEI]**

9 The diagram shows the graph of $y = \sqrt{x} + \dfrac{1}{\sqrt{x}}$

for $x > 0$.

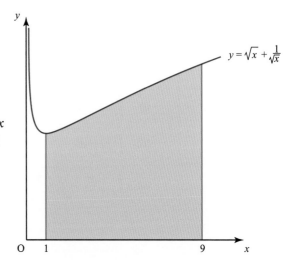

The shaded region is bounded by the curve, the x axis and the lines $x = 1$ and $x = 9$.

Find its area.

10 **(i)** Sketch the graph of $y = (x + 1)^2$ for values of x between $x = -1$ and $x = 4$.

(ii) Shade the area under the curve between $x = 1$, $x = 3$ and the x axis. Calculate this area. [MEI]

11 **(i)** Sketch the curves $y = x^2$ and $y = x^3$ for $0 \leqslant x \leqslant 2$.

(ii) Which is the higher curve within the region $0 < x < 1$?

(iii) Find the area under each curve for $0 \leqslant x \leqslant 1$.

(iv) Which would you expect to be greater, $\int_1^2 x^2 \, dx$ or $\int_1^2 x^3 \, dx$?

Explain your answer in terms of your sketches, and confirm it by calculation.

12 **(i)** Sketch the curve $y = x^2 - 1$ for $-3 \leqslant x \leqslant 3$.

(ii) Find the area of the region bounded by $y = x^2 - 1$, the line $x = 2$ and the x axis.

(iii) Sketch the curve $y = x^2 - 2x$ for $-2 \leqslant x \leqslant 4$.

(iv) Find the area of the region bounded by $y = x^2 - 2x$, the line $x = 3$ and the x axis.

(v) Comment on your answers to parts **(ii)** and **(iv)**.

13 **(i)** Shade, on a suitable sketch, the region with an area given by

$$\int_{-1}^{2} (9 - x^2) \, dx.$$

(ii) Find the area of the shaded region.

14 **(i)** Sketch the curve with equation $y = x^2 + 1$ for $-3 \leqslant x \leqslant 3$.

(ii) Find the area of the region bounded by the curve, the lines $x = 2$ and $x = 3$, and the x axis.

(iii) Predict, with reasons, the value of $\int_{-3}^{-2} (x^2 + 1) \, dx$.

(iv) Evaluate $\int_{-3}^{-2} (x^2 + 1) \, dx$.

15 **(i)** Sketch the curve with equation $y = x^2 - 2x + 1$ for $-1 \leqslant x \leqslant 4$.

(ii) State, with reasons, which area you would expect from your sketch to be larger:

$$\int_{-1}^{3} (x^2 - 2x + 1) \, dx \quad \text{or} \quad \int_{0}^{4} (x^2 - 2x + 1) \, dx.$$

(iii) Calculate the values of the two integrals. Was your answer to part **(ii)** correct?

16 **(i)** Sketch the curve with equation $y = x^3 - 6x^2 + 11x - 6$ for $0 \leqslant x \leqslant 4$.

(ii) Shade the regions with areas given by

(a) $\int_1^2 (x^3 - 6x^2 + 11x - 6)\, dx$

(b) $\int_3^4 (x^3 - 6x^2 + 11x - 6)\, dx.$

(iii) Find the values of these two areas.

(iv) Find the value of $\int_1^{1.5} (x^3 - 6x^2 + 11x - 6)\, dx$.

What does this, taken together with one of your answers to part **(iii)**, indicate to you about the position of the maximum point between $x = 1$ and $x = 2$?

17 Find the area of the region enclosed by the curve $y = 3\sqrt{x}$, the x axis and the lines $x = 0$ and $x = 4$.

18 A curve has equation $y = \dfrac{4}{\sqrt{x}}$.

(i) The normal to the curve at the point $(4, 2)$ meets the x axis at P and the y axis at Q. Find the length of PQ, correct to 3 significant figures.

(ii) Find the area of the region enclosed by the curve, the x axis and the lines $x = 1$ and $x = 4$.

[Cambridge AS & A Level Mathematics 9709, Paper 1 Q9 June 2005]

19 The diagram shows a curve for which $\dfrac{dy}{dx} = -\dfrac{k}{x^3}$, where k is a constant. The curve passes through the points $(1, 18)$ and $(4, 3)$.

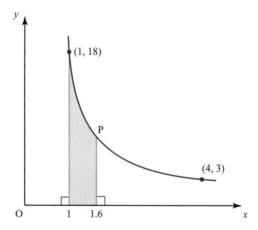

(i) Show, by integration, that the equation of the curve is $y = \dfrac{16}{x^2} + 2$.

The point P lies on the curve and has x co-ordinate 1.6.

(ii) Find the area of the shaded region.

[Cambridge AS & A Level Mathematics 9709, Paper 1 Q9 June 2008]

20 A curve is such that $\dfrac{dy}{dx} = \dfrac{16}{x^3}$, and $(1, 4)$ is a point on the curve.

(i) Find the equation of the curve.

(ii) A line with gradient $-\dfrac{1}{2}$ is a normal to the curve. Find the equation of this normal, giving your answer in the form $ax + by = c$.

(iii) Find the area of the region enclosed by the curve, the *x* axis and the lines $x = 1$ and $x = 2$.

[Cambridge AS & A Level Mathematics 9709, Paper 1 Q10 November 2005]

21 The equation of a curve is $y = 2x + \dfrac{8}{x^2}$.

(i) Obtain expressions for $\dfrac{dy}{dx}$ and $\dfrac{d^2y}{dx^2}$.

(ii) Find the co-ordinates of the stationary point on the curve and determine the nature of the stationary point.

(iii) Show that the normal to the curve at the point $(-2, -2)$ intersects the *x* axis at the point $(-10, 0)$.

(iv) Find the area of the region enclosed by the curve, the *x* axis and the lines $x = 1$ and $x = 2$.

[Cambridge AS & A Level Mathematics 9709, Paper 1 Q10 June 2007]

Areas below the *x* axis

When a graph goes below the *x* axis, the corresponding *y* value is negative and so the value of $y\,\delta x$ is negative (see figure 6.15). So when an integral turns out to be negative you know that the area is below the *x* axis.

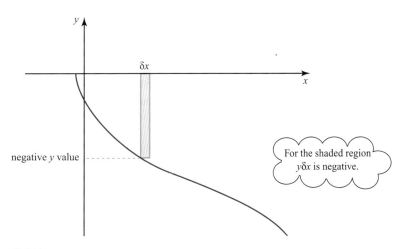

Figure 6.15

EXAMPLE 6.11

Find the area of the region bounded by the curve with equation $y = \dfrac{2}{x^2} - 3$, the lines $x = 2$ and $x = 4$, and the x axis.

SOLUTION

The region in question is shaded in figure 6.16.

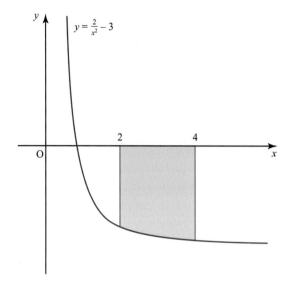

Figure 6.16

The shaded area is

$$A = \int_2^4 \left(\frac{2}{x^2} - 3 \right) dx$$

$$= \int_2^4 \left(2x^{-2} - 3 \right) dx$$

$$= \left[\frac{2x^{-1}}{(-1)} - 3x \right]_2^4$$

$$= \left[-\frac{2}{x} - 3x \right]_2^4$$

$$= \left(-\frac{1}{2} - 12 \right) - (-1 - 6)$$

$$= -5.5$$

Therefore the shaded area is 5.5 square units, and it is below the x axis.

EXAMPLE 6.12 Find the area between the curve and the x axis for the function $y = x^2 + 3x$ between $x = -1$ and $x = 2$.

SOLUTION

The first step is to draw a sketch of the function to see whether the curve goes below the x axis (see figure 6.17).

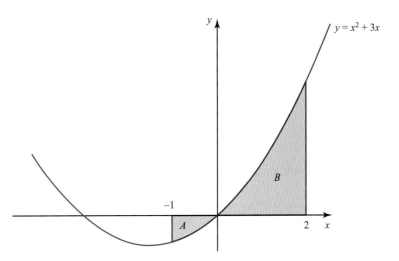

Figure 6.17

This shows that the y values are positive for $0 < x < 2$ and negative for $-1 < x < 0$.

You therefore need to calculate the area in two parts.

$$\text{Area } A = \int_{-1}^{0} (x^2 + 3x)\,dx$$

$$= \left[\frac{x^3}{3} + \frac{3x^2}{2} \right]_{-1}^{0}$$

$$= 0 - \left(-\frac{1}{3} + \frac{3}{2} \right)$$

$$= -\frac{7}{6}.$$

$$\text{Area } B = \int_{0}^{2} (x^2 + 3x)\,dx$$

$$= \left[\frac{x^3}{3} + \frac{3x^2}{2} \right]_{0}^{2}$$

$$= \left(\frac{8}{3} + 6 \right) - 0$$

$$= \frac{26}{3}.$$

$$\text{Total area} = \frac{7}{6} + \frac{26}{3}$$

$$= \frac{59}{6} \text{ square units.}$$

EXERCISE 6C

1 Sketch each of these curves and find the area between the curve and the x axis between the given bounds.

(i) $y = x^3$ between $x = -3$ and $x = 0$.

(ii) $y = x^2 - 4$ between $x = -1$ and $x = 2$.

(iii) $y = x^5 - 2$ between $x = -1$ and $x = 0$.

(iv) $y = 3x^2 - 4x$ between $x = 0$ and $x = 1$.

(v) $y = x^4 - x^2$ between $x = -1$ and $x = 1$.

(vi) $y = 4x^3 - 3x^2$ between $x = -1$ and $x = 0.5$.

(vii) $y = x^5 - x^3$ between $x = -1$ and $x = 1$.

(viii) $y = x^2 - x - 2$ between $x = -2$ and $x = 3$.

(ix) $y = x^3 + x^2 - 2x$ between $x = -3$ and $x = 2$.

(x) $y = x^3 + x^2$ between $x = -2$ and $x = 2$.

2 The diagram shows a sketch of part of the curve with equation $y = 5x^4 - x^5$.

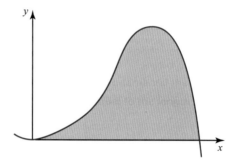

(i) Find $\dfrac{dy}{dx}$.

Calculate the co-ordinates of the stationary points.

(ii) Calculate the area of the shaded region enclosed by the curve and the x axis.

(iii) Evaluate $\int_0^6 x^4(5 - x)\,dx$ and comment on your result.

[MEI]

3 (i) (a) Find $\int_{\frac{1}{4}}^{\frac{1}{2}} \left(\dfrac{1}{x^3} - 8\right) dx$.

(b) Find $\int_{\frac{1}{2}}^{1} \left(\dfrac{1}{x^3} - 8\right) dx$.

(ii) Hence find the total area of the regions bounded by the curve $y = \dfrac{1}{x^3} - 8$, the lines $x = \dfrac{1}{4}$ and $x = 1$ and the x axis.

4 (i) (a) Find $\int_0^4 2x\left(\sqrt{x} - 2\right) dx$.

(b) Find $\int_4^9 2x\left(\sqrt{x} - 2\right) dx$.

(ii) Hence find the total area of the regions bounded by the curve $y = 2x\left(\sqrt{x} - 2\right)$, the line $x = 9$ and the x axis.

The area between two curves

EXAMPLE 6.13   Find the area enclosed by the line $y = x + 1$ and the curve $y = x^2 - 2x + 1$.

SOLUTION

First draw a sketch showing where these graphs intersect (see figure 6.18).

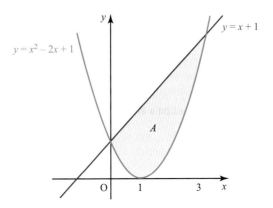

Figure 6.18

When they intersect

$$x^2 - 2x + 1 = x + 1$$
$$\Rightarrow \qquad x^2 - 3x = 0$$
$$\Rightarrow \qquad x(x - 3) = 0$$
$$\Rightarrow \qquad x = 0 \text{ or } x = 3.$$

The shaded area can now be found in one of two ways.

Method 1

Area A can be treated as the difference between the two areas, B and C, shown in figure 6.19.

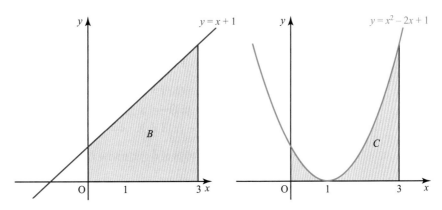

Figure 6.19

$$A = B - C$$

$$= \int_0^3 (x+1)\,\mathrm{d}x - \int_0^3 (x^2 - 2x + 1)\,\mathrm{d}x$$

$$= \left[\frac{x^2}{2} + x\right]_0^3 - \left[\frac{x^3}{3} - x^2 + x\right]_0^3$$

$$= \left[\left(\tfrac{9}{2} + 3\right) - 0\right] - \left[\left(\tfrac{27}{3} - 9 + 3\right) - 0\right]$$

$$= \tfrac{9}{2}\text{ square units.}$$

Method 2

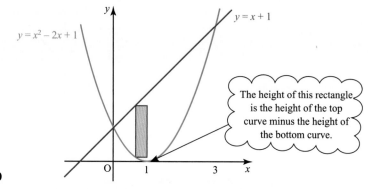

$y = x^2 - 2x + 1$

$y = x + 1$

The height of this rectangle is the height of the top curve minus the height of the bottom curve.

Figure 6.20

$$A = \int_0^3 \{\text{top curve} - \text{bottom curve}\}\,\mathrm{d}x$$

$$= \int_0^3 \left((x+1) - (x^2 - 2x + 1)\right)\mathrm{d}x$$

$$= \int_0^3 (3x - x^2)\,\mathrm{d}x$$

$$= \left[\frac{3x^2}{2} - \frac{x^3}{3}\right]_0^3$$

$$= \left[\tfrac{27}{2} - 9\right] - [0]$$

$$= \tfrac{9}{2}\text{ square units.}$$

EXERCISE 6D

1 The diagram shows the curve $y = x^2$ and the line $y = 9$. The enclosed region has been shaded.

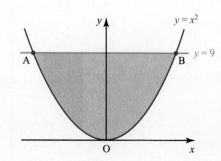

(i) Find the two points of intersection (labelled A and B).

(ii) Using integration, show that the area of the shaded region is 36 square units.

2 **(i)** Sketch the curves with equations $y = x^2 + 3$ and $y = 5 - x^2$ on the same axes, and shade the enclosed region.

    (ii) Find the co-ordinates of the points of intersection of the curves.

    (iii) Find the area of the shaded region.

3 **(i)** Sketch the curve $y = x^3$ and the line $y = 4x$ on the same axes.

    (ii) Find the co-ordinates of the points of intersection of the curve $y = x^3$ and the line $y = 4x$.

    (iii) Find the total area of the region bounded by $y = x^3$ and $y = 4x$.

4 **(i)** Sketch the curves with equations $y = x^2$ and $y = 4x - x^2$.

    (ii) Find the co-ordinates of the points of intersection of the curves.

    (iii) Find the area of the region enclosed by the curves.

5 **(i)** Sketch the curves $y = x^2$ and $y = 8 - x^2$ and the line $y = 4$ on the same axes.

    (ii) Find the area of the region enclosed by the line $y = 4$ and the curve $y = x^2$.

    (iii) Find the area of the region enclosed by the line $y = 4$ and the curve $y = 8 - x^2$.

    (iv) Find the area enclosed by the curves $y = x^2$ and $y = 8 - x^2$.

6 **(i)** Sketch the curve $y = x^2 - 6x$ and the line $y = -5$.

    (ii) Find the co-ordinates of the points of intersection of the line and the curve.

    (iii) Find the area of the region enclosed by the line and the curve.

7 **(i)** Sketch the curve $y = x(4 - x)$ and the line $y = 2x - 3$.

    (ii) Find the co-ordinates of the points of intersection of the line and the curve.

    (iii) Find the area of the region enclosed by the line and the curve.

8 Find the area of the region enclosed by the curves with equations $y = x^2 - 16$ and $y = 4x - x^2$.

9 Find the area of the region enclosed by the curves with equations $y = -x^2 - 1$ and $y = -2x^2$.

10 **(i)** Sketch the curve with equation $y = x^3 + 1$ and the line $y = 4x + 1$.

    (ii) Find the areas of the two regions enclosed by the line and the curve.

11 The diagram shows the curve $y = 5x - x^2$ and the line $y = 4$.

Find the area of the shaded region.

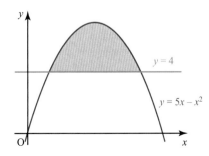

12 The diagram shows the curve with equation $y = x^2(3 - 2x - x^2)$. P and Q are points on the curve with co-ordinates $(-2, 12)$ and $(1, 0)$ respectively.

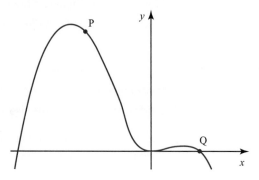

(i) Find $\dfrac{dy}{dx}$.

(ii) Find the equation of the line PQ.

(iii) Prove that the line PQ is a tangent to the curve at both P and Q.

(iv) Find the area of the region bounded by the line PQ and that part of the curve for which $-2 \leqslant x \leqslant 1$.

[MEI]

13 The diagram shows the graph of $y = 4x - x^3$. The point A has co-ordinates $(2, 0)$.

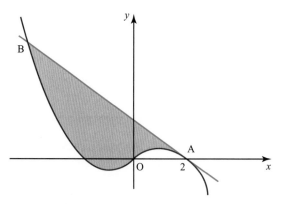

(i) Find $\dfrac{dy}{dx}$.

Then find the equation of the tangent to the curve at A.

(ii) The tangent at A meets the curve again at the point B.

Show that the x co-ordinate of B satisfies the equation $x^3 - 12x + 16 = 0$.

Find the co-ordinates of B.

(iii) Calculate the area of the shaded region between the straight line AB and the curve.

[MEI]

14 The diagram shows the curve $y = (x-2)^2$ and the line $y + 2x = 7$, which intersect at points A and B.

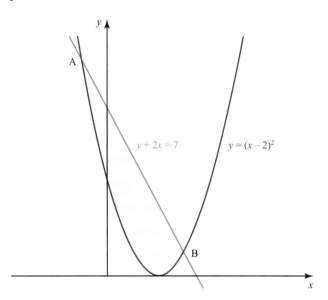

Find the area of the shaded region.

[Cambridge AS & A Level Mathematics 9709, Paper 12 Q9 June 2010]

15 The diagram shows the curve $y = x^3 - 6x^2 + 9x$ for $x \geqslant 0$. The curve has a maximum point at A and a minimum point on the x axis at B. The normal to the curve at C(2, 2) meets the normal to the curve at B at the point D.

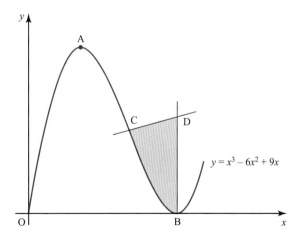

(i) Find the co-ordinates of A and B.

(ii) Find the equation of the normal to the curve at C.

(iii) Find the area of the shaded region.

[Cambridge AS & A Level Mathematics 9709, Paper 1 Q11 June 2009]

The area between a curve and the *y* axis

So far you have calculated areas between curves and the *x* axis. You can also use integration to calculate the area between a curve and the *y* axis. In such cases, the integral involves d*y* and not d*x*. It is therefore necessary to write *x* in terms of *y* wherever it appears. The integration is then said to be carried out *with respect to y* instead of *x*.

EXAMPLE 6.14　Find the area between the curve *y* = *x* − 1 and the *y* axis between *y* = 0 and *y* = 4.

SOLUTION

Instead of strips of width δ*x* and height *y*, you now sum strips of width δ*y* and length *x* (see figure 6.21).

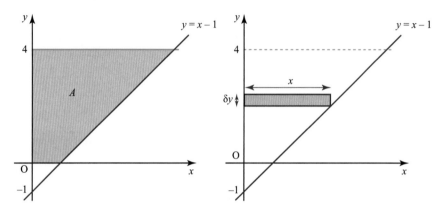

Figure 6.21

You write

$$A = \lim_{\delta y \to 0} \sum_{\substack{\text{over all} \\ \text{rectangles}}} x \, \delta y$$

$$= \int_0^4 x \, dy$$

$$= \int_0^4 (y+1) \, dy$$

To integrate *x* with respect to *y*, write *x* in terms of *y*. For this graph *y* = *x* − 1 so *x* = *y* + 1.

$$= \left[\frac{y^2}{2} + y \right]_0^4$$

= 12 square units.

EXAMPLE 6.15   Find the area between the curve $y = \sqrt{x}$ and the y axis between $y = 0$ and $y = 3$.

SOLUTION

$A = \int_0^3 x\,dy$

$\boxed{\text{Since } y = \sqrt{x},\, x = y^2}$

$= \int_0^3 y^2\,dy$

$= \left[\dfrac{y^3}{3} \right]_0^3$

$= 9$ square units.

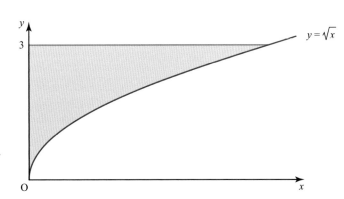

Figure 6.22

EXERCISE 6E   Find the area of the region bounded by each of these curves, the y axis and the lines $y = a$ and $y = b$.

1 $y = 3x + 1$, $a = 1$, $b = 7$.   **2** $y = \sqrt{x - 2}$, $a = 0$, $b = 2$.

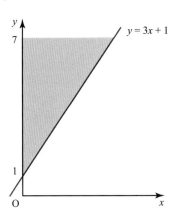

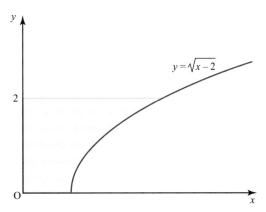

3 $y = \sqrt[3]{x}$, $a = 0$, $b = 2$.   **4** $y = \sqrt{x} - 1$, $a = 0$, $b = 2$.

5 $y = \sqrt[4]{x}$, $a = 1$, $b = 2$.   **6** $y = \sqrt[3]{x} - 2$, $a = -1$, $b = 1$.

The reverse chain rule

$\boxed{\text{You can think of the chain rule as being: '}\textit{the derivative of the bracket} \times \textit{the derivative of the inside of the bracket}\text{'.}}$

ACTIVITY 6.3   **(i)** Use the chain rule to differentiate these.

   (a) $(x - 2)^4$ **(b)** $(2x + 5)^7$

   (c) $\dfrac{1}{(2x - 1)^3}$ **(d)** $\sqrt{(1 - 8x)}$

(ii) Use your answers to part **(i)** to find these.

(a) $\int 4(x-2)^3\,dx$

(b) $\int (x-2)^3\,dx$

(c) $\int 7(2x+5)^6\,dx$

(d) $\int 28(2x+5)^6\,dx$

(e) $\int 6(2x-1)^{-4}\,dx$

(f) $\int \dfrac{1}{(2x-1)^4}\,dx$

(g) $\int \dfrac{-4}{\sqrt{1-8x}}\,dx$

(h) $\int \dfrac{8}{\sqrt{1-8x}}\,dx$

In the activity, you saw that you can use the chain rule in reverse to integrate functions in the form $(ax+b)^n$.

For example, $\qquad \dfrac{d(3x+2)^5}{dx} = 5 \times 3 \times (3x+2)^4$

$$= 15(3x+2)^4$$

This tells you that $\quad \int 15(3x+2)^4\,dx = (3x+2)^5 + c$

$$\Rightarrow \int (3x+2)^4\,dx = \tfrac{1}{15}(3x+2)^5 + c.$$

EXAMPLE 6.16

Find $\int \dfrac{3}{\sqrt{5-2x}}\,dx$.

SOLUTION

$$\int \dfrac{3}{\sqrt{5-2x}}\,dx = \int 3(5-2x)^{-\frac{1}{2}}\,dx$$

Use the reverse chain rule to find the function which differentiates to give $3(5-2x)^{-\frac{1}{2}}$.

This function must be related to $(5-2x)^{\frac{1}{2}}$.

> Increasing the power of the bracket by 1.

The derivative of $(5-2x)^{\frac{1}{2}}$ is $\tfrac{1}{2} \times -2(5-2x)^{-\frac{1}{2}} = -(5-2x)^{-\frac{1}{2}}$

So the derivative of $-3(5-2x)^{\frac{1}{2}}$ is $3(5-2x)^{-\frac{1}{2}}$

$$\Rightarrow \int 3(5-2x)^{-\frac{1}{2}}\,dx = -3(5-2x)^{\frac{1}{2}} + c$$

$$= -3\sqrt{5-2x} + c.$$

In general, $\dfrac{d(ax+b)^{n+1}}{dx} = a(n+1)(ax+b)^n$

Since integration is the reverse of differentiation, you can write:

$$\int a(n+1)(ax+b)^n\,dx = (ax+b)^{n+1} + c$$

$$\Rightarrow \int (ax+b)^n\,dx = \dfrac{1}{a(n+1)}(ax+b)^{n+1} + c.$$

EXERCISE 6F

1 Evaluate the following indefinite integrals.

   (i) $\int (x+5)^4 \, dx$ **(ii)** $\int (x+7)^8 \, dx$

   (iii) $\int \dfrac{1}{(x-2)^6} \, dx$ **(iv)** $\int \sqrt{x-4} \, dx$

   (v) $\int (3x-1)^3 \, dx$ **(vi)** $\int (5x-2)^6 \, dx$

   (vii) $\int 3(2x-4)^5 \, dx$ **(viii)** $\int \sqrt{4x-2} \, dx$

   (ix) $\int \dfrac{4}{(8-x)^2} \, dx$ **(x)** $\int \dfrac{3}{\sqrt{2x-1}} \, dx$

2 Evaluate the following definite integrals.

   (i) $\int_1^5 \sqrt{x-1} \, dx$ **(ii)** $\int_1^3 (x+1)^3 \, dx$

   (iii) $\int_{-1}^4 (x-3)^4 \, dx$ **(iv)** $\int_0^3 (4-2x)^5 \, dx$

   (v) $\int_5^9 \sqrt{x-5} \, dx$ **(vi)** $\int_2^{10} \sqrt{x-1} \, dx$

3 The graph of $y = (x-2)^3$ is shown here.

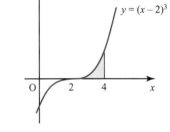

   (i) Evaluate $\int_2^4 (x-2)^3 \, dx$.

   (ii) Without doing any calculations, state what you think the value of $\int_0^2 (x-2)^3 \, dx$ would be. Give reasons.

   (iii) Confirm your answer by carrying out the integration.

4 The graph of $y = (x-1)^4 - 1$ is shown here.

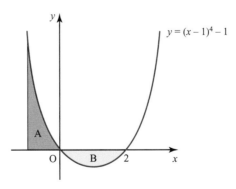

   (i) Find the area of the shaded region A by evaluating $\int_{-1}^0 \left((x-1)^4 - 1 \right) dx$.

   (ii) Find the area of the shaded region B by evaluating an appropriate integral.

   (iii) Write down the area of the total shaded region.

   (iv) Why could you not just evaluate $\int_{-1}^2 \left((x-1)^4 - 1 \right) dx$ to find the total area?

5 Find the area of the shaded region for each of the following graphs.

(i)

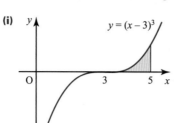

(ii)

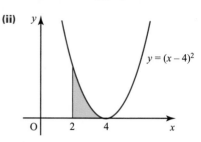

6 The equation of a curve is such that $\dfrac{dy}{dx} = \dfrac{6}{\sqrt{3x-2}}$. Given that the curve passes through the point P(2, 9), find

    (i) the equation of the normal to the curve at P

    (ii) the equation of the curve.

7 A curve is such that $\dfrac{dy}{dx} = \dfrac{4}{\sqrt{6-2x}}$, and P(1, 8) is a point on the curve.

    (i) The normal to the curve at the point P meets the co-ordinate axes at Q and at R. Find the co-ordinates of the mid-point of QR.

    (ii) Find the equation of the curve.

[Cambridge AS & A Level Mathematics 9709, Paper 1 Q9 June 2006]

Improper integrals

ACTIVITY 6.4   Here is the graph of $y = \dfrac{1}{x^2}$. The shaded region is given by $\displaystyle\int_1^{\infty} \dfrac{1}{x^2}\,dx$.

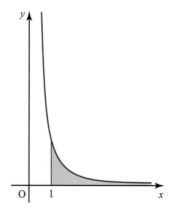

Figure 6.23

    (i) Work out the value of $\displaystyle\int_1^b \dfrac{1}{x^2}\,dx$ when

        (a) $b = 2$ **(b)** $b = 3$ **(c)** $b = 10$ **(d)** $b = 100$ **(e)** $b = 10\,000$.

    (ii) What do you think the value of $\displaystyle\int_1^{\infty} \dfrac{1}{x^2}\,dx$ is?

At first sight, $\int_1^\infty \frac{1}{x^2}\, dx = \left[-\frac{1}{x} \right]_1^\infty$ doesn't look like a particularly daunting integral. However, the upper limit is infinity, which is not a number; so when you get an answer of $1 - \frac{1}{\infty}$, you cannot work it out. Instead, you should start by looking at the case where you are finding the finite area between 1 and b (as you did in the activity). You can then say what happens to the value of $1 - \frac{1}{b}$ as b approaches (or tends to) infinity. This process of taking ever larger values of b, is called taking a limit. In this case you are finding the value of $1 - \frac{1}{b}$ in the limit as b tends to ∞.

You can write this formally as: $\int_1^b \frac{1}{x^2}\, dx = \left[-\frac{1}{x} \right]_1^b$

$$= \left(-\frac{1}{b} \right) - \left(-\frac{1}{1} \right)$$

$$= \left(-\frac{1}{b} \right) + 1$$

As $b \to \infty$ then $\int_1^b \frac{1}{x^2}\, dx$ becomes $\lim_{b \to \infty} \int_1^b \frac{1}{x^2}\, dx = \lim_{b \to \infty} \left(-\frac{1}{b} + 1 \right) = 1.$

❓ What is the value of $\int_a^\infty \frac{1}{x^2}\, dx$?

What can you say about $\int_0^\infty \frac{1}{x^2}\, dx$?

Integrals where one of the limits is infinity are called *improper integrals*.

There is a second type of improper integral, which is when the expression you want to integrate is not defined over the whole region between the two limits. In the example that follows the expression is $\frac{1}{\sqrt{x}}$ and it is not defined when $x = 0$.

EXAMPLE 6.17

Evaluate $\int_0^9 \frac{1}{\sqrt{x}}\, dx$.

SOLUTION

The diagram shows the graph of $y = \frac{1}{\sqrt{x}}$.

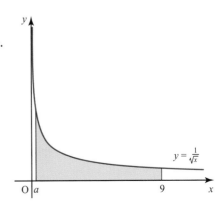

Figure 6.24

You can see that the expression is undefined at $x = 0$, so you need to find the integral from a to 9 and then take the limit as $a \rightarrow 0$ from above.

You can write: $\int_a^9 \frac{1}{\sqrt{x}} dx = \left[2x^{\frac{1}{2}} \right]_a^9$

$$= \left(2 \times 9^{\frac{1}{2}} \right) - \left(2a^{\frac{1}{2}} \right)$$

$$= 6 - 2a^{\frac{1}{2}}$$

So as a tends to zero, the integral tends to 6, and $\int_0^9 \frac{1}{\sqrt{x}} dx = 6$.

Notice, although the left-hand side of the curve is infinitely high, it has a finite area.

EXERCISE 6G

Evaluate the following improper integrals.

1 $\int_0^1 \frac{1}{\sqrt{x}} dx$

2 $\int_1^{\infty} \frac{1}{x^3} dx$

3 $\int_1^{\infty} \frac{2}{x^2} dx$

4 $\int_{-\infty}^{-2} \frac{2}{x^3} dx$

5 $\int_1^{\infty} -\frac{1}{x^2} dx$

6 $\int_0^4 \frac{6}{\sqrt{x}} dx$

Finding volumes by integration

When the shaded region in figure 6.25 is rotated through 360° about the x axis, the solid obtained, illustrated in figure 6.26, is called a *solid of revolution*.

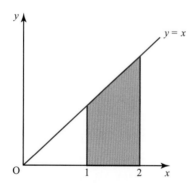

Figure 6.25   **Figure 6.26**

In this particular case, the volume of the solid could be calculated as the difference between the volumes of two cones $\left(\text{using } V = \frac{1}{3}\pi r^2 h \right)$, but if the line $y = x$ in figure 6.25 was replaced by a curve, such a simple calculation would no longer be possible.

1 Describe the solid of revolution obtained by a rotation through 360° of

(i) a rectangle about one side

(ii) a semi-circle about its diameter

(iii) a circle about a line outside the circle.

2 Calculate the volume of the solid obtained in figure 6.26, leaving your answer as a multiple of π.

Solids formed by rotation about the *x* axis

Now look at the solid formed by rotating the shaded region in figure 6.27 through 360° about the *x* axis.

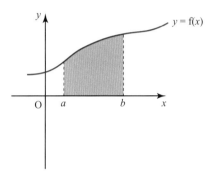

Figure 6.27　　　　　　　　**Figure 6.28**

The volume of the solid of revolution (which is usually called the *volume of revolution*) can be found by imagining that the solid can be sliced into thin discs.

The disc shown in figure 6.28 is approximately cylindrical with radius *y* and thickness δ*x*, so its volume is given by

$$\delta V = \pi y^2 \delta x.$$

The volume of the solid is the limit of the sum of all these elementary discs as δ*x* → 0,

i.e. the limit as δ*x* → 0 of $\displaystyle\sum_{\substack{\text{over all}\\\text{discs}}} \delta V$

$$= \sum_{x=a}^{x=b} \pi y^2 \, \delta x.$$

The limiting values of sums such as these are integrals so

$$V = \int_a^b \pi y^2 \, \mathrm{d}x$$

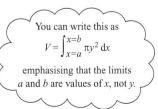

You can write this as

$$V = \int_{x=a}^{x=b} \pi y^2 \, \mathrm{d}x$$

emphasising that the limits *a* and *b* are values of *x*, not *y*.

The limits are *a* and *b* because *x* takes values from *a* to *b*.

Since the integration is 'with respect to x', indicated by the dx and the fact that the limits a and b are values of x, it cannot be evaluated unless the function y is also written in terms of x.

EXAMPLE 6.18

The region between the curve $y = x^2$, the x axis and the lines $x = 1$ and $x = 3$ is rotated through $360°$ about the x axis.

Find the volume of revolution which is formed.

SOLUTION

The region is shaded in figure 6.29.

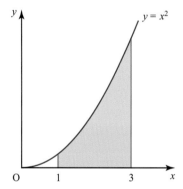

Figure 6.29

Using $V = \displaystyle\int_a^b \pi y^2 \, dx$

$$\text{volume} = \int_1^3 \pi (x^2)^2 \, dx$$

Since in this case $y = x^2$
$y^2 = (x^2)^2 = x^4$.

$$= \int_1^3 \pi x^4 \, dx$$

$$= \left[\frac{\pi x^5}{5} \right]_1^3$$

$$= \frac{\pi}{5}(243 - 1)$$

$$= \frac{242\pi}{5}.$$

The volume is $\dfrac{242\pi}{5}$ cubic units or 152 cubic units (3 s.f.).

 Unless a decimal answer is required, it is usual to leave π in the answer, which is then exact.

Solids formed by rotation about the *y* axis

When a region is rotated about the *y* axis a very different solid is obtained.

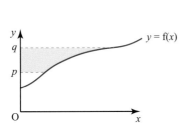

Figure 6.30　　　　　　　**Figure 6.31**

Notice the difference between the solid obtained in figure 6.31 and that in figure 6.28.

For rotation about the *x* axis you obtained the formula

$$V_{x \text{ axis}} = \int_a^b \pi y^2 \, dx.$$

In a similar way, the formula for rotation about the *y* axis

$$V_{y \text{ axis}} = \int_p^q \pi x^2 \, dy \text{ can be obtained.}$$

In this case you will need to substitute for x^2 in terms of *y*.

(p) How would you prove this result?

EXAMPLE 6.19

The region between the curve $y = x^2$, the *y* axis and the lines $y = 2$ and $y = 5$ is rotated through 360° about the *y* axis.
Find the volume of revolution which is formed.

SOLUTION

The region is shaded in figure 6.32.

Using $V = \int_p^q \pi x^2 \, dy$

$$\text{volume} = \int_2^5 \pi y \, dy \text{ since } x^2 = y$$

$$= \left[\frac{\pi y^2}{2} \right]_2^5$$

$$= \frac{\pi}{2} (25 - 4)$$

$$= \frac{21\pi}{2} \text{ cubic units.}$$

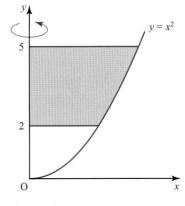

Figure 6.32

1   Name six common objects which are solids of revolution.

2   In each part of this question a region is defined in terms of the lines which form its boundaries. Draw a sketch of the region and find the volume of the solid obtained by rotating it through 360° about the x axis.

(i) $y = 2x$, the x axis and the lines $x = 1$ and $x = 3$

(ii) $y = x + 2$, the x axis, the y axis and the line $x = 2$

(iii) $y = x^2 + 1$, the x axis and the lines $x = -1$ and $x = 1$

(iv) $y = \sqrt{x}$, the x axis and the line $x = 4$

3   (i)   Sketch the line $4y = 3x$ for $x \geqslant 0$.

(ii) Identify the area between this line and the x axis which, when rotated through 360° about the x axis, would give a cone of base radius 3 and height 4.

(iii) Calculate the volume of the cone using

(a) integration

(b) a formula.

4   In each part of this question a region is defined in terms of the lines which form its boundaries. Draw a sketch of the region and find the volume of the solid obtained by rotating through 360° about the y axis.

(i) $y = 3x$, the y axis and the lines $y = 3$ and $y = 6$

(ii) $y = x - 3$, the y axis, the x axis and the line $y = 6$

(iii) $y = x^2 - 2$, the y axis and the line $y = 4$

5   A mathematical model for a large garden pot is obtained by rotating through 360° about the y axis the part of the curve $y = 0.1x^2$ which is between $x = 10$ and $x = 25$ and then adding a flat base. Units are in centimetres.

(i)   Draw a sketch of the curve and shade in the cross-section of the pot, indicating which line will form its base.

(ii) Garden compost is sold in litres. How many litres will be required to fill the pot to a depth of 45 cm? (Ignore the thickness of the pot.)

6 The graph shows the curve $y = x^2 - 4$. The region R is formed by the line $y = 12$, the x axis, the y axis and the curve $y = x^2 - 4$ for positive values of x.

(i) Copy the sketch graph and shade the region R.

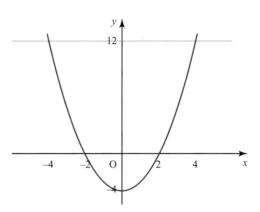

The inside of a vase is formed by rotating the region R through $360°$ about the y axis. Each unit of x and y represents $2\,\text{cm}$.

(ii) Write down an expression for the volume of revolution of the region R about the y axis.

(iii) Find the capacity of the vase in litres.

(iv) Show that when the vase is filled to $\frac{5}{6}$ of its internal height it is three-quarters full.

[MEI]

7 The diagram shows the curve $y = 3x^{\frac{1}{4}}$. The shaded region is bounded by the curve, the x axis and the lines $x = 1$ and $x = 4$.

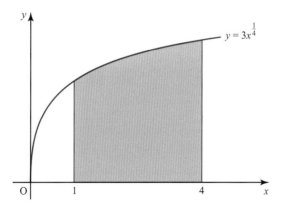

Find the volume of the solid obtained when this shaded region is rotated completely about the x axis, giving your answer in terms of π.

[Cambridge AS & A Level Mathematics 9709, Paper 1 Q2 June 2007]

8 The diagram shows part of the curve $y = \dfrac{a}{x}$, where a is a positive constant.

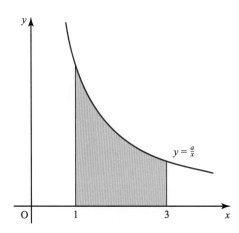

Given that the volume obtained when the shaded region is rotated through 360° about the x axis is 24π, find the value of a.

[Cambridge AS & A Level Mathematics 9709, Paper 12 Q2 June 2010]

KEY POINTS

1 $\dfrac{dy}{dx} = x^n \quad \Rightarrow \quad y = \dfrac{x^{n+1}}{n+1} + c \qquad n \neq -1$

2 $\displaystyle\int_a^b x^n \, dx = \left[\dfrac{x^{n+1}}{n+1} \right]_a^b = \dfrac{b^{n+1} - a^{n+1}}{n+1} \qquad n \neq -1$

3 Area $A = \displaystyle\int_a^b y \, dx$

$\qquad\quad = \displaystyle\int_a^b f(x) \, dx$

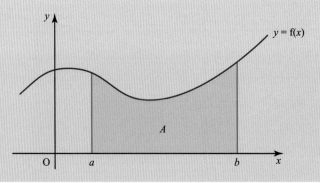

4 Area $B = \int_a^b (f(x) - g(x))\, dx$

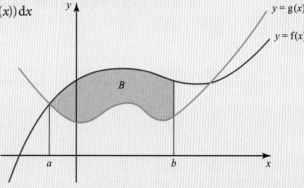

5 Area $C = \int_p^q x\, dy$

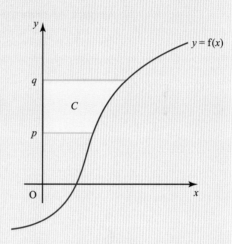

6 **Volumes of revolution**

About the x axis $V = \int_a^b \pi y^2\, dx$

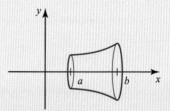

About the y axis $V = \int_p^q \pi x^2\, dy$

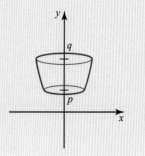

Trigonometry

**I must go down to the seas again, to the lonely sea and the sky,
And all I ask is a tall ship and a star to steer her by.**

John Masefield

ⓑ Trigonometry background

Angles of elevation and depression

The angle of elevation is the angle between the horizontal and a direction above the horizontal (see figure 7.1). The angle of depression is the angle between the horizontal and a direction below the horizontal (see figure 7.2).

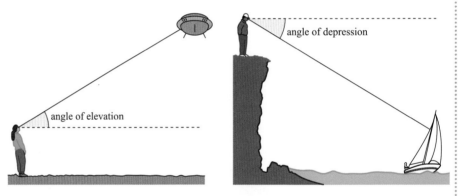

Figure 7.1   **Figure 7.2**

Bearing

The bearing (or compass bearing) is the direction measured as an angle from north, clockwise (see figure 7.3).

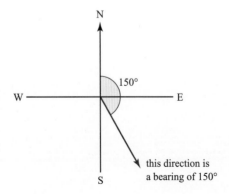

Figure 7.3

Trigonometrical functions

The simplest definitions of the trigonometrical functions are given in terms of the ratios of the sides of a right-angled triangle, for values of the angle θ between 0° and 90°.

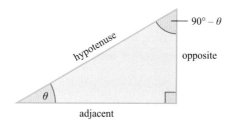

Figure 7.4

In figure 7.4

$$\sin\theta = \frac{\text{opposite}}{\text{hypotenuse}} \qquad \cos\theta = \frac{\text{adjacent}}{\text{hypotenuse}} \qquad \tan\theta = \frac{\text{opposite}}{\text{adjacent}}.$$

Sin is an abbreviation of sine, cos of cosine and tan of tangent. You will see from the triangle in figure 7.4 that

$$\sin\theta = \cos(90° - \theta) \text{ and } \cos\theta = \sin(90° - \theta).$$

Special cases

Certain angles occur frequently in mathematics and you will find it helpful to know the value of their trigonometrical functions.

(i) The angles 30° and 60°

In figure 7.5, triangle ABC is an equilateral triangle with side 2 units, and AD is a line of symmetry.

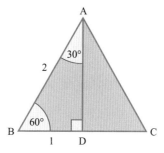

Figure 7.5

Using Pythagoras' theorem

$$AD^2 + 1^2 = 2^2 \implies AD = \sqrt{3}.$$

From triangle ABD,

$$\sin 60° = \frac{\sqrt{3}}{2}; \qquad \cos 60° = \frac{1}{2}; \qquad \tan 60° = \sqrt{3};$$

$$\sin 30° = \frac{1}{2}; \qquad \cos 30° = \frac{\sqrt{3}}{2}; \qquad \tan 30° = \frac{1}{\sqrt{3}}.$$

EXAMPLE 7.1

Without using a calculator, find the value of $\cos 60° \sin 30° + \cos^2 30°$.
(Note that $\cos^2 30°$ means $(\cos 30°)^2$.)

SOLUTION

$$\cos 60° \sin 30° + \cos^2 30° = \frac{1}{2} \times \frac{1}{2} + \left(\frac{\sqrt{3}}{2}\right)^2$$

$$= \frac{1}{4} + \frac{3}{4}$$

$$= 1.$$

(ii) The angle 45°

In figure 7.6, triangle PQR is a right-angled isosceles triangle with equal sides of length 1 unit.

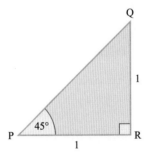

Figure 7.6

Using Pythagoras' theorem, $PQ = \sqrt{2}$.

This gives

$$\sin 45° = \frac{1}{\sqrt{2}}; \qquad \cos 45° = \frac{1}{\sqrt{2}}; \qquad \tan 45° = 1.$$

(iii) The angles 0° and 90°

Although you cannot have an angle of 0° in a triangle (because one side would be lying on top of another), you can still imagine what it might look like. In figure 7.7, the hypotenuse has length 1 unit and the angle at X is very small.

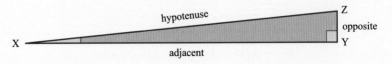

Figure 7.7

If you imagine the angle at X becoming smaller and smaller until it is zero, you can deduce that

$$\sin 0° = \frac{0}{1} = 0; \qquad \cos 0° = \frac{1}{1} = 1; \qquad \tan 0° = \frac{0}{1} = 0.$$

If the angle at X is 0°, then the angle at Z is 90°, and so you can also deduce that

$$\sin 90° = \frac{1}{1} = 1; \qquad \cos 90° = \frac{0}{1} = 0.$$

However when you come to find tan 90°, there is a problem. The triangle suggests this has value $\frac{1}{0}$, but you cannot divide by zero.

If you look at the triangle XYZ, you will see that what we actually did was to draw it with angle X not zero but just very small, and to argue:

'We can see from this what will happen if the angle becomes smaller and smaller so that it is effectively zero.'

? Compare this argument with the ideas about limits which you met in Chapters 5 and 6 on differentiation and integration.

In this case we are looking at the limits of the values of sin θ, cos θ and tan θ as the angle θ approaches zero. The same approach can be used to look again at the problem of tan 90°.

If the angle X is not quite zero, then the side ZY is also not quite zero, and tan Z is 1 (XY is almost 1) divided by a very small number and so is large. The smaller the angle X, the smaller the side ZY and so the larger the value of tan Z. We conclude that in the limit when angle X becomes zero and angle Z becomes 90°, tan Z is infinitely large, and so we say

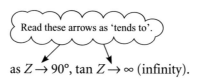

Read these arrows as 'tends to'.

as $Z \to 90°$, tan $Z \to \infty$ (infinity).

You can see this happening in the table of values below.

Z	tan Z
80°	5.67
89°	57.29
89.9°	572.96
89.99°	5729.6
89.999°	57 296

When Z actually equals 90°, we say that tan Z is *undefined*.

Positive and negative angles

Unless given in the form of bearings, angles are measured from the x axis (see figure 7.8). Anticlockwise is taken to be positive and clockwise to be negative.

Figure 7.8

EXAMPLE 7.2

In the diagram, angles ADB and CBD are right angles, angle BAD = 60°, AB = 2l and BC = 3l.

Find the angle θ.

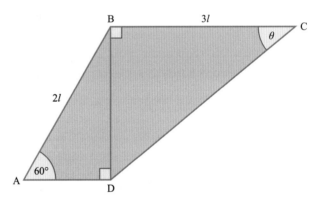

Figure 7.9

SOLUTION

First, find an expression for BD.

In triangle ABD, $\dfrac{BD}{AB} = \sin 60°$ — AB = 2l

$\Rightarrow \qquad BD = 2l\sin 60°$

$= 2l \times \dfrac{\sqrt{3}}{2}$

$= \sqrt{3}l$

In triangle BCD, $\tan\theta = \dfrac{BD}{BC}$

$$= \frac{\sqrt{3}l}{3l}$$

$$= \frac{1}{\sqrt{3}}$$

$$\Rightarrow \qquad \theta = \tan^{-1}\left(\frac{1}{\sqrt{3}}\right)$$

$$= 30°$$

EXERCISE 7A

1 In the triangle PQR, PQ = 17 cm, QR = 15 cm and PR = 8 cm.

  (i) Show that the triangle is right-angled.

  (ii) Write down the values of sin Q, cos Q and tan Q, leaving your answers as fractions.

  (iii) Use your answers to part **(ii)** to show that

    (a) $\sin^2 Q + \cos^2 Q = 1$

    (b) $\tan Q = \dfrac{\sin Q}{\cos Q}$

2 Without using a calculator, show that:

  (i) $\sin 60°\cos 30° + \cos 60°\sin 30° = 1$

  (ii) $\sin^2 30° + \sin^2 45° = \sin^2 60°$

  (iii) $3\sin^2 30° = \cos^2 30°$.

3 In the diagram, AB = 10 cm, angle BAC = 30°, angle BCD = 45° and angle BDC = 90°.

  (i) Find the length of BD.

  (ii) Show that AC = $5\left(\sqrt{3} - 1\right)$ cm.

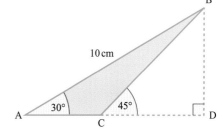

4 In the diagram, OA = 1 cm, angle AOB = angle BOC = angle COD = 30° and angle OAB = angle OBC = angle OCD = 90°.

  (i) Find the length of OD giving your answer in the form $a\sqrt{3}$.

  (ii) Show that the perimeter of OABCD is $\dfrac{5}{3}\left(1 + \sqrt{3}\right)$ cm.

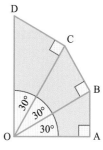

5 In the diagram, ABED is a trapezium with right angles at E and D, and CED is a straight line. The lengths of AB and BC are $2d$ and $\left(2\sqrt{3}\right)d$ respectively, and angles BAD and CBE are 30° and 60° respectively.

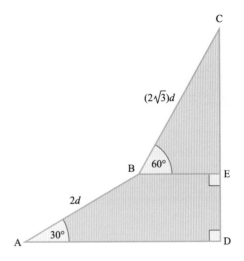

(i) Find the length of CD in terms of d.

(ii) Show that angle CAD $= \tan^{-1}\left(\dfrac{2}{\sqrt{3}}\right)$.

[Cambridge AS & A Level Mathematics 9709, Paper 1 Q3 November 2005]

6 In the diagram, ABC is a triangle in which AB = 4 cm, BC = 6 cm and angle ABC = 150°. The line CX is perpendicular to the line ABX.

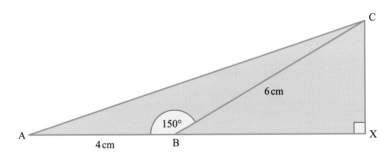

(i) Find the exact length of BX and show that angle CAB $= \tan^{-1}\left(\dfrac{3}{4 + 3\sqrt{3}}\right)$.

(ii) Show that the exact length of AC is $\sqrt{(52 + 24\sqrt{3})}$ cm.

[Cambridge AS & A Level Mathematics 9709, Paper 1 Q6 June 2006]

Trigonometrical functions for angles of any size

Is it possible to extend the use of the trigonometrical functions to angles greater than 90°, like sin 120°, cos 275° or tan 692°? The answer is yes – provided you change the definition of sine, cosine and tangent to one that does not require the angle to be in a right-angled triangle. It is not difficult to extend the definitions, as follows.

First look at the right-angled triangle in figure 7.10 which has hypotenuse of unit length.

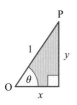

Figure 7.10

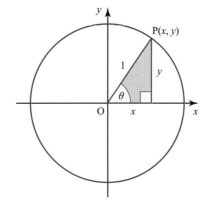

Figure 7.11

This gives rise to the definitions:

$$\sin\theta = \frac{y}{1} = y; \qquad \cos\theta = \frac{x}{1} = x; \qquad \tan\theta = \frac{y}{x}.$$

Now think of the angle θ being situated at the origin, as in figure 7.11, and allow θ to take any value. The vertex marked P has co-ordinates (x, y) and can now be anywhere on the unit circle.

You can now see that the definitions above can be applied to *any* angle θ, whether it is positive or negative, and whether it is less than or greater than 90°

$$\sin\theta = y, \qquad \cos\theta = x, \qquad \tan\theta = \frac{y}{x}.$$

For some angles, x or y (or both) will take a negative value, so the sign of $\sin\theta$, $\cos\theta$ and $\tan\theta$ will vary accordingly.

ACTIVITY 7.1 Draw x and y axes. For each of the four quadrants formed, work out the sign of $\sin\theta$, $\cos\theta$ and $\tan\theta$, from the definitions above.

Identities involving sin θ, cos θ and tan θ

Since $\tan\theta = \frac{y}{x}$ and $y = \sin\theta$ and $x = \cos\theta$ it follows that

$$\tan\theta = \frac{\sin\theta}{\cos\theta}.$$

It would be more accurate here to use the identity sign, ≡, since the relationship is true for all values of θ

$$\tan\theta \equiv \frac{\sin\theta}{\cos\theta}.$$

An *identity* is different from an equation since an equation is only true for certain values of the variable, called the *solution* of the equation. For example, $\tan\theta = 1$ is an equation: it is true when $\theta = 45°$ or $225°$, but not when it takes any other value in the range $0° \leqslant \theta \leqslant 360°$.

By contrast, an *identity* is true for all values of the variable, for example

$$\tan 30° = \frac{\sin 30°}{\cos 30°}, \qquad \tan 72° = \frac{\sin 72°}{\cos 72°}, \qquad \tan(-339°) = \frac{\sin(-399°)}{\cos(-399°)},$$

and so on for all values of the angle.

In this book, as in mathematics generally, we often use an equals sign where it would be more correct to use an identity sign. The identity sign is kept for situations where we really want to emphasise that the relationship is an identity and not an equation.

Another useful identity can be found by applying Pythagoras' theorem to any point $P(x, y)$ on the unit circle

$$y^2 + x^2 \equiv OP^2$$

$$(\sin \theta)^2 + (\cos \theta)^2 \equiv 1.$$

This is written as

$$\sin^2 \theta + \cos^2 \theta \equiv 1.$$

You can use the identities $\tan \theta \equiv \dfrac{\sin \theta}{\cos \theta}$ and $\sin^2 \theta + \cos^2 \theta \equiv 1$ to prove other identities are true.

There are two methods you can use to prove an identity; you can use either method or a mixture of both.

Method 1

When both sides of the identity look equally complicated you can work with both the left-hand side (LHS) and the right-hand side (RHS) and show that LHS – RHS = 0.

EXAMPLE 7.3

Prove the identity $\cos^2 \theta - \sin^2 \theta \equiv 2\cos^2 \theta - 1$.

SOLUTION

Both sides look equally complicated, so show LHS – RHS = 0.

So you need to show $\cos^2 \theta - \sin^2 \theta - 2\cos^2 \theta + 1 \equiv 0$.

Simplifying:

$$\begin{aligned}
\cos^2 \theta - \sin^2 \theta - 2\cos^2 \theta + 1 &\equiv -\cos^2 \theta - \sin^2 \theta + 1 \\
&\equiv -(\cos^2 \theta + \sin^2 \theta) + 1 \\
&\equiv -1 + 1 \quad \longleftarrow \text{Using } \sin^2\theta + \cos^2\theta = 1. \\
&\equiv 0 \text{ as required}
\end{aligned}$$

Method 2

When one side of the identity looks more complicated than the other side, you can work with this side until you end up with the same as the simpler side.

EXAMPLE 7.4

Prove the identity $\dfrac{\cos\theta}{1-\sin\theta} - \dfrac{1}{\cos\theta} \equiv \tan\theta$.

SOLUTION

The LHS of this identity is more complicated, so manipulate the LHS until you end up with $\tan\theta$.

Write the LHS as a single fraction:

$$\frac{\cos\theta}{1-\sin\theta} - \frac{1}{\cos\theta} \equiv \frac{\cos^2\theta - (1-\sin\theta)}{\cos\theta(1-\sin\theta)}$$

$$\equiv \frac{\cos^2\theta + \sin\theta - 1}{\cos\theta(1-\sin\theta)}$$

Since $\sin^2\theta + \cos^2\theta \equiv 1$, $\cos^2\theta \equiv 1 - \sin^2\theta$

$$\equiv \frac{1 - \sin^2\theta + \sin\theta - 1}{\cos\theta(1-\sin\theta)}$$

$$\equiv \frac{\sin\theta - \sin^2\theta}{\cos\theta(1-\sin\theta)} \equiv \frac{\sin\theta(1-\sin\theta)}{\cos\theta(1-\sin\theta)}$$

$$\equiv \frac{\sin\theta}{\cos\theta}$$

$$\equiv \tan\theta \text{ as required}$$

EXERCISE 7B

Prove each of the following identities.

1 $1 - \cos^2\theta \equiv \sin^2\theta$

2 $(1 - \sin^2\theta)\tan\theta \equiv \cos\theta\sin\theta$

3 $\dfrac{1}{\sin^2\theta} - \dfrac{\cos^2\theta}{\sin^2\theta} \equiv 1$

4 $\tan^2\theta \equiv \dfrac{1}{\cos^2\theta} - 1$

5 $\dfrac{\sin^2\theta - 3\cos^2\theta + 1}{\sin^2\theta - \cos^2\theta} \equiv 2$

6 $\dfrac{1}{\cos^2\theta} + \dfrac{1}{\sin^2\theta} \equiv \dfrac{1}{\cos^2\theta\sin^2\theta}$

7 $\tan\theta + \dfrac{\cos\theta}{\sin\theta} \equiv \dfrac{1}{\sin\theta\cos\theta}$

8 $\dfrac{1}{1+\sin\theta} + \dfrac{1}{1-\sin\theta} \equiv \dfrac{2}{\cos^2\theta}$

9 Prove the identity $\dfrac{1 - \tan^2 x}{1 + \tan^2 x} \equiv 1 - 2\sin^2 x$.

[Cambridge AS & A Level Mathematics 9709, Paper 1 Q3 June 2007]

225

10 Prove the identity $\dfrac{1+\sin x}{\cos x} + \dfrac{\cos x}{1+\sin x} \equiv \dfrac{2}{\cos x}$

[Cambridge AS & A Level Mathematics 9709, Paper 1 Q2 November 2008]

11 Prove the identity $\dfrac{\sin x}{1-\sin x} - \dfrac{\sin x}{1+\sin x} \equiv 2\tan^2 x.$

[Cambridge AS & A Level Mathematics 9709, Paper 1 Q1 June 2009]

The sine and cosine graphs

In figure 7.12, angles have been drawn at intervals of 30° in the unit circle, and the resulting y co-ordinates plotted relative to the axes on the right. They have been joined with a continuous curve to give the graph of $\sin \theta$ for $0° \leqslant \theta \leqslant 360°$.

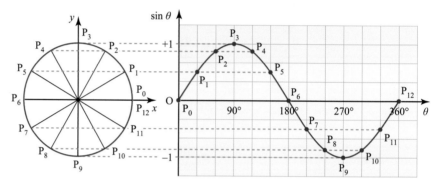

Figure 7.12

The angle 390° gives the same point P_1 on the circle as the angle 30°, the angle 420° gives point P_2 and so on. You can see that for angles from 360° to 720° the sine wave will simply repeat itself, as shown in figure 7.13. This is true also for angles from 720° to 1080° and so on.

Since the curve repeats itself every 360° the sine function is described as *periodic*, with *period* 360°.

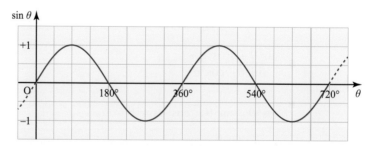

Figure 7.13

In a similar way you can transfer the x co-ordinates on to a set of axes to obtain the graph of $\cos \theta$. This is most easily illustrated if you first rotate the circle through 90° anticlockwise.

Figure 7.14 shows the circle in this new orientation, together with the resulting graph.

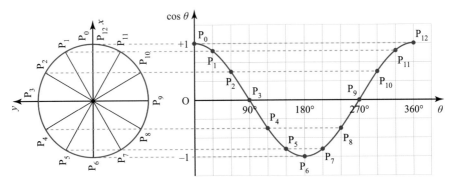

Figure 7.14

For angles in the interval $360° < \theta < 720°$, the cosine curve will repeat itself. You can see that the cosine function is also periodic with a period of $360°$.

Notice that the graphs of $\sin \theta$ and $\cos \theta$ have exactly the same shape. The cosine graph can be obtained by translating the sine graph $90°$ to the left, as shown in figure 7.15.

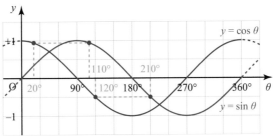

Figure 7.15

From the graphs it can be seen that, for example

$$\cos 20° = \sin 110°, \cos 90° = \sin 180°, \cos 120° = \sin 210°, \text{ etc.}$$

In general

$$\cos \theta \equiv \sin (\theta + 90°).$$

1 What do the graphs of $\sin \theta$ and $\cos \theta$ look like for negative angles?

2 Draw the curve of $\sin \theta$ for $0° \leqslant \theta \leqslant 90°$.

Using only reflections, rotations and translations of this curve, how can you generate the curves of $\sin \theta$ and $\cos \theta$ for $0° \leqslant \theta \leqslant 360°$?

The tangent graph

The value of $\tan\theta$ can be worked out from the definition $\tan\theta = \dfrac{y}{x}$ or by using $\tan\theta = \dfrac{\sin\theta}{\cos\theta}$.

You have already seen that $\tan\theta$ is undefined for $\theta = 90°$. This is also the case for all other values of θ for which $\cos\theta = 0$, namely 270°, 450°, …, and −90°, −270°, …

The graph of $\tan\theta$ is shown in figure 7.16. The dotted lines $\theta = \pm90°$ and $\theta = 270°$ are *asymptotes*. They are not actually part of the curve. The branches of the curve get closer and closer to them without ever quite reaching them.

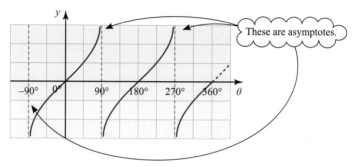

These are asymptotes.

Figure 7.16

> *Note*
>
> The graph of $\tan\theta$ is periodic, like those for $\sin\theta$ and $\cos\theta$, but in this case the period is 180°. Again, the curve for $0 \leqslant \theta < 90°$ can be used to generate the rest of the curve using rotations and translations.

ACTIVITY 7.2

Draw the graphs of $y = \sin\theta$, $y = \cos\theta$, and $y = \tan\theta$ for values of θ between −90° and 450°.

These graphs are very important. Keep them handy because they will be useful for solving trigonometrical equations.

> *Note*
>
> Some people use this diagram to help them remember when sin, cos and tan are positive, and when they are negative. A means all positive in this quadrant, S means sin positive, cos and tan negative, etc.

S	A
T	C

Figure 7.17

Solving equations using graphs of trigonometrical functions

Suppose that you want to solve the equation $\cos\theta = 0.5$.

You press the calculator keys for $\cos^{-1} 0.5$ (or arccos 0.5 or invcos 0.5), and the answer comes up as 60°.

However, by looking at the graph of $y = \cos\theta$ (your own or figure 7.18) you can see that there are in fact infinitely many roots to this equation.

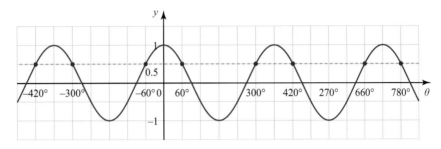

Figure 7.18

You can see from the graph of $y = \cos\theta$ that the roots for $\cos\theta = 0.5$ are:

$$\theta = ..., -420°, -300°, -60°, 60°, 300°, 420°, 660°, 780°, ...$$

The functions cosine, sine and tangent are all many-to-one mappings, so their inverse mappings are one-to-many. Thus the problem 'find cos 60°' has only one solution, 0.5, whilst 'find θ such that $\cos\theta = 0.5$' has infinitely many solutions.

Remember, that a function has to be either one-to-one or many-to-one; so in order to define inverse functions for cosine, sine and tangent, a restriction has to be placed on the domain of each so that it becomes a one-to-one mapping. This means your calculator only gives one of the infinitely many solutions to the equation $\cos\theta = 0.5$. In fact, your calculator will always give the value of the solution between:

$$0° \leqslant \theta \leqslant 180° \quad (\cos)$$
$$-90° \leqslant \theta \leqslant 90° \quad (\sin)$$
$$-90° < \theta < 90° \quad (\tan).$$

The solution that your calculator gives you is called *principal value*.

Figure 7.19 shows the graphs of cosine, sine and tangent together with their principal values. You can see from the graph that the principal values cover the whole of the range (y values) for each function.

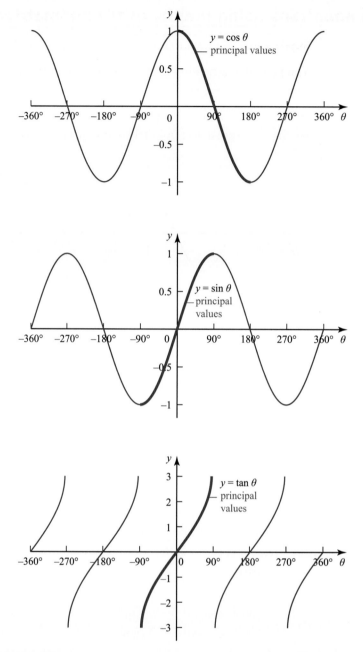

Figure 7.19

EXAMPLE 7.5

Find values of θ in the interval $-360° \le \theta \le 360°$ for which $\sin \theta = 0.5$.

SOLUTION

$\sin \theta = 0.5 \Rightarrow \sin^{-1} 0.5 = 30° \Rightarrow \theta = 30°$. Figure 7.20 shows the graph of $\sin \theta$.

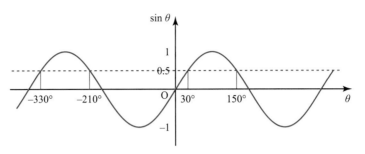

Figure 7.20

The values of θ for which $\sin \theta = 0.5$ are $-330°$, $-210°$, $30°$, $150°$.

EXAMPLE 7.6

Solve the equation $3\tan \theta = -1$ for $-180° \le \theta \le 180°$.

SOLUTION

$$3\tan \theta = -1$$
$$\Rightarrow \quad \tan \theta = -\tfrac{1}{3}$$
$$\Rightarrow \quad \theta = \tan^{-1}\left(-\tfrac{1}{3}\right)$$
$$\Rightarrow \quad \theta = -18.4° \text{ to 1 d.p. (calculator).}$$

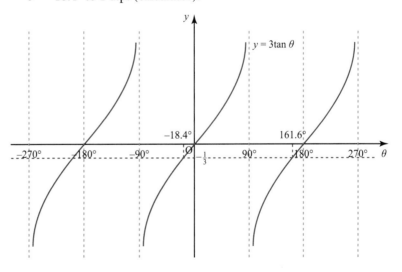

Figure 7.21

From figure 7.21, the other answer in the range is

$$\theta = -18.4° + 180°$$
$$= 161.6°$$

The values of θ are $-18.4°$ or $161.6°$ to 1 d.p.

How can you find further roots of the equation $3\tan\theta = -1$, outside the range $-180° \leq \theta \leq 180°$?

EXAMPLE 7.7

Find values of θ in the interval $0° \leq \theta \leq 360°$ for which $\tan^2\theta - \tan\theta = 2$.

SOLUTION

First rearrange the equation.

$$\tan^2\theta - \tan\theta = 2$$

$$\Rightarrow \qquad \tan^2\theta - \tan\theta - 2 = 0$$

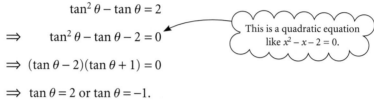

This is a quadratic equation like $x^2 - x - 2 = 0$.

$$\Rightarrow (\tan\theta - 2)(\tan\theta + 1) = 0$$

$$\Rightarrow \tan\theta = 2 \text{ or } \tan\theta = -1.$$

$\tan\theta = 2 \quad \Rightarrow \quad \theta = 63.4° \text{ (calculator)}$

$\qquad\qquad\qquad$ or $\theta = 63.4° + 180°$ (see figure 7.22)

$\qquad\qquad\qquad\qquad = 243.4°.$

$\tan\theta = -1 \quad \Rightarrow \quad \theta = -45° \text{ (calculator)}.$

This is not in the range $0° \leq \theta \leq 360°$ so figure 7.22 is used to give

$$\theta = -45° + 180° = 135°$$

or $\qquad\qquad\qquad \theta = -45° + 360° = 315°.$

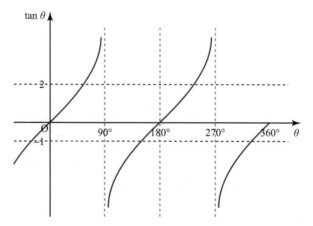

Figure 7.22

The values of θ are 63.4°, 135°, 243.4°, 315°.

EXAMPLE 7.8

Solve the equation $2\sin^2\theta = \cos\theta + 1$ for $0° \leqslant \theta \leqslant 360°$.

SOLUTION

First use the identity $\sin^2\theta + \cos^2\theta = 1$ to obtain an equation containing only one trigonometrical function.

$$2\sin^2\theta = \cos\theta + 1$$

$$\Rightarrow \quad 2(1 - \cos^2\theta) = \cos\theta + 1$$

$$\Rightarrow \quad 2 - 2\cos^2\theta = \cos\theta + 1$$

$$\Rightarrow \quad 0 = 2\cos^2\theta + \cos\theta - 1$$

$$\Rightarrow \quad 0 = (2\cos\theta - 1)(\cos\theta + 1)$$

$$\Rightarrow \quad 2\cos\theta - 1 = 0 \text{ or } \cos\theta + 1 = 0$$

$$\Rightarrow \quad \cos\theta = \tfrac{1}{2} \text{ or } \cos\theta = -1.$$

> This is a quadratic equation in $\cos\theta$. Rearrange it to equal zero and factorise it to solve the equation.

$\cos\theta = \tfrac{1}{2} \quad \Rightarrow \quad \theta = 60°$

$\qquad$ or $\theta = 360° - 60° = 300°$ (see figure 7.23).

$\cos\theta = -1 \quad \Rightarrow \quad \theta = 180°.$

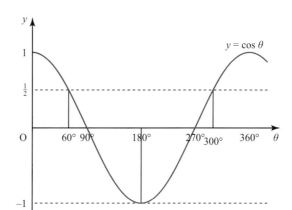

Figure 7.23

The values of θ are $60°$, $180°$ or $300°$.

EXERCISE 7C

1 (i) Sketch the curve $y = \sin x$ for $0° \leqslant x \leqslant 360°$.

(ii) Solve the equation $\sin x = 0.5$ for $0° \leqslant x \leqslant 360°$, and illustrate the two roots on your sketch.

(iii) State the other roots for $\sin x = 0.5$, given that x is no longer restricted to values between $0°$ and $360°$.

(iv) Write down, without using your calculator, the value of $\sin 330°$.

2 (i) Sketch the curve $y = \cos x$ for $-90° \leqslant x \leqslant 450°$.

(ii) Solve the equation $\cos x = 0.6$ for $-90° \leqslant x \leqslant 450°$, and illustrate all the roots on your sketch.

(iii) Sketch the curve $y = \sin x$ for $-90° \leqslant x \leqslant 450°$.

(iv) Solve the equation $\sin x = 0.8$ for $-90° \leqslant x \leqslant 450°$, and illustrate all the roots on your sketch.

(v) Explain why some of the roots of $\cos x = 0.6$ are the same as those for $\sin x = 0.8$, and why some are different.

3 Solve the following equations for $0° \leqslant x \leqslant 360°$.

(i) $\tan x = 1$ **(ii)** $\cos x = 0.5$ **(iii)** $\sin x = -\dfrac{\sqrt{3}}{2}$

(iv) $\tan x = -1$ **(v)** $\cos x = -0.9$ **(vi)** $\cos x = 0.2$

(vii) $\sin x = -0.25$ **(viii)** $\cos x = -1$

4 Write the following as integers, fractions, or using square roots. You should not need your calculator.

(i) $\sin 60°$ **(ii)** $\cos 45°$ **(iii)** $\tan 45°$

(iv) $\sin 150°$ **(v)** $\cos 120°$ **(vi)** $\tan 180°$

(vii) $\sin 390°$ **(viii)** $\cos (-30°)$ **(ix)** $\tan 315°$

5 In this question all the angles are in the interval $-180°$ to $180°$. Give all answers correct to 1 decimal place.

(i) Given that $\sin \alpha < 0$ and $\cos \alpha = 0.5$, find α.

(ii) Given that $\tan \beta = 0.4463$ and $\cos \beta < 0$, find β.

(iii) Given that $\sin \gamma = 0.8090$ and $\tan \gamma > 0$, find γ.

6 (i) Draw a sketch of the graph $y = \sin x$ and use it to demonstrate why $\sin x = \sin (180° - x)$.

(ii) By referring to the graphs of $y = \cos x$ and $y = \tan x$, state whether the following are true or false.

(a) $\cos x = \cos (180° - x)$ **(b)** $\cos x = -\cos (180° - x)$

(c) $\tan x = \tan (180° - x)$ **(d)** $\tan x = -\tan (180° - x)$

7 (i) For what values of α are $\sin \alpha$, $\cos \alpha$ and $\tan \alpha$ all positive?

(ii) Are there any values of α for which $\sin \alpha$, $\cos \alpha$ and $\tan \alpha$ are all negative? Explain your answer.

(iii) Are there any values of α for which $\sin \alpha$, $\cos \alpha$ and $\tan \alpha$ are all equal? Explain your answer.

8 Solve the following equations for $0° \leqslant x \leqslant 360°$.

(i) $\sin x = 0.1$ **(ii)** $\cos x = 0.5$

(iii) $\tan x = -2$ **(iv)** $\sin x = -0.4$

(v) $\sin^2 x = 1 - \cos x$ **(vi)** $\sin^2 x = 1$

(vii) $1 - \cos^2 x = 2\sin x$ **(viii)** $\sin^2 x = 2\cos^2 x$

(ix) $2\sin^2 x = 3\cos x$ **(x)** $3\tan^2 x - 10\tan x + 3 = 0$

9 The diagram shows part of the curves $y = \cos x°$ and $y = \tan x°$ which intersect at the points A and B. Find the co-ordinates of A and B.

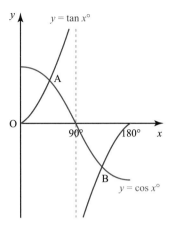

10 (i) Show that the equation $3(2\sin x - \cos x) = 2(\sin x - 3\cos x)$ can be written in the form $\tan x = -\frac{3}{4}$.

(ii) Solve the equation $3(2\sin x - \cos x) = 2(\sin x - 3\cos x)$, for $0° \leqslant x \leqslant 360°$.

[Cambridge AS & A Level Mathematics 9709, Paper 12 Q1 June 2010]

11 (i) Prove the identity $(\sin x + \cos x)(1 - \sin x \cos x) \equiv \sin^3 x + \cos^3 x$.

(ii) Solve the equation $(\sin x + \cos x)(1 - \sin x \cos x) = 9\sin^3 x$ for $0° \leqslant x \leqslant 360°$.

[Cambridge AS & A Level Mathematics 9709, Paper 12 Q5 November 2009]

12 (i) Show that the equation $\sin\theta + \cos\theta = 2(\sin\theta - \cos\theta)$ can be expressed as $\tan\theta = 3$.

(ii) Hence solve the equation $\sin\theta + \cos\theta = 2(\sin\theta - \cos\theta)$, for $0° \leqslant \theta \leqslant 360°$

[Cambridge AS & A Level Mathematics 9709, Paper 1 Q3 June 2005]

13 Solve the equation $3\sin^2\theta - 2\cos\theta - 3 = 0$, for $0° \leqslant x \leqslant 180°$.

[Cambridge AS & A Level Mathematics 9709, Paper 1 Q1 November 2005]

Circular measure

Have you ever wondered why angles are measured in degrees, and why there are 360° in one revolution?

There are various legends to support the choice of 360, most of them based in astronomy. One of these is that since the shepherd-astronomers of Sumeria thought that the solar year was 360 days long, this number was then used by the ancient Babylonian mathematicians to divide one revolution into 360 equal parts.

Degrees are not the only way in which you can measure angles. Some calculators have modes which are called 'rad' and 'gra' (or 'grad'); if yours is one of these, you have probably noticed that these give different answers when you are using the sin, cos or tan keys. These answers are only wrong when the calculator mode is different from the units being used in the calculation.

The *grade* (mode 'gra') is a unit which was introduced to give a means of angle measurement which was compatible with the metric system. There are 100 grades in a right angle, so when you are in the grade mode, sin 100 = 1, just as when you are in the degree mode, sin 90 = 1. Grades are largely of historical interest and are only mentioned here to remove any mystery surrounding this calculator mode.

By contrast, radians are used extensively in mathematics because they simplify many calculations. The *radian* (mode 'rad') is sometimes referred to as the natural unit of angular measure.

If, as in figure 7.24, the arc AB of a circle centre O is drawn so that it is equal in length to the radius of the circle, then the angle AOB is 1 radian, about 57.3°.

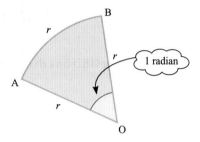

Figure 7.24

You will sometimes see 1 radian written as 1^c, just as 1 degree is written $1°$.

Since the circumference of a circle is given by $2\pi r$, it follows that the angle of a complete turn is 2π radians.

$$360° = 2\pi \text{ radians}$$

Consequently

$$180° = \pi \text{ radians}$$

$$90° = \frac{\pi}{2} \text{ radians}$$

$$60° = \frac{\pi}{3} \text{ radians}$$

$$45° = \frac{\pi}{4} \text{ radians}$$

$$30° = \frac{\pi}{6} \text{ radians}$$

To convert degrees into radians you multiply by $\frac{\pi}{180}$.

To convert radians into degrees multipy by $\frac{180}{\pi}$.

Note

1   If an angle is a simple fraction or multiple of 180° and you wish to give its value in radians, it is usual to leave the answer as a fraction of π.

2   When an angle is given as a multiple of π it is assumed to be in radians.

EXAMPLE 7.9

(i) Express in radians   **(a)** 30°   **(b)** 315°   **(c)** 29°.

(ii) Express in degrees   **(a)** $\dfrac{\pi}{12}$ **(b)** $\dfrac{8\pi}{3}$ **(c)** 1.2 radians.

SOLUTION

(i) **(a)** $30° = 30 \times \dfrac{\pi}{180} = \dfrac{\pi}{6}$

    (b) $315° = 315 \times \dfrac{\pi}{180} = \dfrac{7\pi}{4}$

    (c) $29° = 29 \times \dfrac{\pi}{180} = 0.506$ radians (to 3 s.f.).

(ii) **(a)** $\dfrac{\pi}{12} = \dfrac{\pi}{12} \times \dfrac{180}{\pi} = 15°$

    (b) $\dfrac{8\pi}{3} = \dfrac{8\pi}{3} \times \dfrac{180}{\pi} = 480°$

    (c) 1.2 radians $= 1.2 \times \dfrac{180}{\pi} = 68.8°$ (to 3 s.f.).

Using your calculator in radian mode

If you wish to find the value of, say, $\sin 1.4^c$ or $\cos \dfrac{\pi}{12}$, use the 'rad' mode on your calculator. This will give the answers directly – in these examples 0.9854... and 0.9659... .

You could alternatively convert the angles into degrees $\left(\text{by multiplying by } \dfrac{180}{\pi}\right)$ but this would usually be a clumsy method. It is much better to get into the habit of working in radians.

EXAMPLE 7.10

Solve $\sin\theta = \tfrac{1}{2}$ for $0 < \theta < 2\pi$ giving your answers as multiples of π.

SOLUTION

Since the answers are required as multiples of π it is easier to work in degrees first.

$\sin\theta = \tfrac{1}{2} \Rightarrow \theta = 30°$

$\theta = 30 \times \dfrac{\pi}{180} = \dfrac{\pi}{6}.$

From figure 7.25 there is a second value

$\theta = 150° = \dfrac{5\pi}{6}.$

The values of θ are $\dfrac{\pi}{6}$ and $\dfrac{5\pi}{6}.$

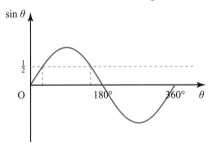

Figure 7.25

EXAMPLE 7.11

Solve $\tan^2 \theta = 2$ for $0 < \theta < \pi$.

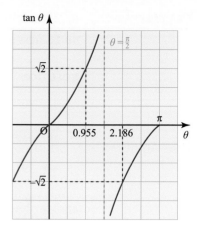

SOLUTION

Here the range $0 < \theta < \pi$ indicates that radians are required.

Since there is no request for multiples of π, set your calculator to radians.

$\tan^2 \theta = 2$

$\Rightarrow \tan \theta = \sqrt{2}$ or $\tan \theta = -\sqrt{2}$.

$\tan \theta = \sqrt{2} \quad \Rightarrow \theta = 0.955$ radians

$\tan \theta = -\sqrt{2} \quad \Rightarrow \theta = -0.955$ (not in range)

Figure 7.26

or $\quad \theta = -0.955 + \pi = 2.186$ radians.

The values of θ are 0.955 radians and 2.186 radians.

EXERCISE 7D

1 Express the following angles in radians, leaving your answers in terms of π where appropriate.

(i) 45°   (ii) 90°   (iii) 120°   (iv) 75°

(v) 300°   (vi) 23°   (vii) 450°   (viii) 209°

(ix) 150°   (x) 7.2°

2 Express the following angles in degrees, using a suitable approximation where necessary.

(i) $\dfrac{\pi}{10}$ (ii) $\dfrac{3\pi}{5}$ (iii) 2 radians   (iv) $\dfrac{4\pi}{9}$

(v) 3π (vi) $\dfrac{5\pi}{3}$ (vii) 0.4 radians   (viii) $\dfrac{3\pi}{4}$

(ix) $\dfrac{7\pi}{3}$ (x) $\dfrac{3\pi}{7}$

3 Write the following as fractions, or using square roots. You should not need your calculator.

(i) $\sin \dfrac{\pi}{4}$ (ii) $\tan \dfrac{\pi}{3}$ (iii) $\cos \dfrac{\pi}{6}$ (iv) $\cos \pi$

(v) $\tan \dfrac{3\pi}{4}$ (vi) $\sin \dfrac{2\pi}{3}$ (vii) $\tan \dfrac{4\pi}{3}$ (viii) $\cos \dfrac{3\pi}{4}$

(ix) $\sin \dfrac{5\pi}{6}$ (x) $\cos \dfrac{5\pi}{3}$

4 Solve the following equation for $0 \le \theta \le 2\pi$, giving your answers as multiples of π.

(i) $\cos \theta = \dfrac{\sqrt{3}}{2}$ (ii) $\tan \theta = 1$ (iii) $\sin \theta = \dfrac{1}{\sqrt{2}}$

(iv) $\sin \theta = -\dfrac{1}{2}$ (v) $\cos \theta = -\dfrac{1}{\sqrt{2}}$ (vi) $\tan \theta = \sqrt{3}$

5 Solve the following equations for $-\pi < \theta < \pi$.

   (i) $\sin \theta = 0.2$ (ii) $\cos \theta = 0.74$ (iii) $\tan \theta = 3$

   (iv) $4 \sin \theta = -1$ (v) $\cos \theta = -0.4$ (vi) $2 \tan \theta = -1$

6 Solve $3 \cos^2 \theta + 2 \sin \theta - 3 = 0$ for $0 \leqslant \theta \leqslant \pi$.

The length of an arc of a circle

From the definition of a radian, an angle of 1 radian at the centre of a circle corresponds to an arc of length r (the radius of the circle). Similarly, an angle of 2 radians corresponds to an arc length of $2r$ and, in general, an angle of θ radians corresponds to an arc length of θr, which is usually written $r\theta$ (figure 7.27).

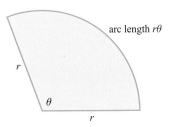

Figure 7.27

The area of a sector of a circle

A *sector* of a circle is the shape enclosed by an arc of the circle and two radii. It is the shape of a piece of cake. If the sector is smaller than a semi-circle it is called a *minor sector*; if it is larger than a semi-circle it is a *major sector*, see figure 7.28.

The area of a sector is a fraction of the area of the whole circle. The fraction is found by writing the angle θ as a fraction of one revolution, i.e. 2π (figure 7.29).

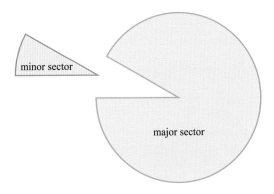

$$\text{Area} = \frac{\theta}{2\pi} \times \pi r^2$$
$$= \tfrac{1}{2} r^2 \theta.$$

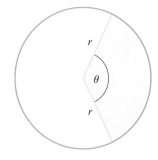

Figure 7.28   Figure 7.29

The following formulae often come in useful when solving problems involving sectors of circles.

For any triangle ABC:

The sine rule: $\dfrac{a}{\sin A} = \dfrac{b}{\sin B} = \dfrac{c}{\sin C}$

or $\dfrac{\sin A}{a} = \dfrac{\sin B}{b} = \dfrac{\sin C}{c}$

The cosine rule: $a^2 = b^2 + c^2 - 2bc\cos A$

or $\cos A = \dfrac{b^2 + c^2 - a^2}{2bc}$

The area of any triangle ABC $= \frac{1}{2}ab\sin C$.

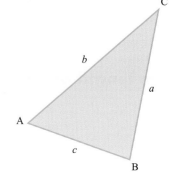

Figure 7.30

EXAMPLE 7.12

Figure 7.31 shows a sector of a circle, centre O, radius 6 cm. Angle AOB $= \dfrac{2\pi}{3}$ radians.

(i) (a) Calculate the arc length, perimeter and area of the sector.

(b) Find the area of the blue region.

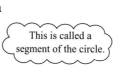
This is called a segment of the circle.

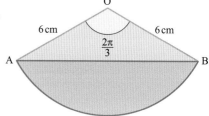

(ii) Find the exact length of the chord AB.

Figure 7.31

SOLUTION

(i) (a) Arc length $= r\theta$

$= 6 \times \dfrac{2\pi}{3}$

$= 4\pi$ cm

Perimeter $= 4\pi + 6 + 6 = 4\pi + 12$ cm

Area $= \frac{1}{2}r^2\theta = \frac{1}{2} \times 6^2 \times \dfrac{2\pi}{3} = 12\pi$ cm^2

(b) Area of segment = area of sector AOB – area of triangle AOB

The area of any triangle ABC $= \frac{1}{2}ab\sin C$.

Area of triangle AOB $= \frac{1}{2} \times 6 \times 6\sin\dfrac{2\pi}{3} = 18\dfrac{\sqrt{3}}{2} = 9\sqrt{3}$ cm^2

So area of segment $= 12\pi - 9\sqrt{3}$

$= 22.1$ cm^2

(ii) Use the cosine rule to find the length of the chord AB

$$a^2 = b^2 + c^2 - 2bc\cos A$$

Substitute in $b = 6$, $c = 6$ and $A = \dfrac{2\pi}{3}$

So $a^2 = 6^2 + 6^2 - 2 \times 6 \times 6\cos\dfrac{2\pi}{3}$

$$= 72 - 72 \times \left(-\tfrac{1}{2}\right) = 108$$

$$a = \sqrt{108} = 6\sqrt{3}\,\text{cm}$$

? How else could you find the area of triangle AOB and the length of AB?

EXERCISE 7E

1 Each row of the table gives dimensions of a sector of a circle of radius r cm. The angle subtended at the centre of the circle is θ radians, the arc length of the sector is s cm and its area is A cm^2. Copy and complete the table.

r (cm)	θ (rad)	s (cm)	A (cm^2)
5	$\dfrac{\pi}{4}$		
8	1		
4		2	
	$\dfrac{\pi}{3}$	$\dfrac{\pi}{2}$	
5			10
	0.8	1.5	
	$\dfrac{2\pi}{3}$		4π

2 (i) (a) Find the area of the sector OAB in the diagram.

(b) Show that the area of triangle OAB is $16\sin\dfrac{5\pi}{12}\cos\dfrac{5\pi}{12}$.

(c) Find the shaded area.

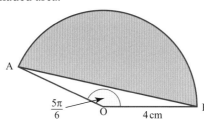

(ii) The diagram shows two circles, each of radius 4 cm, with each one passing through the centre of the other. Calculate the shaded area. (Hint: Add the common chord AB to the sketch.)

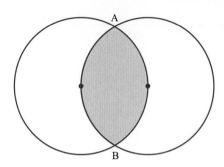

3 The diagram shows the cross-section of three pencils, each of radius 3.5 mm, held together by a stretched elastic band. Find

(i) the shaded area

(ii) the stretched length of the band.

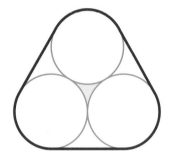

4 A circle, centre O, has two radii OA and OB. The line AB divides the circle into two regions with areas in the ratio 3:1.
If the angle AOB is θ (radians), show that

$$\theta - \sin\theta = \frac{\pi}{2}.$$

5 In a cricket match, a particular cricketer generally hits the ball anywhere in a sector of angle 100°. If the boundary (assumed circular) is 80 yards away, find

(i) the length of boundary which the fielders should patrol

(ii) the area of the ground which the fielders need to cover.

6 In the diagram, ABC is a semi-circle, centre O and radius 9 cm. The line BD is perpendicular to the diameter AC and angle AOB = 2.4 radians.

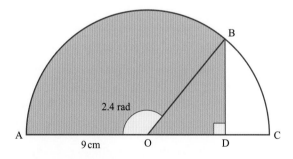

(i) Show that BD = 6.08 cm, correct to 3 significant figures.

(ii) Find the perimeter of the shaded region.

(iii) Find the area of the shaded region.

[Cambridge AS & A Level Mathematics 9709, Paper 1 Q8 June 2005]

7 In the diagram, OAB and OCD are radii of a circle, centre O and radius 16 cm. Angle AOC = α radians. AC and BD are arcs of circles, centre O and radii 10 cm and 16 cm respectively.

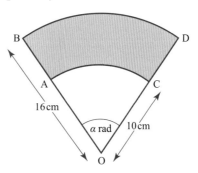

(i) In the case where $\alpha = 0.8$, find the area of the shaded region.

(ii) Find the value of α for which the perimeter of the shaded region is 28.9 cm.

[Cambridge AS & A Level Mathematics 9709, Paper 1 Q2 November 2005]

8 In the diagram, OAB is a sector of a circle with centre O and radius 12 cm. The lines AX and BX are tangents to the circle at A and B respectively. Angle AOB = $\frac{1}{3}\pi$ radians.

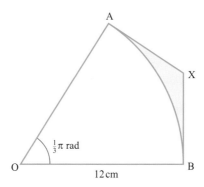

(i) Find the exact length of AX, giving your answer in terms of $\sqrt{3}$.

(ii) Find the area of the shaded region, giving your answer in terms of π and $\sqrt{3}$.

[Cambridge AS & A Level Mathematics 9709, Paper 1 Q5 June 2007]

9 In the diagram, the circle has centre O and radius 5 cm. The points P and Q lie on the circle, and the arc length PQ is 9 cm. The tangents to the circle at P and Q meet at the point T. Calculate

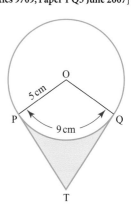

(i) angle POQ in radians

(ii) the length of PT

(iii) the area of the shaded region.

[Cambridge AS & A Level Mathematics 9709, Paper 1 Q6 November 2008]

10 In the diagram, AB is an arc of a circle, centre O and radius $r$cm, and angle AOB $= \theta$ radians. The point X lies on OB and AX is perpendicular to OB.

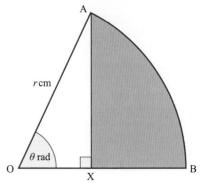

(i) Show that the area, Acm², of the shaded region AXB is given by

$$A = \tfrac{1}{2}r^2\left(\theta - \sin\theta\cos\theta\right)$$

(ii) In the case where $r = 12$ and $\theta = \tfrac{1}{6}\pi$, find the perimeter of the shaded region AXB, leaving your answer in terms of $\sqrt{3}$ and π.

[Cambridge AS & A Level Mathematics 9709, Paper 1 Q7 November 2007]

Other trigonometrical functions

You need to be able to sketch and work with other trigonometrical functions. Using transformations often helps you to do this.

e Transforming trigonometric functions

Translations

You have already seen in figure 7.15 that translating the sine graph 90° to the left gives the cosine graph.

In general, a translation of $\begin{pmatrix} -90° \\ 0 \end{pmatrix}$ moves the graph of $y = f(\theta)$ to $y = f(\theta + 90°)$.

So $\cos\theta = \sin(\theta + 90°)$.

Results from translations can also be used in plotting graphs such as $y = \sin\theta + 1$. This is the graph of $y = \sin\theta$ translated by 1 unit upwards, as shown in figure 7.32.

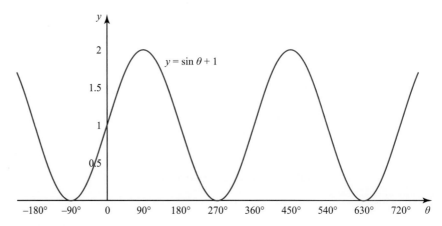

Figure 7.32

ACTIVITY 7.3   Figure 7.33 shows the graphs of $y = \sin x$ and $y = 2 + \sin x$ for $0° \leqslant x \leqslant 360°$.

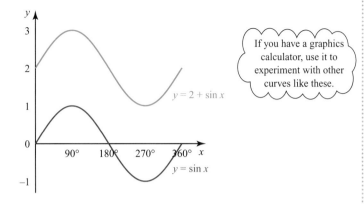

Figure 7.33

Describe the transformation that maps the curve $y = \sin x$ on to the curve $y = 2 + \sin x$.

Complete this statement.

'In general, the curve $y = f(x) + s$ is obtained from $y = f(x)$ by ... .'

ACTIVITY 7.4   Figure 7.34 shows the graphs of $y = \sin x$ and $y = \sin (x - 45°)$ for $0° \leqslant x \leqslant 360°$.

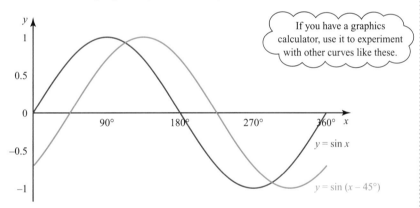

Figure 7.34

Describe the transformation that maps the curve $y = \sin x$ on to the curve $y = \sin (x - 45°)$.

Complete this statement.

'In general, the curve $y = f(x - t)$ is obtained from $y = f(x)$ by ... .'

Reflections

ACTIVITY 7.5   Figure 7.35 shows the graphs of $y = \sin x$ and $y = -\sin x$ for $0° \leqslant x \leqslant 360°$.

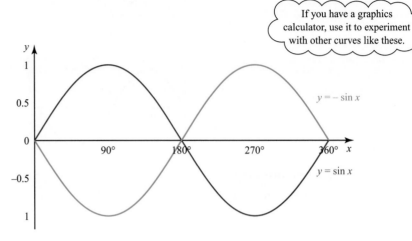

> If you have a graphics calculator, use it to experiment with other curves like these.

Figure 7.35

Describe the transformation that maps the curve $y = \sin x$ on to the curve $y = -\sin x$.

Complete this statement.

'In general, the curve $y = -f(x)$ is obtained from $y = f(x)$ by ... .'

One-way stretches

ACTIVITY 7.6   Figure 7.36 shows the graphs of $y = \sin x$ and $y = 2 \sin x$ for $0° \leqslant x \leqslant 180°$.

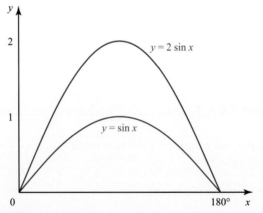

> If you have a graphics calculator, use it to experiment with other curves like these.

Figure 7.36

What do you notice about the value of the y co-ordinate of a point on the curve $y = \sin x$ and the y co-ordinate of a point on the curve $y = 2 \sin x$ for any value of x?

Can you describe the transformation that maps the curve $y = \sin x$ on to the curve $y = 2 \sin x$?

ACTIVITY 7.7

Figure 7.37 shows the graphs of $y = \sin x$ and $y = \sin 2x$ for $0° \leqslant x \leqslant 360°$.

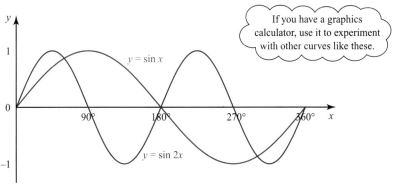

If you have a graphics calculator, use it to experiment with other curves like these.

Figure 7.37

What do you notice about the value of the x co-ordinate of a point on the curve $y = \sin x$ and the x co-ordinate of a point on the curve $y = \sin 2x$ for any value of y?

Can you describe the transformation that maps the curve $y = \sin x$ on to the curve $y = \sin 2x$?

EXAMPLE 7.13

Starting with the curve $y = \cos x$, show how transformations can be used to sketch these curves.

(i) $y = \cos 3x$ (ii) $y = 3 + \cos x$

(iii) $y = \cos (x - 60°)$ (iv) $y = 2 \cos x$

SOLUTION

(i) The curve with equation $y = \cos 3x$ is obtained from the curve with equation $y = \cos x$ by a stretch of scale factor $\frac{1}{3}$ parallel to the x axis. There will therefore be one complete oscillation of the curve in 120° (instead of 360°). This is shown in figure 7.38.

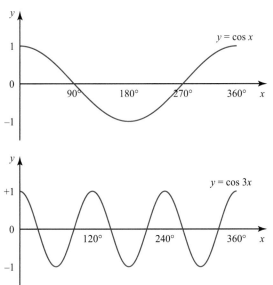

Figure 7.38

(ii) The curve of $y = 3 + \cos x$ is obtained from that of $y = \cos x$ by a translation $\begin{pmatrix} 0 \\ 3 \end{pmatrix}$.

The curve therefore oscillates between $y = 4$ and $y = 2$ (see figure 7.39).

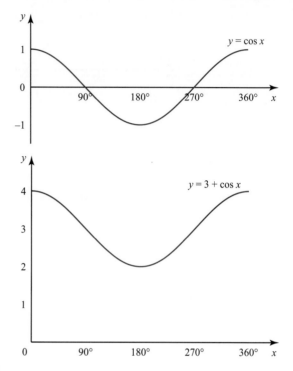

Figure 7.39

(iii) The curve of $y = \cos (x - 60°)$ is obtained from that of $y = \cos x$ by a

translation of $\begin{pmatrix} 60° \\ 0 \end{pmatrix}$ (see figure 7.40).

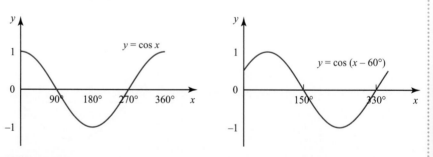

Figure 7.40

(iv) The curve of $y = 2\cos x$ is obtained from that of $y = \cos x$ by a stretch of scale factor 2 parallel to the y axis. The curve therefore oscillates between $y = 2$ and $y = -2$ (instead of between $y = 1$ and $y = -1$). This is shown in figure 7.41.

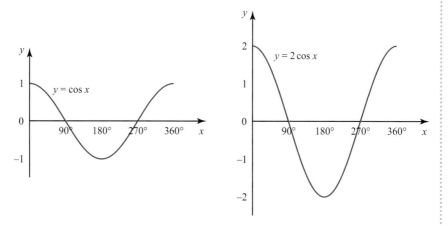

Figure 7.41

 It is always a good idea to check your results using a graphic calculator whenever possible.

EXAMPLE 7.14

(i) The function $\mathrm{f} : x \mapsto a + b\sin x$ is defined for $0 \leqslant x \leqslant 2\pi$.
Given that $\mathrm{f}(0) = 4$ and $\mathrm{f}\!\left(\dfrac{\pi}{6}\right) = 5$,

  (a) find the values of a and b

  (b) the range of f

  (c) sketch the graph of $y = a + b\sin x$ for $0 \leqslant x \leqslant 2\pi$.

(ii) The function $\mathrm{g} : x \mapsto a + b\sin x$, where a and b have the same value as found in part **(i)** is defined for the domain $\dfrac{\pi}{2} \leqslant x \leqslant k$. Find the largest value of k for which $\mathrm{g}(x)$ has an inverse.

SOLUTION

(i) **(a)** $\mathrm{f}(0) = 4 \Rightarrow a + b\sin 0 = 4$

            $\Rightarrow a = 4$ since $\sin 0 = 0$

      $\mathrm{f}\!\left(\dfrac{\pi}{6}\right) = 5 \Rightarrow 4 + b\sin\left(\dfrac{\pi}{6}\right) = 5$

                  $\Rightarrow 4 + \tfrac{1}{2}b = 5$

                  $\Rightarrow b = 2$ $\sin\left(\dfrac{\pi}{6}\right) = \dfrac{1}{2}$

(b) $f : x \mapsto 4 + 2\sin x$

The maximum value of $\sin x$ is 1.

So the maximum value of f is $4 + 2 \times 1 = 6$.

The minimum value of $\sin x$ is -1.

So the minimum value of f is $4 + 2 \times (-1) = 2$.

So the range of f is $2 \leqslant f(x) \leqslant 6$.

(c) As $a = 4$ and $b = 2$,

$y = a + b\sin x$ is

$y = 4 + 2\sin x$.

Figure 7.42 shows the graph of

$y = 4 + 2\sin x$.

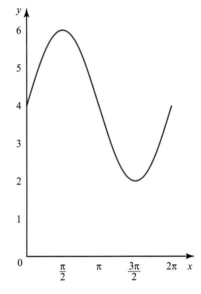

Figure 7.42

(ii) For a function to have an inverse it must be one-to-one.

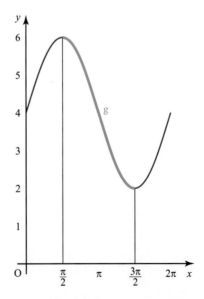

Figure 7.43

The domain of g starts at $\dfrac{\pi}{2}$ and must end at $\dfrac{3\pi}{2}$, as the curve turns here.

So $k = \dfrac{3\pi}{2}$.

1 Starting with the graph of $y = \sin x$, state the transformations which can be used to sketch each of the following curves.

(i) $y = \sin (x - 90°)$

(ii) $y = \sin 3x$

(iii) $2y = \sin x$

(iv) $y = \sin \dfrac{x}{2}$

(v) $y = 2 + \sin x$

2 Starting with the graph of $y = \cos x$, state the transformations which can be used to sketch each of the following curves.

(i) $y = \cos (x + 60°)$

(ii) $3y = \cos x$

(iii) $y = \cos x + 1$

(iv) $y = \cos 2x$

3 For each of the following curves

(a) sketch the curve

(b) identify the curve as being the same as one of the following:

$y = \pm \sin x$, $y = \pm \cos x$,   or $y = \pm \tan x$.

(i) $y = \sin (x + 360°)$

(ii) $y = \sin (x + 90°)$

(iii) $y = \tan (x - 180°)$

(iv) $y = \cos (x - 90°)$

(v) $y = \cos (x + 180°)$

4 Starting with the graph of $y = \tan x$, find the equation of the graph and sketch the graph after the following transformations.

(i) Translation of $\begin{pmatrix} 0 \\ 4 \end{pmatrix}$

(ii) Translation of $\begin{pmatrix} -30° \\ 0 \end{pmatrix}$

(iii) One-way stretch with scale factor 2 parallel to the x axis

5 The graph of $y = \sin x$ is stretched with scale factor 4 parallel to the y axis.

(i) State the equation of the new graph.

(ii) Find the exact value of y on the new graph when $x = 240°$.

6 The function f is defined by $f(x) = a + b \cos 2x$, for $0 \leqslant x \leqslant \pi$. It is given that $f(0) = -1$ and $f\left(\frac{1}{2}\pi\right) = 7$.

(i) Find the values of a and b.

(ii) Find the x co-ordinates of the points where the curve $y = f(x)$ intersects the x axis.

(iii) Sketch the graph of $y = f(x)$.

[Cambridge AS & A Level Mathematics 9709, Paper 1 Q8 June 2007]

7 The function f is such that $f(x) = a - b\cos x$ for $0° \leqslant x \leqslant 360°$, where a and b are positive constants. The maximum value of $f(x)$ is 10 and the minimum value is −2.

   (i) Find the values of a and b.

   (ii) Solve the equation $f(x) = 0$.

   (iii) Sketch the graph of $y = f(x)$.

[Cambridge AS & A Level Mathematics 9709, Paper 1 Q5 November 2008]

8 The diagram shows the graph of $y = a\sin(bx) + c$ for $0 \leqslant x \leqslant 2\pi$.

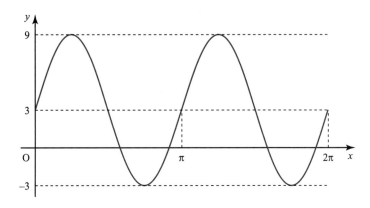

   (i) Find the values of a, b and c.

   (ii) Find the smallest value of x in the interval $0 \leqslant x \leqslant 2\pi$ for which $y = 0$.

[Cambridge AS & A Level Mathematics 9709, Paper 1 Q4 June 2009]

9 The function f is defined by $f : x \mapsto 5 - 3\sin 2x$ for $0 \leqslant x \leqslant \pi$.

   (i) Find the range of f.

   (ii) Sketch the graph of $y = f(x)$.

   (iii) State, with a reason, whether f has an inverse.

[Cambridge AS & A Level Mathematics 9709, Paper 12 Q4 November 2009]

10 The function $f : x \mapsto 4 - 3\sin x$ is defined for the domain $0 \leqslant x \leqslant 2\pi$.

   (i) Solve the equation $f(x) = 2$.

   (ii) Sketch the graph of $y = f(x)$.

   (iii) Find the set of values of k for which the equation $f(x) = k$ has no solution.

The function $g : x \mapsto 4 - 3\sin x$ is defined for the domain $\frac{1}{2}\pi \leqslant x \leqslant A$.

   (iv) State the largest value of A for which g has an inverse.

   (v) For this value of A, find the value of $g^{-1}(3)$.

[Cambridge AS & A Level Mathematics 9709, Paper 12 Q11 June 2010]

1   The point (x, y) at angle θ on the unit circle centre $(0, 0)$ has co-ordinates $(\cos\theta, \sin\theta)$ for all θ.

2   The graphs of $\sin\theta$, $\cos\theta$ and $\tan\theta$ are as shown below.

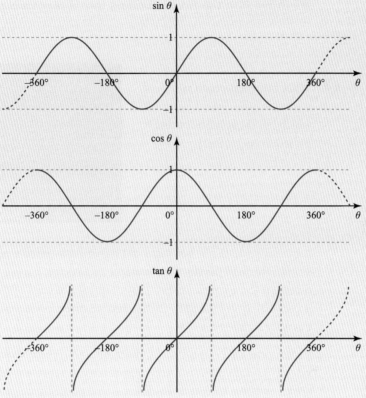

3   $\tan\theta \equiv \dfrac{\sin\theta}{\cos\theta}$

4   $\sin^2\theta + \cos^2\theta \equiv 1$.

5   Angles can be measured in radians. π radians $= 180°$.

6   For a circle of radius r, arc length $= r\theta$
    area of sector $= \frac{1}{2}r^2\theta$ $\Big\}$ (θ in radians).

7   The graph of $y = \mathrm{f}(x) + s$ is a translation of the graph of $y = \mathrm{f}(x)$ by $\begin{pmatrix} 0 \\ s \end{pmatrix}$.

8   The graph of $y = \mathrm{f}(x - t)$ is a translation of the graph of $y = \mathrm{f}(x)$ by $\begin{pmatrix} t \\ 0 \end{pmatrix}$.

9   The graph of $y = -\mathrm{f}(x)$ is a reflection of the graph of $y = \mathrm{f}(x)$ in the x axis.

10 The graph of $y = a\mathrm{f}(x)$ is a one-way stretch of the graph of $y = \mathrm{f}(x)$ with scale factor a parallel to the y axis.

11 The graph of $y = \mathrm{f}(ax)$ is a one-way stretch of the graph of $y = \mathrm{f}(x)$ with scale factor $\dfrac{1}{a}$ parallel to the x axis.

8 Vectors

We drove into the future looking into a rear view mirror.

Herbert Marshall McLuhan

❓ What information do you need to decide how close the aircraft which left these vapour trails passed to each other?

A quantity which has both size and direction is called a *vector*. The velocity of an aircraft through the sky is an example of a vector, having size (e.g. 600 mph) and direction (on a course of 254°). By contrast the mass of the aircraft (100 tonnes) is completely described by its size and no direction is associated with it; such a quantity is called a *scalar*.

Vectors are used extensively in mechanics to represent quantities such as force, velocity and momentum, and in geometry to represent displacements. They are an essential tool in three-dimensional co-ordinate geometry and it is this application of vectors which is the subject of this chapter. However, before coming on to this, you need to be familiar with the associated vocabulary and notation, in two and three dimensions.

ⓑ Vectors in two dimensions

Terminology

In two dimensions, it is common to represent a vector by a drawing of a straight line with an arrowhead. The length represents the size, or magnitude, of the vector and the direction is indicated by the line and the arrowhead. Direction is usually given as the angle the vector makes with the positive x axis, with the anticlockwise direction taken to be positive.

The vector in figure 8.1 has magnitude 5, direction +30°. This is written (5, 30°) and said to be in *magnitude–direction form* or in *polar form*. The general form of a vector written in this way is (r, θ) where r is its magnitude and θ its direction.

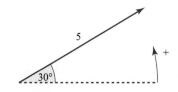

Figure 8.1

Note

In the special case when the vector is representing real travel, as in the case of the velocity of an aircraft, the direction may be described by a compass bearing with the angle measured from north, clockwise. However, this is not done in this chapter, where directions are all taken to be measured anticlockwise from the positive *x* direction.

An alternative way of describing a vector is in terms of *components* in given directions. The vector in figure 8.2 is 4 units in the *x* direction, and 2 in the *y* direction, and this is denoted by $\begin{pmatrix} 4 \\ 2 \end{pmatrix}$.

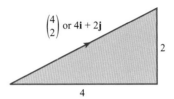

Figure 8.2

This may also be written as $4\mathbf{i} + 2\mathbf{j}$, where $\mathbf{i}$ is a vector of magnitude 1, a *unit vector*, in the *x* direction and $\mathbf{j}$ is a unit vector in the *y* direction (figure 8.3).

Figure 8.3

In a book, a vector may be printed in bold, for example **p** or **OP**, or as a line between two points with an arrow above it to indicate its direction, such as $\overrightarrow{OP}$. When you write a vector by hand, it is usual to underline it, for example, $\underline{p}$ or $\underline{OP}$, or to put an arrow above it, as in $\overrightarrow{OP}$.

To convert a vector from component form to magnitude–direction form, or vice versa, is just a matter of applying trigonometry to a right-angled triangle.

EXAMPLE 8.1

Write the vector $\mathbf{a} = 4\mathbf{i} + 2\mathbf{j}$ in magnitude–direction form.

SOLUTION

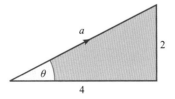

Figure 8.4

The magnitude of **a** is given by the length a in figure 8.4.

$$a = \sqrt{4^2 + 2^2} \qquad \text{(using Pythagoras' theorem)}$$

$$= 4.47 \qquad \text{(to 3 significant figures)}$$

The direction is given by the angle θ.

$$\tan \theta = \frac{2}{4} = 0.5$$

$$\theta = 26.6° \qquad \text{(to 3 significant figures)}$$

The vector **a** is (4.47, 26.6°).

The magnitude of a vector is also called its *modulus* and denoted by the symbols | |. In the example **a** = 4**i** + 2**j**, the modulus of **a**, written | **a** |, is 4.47. Another convention for writing the magnitude of a vector is to use the same letter, but in italics and not bold type; thus the magnitude of **a** may be written a.

EXAMPLE 8.2 Write the vector (5, 60°) in component form.

SOLUTION

In the right-angled triangle OPX

$$OX = 5 \cos 60° = 2.5$$

$$XP = 5 \sin 60° = 4.33$$
$$\text{(to 2 decimal places)}$$

$\overrightarrow{OP}$ is $\begin{pmatrix} 2.5 \\ 4.33 \end{pmatrix}$ or 2.5**i** + 4.33**j**.

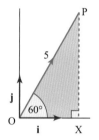

Figure 8.5

This technique can be written as a general rule, for all values of θ.

$$(r, \theta) \rightarrow \begin{pmatrix} r\cos\theta \\ r\sin\theta \end{pmatrix} = (r\cos\theta)\mathbf{i} + (r\sin\theta)\mathbf{j}$$

EXAMPLE 8.3 Write the vector (10, 290°) in component form.

SOLUTION

In this case $r = 10$ and $\theta = 290°$.

$$(10, 290°) \rightarrow \begin{pmatrix} 10\cos 290° \\ 10\sin 290° \end{pmatrix} = \begin{pmatrix} 3.42 \\ -9.40 \end{pmatrix} \text{ to 2 decimal places.}$$

This may also be written 3.42**i** − 9.40**j**.

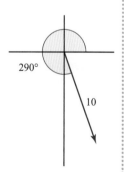

Figure 8.6

In Example 8.3 the signs looked after themselves. The component in the **i** direction came out positive, that in the **j** direction negative, as must be the case for a direction in the fourth quadrant ($270° < \theta < 360°$). This will always be the case when the conversion is from magnitude–direction form into component form.

The situation is not quite so straightforward when the conversion is carried out the other way, from component form to magnitude–direction form. In that case, it is best to draw a diagram and use it to see the approximate size of the angle required. This is shown in the next example.

EXAMPLE 8.4

Write $-5\mathbf{i} + 4\mathbf{j}$ in magnitude–direction form.

SOLUTION

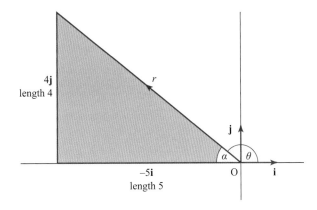

Figure 8.7

In this case, the magnitude $r = \sqrt{5^2 + 4^2}$

$$= \sqrt{41}$$
$$= 6.40 \qquad \text{(to 2 decimal places).}$$

The direction is given by the angle θ in figure 8.7, but first find the angle α.

$$\tan \alpha = \tfrac{4}{5} \qquad \Rightarrow \qquad \alpha = 38.7° \qquad \text{(to nearest 0.1°)}$$

so $\qquad \theta = 180 - \alpha = 141.3°$

The vector is $(6.40, 141.3°)$ in magnitude–direction form.

Vectors in three dimensions

Points

In three dimensions, a point has three co-ordinates, usually called x, y and z.

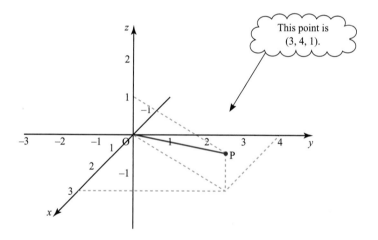

This point is (3, 4, 1).

Figure 8.8

The axes are conventionally arranged as shown in figure 8.8, where the point P is (3, 4, 1). Even on correctly drawn three-dimensional grids, it is often hard to see the relationship between the points, lines and planes, so it is seldom worth your while trying to plot points accurately.

The unit vectors $\mathbf{i}$, $\mathbf{j}$ and $\mathbf{k}$ are used to describe vectors in three dimensions.

Equal vectors

The statement that two vectors **a** and **b** are equal means two things.

- The direction of **a** is the same as the direction of **b**.

- The magnitude of **a** is the same as the magnitude of **b**.

If the vectors are given in component form, each component of **a** equals the corresponding component of **b**.

Position vectors

Saying the vector **a** is given by $3\mathbf{i} + 4\mathbf{j} + \mathbf{k}$ tells you the components of the vector, or equivalently its magnitude and direction. It does not tell you where the vector is situated; indeed it could be anywhere.

All of the lines in figure 8.9 represent the vector **a**.

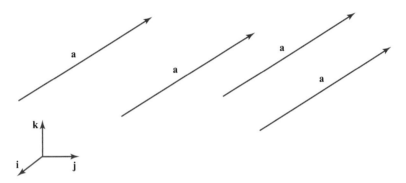

Figure 8.9

There is, however, one special case which is an exception to the rule, that of a vector which starts at the origin. This is called a *position vector*. Thus the line joining the origin to the point P(3, 4, 1) is the position vector $\begin{pmatrix} 3 \\ 4 \\ 1 \end{pmatrix}$ or $3\mathbf{i} + 4\mathbf{j} + \mathbf{k}$.

Another way of expressing this is to say that the point P(3, 4, 1) has the position vector $\begin{pmatrix} 3 \\ 4 \\ 1 \end{pmatrix}$.

EXAMPLE 8.5

Points L, M and N have co-ordinates (4, 3), (−2, −1) and (2, 2).

(i) Write down, in component form, the position vector of L and the vector $\overrightarrow{MN}$.

(ii) What do your answers to part (i) tell you about the lines OL and MN?

SOLUTION

(i) The position vector of L is $\overrightarrow{OL} = \begin{pmatrix} 4 \\ 3 \end{pmatrix}$.

The vector $\overrightarrow{MN}$ is also $\begin{pmatrix} 4 \\ 3 \end{pmatrix}$ (see figure 8.10).

(ii) Since $\overrightarrow{OL} = \overrightarrow{MN}$, lines OL and MN are parallel and equal in length.

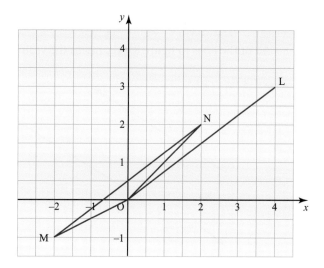

Figure 8.10

Note

A line joining two points, like MN in figure 8.10, is often called a *line segment*, meaning that it is just that particular part of the infinite straight line that passes through those two points.

The vector $\overrightarrow{MN}$ is an example of a displacement vector. Its length represents the magnitude of the displacement when you move from M to N.

The length of a vector

In two dimensions, the use of Pythagoras' theorem leads to the result that a vector $a_1\mathbf{i} + a_2\mathbf{j}$ has length $|\mathbf{a}|$ given by

$$|\mathbf{a}| = \sqrt{a_1^2 + a_2^2}.$$

Ⓟ Show that the length of the three-dimensional vector $a_1\mathbf{i} + a_2\mathbf{j} + a_3\mathbf{k}$ is given by

$$|\mathbf{a}| = \sqrt{a_1^2 + a_2^2 + a_3^2}.$$

EXAMPLE 8.6

Find the magnitude of the vector $\mathbf{a} = \begin{pmatrix} 2 \\ -5 \\ 3 \end{pmatrix}$.

SOLUTION

$$|\mathbf{a}| = \sqrt{2^2 + (-5)^2 + 3^2}$$

$$= \sqrt{4 + 25 + 9}$$

$$= \sqrt{38}$$

$$= 6.16 \text{ (to 2 d.p.)}$$

EXERCISE 8A

1 Express the following vectors in component form.

(i)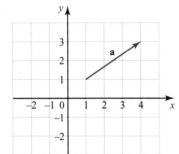

(ii)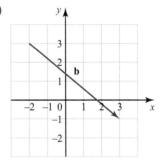

(iii)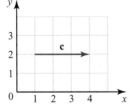

(iv)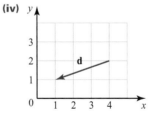

2 Draw diagrams to show these vectors and then write them in magnitude–direction form.

(i) $2\mathbf{i} + 3\mathbf{j}$

(ii) $\begin{pmatrix} 3 \\ -2 \end{pmatrix}$

(iii) $\begin{pmatrix} -4 \\ -4 \end{pmatrix}$

(iv) $-\mathbf{i} + 2\mathbf{j}$

(v) $3\mathbf{i} - 4\mathbf{j}$

3 Find the magnitude of these vectors.

(i) $\begin{pmatrix} 1 \\ -2 \\ 3 \end{pmatrix}$

(ii) $\begin{pmatrix} 4 \\ 0 \\ -2 \end{pmatrix}$

(iii) $2\mathbf{i} + 4\mathbf{j} + 2\mathbf{k}$

(iv) $\mathbf{i} + \mathbf{j} - 3\mathbf{k}$

(v) $\begin{pmatrix} 6 \\ -2 \\ -3 \end{pmatrix}$

(vi) $\mathbf{i} - 2\mathbf{k}$

4 Write, in component form, the vectors represented by the line segments joining the following points.

(i) $(2, 3)$ to $(4, 1)$

(iii) $(0, 0)$ to $(0, -4)$

(v) $(0, 0, 0)$ to $(0, 0, 5)$

(vii) $(-1, -2, 3)$ to $(0, 0, 0)$

(ix) $(1, 2, 3)$ to $(3, 2, 1)$

(ii) $(4, 0)$ to $(6, 0)$

(iv) $(0, -4)$ to $(0, 0)$

(vi) $(0, 0, 0)$ to $(-1, -2, 3)$

(viii) $(0, 2, 0)$ to $(4, 0, 4)$

(x) $(4, -5, 0)$ to $(-4, 5, 1)$

5 The points A, B and C have co-ordinates $(2, 3)$, $(0, 4)$ and $(-2, 1)$.

(i) Write down the position vectors of A and C.

(ii) Write down the vectors of the line segments joining AB and CB.

(iii) What do your answers to parts **(i)** and **(ii)** tell you about

   (a) AB and OC

   (b) CB and OA?

(iv) Describe the quadrilateral OABC.

Vector calculations

Multiplying a vector by a scalar

When a vector is multiplied by a number (a scalar) its length is altered but its direction remains the same.

The vector 2**a** in figure 8.11 is twice as long as the vector **a** but in the same direction.

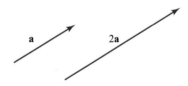

Figure 8.11

When the vector is in component form, each component is multiplied by the number. For example:

$$2 \times (3\mathbf{i} - 5\mathbf{j} + \mathbf{k}) = 6\mathbf{i} - 10\mathbf{j} + 2\mathbf{k}$$

$$2 \times \begin{pmatrix} 3 \\ -5 \\ 1 \end{pmatrix} = \begin{pmatrix} 6 \\ -10 \\ 2 \end{pmatrix}.$$

The negative of a vector

In figure 8.12 the vector $-\mathbf{a}$ has the same length as the vector **a** but the opposite direction.

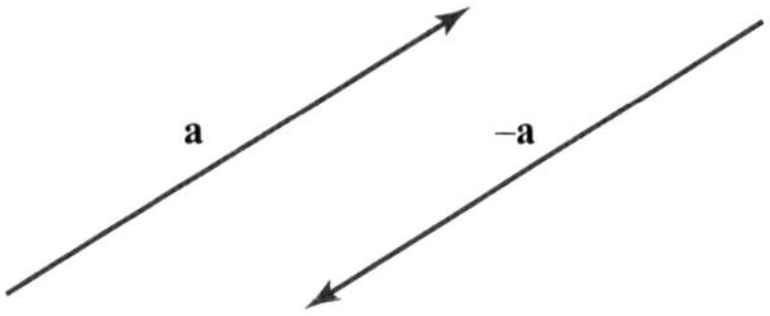

Figure 8.12

When **a** is given in component form, the components of −**a** are the same as those for **a** but with their signs reversed. So

$$-\begin{pmatrix} 23 \\ 0 \\ -11 \end{pmatrix} = \begin{pmatrix} -23 \\ 0 \\ +11 \end{pmatrix}$$

Adding vectors

When vectors are given in component form, they can be added component by component. This process can be seen geometrically by drawing them on graph paper, as in the example below.

EXAMPLE 8.7

Add the vectors 2**i** − 3**j** and 3**i** + 5**j**.

SOLUTION

2**i** − 3**j** + 3**i** + 5**j** = 5**i** + 2**j**

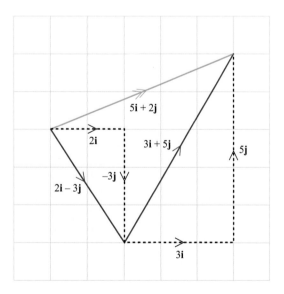

Figure 8.13

The sum of two (or more) vectors is called the *resultant* and is usually indicated by being marked with two arrowheads.

Adding vectors is like adding the legs of a journey to find its overall outcome (see figure 8.14).

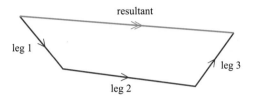

Figure 8.14

When vectors are given in magnitude–direction form, you can find their resultant by making a scale drawing, as in figure 8.14. If, however, you need to calculate their resultant, it is usually easiest to convert the vectors into component form, add component by component, and then convert the answer back to magnitude–direction form.

Subtracting vectors

Subtracting one vector from another is the same as adding the negative of the vector.

EXAMPLE 8.8

Two vectors **a** and **b** are given by

$$\mathbf{a} = 2\mathbf{i} + 3\mathbf{j} \qquad \mathbf{b} = -\mathbf{i} + 2\mathbf{j}.$$

(i) Find **a** – **b**.

(ii) Draw diagrams showing **a**, **b**, **a** – **b**.

SOLUTION

(i) $\mathbf{a} - \mathbf{b} = (2\mathbf{i} + 3\mathbf{j}) - (-\mathbf{i} + 2\mathbf{j})$
$\qquad = 3\mathbf{i} + \mathbf{j}$

(ii)

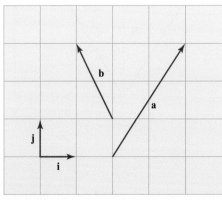

Figure 8.15

When you find the vector represented by the line segment joining two points, you are in effect subtracting their position vectors. If, for example,

P is the point (2, 1) and Q is the point (3, 5), $\overrightarrow{PQ}$ is $\begin{pmatrix} 1 \\ 4 \end{pmatrix}$, as figure 8.16 shows.

You find this by saying

$$\overrightarrow{PQ} = \overrightarrow{PO} + \overrightarrow{OQ} = -\mathbf{p} + \mathbf{q}.$$

In this case, this gives

$$\overrightarrow{PQ} = -\begin{pmatrix} 2 \\ 1 \end{pmatrix} + \begin{pmatrix} 3 \\ 5 \end{pmatrix} = \begin{pmatrix} 1 \\ 4 \end{pmatrix}$$

as expected.

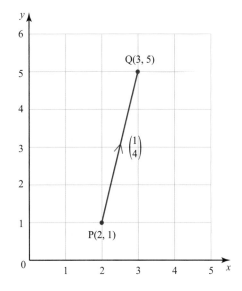

Figure 8.16

This is an important result:

$$\overrightarrow{PQ} = \mathbf{q} - \mathbf{p}$$

where **p** and **q** are the position vectors of P and Q.

Geometrical figures

It is often useful to be able to express lines in a geometrical figure in terms of given vectors.

ACTIVITY 8.1   The diagram shows a cuboid OABCDEFG. P, Q, R, S and T are the mid-points of the edges they lie on. The origin is at O and the axes lie along OA, OC and OD, as shown in figure 8.17.

$$\overrightarrow{OA} = \begin{pmatrix} 6 \\ 0 \\ 0 \end{pmatrix}, \overrightarrow{OC} = \begin{pmatrix} 0 \\ 5 \\ 0 \end{pmatrix}, \overrightarrow{OD} = \begin{pmatrix} 0 \\ 0 \\ 4 \end{pmatrix}$$

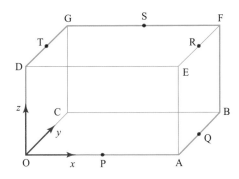

Figure 8.17

(i) Name the points with the following co-ordinates.

(a) $(6, 5, 4)$ (b) $(0, 5, 0)$ (c) $(6, 2.5, 0)$

(d) $(0, 2.5, 4)$ (e) $(3, 5, 4)$

(ii) Use the letters in the diagram to give displacements which are equal to the following vectors. Give all possible answers; some of them have more than one.

(a) $\begin{pmatrix} 6 \\ 5 \\ 4 \end{pmatrix}$ (b) $\begin{pmatrix} 6 \\ 0 \\ 4 \end{pmatrix}$ (c) $\begin{pmatrix} 0 \\ 5 \\ 4 \end{pmatrix}$ (d) $\begin{pmatrix} -6 \\ -5 \\ 4 \end{pmatrix}$ (e) $\begin{pmatrix} -3 \\ 2.5 \\ 4 \end{pmatrix}$

EXAMPLE 8.9

Figure 8.18 shows a hexagonal prism.

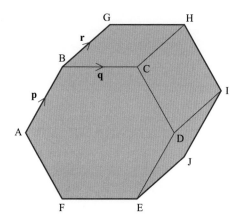

Figure 8.18

The hexagonal cross-section is regular and consequently $\overrightarrow{AD} = 2\overrightarrow{BC}$.

$\overrightarrow{AB} = \mathbf{p}$, $\overrightarrow{BC} = \mathbf{q}$ and $\overrightarrow{BG} = \mathbf{r}$. Express the following in terms of $\mathbf{p}$, $\mathbf{q}$ and $\mathbf{r}$.

(i) $\overrightarrow{AC}$ (ii) $\overrightarrow{AD}$ (iii) $\overrightarrow{HI}$ (iv) $\overrightarrow{IJ}$

(v) $\overrightarrow{EF}$ (vi) $\overrightarrow{BE}$ (vii) $\overrightarrow{AH}$ (viii) $\overrightarrow{FI}$

SOLUTION

(i) $\overrightarrow{AC} = \overrightarrow{AB} + \overrightarrow{BC}$

        $= \mathbf{p} + \mathbf{q}$

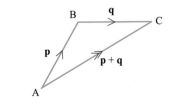

(ii) $\overrightarrow{AD} = 2\overrightarrow{BC} = 2\mathbf{q}$

(iii) $\overrightarrow{HI} = \overrightarrow{CD}$

       Since $\overrightarrow{AC} + \overrightarrow{CD} = \overrightarrow{AD}$

           $\mathbf{p} + \mathbf{q} + \overrightarrow{CD} = 2\mathbf{q}$

              $\overrightarrow{CD} = \mathbf{q} - \mathbf{p}$

     So $\overrightarrow{HI} = \mathbf{q} - \mathbf{p}$

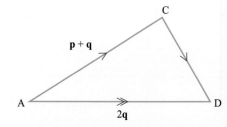

(iv) $\overrightarrow{IJ} = \overrightarrow{DE}$

$= -\overrightarrow{AB}$

$= -\mathbf{p}$

(v) $\overrightarrow{EF} = -\overrightarrow{BC}$

$= -\mathbf{q}$

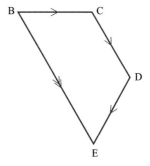

(vi) $\overrightarrow{BE} = \overrightarrow{BC} + \overrightarrow{CD} + \overrightarrow{DE}$

$= \mathbf{q} + (\mathbf{q} - \mathbf{p}) + -\mathbf{p}$

$= 2\mathbf{q} - 2\mathbf{p}$

Figure 8.19

Notice that $\overrightarrow{BE} = 2\overrightarrow{CD}$.

(vii) $\overrightarrow{AH} = \overrightarrow{AB} + \overrightarrow{BC} + \overrightarrow{CH}$ ◄——— $\overrightarrow{CH} = \overrightarrow{BG}$

$= \mathbf{p} + \mathbf{q} + \mathbf{r}$

(viii) $\overrightarrow{FI} = \overrightarrow{FE} + \overrightarrow{EJ} + \overrightarrow{JI}$ ◄——— $\overrightarrow{FE} = \overrightarrow{BC}, \overrightarrow{EJ} = \overrightarrow{BG}, \overrightarrow{JI} = \overrightarrow{AB}$

$= \mathbf{q} + \mathbf{r} + \mathbf{p}$

Unit vectors

A unit vector is a vector with a magnitude of 1, like $\mathbf{i}$ and $\mathbf{j}$. To find the unit vector in the same direction as a given vector, divide that vector by its magnitude.

Thus the vector $3\mathbf{i} + 5\mathbf{j}$ (in figure 8.20) has magnitude $\sqrt{3^2 + 5^2} = \sqrt{34}$, and so the vector $\dfrac{3}{\sqrt{34}}\mathbf{i} + \dfrac{5}{\sqrt{34}}\mathbf{j}$ is a unit vector. It has magnitude 1.

The unit vector in the direction of vector $\mathbf{a}$ is written as $\hat{\mathbf{a}}$ and read as 'a hat'.

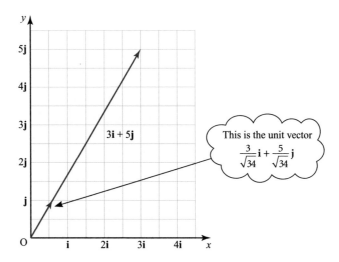

Figure 8.20

EXAMPLE 8.10 Relative to an origin O, the position vectors of the points A, B and C are given by

$$\overrightarrow{OA} = \begin{pmatrix} -2 \\ 3 \\ -2 \end{pmatrix}, \ \overrightarrow{OB} = \begin{pmatrix} 0 \\ 1 \\ -3 \end{pmatrix} \text{ and } \overrightarrow{OC} = \begin{pmatrix} -2 \\ 3 \\ 1 \end{pmatrix}.$$

(i) Find the unit vector in the direction $\overrightarrow{AB}$.

(ii) Find the perimeter of triangle ABC.

SOLUTION

For convenience call $\overrightarrow{OA} = \mathbf{a}$, $\overrightarrow{OB} = \mathbf{b}$ and $\overrightarrow{OC} = \mathbf{c}$.

(i) $\overrightarrow{AB} = \mathbf{b} - \mathbf{a} = \begin{pmatrix} 0 \\ 1 \\ -3 \end{pmatrix} - \begin{pmatrix} -2 \\ 3 \\ -2 \end{pmatrix} = \begin{pmatrix} 2 \\ -2 \\ -1 \end{pmatrix}$

To find the unit vector in the direction $\overrightarrow{AB}$, you need to divide $\overrightarrow{AB}$ by its magnitude.

$$|\overrightarrow{AB}| = \sqrt{2^2 + (-2)^2 + (-1)^2}$$

$$= \sqrt{9}$$

$$= 3 \leftarrow$$

This is the magnitude of $\overrightarrow{AB}$.

So the unit vector in the direction $\overrightarrow{AB}$ is $\frac{1}{3}\begin{pmatrix} 2 \\ -2 \\ -1 \end{pmatrix} = \begin{pmatrix} \frac{2}{3} \\ -\frac{2}{3} \\ -\frac{1}{3} \end{pmatrix}$

(ii) The perimeter of the triangle is given by $|\overrightarrow{AB}| + |\overrightarrow{AC}| + |\overrightarrow{BC}|$.

$$\overrightarrow{AC} = \mathbf{c} - \mathbf{a} = \begin{pmatrix} -2 \\ 3 \\ 1 \end{pmatrix} - \begin{pmatrix} -2 \\ 3 \\ -2 \end{pmatrix} = \begin{pmatrix} 0 \\ 0 \\ 3 \end{pmatrix}$$

$$\Rightarrow |\overrightarrow{AC}| = \sqrt{0^2 + 0^2 + 3^2}$$

$$= 3$$

$$\overrightarrow{BC} = \mathbf{c} - \mathbf{b} = \begin{pmatrix} -2 \\ 3 \\ 1 \end{pmatrix} - \begin{pmatrix} 0 \\ 1 \\ -3 \end{pmatrix} = \begin{pmatrix} -2 \\ 2 \\ 4 \end{pmatrix}$$

$$\Rightarrow |\overrightarrow{BC}| = \sqrt{(-2)^2 + 2^2 + 4^2}$$

$$= \sqrt{24}$$

Perimeter of ABC $= |\overrightarrow{AB}| + |\overrightarrow{AC}| + |\overrightarrow{BC}|$

$$= 3 + 3 + \sqrt{24}$$

$$= 10.9$$

EXERCISE 8B

1 Simplify the following.

(i) $\begin{pmatrix} 2 \\ 3 \end{pmatrix} + \begin{pmatrix} 4 \\ 5 \end{pmatrix}$

(ii) $\begin{pmatrix} 2 \\ -1 \end{pmatrix} + \begin{pmatrix} -1 \\ 2 \end{pmatrix}$

(iii) $\begin{pmatrix} 3 \\ 4 \end{pmatrix} + \begin{pmatrix} -3 \\ -4 \end{pmatrix}$

(iv) $3\begin{pmatrix} 2 \\ 1 \end{pmatrix} + 2\begin{pmatrix} 1 \\ -2 \end{pmatrix}$

(v) $6(3\mathbf{i} - 2\mathbf{j}) - 9(2\mathbf{i} - \mathbf{j})$

2 The vectors $\mathbf{p}$, $\mathbf{q}$ and $\mathbf{r}$ are given by

$$\mathbf{p} = 3\mathbf{i} + 2\mathbf{j} + \mathbf{k} \qquad \mathbf{q} = 2\mathbf{i} + 2\mathbf{j} + 2\mathbf{k} \qquad \mathbf{r} = -3\mathbf{i} - \mathbf{j} - 2\mathbf{k}.$$

Find, in component form, the following vectors.

(i) $\mathbf{p} + \mathbf{q} + \mathbf{r}$ (ii) $\mathbf{p} - \mathbf{q}$ (iii) $\mathbf{p} + \mathbf{r}$

(iv) $3(\mathbf{p} - \mathbf{q}) + 2(\mathbf{p} + \mathbf{r})$ (v) $4\mathbf{p} - 3\mathbf{q} + 2\mathbf{r}$

3 In the diagram, PQRS is a parallelogram and $\overrightarrow{PQ} = \mathbf{a}$, $\overrightarrow{PS} = \mathbf{b}$.

(i) Write, in terms of $\mathbf{a}$ and $\mathbf{b}$, the following vectors.

(a) $\overrightarrow{QR}$ (b) $\overrightarrow{PR}$

(c) $\overrightarrow{QS}$

(ii) The mid-point of PR is M. Find

(a) $\overrightarrow{PM}$ (b) $\overrightarrow{QM}$.

(iii) Explain why this shows you that the diagonals of a parallelogram bisect each other.

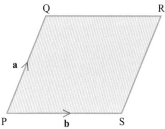

4 In the diagram, ABCD is a kite. AC and BD meet at M.

$$\overrightarrow{AB} = \mathbf{i} + \mathbf{j} \qquad \text{and}$$
$$\overrightarrow{AD} = \mathbf{i} - 2\mathbf{j}$$

(i) Use the facts that the diagonals of a kite meet at right angles and that M is the mid-point of AC to find, in terms of $\mathbf{i}$ and $\mathbf{j}$,

(a) $\overrightarrow{AM}$ (b) $\overrightarrow{AC}$

(c) $\overrightarrow{BC}$ (d) $\overrightarrow{CD}$.

(ii) Verify that $\left| \overrightarrow{AB} \right| = \left| \overrightarrow{BC} \right|$ and $\left| \overrightarrow{AD} \right| = \left| \overrightarrow{CD} \right|$.

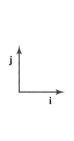

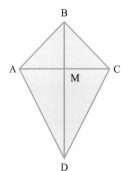

5 In the diagram, ABC is a triangle.
L, M and N are the mid-points of
the sides BC, CA and AB.

$$\overrightarrow{AB} = \mathbf{p} \qquad \text{and} \qquad \overrightarrow{AC} = \mathbf{q}$$

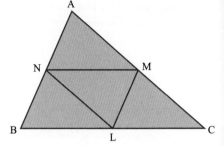

(i) Find, in terms of $\mathbf{p}$ and $\mathbf{q}$, $\overrightarrow{BC}$,
$\overrightarrow{MN}$, $\overrightarrow{LM}$ and $\overrightarrow{LN}$.

(ii) Explain how your results from part (i) show you that the sides of triangle
LMN are parallel to those of triangle ABC, and half their lengths.

6 Find unit vectors in the same directions as the following vectors.

(i) $\begin{pmatrix} 2 \\ 3 \end{pmatrix}$ 　　　(ii) $3\mathbf{i} + 4\mathbf{j}$ 　　　(iii) $\begin{pmatrix} -2 \\ -2 \end{pmatrix}$ 　　　(iv) $5\mathbf{i} - 12\mathbf{j}$

7 Find unit vectors in the same direction as the following vectors.

(i) $\begin{pmatrix} 1 \\ 2 \\ 3 \end{pmatrix}$ 　　　(ii) $2\mathbf{i} - 2\mathbf{j} + \mathbf{k}$ 　　　(iii) $3\mathbf{i} - 4\mathbf{k}$

(iv) $\begin{pmatrix} -2 \\ 4 \\ -3 \end{pmatrix}$ 　　　(v) $5\mathbf{i} - 3\mathbf{j} + 2\mathbf{k}$ 　　　(vi) $\begin{pmatrix} 4 \\ 0 \\ 0 \end{pmatrix}$

8 Relative to an origin O, the position vectors of the points A, B and C are
given by

$$\overrightarrow{OA} = \begin{pmatrix} 2 \\ 1 \\ 3 \end{pmatrix}, \ \overrightarrow{OB} = \begin{pmatrix} -2 \\ 4 \\ 3 \end{pmatrix} \text{ and } \overrightarrow{OC} = \begin{pmatrix} -1 \\ 2 \\ 1 \end{pmatrix}.$$

Find the perimeter of triangle ABC.

9 Relative to an origin O, the position vectors of the points P and Q are given
by $\overrightarrow{OP} = 3\mathbf{i} + \mathbf{j} + 4\mathbf{k}$ and $\overrightarrow{OQ} = \mathbf{i} + x\mathbf{j} - 2\mathbf{k}$.

Find the values of x for which the magnitude of PQ is 7.

10 Relative to an origin O, the position vectors of the points A and B are given by

$$\overrightarrow{OA} = \begin{pmatrix} 4 \\ 1 \\ -2 \end{pmatrix} \qquad \text{and} \qquad \overrightarrow{OB} = \begin{pmatrix} 3 \\ 2 \\ -4 \end{pmatrix}.$$

(i) Given that C is the point such that $\overrightarrow{AC} = 2\overrightarrow{AB}$, find the unit vector in the
direction of $\overrightarrow{OC}$.

The position vector of the point D is given by $\overrightarrow{OD} = \begin{pmatrix} 1 \\ 4 \\ k \end{pmatrix}$, where k is a

constant, and it is given that $\overrightarrow{OD} = m\overrightarrow{OA} + n\overrightarrow{OB}$, where m and n are constants.

(ii) Find the values of m, n and k.

[Cambridge AS & A Level Mathematics 9709, Paper 1 Q9 June 2007]

The angle between two vectors

P As you work through the proof in this section, make a list of all the results that you are assuming.

To find the angle θ between the two vectors

$$\overrightarrow{OA} = \mathbf{a} = a_1\mathbf{i} + a_2\mathbf{j}$$

and

$$\overrightarrow{OB} = \mathbf{b} = b_1\mathbf{i} + b_2\mathbf{j}$$

start by applying the cosine rule to triangle OAB in figure 8.21.

$$\cos\theta = \frac{OA^2 + OB^2 - AB^2}{2OA \times OB}$$

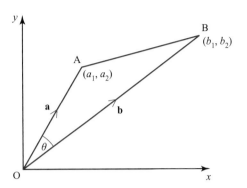

Figure 8.21

In this, OA, OB and AB are the lengths of the vectors $\overrightarrow{OA}$, $\overrightarrow{OB}$ and $\overrightarrow{AB}$, and so

$$OA = |\mathbf{a}| = \sqrt{a_1^2 + a_2^2} \quad \text{and} \quad OB = |\mathbf{b}| = \sqrt{b_1^2 + b_2^2}.$$

The vector $\overrightarrow{AB} = \mathbf{b} - \mathbf{a} = (b_1\mathbf{i} + b_2\mathbf{j}) - (a_1\mathbf{i} + a_2\mathbf{j})$

$$= (b_1 - a_1)\mathbf{i} + (b_2 - a_2)\mathbf{j}$$

and so its length is given by

$$AB = |\mathbf{b} - \mathbf{a}| = \sqrt{(b_1 - a_1)^2 + (b_2 - a_2)^2}.$$

Substituting for OA, OB and AB in the cosine rule gives

$$\cos\theta = \frac{(a_1^2 + a_2^2) + (b_1^2 + b_2^2) - [(b_1 - a_1)^2 + (b_2 - a_2)^2]}{2\sqrt{a_1^2 + a_2^2} \times \sqrt{b_1^2 + b_2^2}}$$

$$= \frac{a_1^2 + a_2^2 + b_1^2 + b_2^2 - \left(b_1^2 - 2a_1b_1 + a_1^2 + b_2^2 - 2a_2b_2 + a_2^2\right)}{2|\mathbf{a}||\mathbf{b}|}$$

This simplifies to

$$\cos\theta = \frac{2a_1b_1 + 2a_2b_2}{2|\mathbf{a}||\mathbf{b}|} = \frac{a_1b_1 + a_2b_2}{|\mathbf{a}||\mathbf{b}|}$$

The expression on the top line, $a_1b_1 + a_2b_2$, is called the *scalar product* (or *dot product*) of the vectors $\mathbf{a}$ and $\mathbf{b}$ and is written $\mathbf{a}.\mathbf{b}$. Thus

$$\cos\theta = \frac{\mathbf{a}.\mathbf{b}}{|\mathbf{a}||\mathbf{b}|}.$$

This result is usually written in the form

$$\mathbf{a}.\mathbf{b} = |\mathbf{a}||\mathbf{b}|\cos\theta.$$

The next example shows you how to use it to find the angle between two vectors given numerically.

EXAMPLE 8.11

Find the angle between the vectors $\begin{pmatrix} 3 \\ 4 \end{pmatrix}$ and $\begin{pmatrix} 5 \\ -12 \end{pmatrix}$.

SOLUTION

Let $\quad \mathbf{a} = \begin{pmatrix} 3 \\ 4 \end{pmatrix} \quad \Rightarrow \quad |\mathbf{a}| = \sqrt{3^2 + 4^2} = 5$

and $\quad \mathbf{b} = \begin{pmatrix} 5 \\ -12 \end{pmatrix} \quad \Rightarrow \quad |\mathbf{b}| = \sqrt{5^2 + (-12)^2} = 13.$

The scalar product

$$\begin{pmatrix} 3 \\ 4 \end{pmatrix} \cdot \begin{pmatrix} 5 \\ -12 \end{pmatrix} = 3 \times 5 + 4 \times (-12)$$
$$= 15 - 48$$
$$= -33.$$

Substituting in $\mathbf{a} \cdot \mathbf{b} = |\mathbf{a}||\mathbf{b}| \cos \theta$ gives

$$-33 = 5 \times 13 \times \cos \theta$$
$$\cos \theta = \frac{-33}{65}$$
$$\Rightarrow \qquad \theta = 120.5°.$$

Perpendicular vectors

Since $\cos 90° = 0$, it follows that if vectors $\mathbf{a}$ and $\mathbf{b}$ are perpendicular then $\mathbf{a} \cdot \mathbf{b} = 0$.

Conversely, if the scalar product of two non-zero vectors is zero, they are perpendicular.

EXAMPLE 8.12

Show that the vectors $\mathbf{a} = \begin{pmatrix} 2 \\ 4 \end{pmatrix}$ and $\mathbf{b} = \begin{pmatrix} 6 \\ -3 \end{pmatrix}$ are perpendicular.

SOLUTION

The scalar product of the vectors is

$$\mathbf{a} \cdot \mathbf{b} = \begin{pmatrix} 2 \\ 4 \end{pmatrix} \cdot \begin{pmatrix} 6 \\ -3 \end{pmatrix}$$
$$= 2 \times 6 + 4 \times (-3)$$
$$= 12 - 12 = 0.$$

Therefore the vectors are perpendicular.

Further points concerning the scalar product

- You will notice that the scalar product of two vectors is an ordinary number. It has size but no direction and so is a scalar, rather than a vector. It is for this reason that it is called the scalar product. There is another way of multiplying vectors that gives a vector as the answer; it is called the *vector product*. This is beyond the scope of this book.

- The scalar product is calculated in the same way for three-dimensional vectors. For example:

$$\begin{pmatrix} 2 \\ 3 \\ 4 \end{pmatrix} \cdot \begin{pmatrix} 5 \\ 6 \\ 7 \end{pmatrix} = 2 \times 5 + 3 \times 6 + 4 \times 7 = 56.$$

In general

$$\begin{pmatrix} a_1 \\ a_2 \\ a_3 \end{pmatrix} \cdot \begin{pmatrix} b_1 \\ b_2 \\ b_3 \end{pmatrix} = a_1 b_1 + a_2 b_2 + a_3 b_3$$

- The scalar product of two vectors is commutative. It has the same value whichever of them is on the left-hand side or right-hand side. Thus $\mathbf{a} \cdot \mathbf{b} = \mathbf{b} \cdot \mathbf{a}$, as in the following example.

$$\begin{pmatrix} 2 \\ 3 \end{pmatrix} \cdot \begin{pmatrix} 6 \\ 7 \end{pmatrix} = 2 \times 6 + 3 \times 7 = 33 \qquad \begin{pmatrix} 6 \\ 7 \end{pmatrix} \cdot \begin{pmatrix} 2 \\ 3 \end{pmatrix} = 6 \times 2 + 7 \times 3 = 33.$$

(p) How would you prove this result?

The angle between two vectors

The angle θ between the vectors $\mathbf{a} = a_1 \mathbf{i} + a_2 \mathbf{j}$ and $\mathbf{b} = b_1 \mathbf{i} + b_2 \mathbf{j}$ in two dimensions is given by

$$\cos \theta = \frac{a_1 b_1 + a_2 b_2}{\sqrt{a_1^2 + a_2^2} \times \sqrt{b_1^2 + b_2^2}} = \frac{\mathbf{a} \cdot \mathbf{b}}{|\mathbf{a}||\mathbf{b}|}$$

where $\mathbf{a} \cdot \mathbf{b}$ is the scalar product of $\mathbf{a}$ and $\mathbf{b}$. This result was proved by using the cosine rule on page 271.

(p) Show that the angle between the three-dimensional vectors

$$\mathbf{a} = a_1\mathbf{i} + a_2\mathbf{j} + a_3\mathbf{k} \quad \text{and} \quad \mathbf{b} = b_1\mathbf{i} + b_2\mathbf{j} + b_3\mathbf{k}$$

is also given by

$$\cos\theta = \frac{\mathbf{a}.\mathbf{b}}{|\mathbf{a}||\mathbf{b}|}$$

but that the scalar product $\mathbf{a}.\mathbf{b}$ is now

$$\mathbf{a}.\mathbf{b} = a_1 b_1 + a_2 b_2 + a_3 b_3.$$

Working in three dimensions

When working in two dimensions you found the angle between two lines by using the scalar product. As you have just proved, this method can be extended into three dimensions, and its use is shown in the following example.

EXAMPLE 8.13

The points P, Q and R are (1, 0, −1), (2, 4, 1) and (3, 5, 6). Find ∠QPR.

SOLUTION

The angle between $\overrightarrow{PQ}$ and $\overrightarrow{PR}$ is given by θ in

$$\cos\theta = \frac{\overrightarrow{PQ}.\overrightarrow{PR}}{|\overrightarrow{PQ}||\overrightarrow{PR}|}$$

In this

$$\overrightarrow{PQ} = \begin{pmatrix} 2 \\ 4 \\ 1 \end{pmatrix} - \begin{pmatrix} 1 \\ 0 \\ -1 \end{pmatrix} = \begin{pmatrix} 1 \\ 4 \\ 2 \end{pmatrix} \qquad |\overrightarrow{PQ}| = \sqrt{1^2 + 4^2 + 2^2} = \sqrt{21}$$

Similarly

$$\overrightarrow{PR} = \begin{pmatrix} 3 \\ 5 \\ 6 \end{pmatrix} - \begin{pmatrix} 1 \\ 0 \\ -1 \end{pmatrix} = \begin{pmatrix} 2 \\ 5 \\ 7 \end{pmatrix} \qquad |\overrightarrow{PR}| = \sqrt{2^2 + 5^2 + 7^2} = \sqrt{78}$$

Therefore

$$\overrightarrow{PQ}.\overrightarrow{PR} = \begin{pmatrix} 1 \\ 4 \\ 2 \end{pmatrix}.\begin{pmatrix} 2 \\ 5 \\ 7 \end{pmatrix}$$

$$= 1 \times 2 + 4 \times 5 + 2 \times 7$$
$$= 36$$

Substituting gives

$$\cos\theta = \frac{36}{\sqrt{21} \times \sqrt{78}}$$

$$\Rightarrow \theta = 27.2°$$

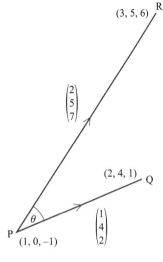

Figure 8.22

⚠ You must be careful to find the correct angle. To find ∠QPR (see figure 8.23), you need the scalar product $\overrightarrow{PQ} \cdot \overrightarrow{PR}$, as in the example above. If you take $\overrightarrow{QP} \cdot \overrightarrow{PR}$, you will obtain ∠Q′PR, which is $(180° - ∠QPR)$.

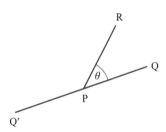

Figure 8.23

1 Find the angles between these vectors.

(i) $2\mathbf{i} + 3\mathbf{j}$ and $4\mathbf{i} + \mathbf{j}$

(ii) $2\mathbf{i} - \mathbf{j}$ and $\mathbf{i} + 2\mathbf{j}$

(iii) $\begin{pmatrix} -1 \\ -1 \end{pmatrix}$ and $\begin{pmatrix} -1 \\ -2 \end{pmatrix}$

(iv) $4\mathbf{i} + \mathbf{j}$ and $\mathbf{i} + \mathbf{j}$

(v) $\begin{pmatrix} 2 \\ 3 \end{pmatrix}$ and $\begin{pmatrix} -6 \\ 4 \end{pmatrix}$

(vi) $\begin{pmatrix} 3 \\ -1 \end{pmatrix}$ and $\begin{pmatrix} -6 \\ 2 \end{pmatrix}$

2 The points A, B and C have co-ordinates (3, 2), (6, 3) and (5, 6), respectively.

(i) Write down the vectors $\overrightarrow{AB}$ and $\overrightarrow{BC}$.

(ii) Show that the angle ABC is 90°.

(iii) Show that $|\overrightarrow{AB}| = |\overrightarrow{BC}|$.

(iv) The figure ABCD is a square.
   Find the co-ordinates of the point D.

3 Three points P, Q and R have position vectors, **p**, **q** and **r** respectively, where

$$\mathbf{p} = 7\mathbf{i} + 10\mathbf{j}, \quad \mathbf{q} = 3\mathbf{i} + 12\mathbf{j}, \quad \mathbf{r} = -\mathbf{i} + 4\mathbf{j}.$$

(i) Write down the vectors $\overrightarrow{PQ}$ and $\overrightarrow{RQ}$, and show that they are perpendicular.

(ii) Using a scalar product, or otherwise, find the angle PRQ.

(iii) Find the position vector of S, the mid-point of PR.

(iv) Show that $|\overrightarrow{QS}| = |\overrightarrow{RS}|$.

Using your previous results, or otherwise, find the angle PSQ.

[MEI]

4 Find the angles between these pairs of vectors.

(i) $\begin{pmatrix} 2 \\ 1 \\ 3 \end{pmatrix}$ and $\begin{pmatrix} 2 \\ -1 \\ 4 \end{pmatrix}$ (ii) $\begin{pmatrix} 1 \\ -1 \\ 0 \end{pmatrix}$ and $\begin{pmatrix} 3 \\ 1 \\ 5 \end{pmatrix}$

(iii) $3\mathbf{i} + 2\mathbf{j} - 2\mathbf{k}$ and $-4\mathbf{i} - \mathbf{j} + 3\mathbf{k}$

5 In the diagram, OABCDEFG is a cube in which each side has length 6. Unit vectors **i**, **j** and **k** are parallel to $\overrightarrow{OA}$, $\overrightarrow{OC}$ and $\overrightarrow{OD}$ respectively. The point P is such that $\overrightarrow{AP} = \frac{1}{3}\overrightarrow{AB}$ and the point Q is the mid-point of DF.

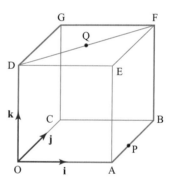

(i) Express each of the vectors $\overrightarrow{OQ}$ and $\overrightarrow{PQ}$ in terms of **i**, **j** and **k**.

(ii) Find the angle OQP.

[Cambridge AS & A Level Mathematics 9709, Paper 12 Q6 November 2009]

6 Relative to an origin O, the position vectors of points A and B are $2\mathbf{i} + \mathbf{j} + 2\mathbf{k}$ and $3\mathbf{i} - 2\mathbf{j} + p\mathbf{k}$ respectively.

(i) Find the value of p for which OA and OB are perpendicular.

(ii) In the case where $p = 6$, use a scalar product to find angle AOB, correct to the nearest degree.

(iii) Express the vector $\overrightarrow{AB}$ in terms of p and hence find the values of p for which the length of AB is 3.5 units.

[Cambridge AS & A Level Mathematics 9709, Paper 1 Q10 June 2008]

7 Relative to an origin O, the position vectors of the points A and B are given by

$$\overrightarrow{OA} = 2\mathbf{i} - 8\mathbf{j} + 4\mathbf{k} \quad \text{and} \quad \overrightarrow{OB} = 7\mathbf{i} + 2\mathbf{j} - \mathbf{k}.$$

(i) Find the value of $\overrightarrow{OA} . \overrightarrow{OB}$ and hence state whether angle AOB is acute, obtuse or a right angle.

(ii) The point X is such that $\overrightarrow{AX} = \frac{2}{5}\overrightarrow{AB}$. Find the unit vector in the direction of OX.

[Cambridge AS & A Level Mathematics 9709, Paper 1 Q6 June 2009]

8 Relative to an origin O, the position vectors of the points A and B are given by

$$\overrightarrow{OA} = 2\mathbf{i} + 3\mathbf{j} - \mathbf{k} \quad \text{and} \quad \overrightarrow{OB} = 4\mathbf{i} - 3\mathbf{j} + 2\mathbf{k}.$$

(i) Use a scalar product to find angle AOB, correct to the nearest degree.

(ii) Find the unit vector in the direction of $\overrightarrow{AB}$.

(iii) The point C is such that $\overrightarrow{OC} = 6\mathbf{j} + p\mathbf{k}$, where p is a constant. Given that the lengths of $\overrightarrow{AB}$ and $\overrightarrow{AC}$ are equal, find the possible values of p.

[Cambridge AS & A Level Mathematics 9709, Paper 1 Q11 June 2005]

9 Relative to an origin O, the position vectors of the points P and Q are given by

$$\overrightarrow{OP} = \begin{pmatrix} -2 \\ 3 \\ 1 \end{pmatrix} \quad \text{and} \quad \overrightarrow{OQ} = \begin{pmatrix} 2 \\ 1 \\ q \end{pmatrix}, \quad \text{where } q \text{ is a constant.}$$

(i) In the case where $q = 3$, use a scalar product to show that $\cos POQ = \frac{1}{7}$.

(ii) Find the values of q for which the length of $\overrightarrow{PQ}$ is 6 units.

[Cambridge AS & A Level Mathematics 9709, Paper 1 Q4 November 2005]

10 The diagram shows a semi-circular prism with a horizontal rectangular base ABCD. The vertical ends AED and BFC are semi-circles of radius 6 cm. The length of the prism is 20 cm. The mid-point of AD is the origin O, the mid-point of BC is M and the mid-point of DC is N. The points E and F are the highest points of the semi-circular ends of the prism. The point P lies on EF such that EP = 8 cm.

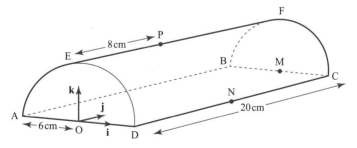

Unit vectors **i**, **j** and **k** are parallel to OD, OM and OE respectively.

(i) Express each of the vectors $\overrightarrow{PA}$ and $\overrightarrow{PN}$ in terms of **i**, **j** and **k**.

(ii) Use a scalar product to calculate angle APN.

[Cambridge AS & A Level Mathematics 9709, Paper 1 Q4 November 2008]

11 The diagram shows the roof of a house. The base of the roof, OABC, is rectangular and horizontal with OA = CB = 14 m and OC = AB = 8 m. The top of the roof DE is 5 m above the base and DE = 6 m. The sloping edges OD, CD, AE and BE are all equal in length.

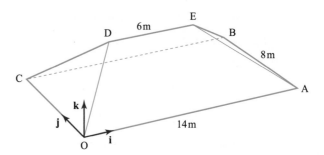

Unit vectors **i** and **j** are parallel to OA and OC respectively and the unit vector **k** is vertically upwards.

(i) Express the vector $\overrightarrow{OD}$ in terms of **i**, **j** and **k**, and find its magnitude.

(ii) Use a scalar product to find angle DOB.

[Cambridge AS & A Level Mathematics 9709, Paper 1 Q8 June 2006]

12 The diagram shows a cube OABCDEFG in which the length of each side is 4 units. The unit vectors **i**, **j** and **k** are parallel to $\overrightarrow{OA}$, $\overrightarrow{OC}$ and $\overrightarrow{OD}$ respectively. The mid-points of OA and DG are P and Q respectively and R is the centre of the square face ABFE.

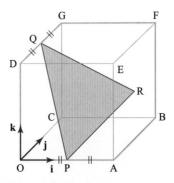

(i) Express each of the vectors $\overrightarrow{PR}$ and $\overrightarrow{PQ}$ in terms of **i**, **j** and **k**.

(ii) Use a scalar product to find angle QPR.

(ii) Find the perimeter of triangle PQR, giving your answer correct to 1 decimal place.

[Cambridge AS & A Level Mathematics 9709, Paper 1 Q10 November 2007]

1 A vector quantity has magnitude and direction.

2 A scalar quantity has magnitude only.

3 Vectors are typeset in bold, **a** or **OA**, or in the form $\overrightarrow{OA}$. They are handwritten either in the underlined form $\underline{a}$, or as $\overrightarrow{OA}$.

4 The length (or modulus or magnitude) of the vector **a** is written as a or as $|\mathbf{a}|$.

5 Unit vectors in the x, y and z directions are denoted by **i**, **j** and **k**, respectively.

6 A vector may be specified in

- magnitude–direction form: (r, θ) (in two dimensions)

- component form: $x\mathbf{i} + y\mathbf{j}$ or $\begin{pmatrix} x \\ y \end{pmatrix}$ (in two dimensions)

$$x\mathbf{i} + y\mathbf{j} + z\mathbf{k} \text{ or } \begin{pmatrix} x \\ y \\ z \end{pmatrix} \text{ (in three dimensions).}$$

7 The position vector $\overrightarrow{OP}$ of a point P is the vector joining the origin to P.

8 The vector $\overrightarrow{AB}$ is $\mathbf{b} - \mathbf{a}$, where **a** and **b** are the position vectors of A and B.

9 The angle between two vectors, **a** and **b**, is given by θ in

$$\cos\theta = \frac{\mathbf{a}.\mathbf{b}}{|\mathbf{a}||\mathbf{b}|}$$

where $\mathbf{a}.\mathbf{b} = a_1 b_1 + a_2 b_2$ (in two dimensions)
$= a_1 b_1 + a_2 b_2 + a_3 b_3$ (in three dimensions).

Answers

Neither University of Cambridge International Examinations nor OCR bear any responsibility for the example answers to questions taken from their past question papers which are contained in this publication.

Chapter 1

❓ (Page 1)

Like terms have the same variable; unlike terms do not.

Note that the power of the variable must also be the same, for example $4x$ and $5x^2$ are unlike terms and cannot be collected.

Exercise 1A (Page 4)

1 (i) $9x$

(ii) $p - 13$

(iii) $k - 4m + 4n$

(iv) 0

(v) $r + 2s - 15t$

2 (i) $4(x + 2y)$

(ii) $3(4a + 5b - 6c)$

(iii) $12(6f - 3g - 4h)$

(iv) $p(p - q + r)$

(v) $12k(k + 12m - 6n)$

3 (i) $28(x + y)$

(ii) $7b + 13c$

(iii) $-p + 24q + 33r$

(iv) $2(5l + 3w - h)$

(v) $2(w + 2v)$

4 (i) $2ab$

(ii) $n(k - m)$

(iii) $q(2p - s)$

(iv) $4(x + 2)$

(v) -2

5 (i) $6x^3y^2$

(ii) $30a^3b^3c^4$

(iii) $k^2m^2n^2$

(iv) $162p^4q^4r^4$

(v) $24r^2s^2t^2u^2$

6 (i) $\dfrac{b}{c}$

(ii) $\dfrac{e}{2f}$

(iii) $\dfrac{x}{5}$

(iv) $2a$

(v) $\dfrac{2}{pr}$

7 (i) 1

(ii) 5

(iii) pq

(iv) $\dfrac{g^2h^3}{3f^2}$

(v) $\dfrac{m^3}{n^2}$

8 (i) $\dfrac{5x}{6}$

(ii) $\dfrac{49x}{60}$

(iii) $\dfrac{z}{3}$

(iv) $\dfrac{5x}{12}$

(v) $\dfrac{27y}{40}$

9 (i) $\dfrac{8}{x}$

(ii) $\dfrac{y + x}{xy}$

(iii) $\dfrac{4y + x^2}{xy}$

(iv) $\dfrac{p^2 + q^2}{pq}$

(v) $\dfrac{bc - ac + ab}{abc}$

10 (i) $\dfrac{3x - 1}{4}$

(ii) $\dfrac{7x + 3}{15}$

(iii) $\dfrac{11x - 29}{12}$

(iv) $\dfrac{76 - 23x}{10}$

(v) $\dfrac{26x - 3}{24}$

11 (i) $\dfrac{1}{2}$

(ii) $\dfrac{2}{(2x + 1)^3}$

(iii) $\dfrac{(y - 3)^3}{4x}$

(iv) 6

(v) $\dfrac{x^3(3x + 2)}{12}$

❓ (Page 6)

A variable is a quantity which can change its value. A constant always has the same value.

❓ (Page 6)

Starting from one vertex, the polygon can be divided into $n - 2$ triangles, each with angle sum 180°.

The angles of the triangles form the angles of the polygon.

❓ (Page 7)

You get $0 = 0$.

Exercise 1B (Page 9)

1 (i) $a = 20$

(ii) $b = 8$

(iii) $c = 0$

(iv) $d = 2$

(v) $e = -5$

(vi) $f = 1.5$

(vii) $g = 14$

(viii) $h = 0$

(ix) $k = 48$

(x) $l = 9$

(xi) $m = 1$

(xii) $n = 0$

2 (i) $a + 6a + 75 = 180$

(ii) $15°, 75°, 90°$

3 (i) $2(r-2) + r = 32$

(ii) $10, 10, 12$

4 (i) $2d + 2(d-40) = 400$

(ii) $d = 120$, area $= 9600 \text{ m}^2$

5 (i) $3x + 49 = 5x + 15$

(ii) $1

6 (i) $6c - q - 25$

(ii) $6c - 47 = 55 : 17$ correct

7 (i) $22m + 36(18 - m)$

(ii) 6 kg

8 (i) $a + 18 = 5(a-2)$

(ii) 7

Exercise 1C (Page 12)

1 (i) $a = \dfrac{v-u}{t}$

(ii) $t = \dfrac{v-u}{a}$

2 $h = \dfrac{V}{lw}$

3 $r = \sqrt{\dfrac{A}{\pi}}$

4 (i) $s = \dfrac{v^2 - u^2}{2a}$

(ii) $u = \pm\sqrt{v^2 - 2as}$

5 $h = \dfrac{A - 2\pi r^2}{2\pi r}$

6 $a = \dfrac{2(s - ut)}{t^2}$

7 $b = \pm\sqrt{h^2 - a^2}$

8 $g = \dfrac{4\pi^2 l}{T^2}$

9 $m = \dfrac{2E}{2gh + v^2}$

10 $R = \dfrac{R_1 R_2}{R_1 + R_2}$

11 $h = \dfrac{2A}{a + b}$

12 $u = \dfrac{fv}{v - f}$

13 $d = \dfrac{u^2}{u - f}$

14 $V = \dfrac{mRT}{M(p_1 - p_2)}$

? (Page 12)

1 Constant acceleration formula

2 Volume of a cuboid

3 Area of a circle

4 Constant acceleration formula

5 Surface area of a closed cylinder

6 Constant acceleration formula

7 Pythagoras' theorem

8 Period of a simple pendulum

9 Energy formula

10 Resistances

11 Area of a trapezium

12 Focal length

13 Focal length

14 Pressure formula

? (Page 17)

100 m

Exercise 1D (Page 18)

1 (i) $(a + b)(l + m)$

(ii) $(p - q)(x + y)$

(iii) $(u - v)(r + s)$

(iv) $(m + p)(m + n)$

(v) $(x + 2)(x - 3)$

(vi) $(y + 7)(y + 3)$

(vii) $(z + 5)(z - 5)$

(viii) $(q - 3)(q - 3) = (q - 3)^2$

(ix) $(2x + 3)(x + 1)$

(x) $(3v - 10)(2v + 1)$

2 (i) $a^2 + 5a + 6$

(ii) $b^2 + 12b + 35$

(iii) $c^2 - 6c + 8$

(iv) $d^2 - 9d + 20$

(v) $e^2 + 5e - 6$

(vi) $g^2 - 9$

(vii) $h^2 + 10h + 25$

(viii) $4i^2 - 12i + 9$

(ix) $ac + ad + bc + bd$

(x) $x^2 - y^2$

---

3 (i) $(x + 2)(x + 4)$

(ii) $(x - 2)(x - 4)$

(iii) $(y + 4)(y + 5)$

(iv) $(r + 5)(r - 3)$

(v) $(r - 5)(r + 3)$

(vi) $(s - 2)^2$

(vii) $(x - 6)(x + 1)$

(viii) $(x + 1)^2$

(ix) $(a + 3)(a - 3)$

(x) $x(x + 6)$

4 (i) $(2x + 1)(x + 2)$

(ii) $(2x - 1)(x - 2)$

(iii) $(5x + 1)(x + 2)$

(iv) $(5x - 1)(x - 2)$

(v) $2(x + 3)(x + 4)$

(vi) $(2x + 7)(2x - 7)$

(vii) $(3x + 2)(2x - 3)$

(viii) $(3x - 1)^2$

(ix) $(t_1 + t_2)(t_1 - t_2)$

(x) $(2x - y)(x - 5y)$

5 (i) $x = 8$ or $x = 3$

(ii) $x = -8$ or $x = -3$

(iii) $x = 2$ or $x = 9$

(iv) $x = 3$ (repeated)

(v) $x = -8$ or $x = 8$

6 (i) $x = \frac{2}{3}$ or $x = 1$

(ii) $x = -\frac{2}{3}$ or $x = -1$

(iii) $x = -\frac{1}{3}$ or $x = 2$

(iv) $x = -\frac{4}{5}$ or $x = \frac{4}{5}$

(v) $x = \frac{2}{3}$ (repeated)

7 (i) $x = -4$ or $x = 5$

(ii) $x = -3$ or $x = \frac{4}{3}$

(iii) $x = 2$ (repeated)

(iv) $x = -3$ or $x = \frac{5}{2}$

(v) $x = -2$ or $x = 3$

(vi) $x = 4$ or $x = \frac{2}{3}$

8 (i) $x = \pm 1$ or $x = \pm 2$

(ii) $x = \pm 1$ or $x = \pm 3$

(iii) $x = \pm\frac{2}{3}$ or $x = \pm 1$

(iv) $x = \pm 1.5$ or $x = \pm 2$

(v) $x = 0$ or $x = \pm 0.4$

(vi) $x = 1$ or $x = 25$

(vii) $x = 1$ or $x = 2$

(viii) $x = 9$ (Note: $\sqrt{4}$ means +2)

9 (i) $x = \pm 1$

(ii) $x = \pm 2$

(iii) $x = \pm 3$

(iv) $x = \pm 2$

(v) $x = \pm 1$ or $x = \pm 1.5$

(vi) $x = 1$ or $x = \sqrt[3]{2}$

(vii) $x = 4$ or $x = 16$

(viii) $x = \frac{1}{4}$ or $x = 9$

10 $x = \pm 3$

11 (i) $w(w + 30)$

(ii) 80 m, 380 m

12 (i) $A = 2\pi rh + 2\pi r^2$

(ii) 3 cm

(iii) 5 cm

13 (ii) 14

(iii) 45

14 $x^2 + (x+1)^2 = 29^2$;
20 cm, 21 cm, 29 cm

? (Page 22)

Since $\left(x + \frac{a}{2}\right)^2 = x^2 + ax + \frac{a^2}{4}$, it
follows that to make $x^2 + ax$ into a
perfect square you must add $\frac{a^2}{4}$ or
$\left(\frac{a}{2}\right)^2$ to it.

Exercise 1E (Page 24)

1 (i) (a) $(x + 2)^2 + 5$

(b) $x = -2; (-2, 5)$

(c)

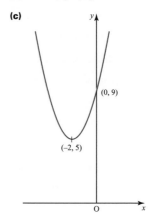

(ii) (a) $(x - 2)^2 + 5$

(b) $x = 2; (2, 5)$

(c)

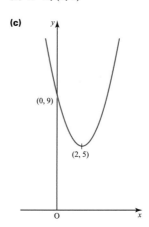

(iii) (a) $(x + 2)^2 - 1$

(b) $x = -2; (-2, -1)$

(c)

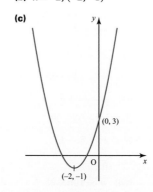

(iv) (a) $(x - 2)^2 - 1$

(b) $x = 2; (2, -1)$

(c)

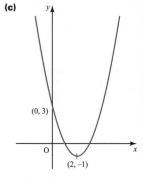

(v) (a) $(x + 3)^2 - 10$

(b) $x = -3; (-3, -10)$

(c)

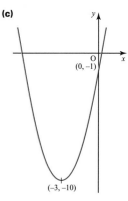

(vi) (a) $(x - 5)^2 - 25$

(b) $x = 5; (5, -25)$

(c)

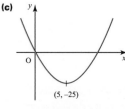

(vii) (a) $\left(x + \frac{1}{2}\right)^2 + 1\frac{3}{4}$

(b) $x = -\frac{1}{2}; \left(-\frac{1}{2}, 1\frac{3}{4}\right)$

(c)

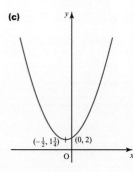

(viii) (a) $\left(x - 1\frac{1}{2}\right)^2 - 9\frac{1}{4}$

(b) $x = 1\frac{1}{2}; \left(1\frac{1}{2}, -9\frac{1}{4}\right)$

(c)

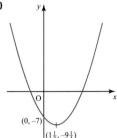

$(0, -7)$
$\left(1\frac{1}{2}, -9\frac{1}{4}\right)$

(ix) (a) $\left(x - \frac{1}{4}\right)^2 + \frac{15}{16}$

(b) $x = \frac{1}{4}; \left(\frac{1}{4}, \frac{15}{16}\right)$

(c)

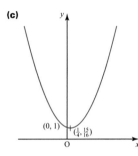

$(0, 1)$
$\left(\frac{1}{4}, \frac{15}{16}\right)$

(x) (a) $(x + 0.05)^2 + 0.0275$

(b) $x = -0.05; (-0.05, 0.0275)$

(c)

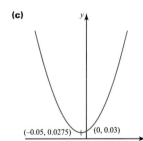

$(-0.05, 0.0275)$
$(0, 0.03)$

2 (i) $x^2 + 4x + 1$

(ii) $x^2 + 8x + 12$

(iii) $x^2 - 2x + 3$

(iv) $x^2 - 20x + 112$

(v) $x^2 - x + 1$

(vi) $x^2 + 0.2x + 1$

3 (i) $2(x + 1)^2 + 4$

(ii) $3(x - 3)^2 - 54$

(iii) $-(x + 1)^2 + 6$

(iv) $-2\left(x + \frac{1}{2}\right)^2 - 1\frac{1}{2}$

(v) $5(x - 1)^2 + 2$

(vi) $4\left(x - \frac{1}{2}\right)^2 - 5$

(vii) $-3(x + 2)^2 + 12$

(viii) $8\left(x + 1\frac{1}{2}\right)^2 - 20$

4 (i) $b = -6, c = 10$

(ii) $b = 2, c = 0$

(iii) $b = -8, c = 16$

(iv) $b = 6, c = 11$

5 (i) $x = 3 \pm \sqrt{6}; x = 5.449$
or $x = 0.551$ to 3 d.p.

(ii) $x = 4 \pm \sqrt{17}; x = 8.123$
or $x = -0.123$ to 3 d.p.

(iii) $x = 1.5 \pm \sqrt{1.25}; x = 2.618$
or $x = 0.382$ to 3 d.p.

(iv) $x = 1.5 \pm \sqrt{1.75}; x = 2.823$
or $x = 0.177$ to 3 d.p.

(v) $x = -0.4 \pm \sqrt{0.56}; x = 0.348$
or $x = -1.148$ to 3 d.p.

Exercise 1F (Page 29)

1 (i) $x = -0.683$ or $x = -7.317$

(ii) No real roots

(iii) $x = 7.525$ or $x = -2.525$

(iv) No real roots

(v) $x = 0.869$ or $x = -1.535$

(vi) $x = 3.464$ or $x = -3.464$

2 (i) -7, no real roots

(ii) 25, two real roots

(iii) 9, two real roots

(iv) -96, no real roots

(v) 4, two real roots

(vi) 0, one repeated root

3 Discriminant $= b^2 + 4a^2$; a^2 and b^2 can never be negative so the discriminant is greater than zero for all values of a and b and hence the equation has real roots.

4 (i) $k = 1$

(ii) $k = 3$

(iii) $k = -\frac{9}{16}$

(iv) $k = \pm 8$

(v) $k = 0$ or $k = -9$

5 (i) $t = 1$ and 2

(ii) $t = 3.065$

(iii) 12.25 m

Exercise 1G (Page 33)

1 (i) $x = 1, y = 2$

(ii) $x = 0, y = 4$

(iii) $x = 2, y = 1$

(iv) $x = 1, y = 1$

(v) $x = 3, y = 1$

(vi) $x = 4, y = 0$

(vii) $x = \frac{1}{2}, y = 1$

(viii) $u = 5, v = -1$

(ix) $l = -1, m = -2$

2 (i) $5p + 8h = 10, 10p + 6h = 10$

(ii) Paperbacks 40c, hardbacks $1

3 (i) $p = a + 5, 8a + 9p = 164$

(ii) Apples 7c, pears 12c

4 (i) $t_1 + t_2 = 4;$
$110t_1 + 70t_2 = 380$

(ii) 275 km motorway,
105 km country roads

5 (i) $x = 3, y = 1$ or $x = 1, y = 3$

(ii) $x = 4, y = 2$
or $x = -20, y = 14$

(iii) $x = -3, y = -2$
or $x = 1\frac{1}{2}, y = 2\frac{1}{2}$

(iv) $k = -1, m = -7$
or $k = 4, m = -2$

(v) $t_1 = -10, t_2 = -5$
or $t_1 = 10, t_2 = 5$

(vi) $p = -3, q = -2$

(vii) $k = -6, m = -4$
or $k = 6, m = 4$

(viii) $p_1 = 1, p_2 = 1$

6 (i) $h + 4r = 100,$
$2\pi rh + 2\pi r^2 = 1400\pi$

(ii) 6000π or $\dfrac{98000\pi}{27}$ cm^3

7 (i) $(3x + 2y)(2x + y)$ m^2

(iii) $x = \frac{1}{2}, y = \frac{1}{4}$

Exercise 1H (Page 37)

1 (i) $a > 6$

(ii) $b \leqslant 2$

(iii) $c > -2$

(iv) $d \leqslant -\frac{4}{3}$

(v) $e > 7$

(vi) $f > -1$

(vii) $g \leqslant 1.4$

(viii) $h < 0$

2 (i) $1 < p < 4$

(ii) $p \leqslant 1$ or $p \geqslant 4$

(iii) $-2 \leqslant x \leqslant -1$

(iv) $x < -2$ or $x > -1$

(v) $y < -1$ or $y > 3$

(vi) $-4 \leqslant z \leqslant 5$

(vii) $q \neq 2$

(viii) $y < -2$ or $y > 4$

(ix) $-2 < x < \frac{1}{3}$

(x) $y \leqslant -\frac{1}{2}$ or $y \geqslant 6$

(xi) $1 \leqslant x \leqslant 3$

(xii) $y < -\frac{1}{2}$ or $y > \frac{3}{5}$

3 (i) $k < \frac{9}{8}$

(ii) $k > -4$

(iii) $k > 10$ or $k < -10$

(iv) $k < 0$ or $k > 3$

4 (i) $k > 9$

(ii) $k < -\frac{1}{8}$

(iii) $-8 < k < 8$

(iv) $0 < k < 8$

Chapter 2

Activity 2.1 (Page 40)

A: $\frac{1}{2}$; B: -1; C: 0; D: ∞

❓ (Page 40)

No, the numerator and denominator of the gradient formula would have the same magnitude but the opposite sign, so m would be unchanged.

Activity 2.2 (Page 41)

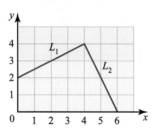

An example of L_2 is the line joining $(4, 4)$ to $(6, 0)$.

$m_1 = \frac{1}{2}, m_2 = -2 \Rightarrow m_1 m_2 = -1.$

Activity 2.3 (Page 41)

$\triangle$ABE $\triangle$BCD

AB = BC

$\angle$AEB = $\angle$BDC

$\angle$BAE = $\angle$CBD

$\Rightarrow$ Triangles ABE and BCD are congruent so BE = CD and AE = BD.

$m_1 = \dfrac{BE}{AE}; m_2 = -\dfrac{BD}{CD}$

$\Rightarrow m_1 m_2 = -\dfrac{BE}{AE} \times \dfrac{BD}{CD} = -1$

Exercise 2A (Page 44)

1 (i) (a) -2

(b) $(1, -1)$

(c) $\sqrt{20}$

(d) $\frac{1}{2}$

(ii) (a) -3

(b) $\left(3\frac{1}{2}, \frac{1}{2}\right)$

(c) $\sqrt{10}$

(d) $\frac{1}{3}$

(iii) (a) 0

(b) $(0, 3)$

(c) 12

(d) Infinite

(iv) (a) $\frac{10}{3}$

(b) $\left(3\frac{1}{2}, -3\right)$

(c) $\sqrt{109}$

(d) $-\frac{3}{10}$

(v) (a) $\frac{3}{2}$

(b) $\left(3, 1\frac{1}{2}\right)$

(c) $\sqrt{13}$

(d) $-\frac{2}{3}$

(vi) (a) Infinite

(b) $(1, 1)$

(c) 6

(d) 0

2 5

3 1

4 (i) AB: $\frac{1}{2}$, BC: $\frac{3}{2}$, CD: $\frac{1}{2}$, DA: $\frac{3}{2}$

(ii) Parallelogram

(iii)

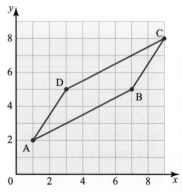

5 (i) 6

(ii) AB = $\sqrt{20}$, BC = $\sqrt{5}$

(iii) 5 square units

6 (i) 18

(ii) −2

(iii) 0 or 8

(iv) 8

7 (i)

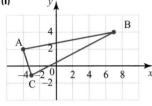

(ii) $AB = BC = \sqrt{125}$

(iii) $\left(-3\frac{1}{2}, \frac{1}{2}\right)$

(iv) 17.5 square units

8 (i) $\dfrac{2y}{x}$

(ii) $(2x, 3y)$

(iii) $\sqrt{4x^2 + 16y^2}$

9 (i)

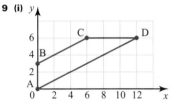

(ii) gradient BC = gradient AD
$= \frac{1}{2}$

(iii) $(6, 3)$

10 (i) 1 or 5

(ii) 7

(iii) 9

(iv) 1

11 Diagonals have gradients $\frac{2}{3}$ and $-\frac{3}{2}$ so are perpendicular.

Mid-points of both diagonals are $(4, 4)$ so they bisect each other.
52 square units

Exercise 2B (Page 49)

1 (i)

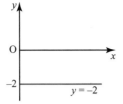

(ii)

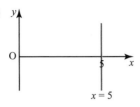

(iii)

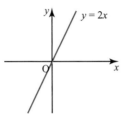

(iv)

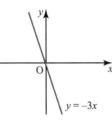

(v)

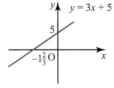

(vi)

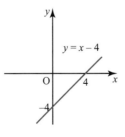

(vii)

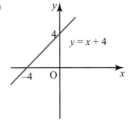

(viii)

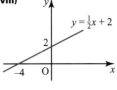

(ix)

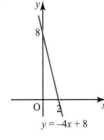

(x)

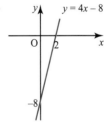

(xi)

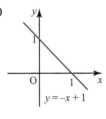

(xii)

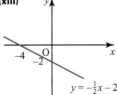

(xiii)

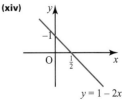

(xiv)

(xv)

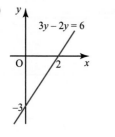

$3y - 2y = 6$

(xvi)

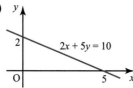

$2x + 5y = 10$

(xvii)

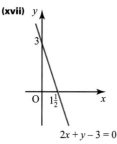

$2x + y - 3 = 0$

(xviii)

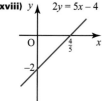

$2y = 5x - 4$

(xix)

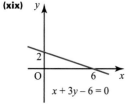

$x + 3y - 6 = 0$

(xx)

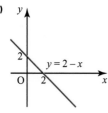

$y = 2 - x$

2 (i) Perpendicular

(ii) Neither

(iii) Perpendicular

(iv) Neither

(v) Neither

(vi) Perpendicular

(vii) Parallel

(viii) Parallel

(ix) Perpendicular

(x) Neither

(xi) Perpendicular

(xii) Neither

? (Page 51)

Take (x_1, y_1) to be $(0, b)$ and (x_2, y_2) to be $(a, 0)$.

The formula gives $\dfrac{y - b}{0 - b} = \dfrac{x - 0}{a - 0}$

which can be rearranged to give

$\dfrac{x}{a} + \dfrac{y}{b} = 1$.

Exercise 2C (Page 54)

1 (i) $x = 7$

(ii) $y = 5$

(iii) $y = 2x$

(iv) $x + y = 2$

(v) $x + 4y + 12 = 0$

(vi) $y = x$

(vii) $x = -4$

(viii) $y = -4$

(ix) $x + 2y = 0$

(x) $x + 3y - 12 = 0$

2 (i) $y = 2x + 3$

(ii) $y = 3x$

(iii) $2x + y + 3 = 0$

(iv) $y = 3x - 14$

(v) $2x + 3y = 10$

(vi) $y = 2x - 3$

3 (i) $x + 3y = 0$

(ii) $x + 2y = 0$

(iii) $x - 2y - 1 = 0$

(iv) $2x + y - 2 = 0$

(v) $3x - 2y - 17 = 0$

(vi) $x + 4y - 24 = 0$

4 (i) $3x - 4y = 0$

(ii) $y = x - 3$

(iii) $x = 2$

(iv) $3x + y - 14 = 0$

(v) $x + 7y - 26 = 0$

(vi) $y = -2$

5 (i)

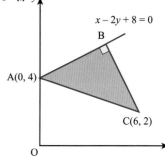

$x - 2y + 8 = 0$

B

A(0, 4)

C(6, 2)

(ii) AC: $x + 3y - 12 = 0$,
BC: $2x + y - 14 = 0$

(iii) AB $= \sqrt{20}$, BC $= \sqrt{20}$,
area = 10 square units

(iv) $\sqrt{10}$

6 (i)

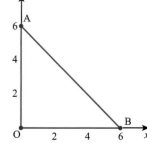

A

B

(ii) $y = x$; $x + 2y - 6 = 0$;
$2x + y - 6 = 0$

7 (i)

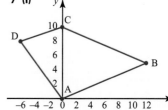

D

C

B

A

(ii) AB: $\frac{5}{12}$, BC: $-\frac{5}{12}$, CD: $\frac{1}{3}$,

    AD: $-\frac{4}{3}$

(iii) AB = 13; BC = 13; CD = $\sqrt{40}$;

    AD = 10

(iv) AB: $5x - 12y = 0$;

    BC: $5x + 12y - 120 = 0$;

    CD: $x - 3y + 30 = 0$;

    AD: $4x + 3y = 0$

(v) 90 square units

❓ (Page 58)

Attempting to solve the equations simultaneously gives 3 = 4 which is clearly false so there is no point of intersection. The lines are parallel.

Exercise 2D (Page 58)

1 (i) A(1, 1); B(5, 3); C(−1, 10)

  (ii) BC = AC = $\sqrt{85}$

2 (i)

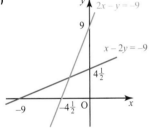

  (ii) (−3, 3)

  (iii) $2x - y = 3$; $x - 2y = 0$

  (iv) (−6, −3); (5, 7)

3 (i) $y = \frac{1}{2}x + 1$, $y = -2x + 6$

  (ii) Gradients = $\frac{1}{2}$ and $-2 \Rightarrow$ AC and BD are perpendicular. Intersection = (2, 2) = mid-point of both AC and BD.

  (iii) AC = BD = $\sqrt{20}$

  (iv) Square

4 (i)

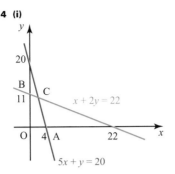

  (ii) A: (4, 0), B: (0, 11), C: (2, 10)

  (iii) 11 square units

  (iv) (−2, 21)

5 (i) (2, 4)

  (ii) (0, 3)

6 (i) $-\frac{1}{2}, \frac{3}{4}, -\frac{1}{2}, \frac{3}{4}$ parallelogram

  (ii) 10

  (iii) $-\frac{4}{3}$, $4x + 3y = 20$

  (iv) (4.4, 0.8)

  (v) 40 square units

7 (i) −3

  (ii) $x - 3y + 5 = 0$

  (iii) $x = 1$

  (iv) (1, 2)

  (vi) 3.75 square units

8 (i) $\frac{1}{2}(-2 + 14) = 6$

  (ii) gradient of AD = $\frac{8}{h}$

    gradient of CD = $\frac{8}{12 - h}$

  (iii) x co-ordinate of D = 16

    x co-ordinate of B = −4

  (iv) 160 square units

9 M(4, 6), A(−8, 0), C(16, 12)

10 (i) $3x + 2y = 31$

  (ii) (7, 5)

11 (i) $2x + 3y = 20$

  (ii) C(10, 0), D(14, 6)

12 (6.2, 9.6)

13 (i) (4, 6)

  (ii) (6, 10)

  (iii) 40.9 units

14 B(6, 5), C(12, 8)

❓ (Page 63)

Even values of n: all values of y are positive; y axis is a line of symmetry.

Odd values of n: origin is the centre of rotational symmetry of order 2.

Exercise 2E (Page 68)

1

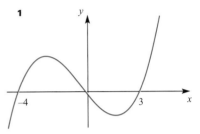

2

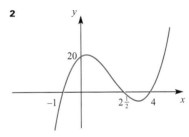

3

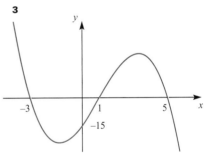

4

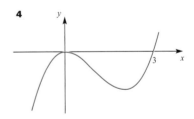

5

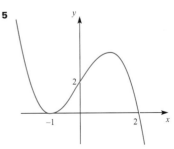

6

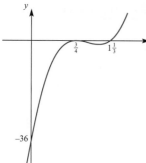

7

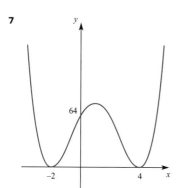

8

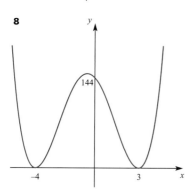

9 $y = (x+1)^2(x-2)^2$

❓ (Page 68)

$(x-a)^3$: crosses the x axis at $(a, 0)$ but is flat at that point.
$(x-a)^4$: touches the x axis at $(a, 0)$.

The same results hold for any odd or even n for $(x-a)^n$.

Exercise 2F (Page 73)

1 $(2, 7)$

2 (i) $(3, 5); (-1, -3)$

  (ii) 8.94

3 (i) $(1, 2); (-5, -10)$

4 $(2, 1)$ and $(12.5, -2.5)$; 11.1

5 $k = \pm 8$

6 $\frac{1}{4}$

7 (i) $(2, 5), (2.5, 4)$

  (ii) $-\sqrt{80} < q < \sqrt{80}$

8 3.75

9 $k < -4$

10 $k > 2, k < -6$

Chapter 3

❓ (Page 75)

(i) (a) Asian Savings

  (b) 80 000, 160 000, 320 000, …

  (c) Exponential geometric sequence

  (d) The sequence could go on but the family will not live forever

(ii) (a) Fish & Chips opening hours

  (b) 10, 10, 10, 10, 12, …

  (c) They go in a cycle, repeating every 7

  (d) Go on forever (or a long time)

(iii) (a) Clock

  (b) 0, −3.5, −5, −3.5, 0, 3.5, …

  (c) A regular pattern, repeating every 8

  (d) Forever

(iv) (a) Steps

  (b) 120, 140, 160, …

  (c) Increasing by a fixed amount (arithmetic sequence)

  (d) The steps won't go on forever

Exercise 3A (Page 81)

1 (i) Yes: $d = 2, u_7 = 39$

  (ii) No

  (iii) No

  (iv) Yes: $d = 4, u_7 = 27$

  (v) Yes: $d = -2, u_7 = -4$

2 (i) 10

  (ii) 37

3 (i) 4

  (ii) 34

4 (i) 5

  (ii) 850

5 (i) 16, 18, 20

  (ii) 324

6 (i) 15

  (ii) 1170

7 (i) First term 4, common difference 6

  (ii) 12

8 (i) 3

  (ii) 165

9 (i) 5000

  (ii) 5100

  (iii) 10 100

  (iv) The 1st sum, 5000, and the 2nd sum, 5100, add up to the third sum, 10 100. This is because the sum of the odd numbers plus the sum of the even numbers from 50 to 150 is the same as the sum of all the numbers from 50 to 150.

10 (i) 22 000

  (ii) The sum becomes negative after the 31st term, i.e. from the 32nd term on.

11 (i) $u_k = 3k + 4$; 23rd term

  (ii) $\frac{n}{2}(11 + 3n)$; 63 terms

12 (i) $16 500

  (ii) 8

13 (i) 49

  (ii) 254.8 km

14 (i) 16

  (ii) 2.5 cm

15 (i) $a = 10, d = 1.5$

  (ii) $n = 27$

16 8

17 (i) 2

(ii) 40

(iii) $\frac{n}{2}(3n+1)$

(iv) $\frac{n}{2}(9n+1)$

18 (i) $a+4d=205;\ a+18d=373$

(ii) 12 tickets; 157

(iii) 28 books

? **(Page 86)**

For example, in column A enter 1 in cell A1 and fill down a series of step 1; then in B1 enter

$=3^\wedge(\text{A1-1})$

then fill down column B. Look for the value 177 147 in column B and read off the value of n in column A.

An alternative approach is to use the IF function to find the correct value.

? **(Page 87)**

3.7×10^{11} tonnes. Less than 1.8×10^{9}; perhaps 10^8 for China.

? **(Page 90)**

The series does not converge so it does not have a sum to infinity.

Exercise 3B (Page 91)

1 (i) Yes: $r=2,\ u_7=320$

(ii) No

(iii) Yes: $r=-1,\ u_7=1$

(iv) Yes: $r=1,\ u_7=5$

(v) No

(vi) Yes: $r=\frac{1}{2},\ u_7=\frac{3}{32}$

(vii) No

2 (i) 384

(ii) 765

3 (i) 4

(ii) 81 920

4 (i) 9

(ii) 10th term

5 (i) 9

(ii) 4088

6 (i) 6

(ii) 267 (to 3 s.f.)

7 (i) 2

(ii) 3

(iii) 3069

8 (i) $\frac{1}{2}$

(ii) 8

9 (i) $\frac{1}{10}$

(ii) $\frac{7}{9}$

(iii) $S_\infty = \frac{7}{11}$

10 (i) 0.9

(ii) 45th

(iii) 1000

(iv) 44

11 (i) 0.2

(ii) 1

12 (i) $r=0.8;\ a=25$

(ii) $a=6;\ r=4$

13 (i) $\frac{16}{3}$

(ii) (a) $x=-8$ or 2

(b) $r=-\frac{1}{2}$ or 2

(iii) (a) 256

(b) $170\frac{2}{3}$

14 (i) $r=\frac{1}{3}$

(ii) $54 \times \left(\frac{1}{3}\right)^{n-1}$

(iii) $81\left(1-\left(\frac{1}{3}\right)^n\right)$

(iv) 81

(v) 11 terms

15 (i) 20, 10, 5, 2.5, 1.25

(ii) 0, 10, 15, 17.5, 18.75

(iii) First series geometric, common ratio $\frac{1}{2}$. Second sequence not geometric as there is no common ratio.

16 (i) 68th swing is the first less than 1°

(ii) 241° (to nearest degree)

17 (i) Height after nth impact $=$
$10 \times \left(\frac{2}{3}\right)^n$

(ii) 59.0m (to 3 s.f.)

19 (i) $\frac{2}{3}$

(ii) 243

(iii) 270

20 (i) $a=117;\ (d=-21)$

(ii) $a=128;\ (r=\frac{3}{4})$

21 (i) $\frac{2}{3}$

(ii) 5150

22 (i) $a+4d;\ a+14d$

(iii) 2.5

Activity 3.1 (Page 98)

(i) $\frac{n-1}{2}$

(ii) $\frac{n-2}{3}$

? **(Page 101)**

1.61051. This is $1 + 5 \times (0.1) +$ $10 \times (0.1)^2 + 10 \times (0.1)^3 + 5 \times (0.1)^4$ $+ 1 \times (0.1)^5$ and 1, 5, 10, 10, 5, 1 are the binominal coefficients for $n=5$.

Exercise 3C (Page 103)

1 (i) $x^4 + 4x^3 + 6x^2 + 4x + 1$

(ii) $1 + 7x + 21x^2 + 35x^3 + 35x^4$ $+ 21x^5 + 7x^6 + x^7$

(iii) $x^5 + 10x^4 + 40x^3 + 80x^2 +$ $80x + 32$

(iv) $64x^6 + 192x^5 + 240x^4 +$ $160x^3 + 60x^2 + 12x + 1$

(v) $16x^4 - 96x^3 + 216x^2 - 216x$ $+ 81$

(vi) $8x^3 + 36x^2y + 54xy^2 + 27y^3$

(vii) $x^3 - 6x + \frac{12}{x} - \frac{8}{x^3}$

(viii) $x^4 + 8x + \frac{24}{x^2} + \frac{32}{x^5} + \frac{16}{x^8}$

(ix) $243x^{10} - 810x^7 + 1080x^4 -$ $720x + \frac{240}{x^2} - \frac{32}{x^5}$

2 (i) 6

   (ii) 15

   (iii) 20

   (iv) 15

   (v) 1

   (vi) 220

3 (i) 56

   (ii) 210

   (iii) 673 596

   (iv) −823 680

   (v) 13 440

4 (i) $6x + 2x^3$

5 $16x^4 - 64x^2 + 96$

6 $64 + 192kx + 240k^2x^2$

7 (i) $1 - 12x + 60x^2$

   (ii) −3136 and 16 128

8 (i) $4096x^6 - 6144kx^3 + 3840k^2$

   (ii) $\pm\frac{1}{4}$

9 (i) $x^{12} - 6x^9 + 15x^6$

   (ii) −20

10 (i) $x^5 - 10x^3 + 40x$

   (ii) 150

11 (ii) $x = 0, -1$ and -2

12 $n = 5, a = -\frac{1}{2}, b = 20$

13 (i) $64 - 192x + 240x^2$

   (ii) 1.25

14 (i) $1 + 5ax + 10a^2x^2$

   (ii) $a = \frac{2}{5}$

   (iii) −2.4

Chapter 4

❓ (Page 108)

(i) (a) One-to-one

   (b) One-to-many

   (c) Many-to-one

   (d) Many-to-many

Exercise 4A (Page 110)

1 (i) One-to-one, yes

   (ii) Many-to-one, yes

   (iii) Many-to-many, no

   (iv) One-to-many, no

   (v) Many-to-many, no

   (vi) One-to-one, yes

   (vii) Many-to-many, no

   (viii) Many-to-one, yes

2 (i) (a) Examples: one $\mapsto 3$, word $\mapsto 4$

   (b) Many-to-one

   (c) Words

   (ii) (a) Examples: $1 \mapsto 4$, $2.1 \mapsto 8.4$

   (b) One-to-one

   (c) $\mathbb{R}^+$

   (iii) (a) Examples: $1 \mapsto 1$, $6 \mapsto 4$

   (b) Many-to-one

   (c) $\mathbb{Z}^+$

   (iv) (a) Examples: $1 \mapsto -3$, $-4 \mapsto -13$

   (b) One-to-one

   (c) $\mathbb{R}$

   (v) (a) Examples: $4 \mapsto 2$, $9 \mapsto 3$

   (b) One-to-one

   (c) $x \geqslant 0$

   (vi) (a) Examples: $36\pi \mapsto 3$, $\frac{9}{2}\pi \mapsto 1.5$

   (b) One-to-one

   (c) $\mathbb{R}^+$

   (vii) (a) Examples: $12\pi \mapsto 3$, $12\pi \mapsto 12$

   (b) Many-to-many

   (c) $\mathbb{R}^+$

   (viii) (a) Examples: $1 \mapsto \frac{3}{2}\sqrt{3}, 4 \mapsto 24\sqrt{3}$

   (b) One-to-one

   (c) $\mathbb{R}^+$

   (ix) (a) Examples: $4 \mapsto 16$, $-0.7 \mapsto 0.49$

   (b) Many-to-one

   (c) $\mathbb{R}$

3 (i) (a) −5

   (b) 9

   (c) −11

   (ii) (a) 3

   (b) 5

   (c) 10

   (iii) (a) 32

   (b) 82.4

   (c) 14

   (d) −40

4 (i) $f(x) \leqslant 2$

   (ii) $0 \leqslant f(\theta) \leqslant 1$

   (iii) $y \in \{2, 3, 6, 11, 18\}$

   (iv) $y \in \mathbb{R}^+$

   (v) $\mathbb{R}$

   (vi) $\left\{\frac{1}{2}, 1, 2, 4\right\}$

   (vii) $0 \leqslant y \leqslant 1$

   (viii) $\mathbb{R}$

   (ix) $0 < f(x) \leqslant 1$

   (x) $f(x) \geqslant 3$

5 For f, every value of x (including $x = 3$) gives a unique output, whereas g(2) can equal either 4 or 6.

❓ (Page 115)

(i) (a) Function with an inverse function.

   (b) f: $C \mapsto \frac{9}{5}C + 32$

   f^{-1}: $F \mapsto \frac{5}{9}(F - 32)$

(ii) (a) Function but no inverse function since one grade corresponds to several marks.

(iii) (a) Function with an inverse function.

   (b) 1 light year $\approx 6 \times 10^{12}$ miles or almost 10^{16} metres.

f: $x \mapsto 10^{16}x$ (approx.)

f^{-1}: $x \mapsto 10^{-16}x$ (approx.)

(iv) (a) Function but no inverse function since fares are banded.

Activity 4.1 (Page 117)

(i)

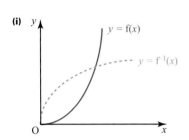

$f(x) = x^2$; $f^{-1}(x) = \sqrt{x}$

(ii)

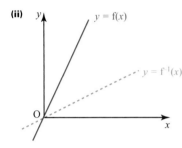

$f(x) = 2x$; $f^{-1}(x) = \frac{1}{2}x$

(iii)

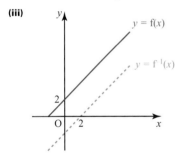

$f(x) = x + 2$; $f^{-1}(x) = x - 2$

(iv)

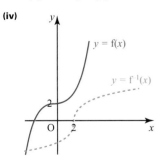

$f(x) = x^3 + 2$; $f^{-1}(x) = \sqrt[3]{x - 2}$

$y = f(x)$ and $y = f^{-1}(x)$ appear to be reflections of each other in $y = x$.

Exercise 4B (Page 120)

1 (i) $8x^3$

   (ii) $2x^3$

   (iii) $(x + 2)^3$

   (iv) $x^3 + 2$

   (v) $8(x + 2)^3$

   (vi) $2(x^3 + 2)$

   (vii) $4x$

   (viii) $[(x + 2)^3 + 2]^3$

   (ix) $x + 4$

2 (i) $f^{-1}(x) = \dfrac{x - 7}{2}$

   (ii) $f^{-1}(x) = 4 - x$

   (iii) $f^{-1}(x) = \dfrac{2x - 4}{x}$

   (iv) $f^{-1}(x) = \sqrt{x + 3}$, $x \geqslant -3$

3 (i), (ii)

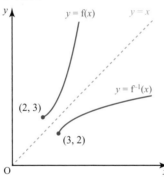

4 (i) fg

   (ii) g^2

   (iii) fg^2

   (iv) gf

5 (i) x

   (ii) $\dfrac{1}{x}$

   (iii) $\dfrac{1}{x}$

   (iv) $\dfrac{1}{x}$

6 (i) $a = 3$

   (ii)

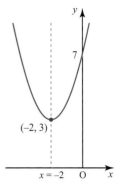

   (iii) $f(x) \geqslant 3$

   (iv) Function f is not one-to-one when domain is $\mathbb{R}$. Inverse exists for function with domain $x \geqslant -2$.

7 f^{-1}: $x \mapsto \sqrt[3]{\dfrac{x - 3}{4}}$, $x \in \mathbb{R}$.

The graphs are reflections of each other in the line $y = x$.

8 (i) $a = 2$, $b = -5$

   (ii) Translation $\begin{pmatrix} -2 \\ -5 \end{pmatrix}$

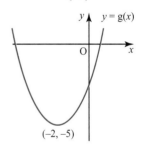

   (iii) $y \geqslant -5$

   (iv) $c = -2$

   (v)

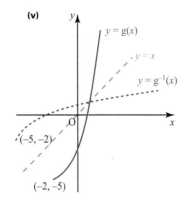

9 **(i)** $f(x) \leqslant 2$

(ii) $k = 13$

10 **(i)** $k = 4$ or -8; $x = 1$ or -5

(ii) 7

(iii) $\dfrac{9 - 2x}{x}$, $x \neq 0$

11 **(i)** $2(x - 2)^2 + 3$

(ii) $f(x) \geqslant 3$

(iii) f is not one-to-one

(iv) 2

(v) $2 - \sqrt{\dfrac{x - 3}{2}}$, $g^{-1}(x) \leqslant 2$

12 **(i)**

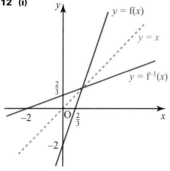

(ii) $-9x^2 + 30x - 16$

(iii) $9 - (x - 3)^2$

(iv) $3 + \sqrt{9 - x}$

Chapter 5

Activity 5.1 (Page 124)

See text that follows.

Activity 5.2 (Page 126)

6.1; 6.01; 6.001

Activity 5.3 (Page 127)

(i) 2

(ii) -4

(iii) 8

Gradient is twice the x co-ordinate.

Exercise 5A (Page 129)

2 $4x^3$

3

$f(x)$	$f'(x)$
x^2	$2x$
x^3	$3x^2$
x^4	$4x^3$
x^5	$5x^4$
x^6	$6x^5$
$\vdots$	
x^n	nx^{n-1}

? **(Page 129)**

When $f(x) = x^n$, then

$f(x + h)$

$= (x + h)^n$

$= x^n + nhx^{n-1}$ + terms of order h^2 and higher powers of h.

The gradient of the chord

$= \dfrac{f(x + h) - f(x)}{h}$

$= nx^{n-1}$ + terms of order h and higher powers of h.

As h tends to zero, the gradient tends to nx^{n-1}.

Hence the gradient of the tangent is nx^{n-1}.

Activity 5.4 (Page 130)

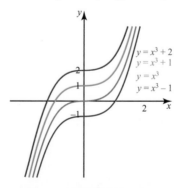

When $x = 0$, all gradients $= 0$

When $x = 1$, all gradients are equal.

i.e. for any x value they all have the same gradient.

Activity 5.5 (Page 130)

$y = x^3 + c \Rightarrow \dfrac{dy}{dx} = 3x^2$, i.e. gradient depends only on the x co-ordinate.

Exercise 5B (Page 133)

1 $5x^4$

2 $8x$

3 $6x^2$

4 $11x^{10}$

5 $40x^9$

6 $15x^4$

7 0

8 7

9 $6x^2 + 15x^4$

10 $7x^6 - 4x^3$

11 $2x$

12 $3x^2 + 6x + 3$

13 $3x^2$

14 $x + 1$

15 $6x + 6$

16 $8\pi r$

17 $4\pi r^2$

18 $\dfrac{1}{2}t$

19 2π

20 $3l^2$

21 $\dfrac{3}{2}x^{\frac{1}{2}}$

22 $-\dfrac{1}{x^2}$

23 $\dfrac{1}{2\sqrt{x}}$

24 $\dfrac{1}{2}x^{\frac{3}{2}}$

25 $-\dfrac{2}{x^3}$

26 $-\dfrac{15}{x^4}$

27 $-x^{-\frac{3}{2}}$

28 $\dfrac{2}{\sqrt{x}} + 4x^{-\frac{3}{2}}$

29 $\dfrac{3}{2}x^{\frac{1}{2}} - \dfrac{3}{2}x^{-\frac{5}{2}}$

30 $\dfrac{5}{3}x^{\frac{2}{3}} + \dfrac{2}{3}x^{-\frac{5}{3}}$

31 $8x - 1$

32 $4x + 5$

33 1

34 $16x^3 - 10x$

35 $\frac{3}{2}x^{\frac{1}{2}}$

36 $\frac{1}{\sqrt{x}}$

37 $\frac{9\sqrt{x}}{2} - \frac{1}{\sqrt{x}}$

38 $\frac{3}{4}x^2 - \frac{1}{2}x + 4$

39 $\frac{3\sqrt{x}}{2}$

40 $\frac{5}{4}x^{\frac{3}{2}} - \frac{3}{2}\sqrt{x} - \frac{2}{\sqrt{x}}$

Exercise 5C (Page 136)

1 (i) (a) $-2x^{-3}$

(b) -128

(ii) (a) $-x^{-2} - 4x^{-5}$

(b) 3

(iii) (a) $-12x^{-4} - 10x^{-6}$

(b) -22

(iv) (a) $12x^3 + 24x^{-4}$

(b) 97.5

(v) (a) $\frac{1}{2\sqrt{x}} + 3$

(b) $3\frac{1}{4}$

(vi) (a) $-2x^{-\frac{3}{2}}$

(b) $-\frac{2}{27}$

2 (i)

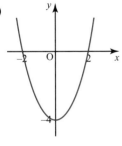

(ii) $(-2, 0), (2, 0)$

(iii) $\frac{\mathrm{d}y}{\mathrm{d}x} = 2x$

(iv) At $(-2, 0), \frac{\mathrm{d}y}{\mathrm{d}x} = -4$;

at $(2, 0), \frac{\mathrm{d}y}{\mathrm{d}x} = 4$

3 (i)

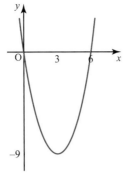

(ii) $\frac{\mathrm{d}y}{\mathrm{d}x} = 2x - 6$

(iii) At $(3, -9), \frac{\mathrm{d}y}{\mathrm{d}x} = 0$

(iv) Tangent is horizontal: curve at a minimum.

4 (i)

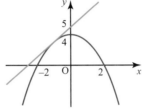

(iii) $\frac{\mathrm{d}y}{\mathrm{d}x} = -2x$: at $(-1, 3), \frac{\mathrm{d}y}{\mathrm{d}x} = 2$

(iv) Yes: the line and the curve both pass through $(-1, 3)$ and they have the same gradient at that point.

(v) Yes, by symmetry.

5 (i)

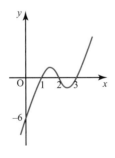

(ii) $\frac{\mathrm{d}y}{\mathrm{d}x} = 3x^2 - 12x + 11$

(iii) $x = 1: \frac{\mathrm{d}y}{\mathrm{d}x} = 2; x = 2: \frac{\mathrm{d}y}{\mathrm{d}x} = -1;$

$x = 3: \frac{\mathrm{d}y}{\mathrm{d}x} = 2$

The tangents at $(1, 0)$ and $(3, 0)$ are therefore parallel.

6 (i)

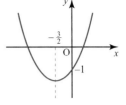

(ii) $\frac{\mathrm{d}y}{\mathrm{d}x} = 2x + 3$

(iii) $(1, 3)$

(iv) No, since the line does not go through $(1, 3)$.

7 (i)

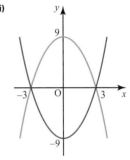

(ii) $\frac{\mathrm{d}y}{\mathrm{d}x} = 2x$

(iii) At $(2, -5), \frac{\mathrm{d}y}{\mathrm{d}x} = 4$;

at $(-2, -5), \frac{\mathrm{d}y}{\mathrm{d}x} = -4$

(iv) At $(2, 5), \frac{\mathrm{d}y}{\mathrm{d}x} = -4$;

at $(-2, 5), \frac{\mathrm{d}y}{\mathrm{d}x} = 4$

(v) A rhombus

8 (i)

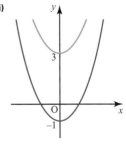

(ii) 4

(iv) $y = x^2 + c, c \in \mathbb{R}$

9 (i) $4a + b - 5 = 0$

(ii) $12a + b = 21$

(iii) $a = 2$ and $b = -3$

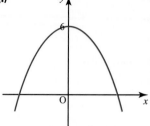

10 (i) $\dfrac{dy}{dx} = -\dfrac{7x}{20}$

(ii) 0.8225 and −0.8225

(iii) $x = \dfrac{10}{7}$

11 (i)

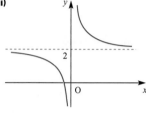

(ii) $\left(-\frac{1}{2}, 0\right)$

(iii) $-\dfrac{1}{x^2}$

(iv) −4

12 (i) $-\dfrac{8}{x^3} + 1$

(iii) 2

(v) 0

(vi) There is a minimum point at $(2, 3)$

13 (i)

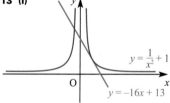

$y = \dfrac{1}{x^2} + 1$

$y = -16x + 13$

(iii) $-\dfrac{2}{x^3}$; −16

(iv) The line $y = -16x + 13$ is a tangent to the curve $y = \dfrac{1}{x^2} + 1$ at $(0.5, 5)$

14 (i)

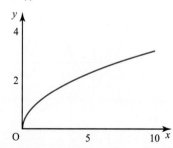

(ii) $\dfrac{dy}{dx} = \frac{1}{2}x^{-\frac{1}{2}}$

(iii) $\frac{1}{6}$

15 (i)

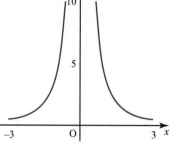

(ii) $\dfrac{dy}{dx} = -\dfrac{8}{x^3}$

(iii) 1

(iv) −1; the curve is symmetrical about the y axis

16 (i) $\dfrac{dy}{dx} = \dfrac{1}{2} + \dfrac{2}{x^2}$

(ii) $x = 2$, gradient $= 1$

17 4

18 $\dfrac{3}{8}$

Exercise 5D (Page 142)

1 (i) $\dfrac{dy}{dx} = 6 - 2x$

(ii) 4

(iii) $y = 4x + 1$

2 (i)

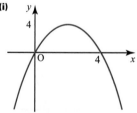

(ii) $\dfrac{dy}{dx} = 4 - 2x$

(iii) 2

(iv) $y = 2x + 1$

3 (i) $\dfrac{dy}{dx} = 3x^2 - 8x$

(ii) −4

(iii) $y = -4x$

(iv) $(0, 0)$

4 (i)

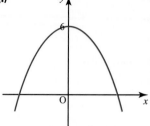

(ii) At $(-1, 5), \dfrac{dy}{dx} = 2$; at $(1, 5), \dfrac{dy}{dx} = -2$

(iii) $y = 2x + 7$, $y = -2x + 7$

(iv) $(0, 7)$

5 (i)

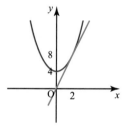

(iii) $y = 4x$ is the tangent to the curve at $(2, 8)$.

6 (i) $y = 6x + 28$

(ii) $(3, 45)$

(iii) $6y = -x + 273$

7 (i) $\dfrac{dy}{dx} = 3x^2 - 8x + 5$

(ii) 4

(iii) 8

(iv) $y = 8x - 20$

(v) $8y = -x + 35$

(vi) $x = 0$ or $x = \frac{8}{3}$

8 (i)

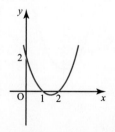

A(1, 0); B(2, 0) or vice versa

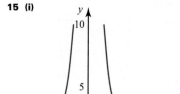

(ii) At $(1, 0)$, $\dfrac{dy}{dx} = -1$

At $(2, 0)$, $\dfrac{dy}{dx} = 1$

(iii) At $(1, 0)$,
tangent is $y = -x + 1$,
normal is $y = x - 1$
At $(2, 0)$,
tangent is $y = x - 2$,
normal is $y = -x + 2$

(iv) A square

9 (i) $(1, -7)$ and $(4, -4)$

(ii) $\dfrac{dy}{dx} = 4x - 9$. At $(1, -7)$,
tangent is $y = -5x - 2$;
at $(4, -4)$, tangent is
$y = 7x - 32$.

(iii) $(2.5, -14.5)$

(iv) No

10 (i) $y = \frac{1}{2}x + \frac{1}{2}$

(ii) $y = 3 - 2x$

(iii) $2\frac{1}{2}$ units

11 (i) $y = -\frac{1}{4}x + 1$

(ii) $y = 4x - 7\frac{1}{2}$

(iii) $8\frac{1}{2}$ square units

12 (i) $\dfrac{1}{2\sqrt{x}}$

(ii) $\left(\frac{1}{16}, -\frac{3}{4}\right)$

(iii) No. Point $\left(\frac{1}{16}, -\frac{3}{4}\right)$ does not
lie on the line $y = 2x - 1$.

13 (i) $y = 5x - \frac{7}{4}$

(ii) $20y + 4x + 9 = 0$

(iii) $\frac{13}{20}$ square units

14 27.4 units

15 (i) $2y = x + 6$

(ii) 9 square units

16 (i) $3 + \dfrac{2}{x^3}$

(ii) 5

(iii) $y = 5x - 3$

17 (i) $2x - \dfrac{1}{x^2}$

(ii) 1

(iv) $(-2.4, 5.4)$, $(0.4, 2.6)$

18 $26\frac{2}{3}$ units

19 (i) (a) $x = 1\frac{1}{2}$ and $x = 3$

(b) $y = 2x - 2$

(c) $36.9°$

(ii) $k < 3.875$

20 (ii) $(-8, 6)$

(iii) 11.2 units

Activity 5.6 (Page 146)

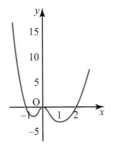

(i) 3

(ii) 0

(iii) $(0, 0)$ maximum; minima to left
and right of this.

(iv) No

(v) No

(vi) About -2.5

Exercise 5E (Page 151)

1 (i) $\dfrac{dy}{dx} = 2x + 8$;

$\dfrac{dy}{dx} = 0$ when $x = -4$

(ii) Minimum

(iv)

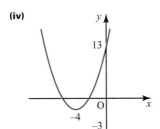

2 (i) $\dfrac{dy}{dx} = 2x + 5$;

$\dfrac{dy}{dx} = 0$ when $x = -2\frac{1}{2}$

(ii) Minimum

(iii) $y = -4\frac{1}{4}$

(iv)

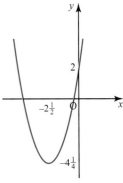

3 (i) $\dfrac{dy}{dx} = 3x^2 - 12$;

$\dfrac{dy}{dx} = 0$ when $x = -2$ or 2

(ii) Minimum at $x = 2$,
maximum at $x = -2$

(iii) When $x = -2$, $y = 18$;
when $x = 2$, $y = -14$

(iv)

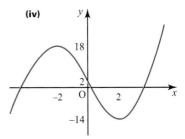

4 (i) A maximum at $(0, 0)$,
a minimum at $(4, -32)$

(ii)

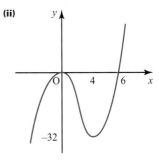

5 $\dfrac{dy}{dx} = 3x^2 - 1$

6 (i) $\dfrac{dy}{dx} = 3x^2 + 4$

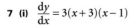
7 (i) $\dfrac{dy}{dx} = 3(x+3)(x-1)$

(ii) $x = -3$ or 1

(v)

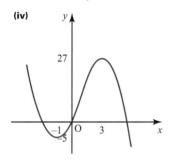

8 (i) $\dfrac{dy}{dx} = -3(x+1)(x-3)$

(ii) Minimum when $x = -1$, maximum when $x = 3$

(iii) When $x = -1$, $y = -5$; when $x = 3$, $y = 27$

(iv)

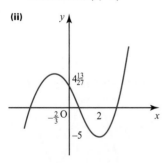

9 (i) Maximum at $\left(-\dfrac{2}{3}, 4\dfrac{13}{27}\right)$, minimum at $(2, -5)$

(ii)

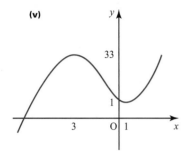

10 (i) Maximum at $(0, 300)$, minimum at $(3, 165)$, minimum at $(-6, -564)$

(ii)

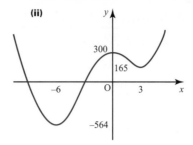

11 (i) $\dfrac{dy}{dx} = 3(x^2 + 1)$

(ii) There are no stationary points.

(iii)

x	-3	-2	-1	0	1	2	3
y	-36	-14	-4	0	4	14	36

(iv)

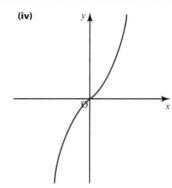

12 (i) $\dfrac{dy}{dx} = 6x^2 + 6x - 72$

(ii) $y = 18$

(iii) $\dfrac{dy}{dx} = 48$; $y = 48x - 174$

(iv) $(-4, 338)$ and $(3, -5)$

13 (i) $\left(\dfrac{1}{2}, 4\right)$ and $\left(-\dfrac{1}{2}, -4\right)$

(ii) $-\dfrac{1}{2} < x < \dfrac{1}{2}$

14 (i) $\dfrac{dy}{dx} = (2x - 3)^2 - 4$

(ii) $2y + 9 = 10x$

(iii) $x > 2\dfrac{1}{2}$ or $x < \dfrac{1}{2}$

15 (ii) $x < 1.5$

(iii) $(-1, 8)$ and $(2, 2)$

(iv) $3\dfrac{3}{4}$

16 (i) $x = 1\dfrac{1}{2}$ and $x = 2$

(ii) $(2, 1)$ is the stationary point

Activity 5.7 (Page 155)

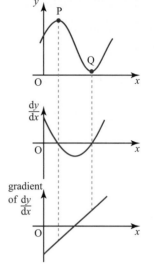

At P (max.) the gradient of $\dfrac{dy}{dx}$ is negative.

At Q (min.) the gradient of $\dfrac{dy}{dx}$ is positive.

Exercise 5F (Page 158)

1 (i) $\dfrac{dy}{dx} = 3x^2$; $\dfrac{d^2y}{dx^2} = 6x$

(ii) $\dfrac{dy}{dx} = 5x^4$; $\dfrac{d^2y}{dx^2} = 20x^3$

(iii) $\dfrac{dy}{dx} = 8x$; $\dfrac{d^2y}{dx^2} = 8$

(iv) $\dfrac{dy}{dx} = -2x^{-3}$; $\dfrac{d^2y}{dx^2} = 6x^{-4}$

(v) $\dfrac{dy}{dx} = \dfrac{3}{2}x^{\frac{1}{2}}$; $\dfrac{d^2y}{dx^2} = \dfrac{3}{4}x^{-\frac{1}{2}}$

(vi) $\dfrac{dy}{dx} = 4x^3 + \dfrac{6}{x^4}$;

$\dfrac{d^2y}{dx^2} = 12x^2 - \dfrac{24}{x^5}$

2 (i) $(-1, 3)$, minimum

(ii) $(3, 9)$, maximum

(iii) $(-1, 2)$, maximum and $(1, -2)$, minimum

(iv) $(0, 0)$, maximum and $(1, -1)$, minimum

(v) $(-1, 2)$, minimum; $\left(-\dfrac{3}{4}, 2.02\right)$, maximum; $(1, -2)$, minimum

(vi) $(1, 2)$, minimum and

$(-1, -2)$, maximum

(vii) $\left(\frac{1}{2}, 12\right)$, minimum

(viii) $\left(\sqrt{2}, 8\sqrt{2}\right)$, minimum and

$\left(-\sqrt{2}, -8\sqrt{2}\right)$, maximum

(ix) $(16, 32)$, maximum

3 (i) $4x(x+2)(x-2)$

(ii) $4(3x^2 - 4)$

(iii) $(-2, -16)$, minimum;

$(0, 0)$, maximum;

$(2, -16)$, minimum

(iv)

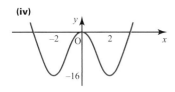

4 (i) $\dfrac{dy}{dx} = (3x-7)(x-1)$

(ii) Maximum at $(1, 0)$;

minimum at $\left(2\frac{1}{3}, -1\frac{5}{27}\right)$

(iii)

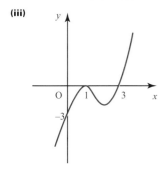

5 (i) $\dfrac{dy}{dx} = 4x(x-1)(x-2)$

(ii) Minimum at $(0, 0)$;

maximum at $(1, 1)$;

minimum at $(2, 0)$

(iii)

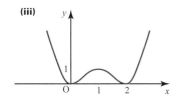

6 (i) $p + q = -1$

(ii) $3p + 2q = 0$

(iii) $p = 2$ and $q = -3$

7 (i) $f'(x) = 8x - \dfrac{1}{x^2}; f''(x) = 8 + \dfrac{2}{x^3}$

(ii) $\left(\frac{1}{2}, 3\right)$, minimum

8 (i) $1 - \dfrac{2}{\sqrt{x}}; x^{-\frac{3}{2}}$

(ii) $(4, -4)$, minimum

9 2

10 (i) 0, 10

(ii) -58.8

Exercise 5G (Page 162)

1 (i) $y = 60 - x$

(ii) $A = 60x - x^2$

(iii) $\dfrac{dA}{dx} = 60 - 2x;$

$\dfrac{d^2A}{dx^2} = -2$

Dimensions 30 m by 30 m,

area 900 m²

2 (i) $V = 4x^3 - 48x^2 + 144x$

(ii) $\dfrac{dV}{dx} = 12x^2 - 96x + 144;$

$\dfrac{d^2V}{dx^2} = 24x - 96$

3 (i) $y = 8 - x$

(ii) $S = 2x^2 - 16x + 64$

(iii) 32

4 (i) $2x + y = 80$

(ii) $A = 80x - 2x^2$

(iii) $x = 20, y = 40$

5 (i) $x(1 - 2x)$

(ii) $V = x^2 - 2x^3$

(iii) $\dfrac{dV}{dx} = 2x - 6x^2;$

$\dfrac{d^2V}{dx^2} = 2 - 12x$

(iv) All dimensions $\frac{1}{3}$ m (a cube);

volume $\frac{1}{27}$ m³

6 (i) (a) $(4 - 2x)$ cm

(b) $(16 - 16x + 4x^2)$ cm²

(iii) $x = 1.143$

(iv) $A = 6.857$

7 (i) $P = 2\pi r, r = \dfrac{15 - 2x}{\pi}$

(iii) $x = \dfrac{30}{4 + \pi}$ cm:

lengths ≈ 16.8 cm and

13.2 cm

8 (i) $h = \dfrac{125}{r} - r$

(ii) $V = 125\pi r - \pi r^3$

(iii) $\dfrac{dV}{dr} = 125\pi - 3\pi r^2;$

$\dfrac{d^2V}{dx^2} = -6\pi r$

(iv) $r = 6.45$ cm; $h = 12.9$ cm

(to 3 s.f.)

9 (i) Area $= xy = 18$

(ii) $T = 2x + y$

(iv) $\dfrac{dT}{dx} = 2 - \dfrac{18}{x^2}; \dfrac{d^2T}{dx^2} = \dfrac{36}{x^3}$

(v) $x = 3$ and $y = 6$

10 (i) $V = x^2 y$

(ii) $A = x^2 + 4xy$

(iii) $A = x^2 + \dfrac{2}{x}$

(iv) $\dfrac{dA}{dx} = 2x - \dfrac{2}{x^2}; \dfrac{d^2A}{dx^2} = 2 + \dfrac{4}{x^3}$

(v) $x = 1$ and $y = \frac{1}{2}$

11 (i) $h = \dfrac{324}{x^2}$

(iii) $\dfrac{dA}{dx} = 12x - \dfrac{2592}{x^2}$; stationary

point when $x = 6$ and $h = 9$

(iv) Minimum area $= 648$ cm²

Dimensions:

6 cm × 18 cm × 9 cm

12 (i) $y = \dfrac{24}{x}$

(ii) $A = 3x + 30 + \dfrac{48}{x}$

(iii) $A = 54$ m²

13 (i) $h = 12 - 2r$

(ii) 64π or 201 cm³

❓ (Page 167)

$\dfrac{dV}{dh}$ is the rate of change of the

volume with respect to the height of

the sand.

$\dfrac{dh}{dt}$ is the rate of change of the height of the sand with respect to time.

$\dfrac{dV}{dh} \times \dfrac{dh}{dt}$ is the rate of change of the volume with respect to time.

ⓟ (Page 169)

$y = (x^2 - 2)^4$

$= (x^2)^4 + 4(x^2)^3(-2) + 6(x^2)^2(-2)^2$
$\quad + 4(x^2)(-2)^3 + (-2)^4$

$= x^8 - 8x^6 + 24x^4 - 32x^2 + 16$

$\dfrac{dy}{dx} = 8x^7 - 48x^5 + 96x^3 - 64x$

$= 8x(x^6 - 6x^4 + 12x^2 - 8)$

$= 8x(x^2 - 2)(x^4 - 4x^2 + 4)$

$= 8x(x^2 - 2)(x^2 - 2)^2$

$= 8x(x^2 - 2)^3$

Exercise 5H (Page 171)

1 (i) $3(x + 2)^2$

(ii) $8(2x + 3)^3$

(iii) $6x(x^2 - 5)^2$

(iv) $15x^2(x^3 + 4)^4$

(v) $-3(3x + 2)^{-2}$

(vi) $\dfrac{-6x}{(x^2 - 3)^4}$

(vii) $3x(x^2 - 1)^{\frac{1}{2}}$

(viii) $3\left(\dfrac{1}{x} + x\right)^2\left(1 - \dfrac{1}{x^2}\right)$

(ix) $\dfrac{2}{\sqrt{x}}\left(\sqrt{x} - 1\right)^3$

2 (i) $9(3x - 5)^2$

(ii) $y = 9x - 17$

3 (i) $8(2x - 1)^3$

(ii) $\left(\frac{1}{2}, 0\right)$, minimum

(iii)

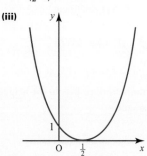

4 (i) $4(2x - 1)(x^2 - x - 2)^3$

(ii) $(-1, 0)$, minimum;

$\left(\frac{1}{2}, \frac{6561}{256}\right)$, maximum;

$(2, 0)$, minimum

(iii)

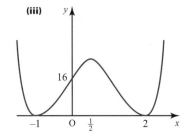

5 $4\ \text{cm}^2\,\text{s}^{-1}$

6 $-0.015\ \text{Ns}^{-1}$

7 $\dfrac{\pi}{10}\ \text{m}^2\,\text{day}^{-1}$

$(= 0.314\ \text{m}^2\,\text{day}^{-1}$ to 3 s.f.$)$

Chapter 6

❓ (Page 173)

The gradient depends only on the x co-ordinate. This is the same for all four curves so at points with the same x co-ordinate the tangents are parallel.

Exercise 6A (Page 177)

1 (i) $y = 2x^3 + 5x + c$

(ii) $y = 2x^3 + 5x + 2$

2 (i) $y = 2x^2 + 3$

(ii) 5

3 (i) $y = 2x^3 - 6$

4 (ii) $t = 4$. Only 4 is applicable here.

5 (i) $y = 5x + c$

(ii) $y = 5x + 3$

(iii)

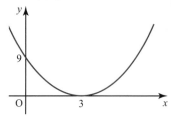

6 (i) $x = 1$ (minimum) and $x = -1$ (maximum)

(ii) $y = x^3 - 3x + 3$

(iii)

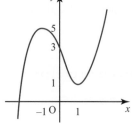

7 (i) $y = x^2 - 6x + 9$

(ii) The curve passes through $(1, 4)$

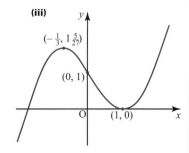

8 (i) $y = x^3 - x^2 - x + 1$

(ii) $\left(-\frac{1}{3}, 1\frac{5}{27}\right)$ and $(1, 0)$

(iii)

9 (i) $y = x^3 - 4x^2 + 5x + 3$

(ii) max $(1, 5)$, min $\left(1\frac{2}{3}, 4\frac{23}{27}\right)$

(iii) $4\frac{23}{27} < k < 5$

(iv) $1 < x < 1\frac{2}{3}$; $x = 1\frac{1}{3}$

10 $y = \frac{2}{3}x^{\frac{3}{2}} + 2$

11 $y = -\dfrac{2}{x} - 3x + 17$

12 $y = \frac{2}{3}x^{\frac{3}{2}} - \dfrac{1}{x} + 5\frac{1}{3}$

13 $y = x^3 + 5x + 2$

14 (i) $y = 2x\sqrt{x} - 9x + 20$

(ii) $x = 9$, minimum

15 $y = 6\sqrt{x} - \dfrac{x^2}{2} + 2$

16 (i) $y = 4x - \dfrac{1}{2}x^2 + 3$

  (ii) $x + 2y = 20$

  (iii) $(7, 6.5)$

Activity 6.1 (Page 183)

The bounds converge on the value
$A = 45\dfrac{1}{3}$.

Activity 6.2 (Page 187)

(i) Area $= \dfrac{1}{2}[3 + (b+3)]b - \dfrac{1}{2}[3 + (a+3)]a$

        $= \dfrac{1}{2}[6b + b^2 - 6a - a^2]$

(ii) $= \left[\dfrac{b^2}{2} + 3b\right] - \left[\dfrac{a^2}{2} + 3a\right]$

        $= \left[\dfrac{x^2}{2} + 3x\right]_a^b$

(iii) $\displaystyle\int_a^b (x+3)\,\mathrm{d}x = \left[\dfrac{x^2}{2} + 3x\right]_a^b$

Exercise 6B (Page 189)

1 (i) $x^3 + c$

  (ii) $x^5 + x^7 + c$

  (iii) $2x^3 + 5x + c$

  (iv) $\dfrac{x^4}{4} + \dfrac{x^3}{3} + \dfrac{x^2}{2} + x + c$

  (v) $x^{11} + x^{10} + c$

  (vi) $x^3 + x^2 + x + c$

  (vii) $\dfrac{x^3}{3} + 5x + c$

  (viii) $5x + c$

  (ix) $2x^3 + 2x^2 + c$

  (x) $\dfrac{x^5}{5} + x^3 + x^2 + x + c$

2 (i) $-\dfrac{10}{3}x^{-3} + c$

  (ii) $x^2 + x^{-3} + c$

  (iii) $2x + \dfrac{x^4}{4} - \dfrac{5}{2}x^{-2} + c$

  (iv) $2x^3 + 7x^{-1} + c$

  (v) $4x^{\frac{5}{4}} + c$

  (vi) $-\dfrac{1}{3x^3} + c$

  (vii) $\dfrac{2}{3}x\sqrt{x} + c$

  (viii) $\dfrac{2x^5}{5} + \dfrac{4}{x} + c$

3 (i)   3

  (ii)   9

  (iii)   27

  (iv)   12

  (v)   12

  (vi)   15

  (vii)   114

  (viii) $\dfrac{1}{6}$

  (ix) $2\dfrac{9}{20}$

  (x)   0

  (xi) $-105\dfrac{3}{4}$

  (xii)   5

4 (i) $2\dfrac{1}{4}$

  (ii) $\dfrac{3}{4}$

  (iii)   56

  (iv) $-2\dfrac{2}{3}$

  (v) $17\dfrac{5}{8}$

  (vi) $10\dfrac{2}{3}$

5 (i)   A: $(2, 4)$; B: $(3, 6)$

  (ii)   5

  (iv)   In this case the area is not a trapezium since the top is curved.

6 (i)

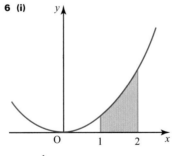

  (ii) $2\dfrac{1}{3}$

7 (i)

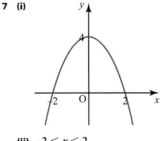

  (ii) $-2 < x < 2$

  (iii) $10\dfrac{2}{3}$

8 (i)

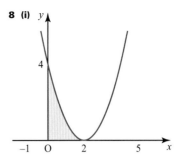

  (ii) $2\dfrac{2}{3}$ square units

9 $21\dfrac{1}{3}$ square units

10 (i)

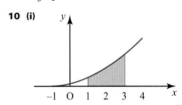

  (ii) $18\dfrac{2}{3}$ square units

11 (i)

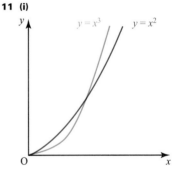

  (ii) $y = x^2$

  (iii) $y = x^2$: area $= \dfrac{1}{3}$ square units

        $y = x^3$: area $= \dfrac{1}{4}$ square units

  (iv) Expect $\displaystyle\int_1^2 x^3\,\mathrm{d}x > \int_1^2 x^2\,\mathrm{d}x$, since the curve $y = x^3$ is above the curve $y = x^2$ between 1 and 2.

        Confirmation: $\displaystyle\int_1^2 x^3\,\mathrm{d}x = 3\dfrac{3}{4}$ and $\displaystyle\int_1^2 x^2\,\mathrm{d}x = 2\dfrac{1}{3}$

12 (i)

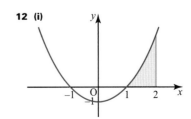

(ii) $1\frac{1}{3}$

(iii)

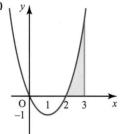

(iv) $1\frac{1}{3}$

(v) The answers are the same, since the second area is a translation of the first.

13 (i)

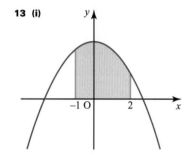

(ii) 24 square units

14 (i)

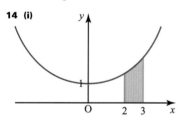

(ii) $7\frac{1}{3}$ square units

(iii) $7\frac{1}{3}$, by symmetry

(iv) $7\frac{1}{3}$

15 (i)

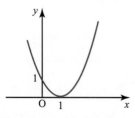

(ii) $\int_0^4 (x^2 - 2x + 1)\,dx$ larger, as area between 3 and 4 is larger than area between −1 and 0.

(iii) $\int_{-1}^{3} (x^2 - 2x + 1)\,dx = 5\frac{1}{3}$;
$\int_0^4 (x^2 - 2x + 1)\,dx = 9\frac{1}{3}$

16 (i) and (ii)

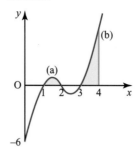

(iii) (a) $\frac{1}{4}$

(b) $2\frac{1}{4}$

(iv) 0.140625. The maximum lies before $x = 1.5$.

17 16 square units

18 (i) 14.4 units

(ii) 8 square units

19 (ii) 7.2 square units

20 (i) $y = -\dfrac{8}{x^2} + 12$

(ii) $x + 2y = 22$

(iii) 8 square units

21 (i) $2 - \dfrac{16}{x^3}, \dfrac{48}{x^4}$

(ii) $(2, 6)$, minimum

(iv) 7 square units

Exercise 6C (Page 196)

1 (i)

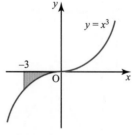

$20\frac{1}{4}$ square units

(ii)

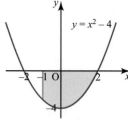

9 square units

(iii)

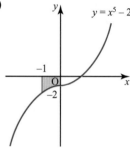

$2\frac{1}{6}$ square units

(iv)

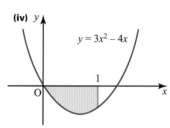

1 square units

(v)

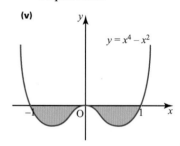

$\frac{4}{15}$ square units

(vi)

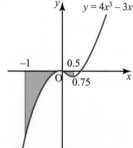

$2\frac{1}{16}$ square units

(vii)

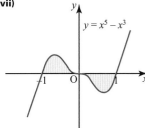
$y = x^5 - x^3$

$\frac{1}{6}$ square units

(viii)

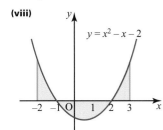
$y = x^2 - x - 2$

$8\frac{1}{6}$ square units

(ix)

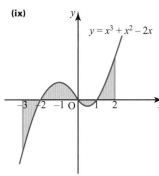
$y = x^3 + x^2 - 2x$

$11\frac{1}{12}$ square units

(x)

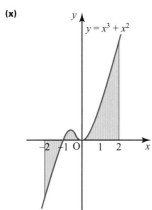
$y = x^3 + x^2$

$8\frac{1}{6}$ square units

2 **(i)** $\frac{\mathrm{d}y}{\mathrm{d}x} = 20x^3 - 5x^4$; $(0, 0)$
and $(4, 256)$

(ii) $520\frac{5}{6}$ square units

(iii) 0. Equal areas above and below the x axis.

3 **(i)** **(a)** 4

(b) -2.5

(ii) 6.5 square units

4 **(i)** **(a)** -6.4

(b) 38.8

(ii) 45.2 square units

Exercise 6D (Page 198)

1 **(i)** A: $(-3, 9)$; B: $(3, 9)$

2 **(i)**

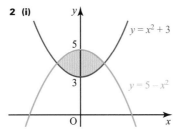
$y = x^2 + 3$
$y = 5 - x^2$

(ii) $(-1, 4)$ and $(1, 4)$

(iii) $2\frac{2}{3}$ square units

3 **(i)**

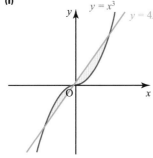
$y = x^3$
$y = 4x$

(ii) $(-2, -8)$, $(0, 0)$ and $(2, 8)$

(iii) 8 square units

4 **(i)**

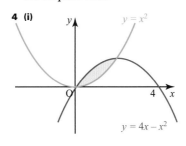
$y = x^2$
$y = 4x - x^2$

(ii) $(0, 0)$ and $(2, 4)$

(iii) $2\frac{2}{3}$ square units

---

5 **(i)**

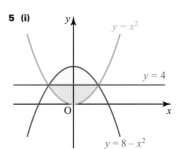
$y = x^2$
$y = 4$
$y = 8 - x^2$

(ii) $10\frac{2}{3}$ square units

(iii) $10\frac{2}{3}$ square units

(iv) $21\frac{1}{3}$ square units

6 **(i)**

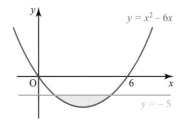
$y = x^2 - 6x$
$y = -5$

(ii) $(1, -5)$ and $(5, -5)$

(iii) $10\frac{2}{3}$ square units

7 **(i)**

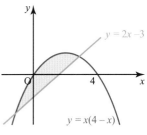
$y = 2x - 3$
$y = x(4 - x)$

(ii) $(-1, -5)$, $(3, 3)$

(iii) $10\frac{2}{3}$ square units

8 72 square units

9 $1\frac{1}{3}$ square units

10 **(i)**

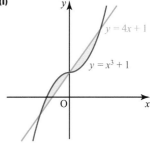
$y = 4x + 1$
$y = x^3 + 1$

(ii) 8 square units (4 each)

11 4.5 square units

12 (i) $\dfrac{dy}{dx} = 6x - 6x^2 - 4x^3$

(ii) $4x + y - 4 = 0$

(iv) 8.1 square units

13 (i) $\dfrac{dy}{dx} = 4 - 3x^2$; $8x + y - 16 = 0$

(ii) $(-4, 48)$

(iii) 108 square units

14 $10\frac{2}{3}$ square units

15 (i) A: $(1, 4)$; B: $(3, 0)$

(ii) $3y = x + 4$

(iii) $\frac{17}{12}$ square units

Exercise 6E (Page 203)

1 6 square units

2 $6\frac{2}{3}$ square units

3 4 square units

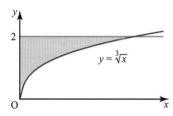

4 $8\frac{2}{3}$ square units

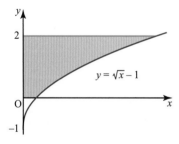

5 $6\frac{1}{5}$ square units

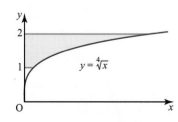

6 20 square units

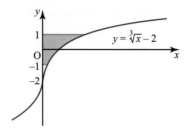

Activity 6.3 (Page 203)

(i) (a) $4(x - 2)^3$

(b) $14(2x + 5)^6$

(c) $\dfrac{-6}{(2x - 1)^4}$

(d) $\dfrac{-4}{\sqrt{1 - 8x}}$

(ii) (a) $(x - 2)^4 + c$

(b) $\frac{1}{4}(x - 2)^4 + c$

(c) $\frac{1}{2}(2x + 5)^7 + c$

(d) $2(2x + 5)^7 + c$

(e) $\dfrac{-1}{(2x - 1)^3} + c$

(f) $\dfrac{-1}{6(2x - 1)^3} + c$

(g) $\sqrt{(1 - 8x)} + c$

(h) $-2\sqrt{(1 - 8x)} + c$

Exercise 6F (Page 205)

1 (i) $\frac{1}{5}(x + 5)^5 + c$

(ii) $\frac{1}{9}(x + 7)^9 + c$

(iii) $\dfrac{-1}{5(x - 2)^5} + c$

(iv) $\frac{2}{3}(x - 4)^{\frac{3}{2}} + c$

(v) $\frac{1}{12}(3x - 1)^4 + c$

(vi) $\frac{1}{35}(5x - 2)^7$

(vii) $\frac{1}{4}(2x - 4)^6 + c$

(viii) $\frac{1}{6}(4x - 2)^{\frac{3}{2}} + c$

(ix) $\dfrac{4}{8 - x} + c$

(x) $3\sqrt{2x - 1} + c$

2 (i) $5\frac{1}{3}$

(ii) 60

(iii) 205

(iv) 336

(v) $5\frac{1}{3}$

(vi) $\frac{52}{3}$

3 (i) 4

(ii) -4; the graph has rotational symmetry about $(2, 0)$.

4 (i) 5.2 square units

(ii) 1.6 square units

(iii) 6.8 square units

(iv) Because region B is below the x axis, so the integral for this part is negative.

5 (i) 4 square units

(ii) $2\frac{2}{3}$ square units

6 (i) $3y + x = 29$

(ii) $y = 4\sqrt{3x - 2} + 1$

7 (i) $(8.5, 4.25)$

(ii) $y = 16 - 4\sqrt{6 - 2x}$

Activity 6.4 (Page 206)

(i) (a) $\frac{1}{2}$

(b) $\frac{2}{3}$

(c) 0.9

(d) 0.99

(e) 0.9999

(ii) 1

? (Page 207)

$\dfrac{1}{a}$; $\displaystyle\int_0^\infty \dfrac{1}{x^2}\,dx$ does not exist since $\dfrac{1}{0}$ is undefined.

Exercise 6G (Page 208)

1 2

2 $\frac{1}{2}$

3 2

4 $-\frac{1}{4}$

5 -1

6 24

? **(Page 209)**

1 (i) A cylinder

  (ii) A sphere

  (iii) A torus

2 $\dfrac{7\pi}{3}$

P **(Page 211)**

Follow the same procedure as that on page 209 but with the solid sliced into horizontal rather than vertical discs.

Exercise 6H (Page 212)

1 For example: ball, top (as in top & whip), roll of sticky tape, pepper mill, bottle of wine/milk etc., tin of soup

2 (i)

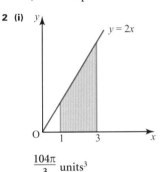

$\dfrac{104\pi}{3}$ units³

  (ii)

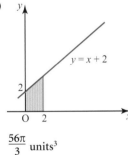

$\dfrac{56\pi}{3}$ units³

  (iii)

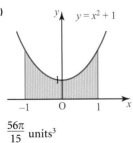

$\dfrac{56\pi}{15}$ units³

(iv)

8π units³

3 (i) (ii)

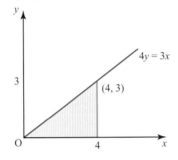

  (iii) 12π units³

4 (i)

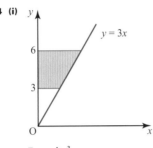

7π units³

  (ii)

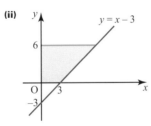

234π units³

  (iii)

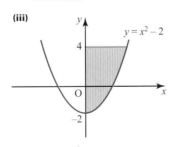

18π units³

5 (i)

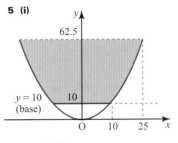

  (ii) 45.9 litres

6 (i)

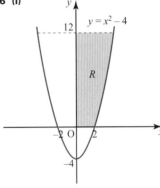

  (ii) $\displaystyle\int_0^{12}\pi(y+4)\,\mathrm{d}y$

  (iii) 3 litres

  (iv) $\displaystyle\int_0^{10}\pi(y+4)\,\mathrm{d}y = 90\pi$
  $= \tfrac{3}{4}$ of 120π

7 42π

8 6

Chapter 7

? **(Page 219)**

When looking at the gradient of a tangent to a curve it was considered as the limit of a chord as the width of the chord tended to zero. Similarly, the region between a curve and an axis was considered as the limit of a series of rectangles as the width of the rectangles tended to zero.

Exercise 7A (Page 221)

1 (i) Converse of Pythagoras' theorem

  (ii) $\tfrac{8}{17}, \tfrac{15}{17}, \tfrac{8}{15}$

3 (i) 5 cm

4 (i) $\frac{8}{9}\sqrt{3}$

5 (i) $4d$

6 (i) $BX = 3\sqrt{3}$

Activity 7.1 (Page 223)

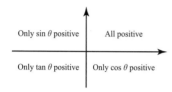

Only sin θ positive	All positive
Only tan θ positive	Only cos θ positive

❓ (Page 227)

1 The oscillations continue to the left.

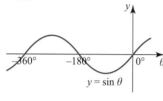

$y = \sin \theta$

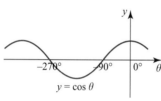

$y = \cos \theta$

2 $y = \sin \theta$:

– reflect in $\theta = 90°$ to give the curve for $90° \leqslant \theta \leqslant 180°$

– rotate the curve for $0 \leqslant \theta \leqslant 180°$ through $180°$, centre $(180°, 0)$ to give the curve for $180° \leqslant \theta \leqslant 360°$.

$y = \cos \theta$:

– translate $\begin{pmatrix} -90° \\ 0 \end{pmatrix}$ and reflect in y axis to give the curve for $0 \leqslant \theta \leqslant 90°$

– rotate this through $180°$, centre $(90°, 0)$ to give the curve for $90° \leqslant \theta \leqslant 180°$

– reflect the curve for $0 \leqslant \theta \leqslant 180°$ in $\theta = 180°$ to give the curve for $180° \leqslant \theta \leqslant 360°$.

Activity 7.2 (Page 228)

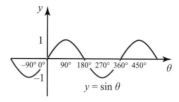

$y = \sin \theta$

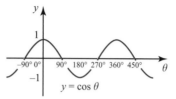

$y = \cos \theta$

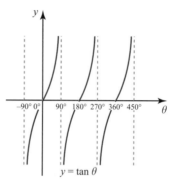

$y = \tan \theta$

❓ (Page 232)

The tangent graph repeats every $180°$ so, to find more solutions, keep adding or subtracting $180°$.

Exercise 7C (Page 233)

1 (i), (ii)

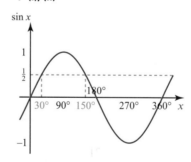

(ii) $30°$, $150°$

(iii) $30°$, $150°$ ($\pm$ multiples of $360°$)

(iv) -0.5

2 (i), (ii)

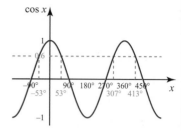

(ii) $x = -53°, 53°, 307°, 413°$
   (to nearest $1°$)

(iii), (iv)

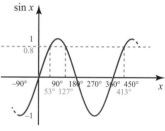

(iv) $x = 53°, 127°, 413°$
   (to nearest $1°$)

(v) For $0 \leqslant x \leqslant 90°$, $\sin x = 0.8$ and $\cos x = 0.6$ have the same root. For $90° \leqslant x \leqslant 360°$, $\sin x$ and $\cos x$ are never both positive.

3 (Where relevant, answers are to the nearest degree.)

(i) $45°$, $225°$

(ii) $60°$, $300°$

(iii) $240°$, $300°$

(iv) $135°$, $315°$

(v) $154°$, $206°$

(vi) $78°$, $282°$

(vii) $194°$, $346°$

(viii) $180°$

4 (i) $\dfrac{\sqrt{3}}{2}$

(ii) $\dfrac{1}{\sqrt{2}}$

(iii) 1

(iv) $\dfrac{1}{2}$

(v) $-\dfrac{1}{2}$

(vi) 0

(vii) $\frac{1}{2}$

(viii) $\frac{\sqrt{3}}{2}$

(ix) -1

5 (i) $-60°$

(ii) $-155.9°$

(iii) $54.0°$

6 (i)

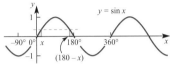

shaded areas are congruent

(ii) **(a)** False

(b) True

(c) False

(d) True

7 (i) α between 0° and 90°, 360° and 450°, 720° and 810°, etc. (and corresponding negative values).

(ii) No: since $\tan\alpha = \dfrac{\sin\alpha}{\cos\alpha}$, all must be positive or one positive and two negative.

(iii) No: $\sin\alpha = \cos\alpha \Rightarrow \alpha = 45°$, 225°, etc. but $\tan\alpha = \pm 1$ for these values of α, and $\sin\alpha = \cos\alpha = \dfrac{1}{\sqrt{2}}$

8 (i) 5.7°, 174.3°

(ii) 60°, 300°

(iii) 116.6°, 296.6°

(iv) 203.6°, 336.4°

(v) 0°, 90°, 270°, 360°

(vi) 90°, 270°

(vii) 0°, 180°, 360°

(viii) 54.7°, 125.3°, 234.7°, 305.3°

(ix) 60°, 300°

(x) 18.4°, 71.6°, 198.4°, 251.6°

9 A: (38.2°, 0.786),
B: (141.8°, −0.786)

10 (ii) $x = 143.1°$ or $x = 323.1°$

11 (ii) $x = 26.6°$ or $x = 206.6°$

12 (ii) $\theta = 71.6°$ or $\theta = 251.6°$

13 $\theta = 90°$ or $\theta = 131.8°$

Exercise 7D (Page 238)

1 (i) $\dfrac{\pi}{4}$

(ii) $\dfrac{\pi}{2}$

(iii) $\dfrac{2\pi}{3}$

(iv) $\dfrac{5\pi}{12}$

(v) $\dfrac{5\pi}{3}$

(vi) 0.4 rad

(vii) $\dfrac{5\pi}{2}$

(viii) 3.65 rad

(ix) $\dfrac{5\pi}{6}$

(x) $\dfrac{\pi}{25}$

2 (i) 18°

(ii) 108°

(iii) 114.6°

(iv) 80°

(v) 540°

(vi) 300°

(vii) 22.9°

(viii) 135°

(ix) 420°

(x) 77.1°

3 (i) $\dfrac{1}{\sqrt{2}}$

(ii) $\sqrt{3}$

(iii) $\dfrac{\sqrt{3}}{2}$

(iv) -1

(v) -1

(vi) $\dfrac{\sqrt{3}}{2}$

(vii) $\sqrt{3}$

(viii) $-\dfrac{1}{\sqrt{2}}$

(ix) $\dfrac{1}{2}$

(x) $\dfrac{1}{2}$

4 (i) $\dfrac{\pi}{6}, \dfrac{11\pi}{6}$

(ii) $\dfrac{\pi}{4}, \dfrac{5\pi}{4}$

(iii) $\dfrac{\pi}{4}, \dfrac{3\pi}{4}$

(iv) $\dfrac{7\pi}{6}, \dfrac{11\pi}{6}$

(v) $\dfrac{3\pi}{4}, \dfrac{5\pi}{4}$

(vi) $\dfrac{\pi}{3}, \dfrac{4\pi}{3}$

5 (i) 0.201 rads, 2.940 rads

(ii) −0.738 rads, 0.738 rads

(iii) −1.893 rads, 1.249 rads

(iv) −2.889 rads, −0.253 rads

(v) −1.982 rads, 1.982 rads

(vi) −0.464 rads, 2.678 rads

6 0 rads, 0.730 rads, 2.412 rads, π rads

? (Page 241)

Draw a line from O to M, the mid-point of AB. Then find the lengths of OM, AM and BM and use them to find the areas of the triangles OAM and OBM, and so that of OAB.

In the same way,
AB = AM + MB = 2AM.

Exercise 7E (Page 241)

1

r (cm)	θ (rad)	s (cm)	A (cm²)
5	$\dfrac{\pi}{4}$	$\dfrac{5\pi}{4}$	$\dfrac{25\pi}{8}$
8	1	8	32
4	$\dfrac{1}{2}$	2	4
$1\frac{1}{2}$	$\dfrac{\pi}{3}$	$\dfrac{\pi}{2}$	$\dfrac{3\pi}{8}$
5	$\dfrac{4}{5}$	4	10
1.875	0.8	1.5	1.41
3.46	$\dfrac{2\pi}{3}$	7.26	4π

2 (i) (a) $\dfrac{20\pi}{3}$ cm^2

 (c) 16.9 cm^2

 (ii) 19.7 cm^2

3 (i) 1.98 mm^2

 (ii) 43.0 mm

5 (i) 140 yards

 (ii) 5585 square yards

6 (ii) 43.3 cm

 (iii) 117 cm^2 (3 s.f.)

7 (i) 62.4 cm^2

 (ii) 0.65

8 (i) $4\sqrt{3}$

 (ii) $48\sqrt{3} - 24\pi$

9 (i) 1.8 radians

 (ii) 6.30 cm

 (iii) 9.00 cm^2

10 (ii) $18 - 6\sqrt{3} + 2\pi$

Activity 7.3 (Page 245)

The transformation that maps the curve $y = \sin x$ on to the curve $y = 2 + \sin x$ is the translation $\begin{pmatrix} 0 \\ 2 \end{pmatrix}$.

In general, the curve $y = f(x) + s$ is obtained from $y = f(x)$ by the translation $\begin{pmatrix} 0 \\ s \end{pmatrix}$.

Activity 7.4 (Page 245)

The transformation that maps the curve $y = \sin x$ on to the curve $y = \sin(x - 45°)$ is the translation $\begin{pmatrix} 45° \\ 0 \end{pmatrix}$.

In general, the curve $y = f(x - t)$ is obtained from $y = f(x)$ by the translation $\begin{pmatrix} t \\ 0 \end{pmatrix}$.

Activity 7.5 (Page 246)

The transformation that maps the curve $y = \sin x$ on to the curve $y = -\sin x$ is a reflection in the x axis.

In general, the curve $y = -f(x)$ is obtained from $y = f(x)$ by a reflection in the x axis.

Activity 7.6 (Page 246)

For any value of x, the y co-ordinate of the point on the curve $y = 2\sin x$ is exactly double that on the curve $y = \sin x$.

This is the equivalent of the curve being stretched parallel to the y axis. Since the y co-ordinate is doubled, the transformation that maps the curve $y = \sin x$ on to the curve $y = 2\sin x$ is called a stretch of scale factor 2 parallel to the y axis.

The equation $y = 2\sin x$ could also be written as $\dfrac{y}{2} = \sin x$, so dividing y by 2 gives a stretch of scale factor 2 in the y direction.

This can be generalised as the curve $y = af(x)$, where a is greater than 0, is obtained from $y = f(x)$ by a stretch of scale factor a parallel to the y axis.

Activity 7.7 (Page 247)

For any value of y, the x co-ordinate of the point on the curve $y = \sin 2x$ is exactly half that on the curve $y = \sin x$.

This is the equivalent of the curve being compressed parallel to the x axis. Since the x co-ordinate is halved, the transformation that maps the curve $y = \sin x$ on to the curve $y = \sin 2x$ is called a stretch of scale factor $\frac{1}{2}$ parallel to the x axis.

Dividing x by a gives a stretch of scale factor a in the x direction, just as dividing y by a gives a stretch of scale factor a in the y direction:

$y = f\left(\dfrac{x}{a}\right)$ corresponds to a stretch of scale factor a parallel to the x axis.

Similarly, the curve $y = f(ax)$, where a is greater than 0, is obtained from $y = f(x)$ by a stretch of scale factor $\dfrac{1}{a}$ parallel to the x axis.

Exercise 7F (Page 251)

1 (i) Translation $\begin{pmatrix} 90° \\ 0 \end{pmatrix}$

 (ii) One-way stretch parallel to x axis of s.f. $\frac{1}{3}$

 (iii) One-way stretch parallel to y axis of s.f. $\frac{1}{2}$

 (iv) One-way stretch parallel to x axis of s.f. 2

 (v) Translation $\begin{pmatrix} 0 \\ 2 \end{pmatrix}$

2 (i) Translation $\begin{pmatrix} -60° \\ 0 \end{pmatrix}$

 (ii) One-way stretch parallel to y axis of s.f. $\frac{1}{3}$

 (iii) Translation $\begin{pmatrix} 0 \\ 1 \end{pmatrix}$

 (iv) One-way stretch parallel to x axis of s.f. $\frac{1}{2}$

3 (i) (a)

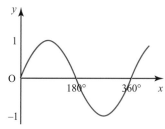

 (b) $y = \sin x$

 (ii) (a)

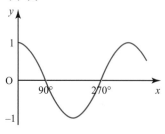

 (b) $y = \cos x$

 (iii) (a)

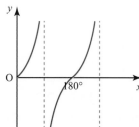

 (b) $y = \tan x$

(iv) (a)

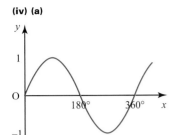

(b) $y = \sin x$

(v) (a)

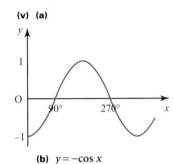

(b) $y = -\cos x$

4 (i) $y = \tan x + 4$

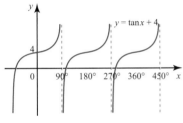

(ii) $y = \tan (x + 30°)$

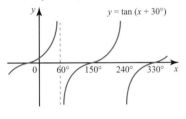

(iii) $y = \tan (0.5x)$

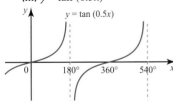

5 (i) $y = 4 \sin x$

(ii) $-2\sqrt{3}$

6 (i) $a = 3, b = -4$

(ii) $x = 0.361$ or $x = 2.78$

(iii)

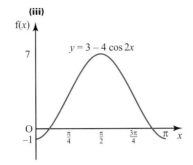

7 (i) $a = 4, b = 6$

(ii) $x = 48.2$ or $x = 311.8$

(iii)

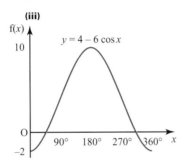

8 (i) $a = 6, b = 2, c = 3$

(ii) $\dfrac{7\pi}{12}$

9 (i) $2 \leqslant f(x) \leqslant 8$

(ii)

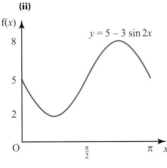

(iii) No, it is a many-to-one function.

10 (i) $x = 0.730$ or $x = 2.41$

(ii)

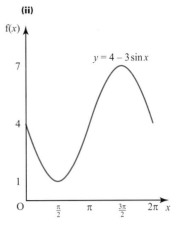

(iii) $k < 1, k > 7$

(iv) $\dfrac{3\pi}{2}$

(v) 2.80

Chapter 8

❓ (Page 254)

To find the distance between the vapour trails you need two pieces of information for each of them: either two points that it goes through, or else one point and its direction. All of these need to be in three dimensions. However, if you want to find the closest approach of the aircraft you also need to know, for each of them, the time at which it was at a given point on its trail and the speed at which it was travelling. (This answer assumes constant speeds and directions.)

℗ (Page 261)

The vector $a_1\mathbf{i} + a_2\mathbf{j} + a_3\mathbf{k}$ is shown in the diagram.

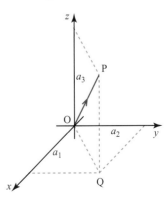

Start with the vector $\overrightarrow{OQ} = a_1\mathbf{i} + a_2\mathbf{j}$.

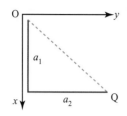

Length $= \sqrt{a_1^2 + a_2^2}$

Now look at the triangle OQP.

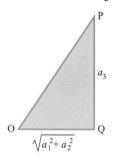

$$OP^2 = OQ^2 + QP^2$$
$$= \left(a_1^2 + a_2^2\right) + a_3^2$$
$$\Rightarrow OP = \sqrt{a_1^2 + a_2^2 + a_3^2}$$

Exercise 8A (Page 261)

1　(i)　$3\mathbf{i} + 2\mathbf{j}$

　　(ii)　$5\mathbf{i} - 4\mathbf{j}$

　　(iii)　$3\mathbf{i}$

　　(iv)　$-3\mathbf{i} - \mathbf{j}$

2　For all question 2:

　(i)

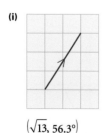

$\left(\sqrt{13},\ 56.3°\right)$

(ii)

$\left(\sqrt{13},\ -33.7°\right)$

(iii)

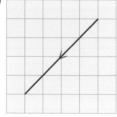

$\left(4\sqrt{2},\ -135°\right)$

(iv)

$\left(\sqrt{5},\ 116.6°\right)$

(v)

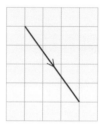

$(5,\ -53.1°)$

3　(i)　3.74

　(ii)　4.47

　(iii)　4.90

　(iv)　3.32

　(v)　7

　(vi)　2.24

4　(i)　$2\mathbf{i} - 2\mathbf{j}$

　(ii)　$2\mathbf{i}$

　(iii)　$-4\mathbf{j}$

　(iv)　$4\mathbf{j}$

　(v)　$5\mathbf{k}$

　(vi)　$-\mathbf{i} - 2\mathbf{j} + 3\mathbf{k}$

　(vii)　$\mathbf{i} + 2\mathbf{j} - 3\mathbf{k}$

　(viii)　$4\mathbf{i} - 2\mathbf{j} + 4\mathbf{k}$

　(ix)　$2\mathbf{i} - 2\mathbf{k}$

　(x)　$-8\mathbf{i} + 10\mathbf{j} + \mathbf{k}$

5　(i)　A: $2\mathbf{i} + 3\mathbf{j}$, C: $-2\mathbf{i} + \mathbf{j}$

　(ii)　$\overrightarrow{AB} = -2\mathbf{i} + \mathbf{j}$, $\overrightarrow{CB} = 2\mathbf{i} + 3\mathbf{j}$

　(iii)　(a)　$\overrightarrow{AB} = \overrightarrow{OC}$

　　　(b)　$\overrightarrow{CB} = \overrightarrow{OA}$

　(iv)　A parallelogram

Activity 8.1 (Page 266)

(i)　(a)　F

　　(b)　C

　　(c)　Q

　　(d)　T

　　(e)　S

(ii)　(a)　$\overrightarrow{OF}$

　　(b)　$\overrightarrow{OE}$, $\overrightarrow{CF}$

　　(c)　$\overrightarrow{OG}$, $\overrightarrow{PS}$, $\overrightarrow{AF}$

　　(d)　$\overrightarrow{BD}$

　　(e)　$\overrightarrow{QS}$, $\overrightarrow{PT}$

Exercise 8B (Page 269)

1　(i)　$\begin{pmatrix} 6 \\ 8 \end{pmatrix}$

　(ii)　$\begin{pmatrix} 1 \\ 1 \end{pmatrix}$

　(iii)　$\begin{pmatrix} 0 \\ 0 \end{pmatrix}$

　(iv)　$\begin{pmatrix} 8 \\ -1 \end{pmatrix}$

　(v)　$-3\mathbf{j}$

2　(i)　$2\mathbf{i} + 3\mathbf{j} + \mathbf{k}$

　(ii)　$\mathbf{i} - \mathbf{k}$

　(iii)　$\mathbf{j} - \mathbf{k}$

　(iv)　$3\mathbf{i} + 2\mathbf{j} - 5\mathbf{k}$

　(v)　$-6\mathbf{k}$

3　(i)　(a)　$\mathbf{b}$

　　(b)　$\mathbf{a} + \mathbf{b}$

　　(c)　$-\mathbf{a} + \mathbf{b}$

　(ii)　(a)　$\frac{1}{2}(\mathbf{a} + \mathbf{b})$

　　(b)　$\frac{1}{2}(-\mathbf{a} + \mathbf{b})$

　(iii)　PQRS is any parallelogram and $\overrightarrow{PM} = \frac{1}{2}\overrightarrow{PR}$, $\overrightarrow{QM} = \frac{1}{2}\overrightarrow{QS}$

4 (i) (a) i

(b) 2i

(c) i − j

(d) −i − 2j

(ii) $|\overrightarrow{AB}| = |\overrightarrow{BC}| = \sqrt{2}$,
$|\overrightarrow{AD}| = |\overrightarrow{CD}| = \sqrt{5}$

5 (i) $-\mathbf{p} + \mathbf{q}, \frac{1}{2}\mathbf{p} - \frac{1}{2}\mathbf{q}, -\frac{1}{2}\mathbf{p}, -\frac{1}{2}\mathbf{q}$

(ii) $\overrightarrow{NM} = \frac{1}{2}\overrightarrow{BC}, \overrightarrow{NL} = \frac{1}{2}\overrightarrow{AC},$
$\overrightarrow{ML} = \frac{1}{2}\overrightarrow{AB}$

6 (i) $\begin{pmatrix} \frac{2}{\sqrt{13}} \\ \frac{3}{\sqrt{13}} \end{pmatrix}$

(ii) $\frac{3}{5}\mathbf{i} + \frac{4}{5}\mathbf{j}$

(iii) $\begin{pmatrix} \frac{-1}{\sqrt{2}} \\ \frac{-1}{\sqrt{2}} \end{pmatrix}$

(iv) $\frac{5}{13}\mathbf{i} - \frac{12}{13}\mathbf{j}$

7 (i) $\begin{pmatrix} \frac{1}{\sqrt{14}} \\ \frac{2}{\sqrt{14}} \\ \frac{3}{\sqrt{14}} \end{pmatrix}$

(ii) $\frac{2}{3}\mathbf{i} - \frac{2}{3}\mathbf{j} + \frac{1}{3}\mathbf{k}$

(iii) $\frac{3}{5}\mathbf{i} - \frac{4}{5}\mathbf{k}$

(iv) $\begin{pmatrix} \frac{-2}{\sqrt{29}} \\ \frac{4}{\sqrt{29}} \\ \frac{-3}{\sqrt{29}} \end{pmatrix}$

(v) $\frac{5}{\sqrt{38}}\mathbf{i} - \frac{3}{\sqrt{38}}\mathbf{j} + \frac{2}{\sqrt{38}}\mathbf{k}$

(vi) $\begin{pmatrix} 1 \\ 0 \\ 0 \end{pmatrix}$

8 11.74

9 $x = 4$ or $x = -2$

---

10 (i) $\frac{1}{7}\begin{pmatrix} 2 \\ 3 \\ -6 \end{pmatrix}$

(ii) $m = -2, n = 3, k = -8$

ⓟ (Page 271)

The cosine rule
Pythagoras' theorem

ⓟ (Page 273)

$\begin{pmatrix} a_1 \\ a_2 \end{pmatrix} \cdot \begin{pmatrix} b_1 \\ b_2 \end{pmatrix} = a_1 b_1 + a_2 b_2$

$\begin{pmatrix} b_1 \\ b_2 \end{pmatrix} \cdot \begin{pmatrix} a_1 \\ a_2 \end{pmatrix} = b_1 a_1 + b_2 a_2$

These are the same because ordinary multiplication is commutative.

ⓟ (Page 274)

Consider the triangle OAB with angle
AOB $= \theta$, as shown in the diagram.

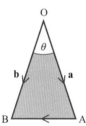

$\mathbf{b} - \mathbf{a} = (b_1 - a_1)\mathbf{i} +$
$(b_2 - a_2)\mathbf{j} + (b_3 - a_3)\mathbf{k}$

$\cos\theta = \dfrac{OA^2 + OB^2 - AB^2}{2 \times OA \times OB}$

$OA^2 = a_1^2 + a_2^2 + a_3^2$
$OB^2 = b_1^2 + b_2^2 + b_3^2$
$AB^2 = (b_1 - a_1)^2 + (b_2 - a_2)^2 + (b_3 - a_3)^2$

$\Rightarrow \quad \cos\theta = \dfrac{2(a_1 b_1 + a_2 b_2 + a_3 b_3)}{2\,|\mathbf{a}||\mathbf{b}|}$

$= \dfrac{\mathbf{a}.\mathbf{b}}{|\mathbf{a}||\mathbf{b}|}$

Exercise 8C (Page 275)

1 (i) 42.3°

(ii) 90°

(iii) 18.4°

(iv) 31.0°

(v) 90°

(vi) 180°

2 (i) $\begin{pmatrix} 3 \\ 1 \end{pmatrix}, \begin{pmatrix} -1 \\ 3 \end{pmatrix}$

(ii) $\overrightarrow{BA} . \overrightarrow{BC} = 0$

(iii) $|\overrightarrow{AB}| = |\overrightarrow{BC}| = \sqrt{10}$

(iv) $(2, 5)$

3 (i) $\overrightarrow{PQ} = -4\mathbf{i} + 2\mathbf{j}; \overrightarrow{RQ} = 4\mathbf{i} + 8\mathbf{j}$

(ii) 26.6°

(iii) $3\mathbf{i} + 7\mathbf{j}$

(iv) 53.1°

4 (i) 29.0°

(ii) 76.2°

(iii) 162.0°

5 (i) $\overrightarrow{OQ} = 3\mathbf{i} + 3\mathbf{j} + 6\mathbf{k},$
$\overrightarrow{PQ} = -3\mathbf{i} + \mathbf{j} + 6\mathbf{k}$

(ii) 53.0°

6 (i) -2

(ii) 40°

(iii) $\overrightarrow{AB} = \mathbf{i} - 3\mathbf{j} + (p-2)\mathbf{k};$
$p = 0.5$ or $p = 3.5$

7 (i) -6, obtuse

(ii) $\begin{pmatrix} \frac{2}{3} \\ -\frac{2}{3} \\ \frac{1}{3} \end{pmatrix}$

8 (i) 99°

(ii) $\frac{1}{7}(2\mathbf{i} - 6\mathbf{j} + 3\mathbf{k})$

(iii) $p = -7$ or $p = 5$

9 (ii) $q = 5$ or $q = -3$

10 (i) $\overrightarrow{PA} = -6\mathbf{i} - 8\mathbf{j} - 6\mathbf{k},$
$\overrightarrow{PN} = 6\mathbf{i} + 2\mathbf{j} - 6\mathbf{k}$

(ii) 99.1°

11 (i) $4\mathbf{i} + 4\mathbf{j} + 5\mathbf{k}$, 7.55 m

(ii) 43.7° (or 0.763 radians)

12 (i) $\overrightarrow{PR} = 2\mathbf{i} + 2\mathbf{j} + 2\mathbf{k},$
$\overrightarrow{PQ} = -2\mathbf{i} + 2\mathbf{j} + 4\mathbf{k}$

(ii) 61.9°

(iii) 12.8 units

Index

Index